FINANCE AND SUSTAINABLE DEVELOPMENT
(With Special Reference to Micro Finance)

FINANCE AND SUSTAINABLE DEVELOPMENT

(With Special Reference to Micro Finance)

Editors

ASHRAF IMAM
PGEDP, MFC
Department of Commerce
Aligarh Muslim University, Aligarh (U.P.)

ABDUL RAHMAN SHAIK
M.Com., MBA, UB, M.Phil.
IIT Kharagpur (W.B.)

AKANSHA BHARGAVA
MBA

REGAL PUBLICATIONS
New Delhi - 110 027

FINANCE AND SUSTAINABLE DEVELOPMENT
(With Special Reference to Micro Finance)

ISBN 978-81-8484-186-2

Typeset by
RAHUL COMPOSERS
358, Pocket-B, Phase-2, Sector-16 B, Dwarka, New Delhi - 110 075

Printed in India at
MAYUR ENTERPRISES
WZ Plot No. 3, Gujjar Market, Tihar Village, New Delhi - 110 018

Published by
REGAL PUBLICATIONS
F-159, Rajouri Garden, New Delhi - 110 027 • Phone : 45546396
E-mail : regalbookspub@yahoo.com

Contents

Acknowledgements

A formal acknowledgement will hardly meet the ends of righteousness in the expression of our deep sense of gratitude and obligation to all those who helped us in the completion of this book. This book is the result of the guidance, assistance and inspiration of several people including the eminent professors from all over India.

We simply whole heartedly express our sincere gratitude to all our Professors like Prof. H.K. Singh, Prof. G. Raju, Dr. Mohd. Shamim, Dr. Nafees A. Khan, Dr. Chandra Shekhar Chaubey, Dr. M. Ashraf Ali, Dr. Imran Saleem, Dr. Pradeep Kamal and Dr. Harish Handa for their valuable suggestions, inspiring guidance and all out support in producing this book. It is their profound subject knowledge that they infused in us and their perpetual guidance that we could deliver the best and for that matter, would remain indebted to them. We also place on record our special thanks to our research collegues like Dr. Shahid Alam, Azeem A. Khan, Mushtaq Ahmad and Mrs. Poonam Sharma for supporting us and sparing their valuable time for us in compilation of papers.

We also extremely thankful to all the contributors of this book for their valuable support and contribution as research papers, review papers and articles.

We also acknowledge with thanks for the support provided by Mr. Pervez Khwaja—Seminar Incharge, Mr. Ali Hasan and Mr. Mohd. Anees. Our heartiest thanks are also due to Mr. Hasnain Saheb for his kind co-operation.

A special thanks goes to Mr. Azam Malik for meticulously working through the book.

We also thank all who have helped us at every step of the project and always backed me up under all circumstances.

ASHRAF IMAM
ABDUL RAHMAN SHAIK
AKANSHA BHARGAVA

List of Contributors

Abdul Ghani Faiyyaz, M.Com. (F), AMU, Aligarh (U.P.).

Abhishek Kumar Chintu, Research Scholar, Economics, FSS JPU, Chapra (Bihar).

Akansha Bhargava, Assistant Professor, New Horizon Institute of Management Studies, Thane (Maharashtra).

Anand Nayyar, Assistant Professor, Department of Computer Applications and I.T., KCL Institute of Management and Technology, Jalandhar (Punjab).

Arif, M.K., M.Com (F), AMU, Aligarh (U.P.).

Arpita Kotnala, Ph.D. Student, Agricultural Economics, G.B. Pant University of Agriculture & Technology, Pantnagar, Udham Singh Nagar (Uttarakhand).

Ca Mitual Parmar, Lecturer, M.S. University, Commerce Department, Baroda (Gujarat).

Devendra Kumar Meena, Ph.D. Student, Dairy Extension Division, N.D.R.I., Karnal (Haryana).

Dr. Amitabh Joshi, Associate Professor, Prestige Institute of Management, Dewas (M.P.).

Dr. Amitava Basu, Assistant Professor of Commerce, B.B. College, Asansol, Burdwan (W.B.).

Dr. Asad Rehman, Associate Professor, Department of Business Administration, Aligarh Muslim University, Aligarh (U.P.).

Dr. Chetna Parmar, Assistant Professor, R.K. University, Rajkot (Gujarat).

Dr. Harish Handa, Associate Professor, Shaheed Bhagat Singh College, Delhi University, Delhi.

Dr. Rajesh Kumar Sharma, Head, Department of Sociology, Government P.G. College, Dholpur (Rajasthan).

Dr. Ramesh Kumar Miryala, Professor, Swami Ramananda Tirtha Institute of Science and Technology, Nalgonda (A.P.).

Dr. Shahid Alam, Guest Faculty, Department of Commerce, Aligarh Muslim University, Aligarh (U.P.).

Dr. Simranjeet Kaur Sandhar, Associate Professor, Indore Institute of Science and Technoogy, Indore (M.P.).

Eliza Sharma, Research Scholar, Jaypee Institute of Information Technology, Noida (U.P.).

G. Prasad Babu, Ph.D. Scholar, National Dairy Research Institute, Karnal (Haryana).

Hari Babu Bathini, Lecturer, V.R. Siddhartha Engineering College, Kanuru, Vijayawada (A.P.).

Jyoti Kumari, Research Scholar, Banasthali Vidyapeeth, Tonk (Rajasthan).

K. Hema Divya, Lecturer, School of Management, K.L. University (A.P.).

K.S. Kadian, Principal Scientist, National Dairy Research Institute, Karnal (Haryana).

Laxmi Rani Dubey, Ph.D., Dairy Economic (First Year), N.D.R.I-Karnal (Haryana).

M. Sayeed Alam, Assistant Professor, Department of Business Administration, East-West University, Dhaka (Bangladesh).

Maansi Kataria, Lecturer, Shobhit University, Meerut (U.P.).

Massoumeh Nasrollah Zadeh, Mashhad, Iran.

Md. Agha Nuruzzaman, Research Scholar, Department of Business Administration, Aligarh Muslim University, Aligarh (U.P.).

Ms. Sumbul Tahir, Assistant Professor, JIMS, Kalkaji, New Delhi.

Ms. Fozia, Research Scholar, Department of Commerce, Aligarh Muslim University, Aligarh (U.P.).

Ms. Nahid, Research Scholar, Department of Commerce, Aligarh Muslim University, Aligarh (U.P.).

Ms. Neha Gupta, Assistant Professor, JIMS, Kalkaji, New Delhi.

Ms. Silky Janglani, Assisstant Professor, Indore Institute of Computer Application, Indore (M.P.).

Mushtaq Ahmad, Research Scholar, Department of Commerce, Aligarh Muslim University, Aligarh (U.P.).

Nandita Majumdar, Ph.D. Student, Acharya Nagarjuna University, Guntur (A.P.).

Neetu Kwatra, Research Scholor, Mahatma Gandhi Chitrakoot Rural University, Satna (M.P.).

Omar Faruq, Assistant Professor, Department of Business Administration, East West University, Dhaka (Bangladesh).

Onkar Nath Mishra, Research Scholar, Economics, FSS, BHU, Varanasi (U.P.).

Pooja Talwar, Assistant Professor, Delhi University, Delhi.

Prof. N.K. Bansal, Head, Department of A.B.S.T., Government P.G. College, Dholpur (Rajasthan).

Raghu Katragadda, Sr. Lecturer, V.R. Siddhartha Engineering College, Kanuru, Vijayawada (A.P.).

S.S. Bhushanam, Management Consultant.

Sabina Sharmin, Assistant Professor, Department of Statistics, Biostatistics and Informatics, University of Dhaka (Bangladesh).

Saswat Barpanda, Research Scholar, IIT, Kharagpur (W.B.).

Tabinda Iqbal, Research Scholar, Department of Education, A.M.U., Aligarh (U.P.).

Talata C. Ratnayake, Department of Animal Production and Health, Sri Lanka and Ph.D. Scholar, NDRI, Karnal (Haryana).

Tosib Alam, Research Scholar, Department of Economics, Aligarh Muslim University, Aligarh (U.P.).

Zeeshan, P.G. Student, Department of Economics, Aligarh Muslim University, Aligarh (U.P.).

Introduction

Financial Sustainability is essential for two reasons. Firstly, the majority of businesses will not pursue sustainability unless they see it as offering them financial benefits. Secondly, financial wealth is an important element of quality of life. However, contrary to traditional belief, the goal of financial profit does not have to be in conflict with the goals of social and environmental profit. Carefully designing products within their business, social and environmental systems can result in solutions that have long-term financial viability and consistently generate financial profit and wealth. All of this can be achieved without damage to society or the environment and can potentially even generate profit in these areas. So, with our authors we have made out many contributions for the sustainability of Indian Economy. Arif, M.K. and Abdul Ghani Faiyyaz has given view on the Sustainable Development in India; Perspectives, Issues and Opportunities.

Emphasises on human rights, labour rights, corporate governance, etc. And 'Not for Profit Organization' (NPO) has to play a key role in the social development activities such as Education, health, social justice, minority welfare, poverty alleviation, religious and cultural values for the healthy economy. Even though government is providing much financial assistance to social organization especially 'Not for Profit Organizations' (NPOs), their performance for upliftment of society is not satisfactory. So some well-planned and innovative schemes should be adopted for sustainable development of the country. Md. Agha Nuruzzaman and Dr. Asad Rehman has given view on Sustainable Development of Indian Derivatives Markets: An Analysis. This chapter attempts to discuss the derivatives trading by tracing its historical development and classification of derivatives. It also looks at regulation and policy developments, future prospects and challenges of futures market in India. They have also talked about the hedgers and speculators in the markets. Ms Akansha Bhargava has taken the heeds towards the Role of FDI in Sustaining with Various Economy of the World Focusing on India.

She developed a simple information-based model of FDI flows in which the abundance of "intangible" capital in the source countries, which generates expertise in cream-skimming investment projects in the host countries and enhances FDI flows. A comparative study has been done with developed and developing nations. Dr. Amitava Basu has focused on the Mutual Fund and the Response of Small Investors: The Indian Context they have discussed the success of mutual fund in todays market with the consideration of the small investors and it is the best source to invest our money even it could be a part of household savings. Mr. Anand Nayyar has talked about Challenges faced by India and how it is playing role in Sustainable Development of Information and Communication Technologies (ICTs) to improve the activities of various government agencies. As India's position in E-Readiness is very low as compared to other countries of the world. The study has implementated the E-Government which has Low-Literacy, Low per capita income and limited financial resources. In this chapter, A Conceptual framework is proposed for the Effective Implementation of E-Government in India. The Conceptual Framework proposed can be validated in Real Life Situation. Mr. S.S. Bhushanam, Sustaining Micro Financing through Re-Engineering and Synergy the vital pre-requisites in working towards increasing the effectiveness of various programs are: programs integration and adapting project management methodologies. He has made an effort to manage micro finance institutions by managing reengineering. The approach suggested to maximize the practical application of management practices into more realistically. Dr. Chetna Parmar and Ca Mitual Parmar BSE and Sectoral Indices: A

Comparative Study the worst strike of BSE among the Indian stock market indices. The other sectoral indices are also following the SENSEX until a revival in the last quarter. Because of the declining trends in the capital markets, it seems that the investors are in a dilemma whether their investments will be safe or not. So they have shown the Free float Market Capitalization, FMCG, BOLT, Free float Factors. Ms. Eliza Sharma an Application of Z-Score Model a Study of Reliance Industries Limited present study to have an insight into the examination of financial health of the organization. The result clearly indicates that the solvency position of the company is healthy. Mr. Mushtaq Ahmad wrote about the Foreign Direct Investment in Indian Retail Sector: Strategic Issues and Implication she has emphasized to analyze the strategic issues concerning the influx of foreign direct investment in the Indian retail industry. Moreover, with the latest move of the government to allow FDI in retailing sector, she has also analyzed the reason why prospects in India foreign retailers are interested in India, the strategies they are adopting to enter India. The findings of the study point out that FDI in retail would undoubtedly enable India Inc. to integrate its economy with that of the global economy. Onkar Nath Mishra and Abhishek Kumar Chintu they propounded about the Forecasting exchange rate: A case study of short-term exchange rate between INR and US Dollar. A reliable forecast of future spot rates provides essentially an informational input for the management of foreign exchange exposure and other financial decisions. In this project an analysis of the short-term exchange rate between the INR and USD has been carried out. Ms. Fozia and Ms. Nahid has written that the globalization of production comprises both international trade and Foreign Direct Investment. They came up with great promise of a new phase of export growth from developing countries, whose addition in the process of opening new market they have said the changing structure of trade and investment create the possibilities for harmonizing economic policies between countries seeking to build closer economic relation, the objective is to eliminate and regulatory "Trade Frictions" restricting expansion of international trade and foreign investment from within countries rather than at their border. Ms. Tabinda Iqbal has taken a different prospect of sustainability, she has given a Study of Sustainable Development of Secondary School Students in Relation to Gender and Religion in which the sustainable development of secondary school student in relation to gender is being taken out. Hari Babu Bathini and Raghu Katragadda has told about the SHG-Bank Linkage Programme in India, an attempt has given by them to review the performance of the programme in different states of India and across three major institutions—commercial banks, cooperatives, and the regional rural banks. The study also presents vital information about the leading NGOs with major credit linkages in Indian states. Dr. Harish Handa and Pooja Talwar has viewed about the Impact of Index Futures on Indian Market Volatility—An Application of Garch, while studying conditional volatility it was observed that the volatility has come down in the post-derivative period. The chapter concludes that the volatility of the market as measured by benchmark indices like S&P CNX NIFTY and S&P CNX NIFTY JUNIOR have fallen in the post-derivatives period.

Ms. Jyoti Kumari had wrote about the Micro Financing Through CBIGA and Rural Women Empowerment: A Case Study to know the empowerment among rural women through CBIGA [Community Based Income Generating Activity—A kind of micro financings] which has been provided by Informal Women Education Centre, Banasthali Vidyapeeth in Tonk district of Rajasthan state in India. 12 rural women from different villages of selected district formed the target group/ case for the study. The design used in the study was the Multiple Case Study Design for the purpose of exploring the phenomenon under study through the use of a replication strategy. A semi-structured interview and observation were used to collect the information. Laxmi Rani Dubey, Massoumeh Nasrollah Zadeh and Arpita Kotnala, Microfinance through SHG—A Way for Sustainable Development SHGs, in many ways, have gone beyond the means of delivering the financial services as a channel and turned out to be focal point for purveying various services to the poor. The programme, over a period, has become the common vehicle in the development process, converging important development programmes. With the small beginning as Pilot Programme launched by NABARD.

Ms. Maansi Kataria Prospects of Green Banking in India, her study tries to explore the need of green banking in the Indian banking industry. It also illustrates few international initiatives been taken world-wide to protect the environment. This chapter investigates the various levels of green banking at which the Indian banks can operate. The study also suggests some products that can be adopted by the Indian banks for promoting green initiatives. Nahid and Fozia, Recent Trends in FDI and its Impact on Growth and Development of India. Their study showed the recent trends in FDI and its impact on growth and development of Indian economy and challenges faced by FDI in India. The chapter findings show that there is a positive correlation between FDI and domestic investment. FDI also has a positive interaction with human capital, sound macroeconomic policies and stability of institutions, thus it contributes towards the enhancement of economic growth and development. Ms. Nandita Majumdar has shown the Mirage of Foreign Direct Investment in Higher Education which indicates the Education institutions in India have witnessed dramatically rapid growth, by doubling the number of universities since 1990-91 and the enrolments being more than double at the expense of quality, decreased flexibility in the course design, poor combination of knowledge and increasing rate of unavailability of laboratories, journals, field work, etc. An average Indian graduate is poorly compared with their equivalent in other developed or for those matters even developing countries. This led to both the ends of the quality, on one hand it enhanced the quality of education by providing standards matching international universities and on the other hand it led to poor first hand information of the country and its economic structure they are living in. Dr. Ramesh Kumar Miryala emphasized on the Need of Financial Inclusion for Poverty Alleviation and GDP Growth has been realized by the policy-makers that increase in GDP alone is not the solution of the deep-rooted problems of poverty. Growth is necessary but not sufficient for the poverty eradication. Inclusive growth can be a solution for poverty removal. In the 1990s, government of India started many programmes which were specially made for enhancing the income level of the poor masses. Consequently, all the major initiatives of government—in agricultural and rural development, in industry and urban development, in infrastructure and services, in education and health care—sought to promote 'inclusive growth'. It is apparent from the study that Inclusive growth is necessary for sustainable development and equitable distribution of wealth and prosperity.

Neetu Kwatra in Integration of Sustainability into the Banking Sector an effort is made to suggest modified procedure for commercial lending by Indian commercial banks to enable them to safeguard their own interests and also help in promoting environmental protection by the industry. Chapter explained the need for environmental protection, need for sensitization of branch managers and requested bankers to be aware of funding environment-related projects. Dr. Rajesh Kumar Sharma and Prof. N.K. Bansal in Financial Assistance and Incentives to the Senior Citizens of India—With Special Reference to the Senior Citizens of Dholpur in Rajasthan, they possess a vast experience.in different walks of life. The youth of today can gain from the experience of the senior citizens in taking the nation to greater heights. At this age of their life, they need to be taken care of and made to feel special. Indian government provides several benefits through its schemes in various sectors of development. With various tax benefits, travel and health care facilities provisioned for them, Indian Government has created reasons for senior citizens to feel happy. This corner on senior citizens is aimed at providing details on various aspects concerning them. M. Sayeed Alam, Sabina Sharmin, Omar Faruq, Do family and experience matter to access finance? A test on women entrepreneurs of Dhaka has been done with the samples, it is found that family support will be helpful to get institutional support whereas experience matter little. This study is concentrated only within Dhaka city and one limited sample so extended areas and more sample size are suggested to generalized the findings. Dr. Shahid Alam's Sustainable Development and the Indian Garments Industry, the increasing presence of foreign retailers in the domestic market is also expected to influence domestic players to improve their operations and offering to the customers. To tap the opportunities and sustain businesses in this changing consumption scenario, companies need to align themselves with the market requirements and develop required competencies. Manufacturers need to get more service-oriented and look to develop a niche positioning for themselves amongst their buyers. With growing competition suppliers also need to have orientation towards innovation across their business in terms of products, processes and adopt best manufacturing practices to increase competitiveness.

Ms. Silky Janglani, Dr. Simranjeet Kaur Sandhar, Dr. Amitabh Joshi has focused on Micro Finance: Innovations and Growth Trends, according to them a need was felt for alternative policies, systems and procedures, savings and loan products, complementary services, and new delivery mechanisms that would fulfil the requirements of the poorest, especially of the women members of such households. Micro finance was one solution to these problems. The study is to analyze various growth trends and innovations in micro finance. It also studies the success of micro finance and its benefits to rural people. Ms. Neha Gupta and Ms. Sumbul Tahir has expressed Road Map to Sustainability Rests on Corporate Governance. It is through effective corporate governance only that the company is held accountable to its residual owners. This ideology has now become ingrained in most corporate cultures. It is further believed that if the company maximizes shareholder value, the returns to other stakeholders will also increase leading to overall development and success. However, in reality, there have been many cases where shareholder interests do no reconcile well with stakeholder's interest. Such scenarios show that overwhelming emphasis on shareholder value may push executives to lean towards short cuts and unethical conduct. Ms. Sumbul Tahir, Sustainability in Higher Education: A New Paradigm Sustainable Development is a burning issue that requires efforts and dialogue from all sections of the society with the onus of responsibility being higher on educational institutions as they are associated with the young of the society. A successful marriage between education and a positive and responsible attitude towards environment will only lead to a lasting impression for the generations to come. Mr. G. Prasad

Babu, Talata C. Ratnayake and K.S. Kadian has viewed about Growth of Banking Sector In India—An Overview for understanding the banking structure in India, it will be essential to first know what constitutes banking activity. The Banking Regulation Act, 1949 defines banking as "accepting for the purposes of lending or investment, deposits of money from the public, repayable on demand or otherwise and withdrawable by cheque, draft, order or otherwise". The definition thus rules out from its scope the vast unorganized network of the indigenous village bankers who do not generally accept deposits and the mostly urban-based financial bodies who accept deposits for the purpose of lending but who do not offer withdrawal either on demand or by cheque and draft.

SHGs and Empowerment of Rural Women: Issues and Challenges by Tosib Alam and Zeeshan, Micro finance in India has gathered momentum to become a major force. Microfinance does not directly address some structural problems facing Indian society and the economy, and it is not yet as efficient as it will be when economies of scale are realised and a more supportive policy environment is created. Microfinance is one of the few markets-based, scalable anti-poverty solutions that are in place in India today, and the argument to scale it up to meet the overwhelming need is compelling. Lastly, Saswat Barpanda has thrown a light on HR issues relating to the MFIs working in India. He presents a brief review of literature on challenges of HR in the growth and transformation of Micro Finance Organizations (MFO) in India.

CHAPTER

1

Sustainable Development in India

Perspectives, Issues and Opportunities

ARIF M.K. AND ABDUL GHANI FAIYYAZ

ABSTRACT

India as a fast growing country in the modern world, sustainability should be there in all spheres of economic as well as social activities. Social sustainability emphasis on human rights, labour rights, corporate governance, etc. And 'Not for Profit Organization' (NPO) has to play key role in social development activities such as Education, health, social justice, minority welfare, poverty alleviation, religious and cultural values for the healthy economy. Even though government is providing much financial assistance to social organization especially 'Not for profit organizations' (NPOs), their performance for upliftment of society is not satisfactory. So some well-planned and innovative schemes should be adopted for sustainable development of the country.

Key Words: Sustainable development, Social sustainability, NPOs and NGOs.

INTRODUCTION

Sustainable Development (*SD*) is a pattern of resource use that aims to meet human needs while preserving the environment, so that these needs can be met not only in the present, but also for the future generations. The term sustainable development was firstly used by the Brundtland Commission, which coined what has become the most often-quoted definition on sustainable development as "development that meets the needs of the present without compromising the ability of future generations to meet their own needs."

This simple definition of sustainable development provided by *World Conference* on *Environment* and *Development (WCED)* in 1987 is immediately seen to contain a distinction and potential conflict between interest of present and those of future generations. The conditions for such future generation encompass all area of human activities including production, trade, technology, politics, etc.

Most definition of sustainable development emphasizes the idea that there are three inter-dependent and mutually reinforcing pillars of sustainable development such as Environment protection, social sustainability and economic development.

Economic Sustainability includes identification of information, integration, and participation as key building blocks to help countries achieve development that recognizes these interdependent pillars. It emphasizes that in sustainable development everyone is a user and provider of information. It stresses the need to change from old sector-centered ways of doing business to new approaches that involve cross-spectral co-ordination and the integration of environmental and social concerns into all development processes.

Environmental Sustainability: According to world summit on sustainable development in Johansberg (2002) "the global environment continue to suffer, loss of biodiversity continues, fish stock continue to be depleted, dissatisfaction claim more and more fertile land. The adverse affect of climate change are all ready evident. Natural disasters are more frequent and devastating and developing countries more vulnerable and are water and marine pollution continues to take millions of decent life." Environmental sustainability can only be achieved by overcoming these challenges.

Social sustainability: It requires the cohesion of society and its ability to work towards common goals should be maintained. Individual needs, such as those for health and well-being, nutrition, shelter, education and cultural expression should be met. It also includes human right; labour right, corporate governance, etc.

History has led to vast inequalities, almost three-forth of world's people living in less developed countries and one fifth living below poverty line. The problem is complex and choice is difficult. As far as India is concerned Eleventh Plan sought to on gain achieved in the tenth plan and shift the economy to the path of faster and more inclusive growth. The programs on education, health, social justice, employment and skill development, handloom and handicraft, women agency and child rights, rural development, special area program governance, poverty reduction are the main head under Planning Commission of India for the social development. Social development only is possible through well-planned implementation of programme in each area.

SOCIAL INDICATORS ON SUSTAINABLE DEVELOPMENT

There are two terms are commonly used on the sustainability, i.e. weak sustainability and strong sustainability. The degree of sustainability can be determined on the performance of social indicators. It includes the following :

- % of population living below poverty line
- Gini index of inequality
- Unemployment rate
- Average female wage to male wage
- Nutritional status of children
- Mortality rate under the age of five
- Infant mortality rate
- Life expectancy at birth
- % with adequate sewage disposal facilities
- Population with access to safe drinking water

- % population with primary health access facility
- Immunization growth inefficiencies childhood diseases
- Contraceptive prevalence rate
- Child reaching grade fine of primary education
- Adult secondary education achievement level
- Adult literacy rate
- Flour area per person
- No. of repeated crimes per thousand population
- Population growth rate
- Sex ratio
- Crude birth rate
- Population of urban and formal and informal settlement

The government plans and policies are much advanced to guide sustainable development especially social sustainability of the economy. But highly populated country like India, it is not possible for Government to fulfil all requirements of the citizens in the country. There are many factors and aspect for inclusive growth and sustainability of the economy. Social and Not for Profit Organization (NPO) has to function an important role in the social development activities such as education, health, social justice, minority welfare, poverty alleviation, religious and culture values for the healthy economy.

SOCIAL AND NOT FOR PROFIT ORGANIZATION

Not for profit organization is an organization establishes for public purpose that does not distribute its surplus funds to owner or shareholders, but instead uses them to help pursue its goal. The distinction between profit and NPO is for profit organization can be privately owned and may be re-distribute taxable wealth to employees and shareholder. By contrast, NPO does not have private owners. They have controlling members and board, but people cannot sell their shares to others or personal benefit in any taxable organization.

NPOs are often charities or service organizations. Sometimes they are also called foundation, or endowment that has large stock funds. Foundation gives and grants NPOs for fellowship and direct grant to participant. However, the name foundation can be used by any not for profit corporate—even volunteer organization or grass root groups. Other name of NPOs includes non-government organization, community, base of organization, civil society organization, etc.

NPOs can be registered in the following four ways :

- Trust
- Society
- Section 25 of Companies Act
- Special licensing

Registration can be done with Registrar of Companies

The following laws or constitutional Articles of the republic of India are relevant to NGOs :

- Articles 19(1) and 30 of the constitution of India
- Income Tax Act, 1961
- Public trust acts of various states
- Societies Registrar Act, 1860
- Section 25 of Indian Companies Act
- Foreign Contract (Regulation) Act, 1976

Even though Not for Profit Organization includes trust, societies, charities, etc., we mainly concentrate on NGOs for the convenience of the study.

NON-GOVERNMENT ORGANISATION

In India NPOs are commonly known as non-government organization. There was an imperative need towards ensuring the development wide-spread and fair. They focus on fostering sustainable economic and social development in most developing countries. Their integration in world economy and poverty alleviation necessitated working with institution other than government.

The "NGOs" phenomenon is recognition of the fact that the state, with limited resource has failed to provide the targeted level of social services, economic opportunities and political empowerment to its people. The market responded with growth of NGOs, to fill vacuum left by absence of state-sponsored services. NGOs became more important in providing social and economic services. They also became more active in setting development agenda. Thus, failure of government policy was not just absence of services, but failure of policy to ensure widespread distribution of resource (services) where they were available.

Role of NPO's In Sustainable Development

The role of NPO's is very wide because it includes NGOs, Trusts, Charity, Societies for Welfare, social organizations and so many other organisations which are not made for profit but to make a welfare state. Role of NGO's can be give under the following headings :

Poverty Alleviation and Skill Development

The Eleventh Plan target was to reduce the percentage of poverty by 10 percentage points over the Plan period, or 2 percentage points per year, which is more than twice the pace observed in the past. Mahatma Gandhi National Rural Employment Guarantee Program (MGNREGP) is one of the most important step in the part of Government India for poverty alleviation. Government program can only be make success for poverty reduction programs, social organization especially NGO has great role in this regard. That is why Government of India is making plan on co-partnership with NGOs. NGOs programs include free supply of equipment, tool for employment purposes, promoting social entrepreneurship, youth entrepreneurship, women entrepreneurship, financial assistance to start small businesses. Beside this social organization or societies are getting many financial assistance within the country as well as outside the country for building houses, education and many activities to poor people. NGO's programs should give attention on traditionally skilled persons like carpenter, painters, etc., their skill on that particular area should be motivated and promoted. NGO's programs on the promotion on job-oriented education should be continued for the social sustainability.

Education

Quality education must be broadened to all sections of the population that could benefit for the new and productive employment opportunities for substantial growth in these areas. It is only through qualitative education India can be sustained. There are many community colleges religious organization starting school and colleges for the development of their community. NGOs are concentrating on elementary education by starting Anganwadi, street schools and other social activities with the help various government programs and schemes.

Health

Human health is one of the important aspects of social development. Access to good quality health service is another critical element of inclusive growth. The deficiencies in Government health centers and hospital are well known. That is it only with the help of NPOs India can succeed for long-term. There are many hospitals running under many charitable institutions and also trusts with an intention to serve the society. They are not concentrating on rural heath. NGO's programs on rural health includes medical camp, health orientation programs Awareness on communicative diseases.

Social Justice

Social justice will be meaningful only when it delivers justice to all particularly disadvantaged groups such as scheduled caste, scheduled tribe and other backward classes of minority. Person with disability senior citizen and other marginalized groups. NGO's programs should give emphasis on promoting and advertising about Fundamental Human Rights, Right to Education Act, Right to Information Act, women reservation, rights of backward communities, etc.

Sports and Culture

NGOs Performance on sports is not up to the mark. Government only promotes cricket and hockey. There are so many players on various sports items which are more popular in the rural areas need to give much attention. India's vision and mission on sports is not getting desired result. There are many sports and arts club for the promotions of sports activities and cultural programs. They should improve their performance.

CRITICISM ON NPOs

The government is providing much financial assistance to social and not for organizations, but performance is not satisfactory up to some extent for sustainable development. There are many reasons for this. We know that number of blacklisted NGOs are increasing day-by-day. There are many reasons for blacklisting of NGOs. Main reasons are :

- Misappropriation of fund is the main important limitation of NGOs facing in India. As we know that corruption and misappropriation of funds are there is in every economic activity, NGOs also facing same problem in this regard.
- Window dressing and manipulation of accounting record is another important reason for black-listing of NGOs.
- As far as NPOs are concerned, they may get fund from their own communities, religion and foreign countries also, but there may be some people who donate funds to these NPOs without disclosing their name and these fund remain unrecorded in the accounts of NPOs.

There are many reasons for unsatisfactory performance of NPOs in India. It can be outlined in following points :

- Planning Commission of India clearly mentions their aim as inclusive growth. Inclusive Growth can only possible by including lower class people in economic and social activities. Most of the programs of social organization are not reaching to the grass-root level up to some extent.
- Most of the volunteers and organizers working in NGOs are unskilled. That is why the organization lacks professional touch.

- NGOs working in one particular project don't concentrate on other areas (e.g. NGOs encaged in education programs are not give attention to health program and *vice versa*.)
- Lack of Continuity of the projects in the same locality, shortage of the projects is another constrains to them.
- Hypocrisy of the volunteer is another question mark. Some persons in NPO are doing work only for name and fame. One case was occurred in a city that one NGO has donated 25 wheel chairs to one hospital but it has been shown 100 in so many newspapers and news channels.
- Even though foreign money is an important and main source of fund for social organization, there are some societies misusing the fund which has been allotted to them for social causes. But it cannot be justified on any ground.
- Some NGOs are resisted by local people in many villages because of the misbehavior of volunteers.
- Many rich people are dealing in with NPOs to get benefit of tax exemption and deduction.
- Information about NGO programs are not known to common people especially lower class people. It is due to lack of proper advertisement and publicity of different programs, etc. and also they are not trying to canvas the common people in social services.
- NGOs giving much attention on oral programs (orientation, speech, awareness) than to perform.
- Main problem of Not for Profit and Social Organization is lack of professional touch in their activities. That is why some times they lose team work and coordination.
- Poverty alleviation programs have no long life, as they have no vision, only targeting short-term. Lack of continuity of the programs and not reviewing the performance on time is another drawback.
- Health programs not giving much attention on malnutrition and other diseases which are only caused because of the illiteracy of the poor parents.

- Most of the welfare organization confined to SC, ST promotion not giving much attention to other backward classes in the country.
- Career counseling programs are not so effective in NGOs.
- By the name of religion some societies are starting educational institution but they are charging high fee from students.

SUGGESTIONS

- There are some NGOs working in USA with an aim of sustainable development only. NGOs in India can also perform in this way.
- In globalised era most of the people are not interested in social service and to join social organization. So much attention should be given to encourage people to come ahead for social services as it's only for their benefit.
- NGOs and NPOs should try to link or connect with NSS, NCC, etc. and social activities of schools and colleges. It is only literate youth can make social sustainability of India.
- Minority college, institutions, community educational institute must try to work for the Upliftment of their community, religion and also try to protect their own culture by keeping secularism in the country.
- Poverty alleviation program should have vision and mission, continuity of project and reviewing of result is also mandatory.
- Social justice program is confine to speeches only there is no productive law education.
- As far as health sector is concerned social organization are doing work on a particular disease or orientation to defend that particular disease. But before that they must give attention on the term "prevention is better than cure" conduct health survey on that particular village on health it may disclose some facts about communicative diseases.

- Accident is increasing day by day in all cities there is no effective arrangement for saving the life in accident cases and giving emergency treatment with the help of Government, NGOs can chalk out some plan including mobile clinic.
- Some state Governments are providing sex education along with their curriculum its responsibility of NPOs to conduct this type of classes.
- With the help of Right To Education Act NGOs should give primary education by starting street school and Anganwadi for highlighting right to education act and preventing child labour by using appropriate clause
- Political interference in any NPOs should be strictly banned.
- NGOs should give emphasis for giving awareness on fundamental human right like Right to Information Act; Right to Education on the lowest class of society by conducting street plays another means.
- Awareness about government program and schemes should be communicated through NPOs.
- Employment programs should include coordinating Entrepreneur of particular area and giving project consultancies services for generating employment opportunities in that village.
- Should promote traditionally skilled workers like carpenter, painter and motivate them for employment.
- Social entrepreneurship is another important element of poverty alleviation.
- Reviewing and monitoring system of NGOs should be appropriate.
- Sports club should give attention on promoting sports activities to student as well as youth.
- Conducting cultural and youth festival once in a year.
- Co ordinate all NGOs working in particular district for getting new project from NPOs.
- Government should restrict on number of NGOs working in specific areas in order to enhance boundary of NGOs.

Vision of Sustainable Development in India through NGO's—A Model

This model suggests that inclusive and sustainable growth of India can only be attained by starting social development programs and schemes from grass-root level. Proper data should be needed for chalking out any plans. Government of India neither collecting data nor making official estimates annually relating social development. Statistics of 2001 census and sample data of Suresh Tendulkar Committee in 2004-05 is using for planning the schemes. That is why first attention given by this model is to collect data on education, health, social justice and poverty on each ward in a Panchayat, Municipality or Corporation.

This model says the importance of having at least one NGO in every Panchayat, Municipality, and Corporation. Most of the NGOs concentrating only to one sector (i.e. education only, health only) but this model concentrates four lines of activity under one NGO with the coordination of respective bodies.

NGO activities should not limited to one area of activity only, that is education, health but it should focus on other social problems which, in fact is a hindrance for sustainable development of the economy. We are suggesting at preliminary level one NGOs working in a Panchayat for education, health, poverty alleviation including employment generation and social justice.

Social sustainability can only be possible by the programs at grass-root level.

After collecting the data on each area it will be submitted in ward meeting. Then only the Organizations can understand the real picture about the village. Its literacy rate, status of higher education, person employed in service sector, private sector, status of male and female, health condition, number of person suffering from particular diseases, etc. By analyzing these reports organization like NGOs can predict the future status of that village. Same thing doing will follow all the wards in that particular Panchayat, municipality, or corporation.

Ward meeting will divide people into four groups, i.e., education, health, poverty alleviation and social justice. Groups can include educational institution representatives, volunteers of clubs, political representatives, etc. Formulated groups with the help of NGOs will suggest appropriate programs for back ward areas. NGOs will propose this to government in the form of project. Panchayat, Corporation, Municipality can effectively

Panchayat/Municipality/Corporation

NGO (One)

Health, Education, Poverty Alleviation, Social Justice, etc.

Ward Survey in each area

Survey Report analysis in ward meeting

Understanding the real picture of the village

Forming groups of people from the villages (with the help of NGO's)

Education, Health, Poverty Alleviation, Social Justice, etc.

NGO's after understanding with groups setting upon project and sumbit to government

Local Bodies of the Government can also corporate with the local NGO's in the policies of the Government to provide Education, health facilities, socio-economic justice and remove poverty, etc.

Review the results quarterly

Annual survey and review

implement government programs for rural and urban development. The formation of group is for giving significance on social services; later on the group can be converted into NGO. Instead of implementing different projects on different areas this model gives long-term vision. Reviewing annual result and annual survey very important for the continuity of the project and also full sustainability of India.

References

1. Srivastava, A.K. (2004), Sustainable Development, APH, New Delhi.
2. Iqbal, Qureshi Zafar (2005), Managing NGOs in Developing Countries: Concept, Framework and Cases, Oxford University Press.
3. Sethi, Harsh, Review: Difficult Times for NGOs, *Economic and Political Weekly*, Vol. 38, No. 46 (Nov. 15-21, 2003).
4. Wallace, Tina, Trends in UK NGOs: A Research Note, Development in Practice, Vol. 13, No. 5 (Nov., 2003), pp. 564-569.
5. Devine, Joseph, The Paradox of Sustainability : Reflections of NGOs in Bangladesh, Annals of the American Academy of Political and Social Science, Vol. 590, Rethinking Sustainable Development (Nov., 2003), pp. 227-42 Published.
6. Simmons, P.J., Learning to Live with NGOs. *Source* : Foreign Policy, No. 112 (Autumn, 1998), pp. 82-96.
7. www.planningcommission.nic.in
8. www.socialjustice.nic.in
9. ngo.india.gov.in

CHAPTER

Role of FDI in Sustaining Various Economy of the World Focusing on India

Akansha Bhargava

ABSTRACT

We develop a simple information-based model of FDI flows in which the abundance of "intangible" capital in the source countries, which generates expertise in cream-skimming investment projects in the host countries and enhances FDI flows. Corporate transparency in the host countries, on the other hand, diminishes the value of this expertise and thereby reduces the flow of FDI. The gains from FDI in the host countries are reflected in a more efficient size of stock of domestic capital and its allocation across firms. These gains depend crucially on the degree of competition among FDI investors.

In recognition of the important role of Foreign Direct Investment (FDI) in the accelerated economic growth of the country, Government of India initiated a slew of economic and financial reforms in 1991. India is now ushering in the second generation reforms aimed at further and faster integration of Indian economy with the global economy. As a result of the various policy initiatives taken, India has been rapidly changing from a restrictive regime to a liberal one, and FDI is encouraged in almost all the economic activities under the automatic route. And so this paper will includes the following heads:

- An introduction of the FDI Sustainability
- History of FDI Sustainability
- Various methods of FDI Sustainability
- FDI Sustainability in the U.S. Economy
- FDI Sustainability in the China Economy
- FDI Sustainability in the Developing World Focusing India
- Conclusion with Final Remarks

INTRODUCTION OF FOREIGN DIRECT INVESTMENT (FDI) SUSTAINABILITY

Over the years, FDI inflow in the country is increasing. However, India has tremendous potential for absorbing greater flow of FDI in the coming years. Serious efforts are being made to attract greater inflow of FDI in the country by taking several actions both on policy-making and implementation front. However, the subject relating to FDI Policy and its promotion and facilitation as also promotion and facilitation of investment by Non-Resident Indians (NRIs) and Overseas Corporate Bodies (OCBs) will continue to be handled by the Department.

Introduction of Foreign Direct Investment (FDI) has been growing faster than world GDP, and is becoming a major component of foreign investment. Indeed, empirical studies distinguish this form of capital flows from other forms, such as portfolio-equity and debt flows. We usually observe both one-way flows of FDI, from developed to developing economies, and two-way flows among developed economies. The purpose of this paper is to explore some unique features of FDI associated with information and transparency, which make it stand out among the various forms of capital flows. FDI flows into the host countries is shown to exist. We incorporate these new considerations in a gravity model of capital flows. Such models have proved

Useful in explaining bilateral trade flows and, more recently, cross-border equity flows. There has been some initial exploration of the determinants of FDI in gravity models but not focusing on the role of information as we do here. We interpret the industry specialization in the source country as providing a comparative advantage to the potential foreign direct investors, in eliciting good investment opportunities in the host country, relative to domestic investors in the latter country. This advantage may stem, for instance, from the ability of FDI investors to apply better industry-specific micro-management standards. In our model this element is captured by assuming a lower cost of cream-skimming. Refers to long-term participation by country A into country B. It usually involves participation in *management, joint-venture, transfer of technology* and *expertise*. There are three types of FDI: inward foreign direct investment and outward foreign direct investment, resulting in a net FDI inflow (positive or negative) and "stock of foreign direct investment", which is the cumulative number for a given period. Direct investment excludes *investment through purchase of shares*.

History

(FDI) is a measure of foreign ownership of productive assets, such as factories, mines and land. Increasing foreign investment can be used as one measure of growing economic globalization. Figure on page no. 20 shows net inflows of foreign direct investment. The largest flows of foreign investment occur between the industrialized countries (*North America, Western Europe* and *Japan*). But flows to non-industrialized countries are increasing sharply.

Types

A foreign direct investor may be classified in any sector of the economy and could be any one of the following:

- an individual;
- a group of related individuals;

- an incorporated or *unincorporated entity;*
- a *public company* or *private company;*
- a group of related enterprises;
- a government body;
- an *estate (law), trust* or other societal organization; or
- Any combination of the above.

Methods

The foreign direct investor may acquire 10% or more of the voting power of an enterprise in an economy through any of the following methods:

- by incorporating a wholly owned *subsidiary* or *company;*
- by acquiring shares in an associated enterprise;
- through a *merger* or an *acquisition* of an unrelated enterprise; and
- participating in an equity *joint venture* with another investor or enterprise.

Foreign direct investment incentives may take the following forms:

- low *corporate tax* and *income tax* rates
- *tax holidays*
- other types of tax concessions
- preferential *tariffs*
- *Special economic zones*
- *EPZ*-Export Processing Zones
- *Bonded Warehouses*
- *Soft loan* or loan *guarantees*
- Free land or land subsidies
- Relocation and expatriation subsidies
- Job training and employment subsidies
- *Infrastructure* subsidies
- RandD support
- Derogation from regulations (usually for very large projects)

SUSTAINABILITY OF FDI IN UNITED STATES

"Invest in America" is an initiative of the *US Department of Commerce* and aimed to promote the arrival of foreign investors to the country.

The "Invest in America" policy is focused on:

- Facilitating *investor* queries.
- Carrying out maneuvers to aid foreign investors.
- Provide support both at local and state levels.
- Address concerns related to the business environment by helping as an *ombudsman* in Washington DC for the international *venture* community.
- Offering policy guidelines and helping getting access to the legal system.

The United States is the world's largest recipient of FDI. More than $ 325.3 billion in FDI flowed into the United States in 2010, which is a 48 percent increase from 2009. The $ 2.1 trillion stock of FDI in the United States at the end of 2008 is the equivalent of approximately 16 percent of U.S. gross domestic product (GDP) 55.

Benefits of FDI in America

In the last 6 years, over 4000 new projects and 630,000 new jobs have been created by foreign companies, resulting in close to $ 314 billion in investment. Unarguably, US affiliates of foreign companies have a history of paying higher wages than US corporations. Foreign companies have in the past supported an annual US payroll of $ 364 billion with an average annual compensation of $ 68,000 per employee. Increased US exports through the use of multinational distribution networks. FDI has resulted in 30% of jobs for Americans in the manufacturing sector, which accounts for 12% of all manufacturing jobs in the US. Affiliates of *foreign corporations* spent more than $34 billion on *research and development* in 2006 and continue to support many national projects. Inward FDI has led to higher productivity through increased capital, which in turn has led to high *living standards*.

SUSTAINABILITY OF FDI IN CHINA

FDI in China has been one of the major successes of the past 3 decades. Starting from a *baseline* of less than $ 19 billion just 20 years ago, FDI in China has grown to over $ 300 billion in the first 10 years. China has continued its massive growth and is the leader among all developing nations in terms of FDI. Even though there was a slight dip in FDI in 2009 as a result of the global slowdown, 2010 has again seen investments increase. The Chinese continue to steamroll with expectations that economic growth will be 10% this year.

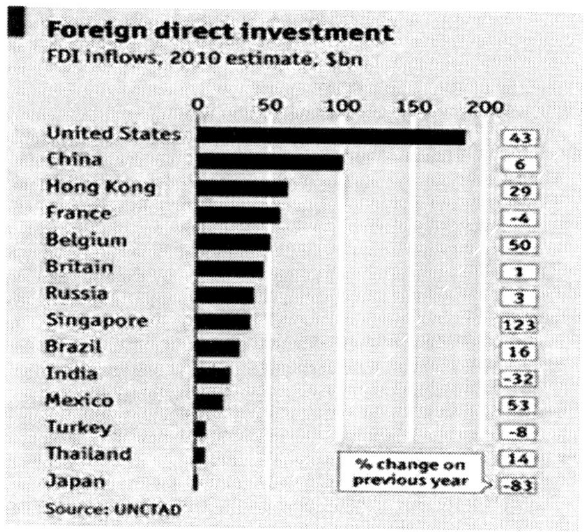

FOREIGN DIRECT INVESTMENT AND THE DEVELOPING WORLD

Foreign investment can be a significant driver of development in poor nations. It provides an inflow of foreign capital and funds, in addition to an increase in the transfer of skills, technology, and job opportunities. Many of the East Asian tigers such as *China, South Korea, Malaysia,* and *Singapore* benefited from investment abroad. The *Commitment to Development Index* ranks the "development-friendliness" of rich country investment policies.

SUSTAINABILITY OF FDI IN INDIA

The constant efforts of the Government of India in making the country an investor-friendly destination are reaping dividends. Alongside the United Nations Conference on Trade and Development (UNCTAD) ranking India at second place in global foreign direct investments (FDI) in 2010, in its report titled, 'World Investment Prospects Survey 2009-2012' has added to the initiative to a great extent. The report further forecasts, India to be among the top five attractive destinations for international investors during 2010-12.

FDI inflow rose by more than 100 percent to US $ 4.66 billion in May 2011, which is the highest monthly inflow in 39 months, while the cumulative amount of FDI equity inflows from April 2000 to May 2011 stood at US $ 205.96 billion, according to the latest data released by the Department of Industrial Policy and Promotion (DIPP). The service (including financial and non-financial) sectors attracted highest FDI equity inflows during April-May 2011-12 at US $ 910 million. India received maximum FDI from countries like Mauritius, Singapore, and the US at US $ 56.31 billion, US $ 13.25 billion and US $ 9.71 billion, respectively, during April 2000-May 2011. India's foreign exchange (Forex) reserves have increased by US $ 2.29 billion for the week ended July 22, 2011, according to the weekly statistical bulletin released by the Reserve Bank of India (RBI). In the week under consideration, foreign currency assets went up by US $ 2.23 billion to US $ 284.53 billion. Furthermore, India may emerge as US Export-Import Bank's (Ex-Im) largest market in next 12-18 months. "During the last nine months, we have approved 173 transactions involving 100 companies and US $ 1.4 billion in financing of US exports to India," as per Fred P. Hochberg, the bank's Chairman and President.

Top Sectors Receiving FDI

Rank	Sector	2010-11 (April-Feb.) in $B
1	Services Sector	3.27
2	Telecommunications	1.41
3	Automobile Industry	1,32
4	Power	1.24
5	Housing and Real Estate	1.1
6	Construction Actitivies	1.07
7	Metallurgical Industris	1.04
8	Computer Software and Hardware	0.76
9	Petroleum and Natural Gas	0.56
10	Chemicals	0.38

Source : Ministry of Commerce and Industry.

Investment Sustainability

The total merger and acquisitions (MandA) and private equity (PE) (including qualified institutional placement (QIP)) deals in the first half of 2011 include 524 deals valued at US $. 32.48 billion, according to data released by Grant Thornton

Top 10 Countries Investing in India

Rank	Country	2010-11 (April-Feb.) in $B
1	Mauritius	6.6
2	Singapore	1.6
3	Japan	1.5
4	Netehrlands	1.1
5	U.S.A.	1.1
6	Cyprus	0.83
7	France	0.71
8	U.K.	0.52
9	U.A.E.	0.32
10	Germany	0.16

Source : Ministry of Commerce and Industry.

India. The global MandA activity has been increasing so far in 2011 (Jan.-June 2011) clocking deals worth US $ 1.5 trillion. In addition, the total value of outbound deals—Indian companies acquiring businesses outside India—in the first half of 2011 was recorded at 86 deals worth US $ 5.89 billion. PE deals amounted to 203 deals worth US $ 5.09 billion in the first half of 2011 as compared to 125 deals worth US $ 2.95 billion during the corresponding period in 2010.

CONCLUSION

We developed a model in which foreign direct investors are better equipped and experienced in skimming the "good" firms than their domestic counterparts. Employing this technology, the foreign direct investors are able to outbid domestic and foreign portfolio investors for the good firms. We emphasize this feature of FDI which is better hands-on management standards that entails a cutting-edge advantage over other investors in reacting in real time to a changing business environment. This feature is more pronounced in high-productivity firms, resulting in "cream-skimming" of domestic firms by FDI investors. Note that this mechanism applies both to mergers and acquisitions and to Greenfield investments. The productivity signal, though, is likely to be coarser in the latter, conveying less information about the true productivity. We view FDI as distinct from portfolio investment with respect to the quality of management.

Foreign direct investors, by definition, acquire some significant control over the firm they invest in. They can then apply hands-on management (micro-management) standards that enable them to react in real time to changing economic environments. This feature may stem from "intangible capital" accumulated through a specialization by the foreign direct investors in certain niche, some micro evidence in support of our theory. In (2010) report that foreign direct investors pick the high-productivity firms in transition economies. We employ a gravity equation in order to shed some empirical evidence on the prediction of our theory. We find that indeed the abundance of "intangible" capital in the source countries is positively correlated with FDI flows to the host countries. Also, the degree of corporate transparency in the host countries is negatively correlated with these flows.

CHAPTER

3

Sustainable Development of Indian Derivatives Markets

An Analysis

MD. AGHA NURUZZAMAN AND ASAD REHMAN

I. BACKGROUND

The present paper attempts to discuss the genesis of derivatives trading by tracing its historical development and classification of derivatives. It also looks at regulation and policy developments, future prospects and challenges of futures market in India.

Derivatives' trading is an integral part of the maturing process of capital market of every nation. Derivatives contracts were introduced just as a risk management tool in the financial market. However, they can be used for price risk as well as to speculate, thereby attracting hedgers and speculators towards the market. Futures act as a double-edged weapon (Bodla and

Jindal, 2008) and even highly expert professionals can lose money in speculative futures trading (Kant, 2008).

Indian futures market is mainly driven by Institutional investor,[1] Retail investor[2] and Proprietary.[3] In 2009-10 (Figure 1) their participation was 13.61%, 54.86% and 31.635 respectively in terms of traded volume. This shows that retail investors have an important role in Indian derivative markets. As their numbers have exploded, it has become increasingly more important to understand the minds, motivations, and decision-making styles of retail investors.

FIG. 1

Participation-wise Futures and Options Turnover during 2009-10

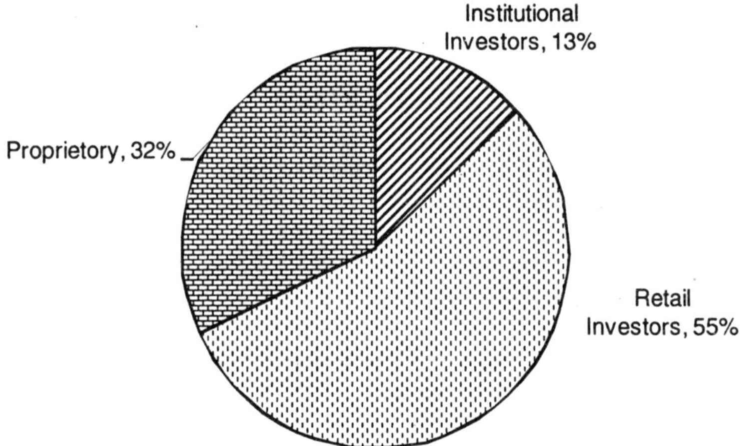

Source : Developed by the researcher.

A retail investor's behavior comprehension happens to be a complex thing. Economists, sociologists and psychologists have all attempted to explain investor behavior in various ways. Economists' enquiry into investors' behavior have focused largely on the 'rationality' or 'irrationality' of investor decision-making process. Sociologists explain investor behavior by focusing on investors' social environments. They suggest that investors may be trying to enhance their stature within a group or society in general. Psychologists have largely focused on the investor's behavior on the basis of their attitudes, perceptions, and personality. But of course, there is a lot of overlap between the disciplines.

2. INVESTMENTS AND ITS OBJECTIVES

Investment is a planned task of construction and management of personal investment portfolio by an individual, and is done as per his/her requirements and life-stage (Figure 2). It is an activity, whose outcome should match the short-term and long-term financial needs of an individual and/ or his/her family (Shrotriya, 2007).

FIG. 2
Motives of Investment

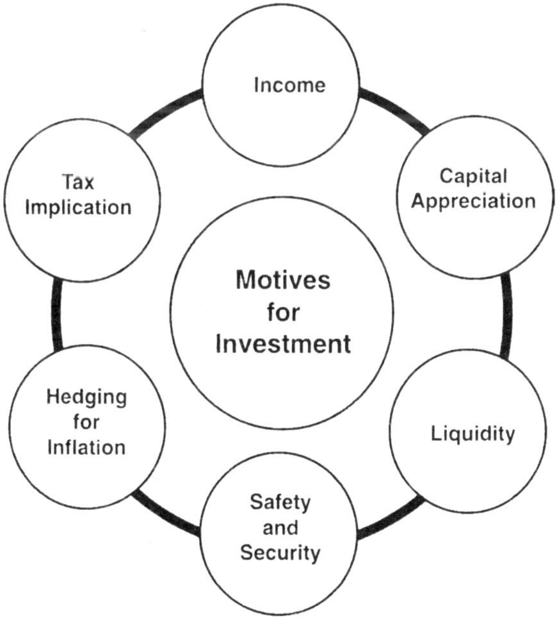

Source : Developed by the researcher.

There are various motives for investment as shown in Figure 2. Some investors wants capital appreciation, whereas some prefer liquidity, some of the investors are interested to invest their funds in tax saving instruments and some focus on safety and security. Apart from this, some of the investors want to hedge their investment against different types of risk associated with their investments. Derivatives (futures/options) are risk minimizing instruments, by using derivatives the risk of the underlying assets can be minimized to a greater extent (Tofano and Haushalter, 1996; Hentschel and Kothari, 2000; Mckenzie *et. al.*, 2000; Rinalini and Kakati, 2007).

To meet the various motives of investment, investors have different investment avenues. In broader sense, they can be divided into two types (Figure 3), investment in physical assets like gold, real estate, etc. and investment in financial assets like government securities, fixed bank deposits, equity shares, etc. Each instrument has its own advantages and disadvantages. Investors invest in these assets to take advantage of them even

FIG. 3
Investment Avenues

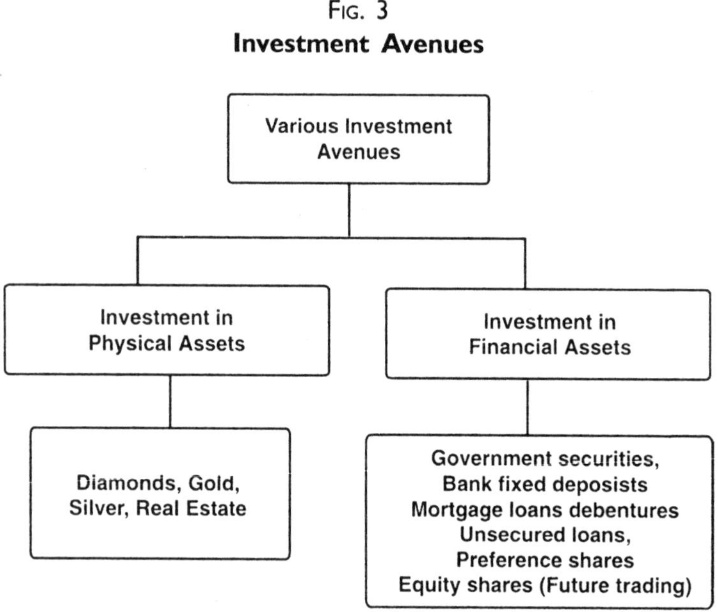

Source : Developed by the Researcher.

though by assuming risks associated with these investment avenues. To protect against the risk of equity shares, investors use single stock futures as well as stock based index futures.

3. CONCEPTS OF DERIVATIVES

The term 'derivatives' refers to a broad class of financial instruments, mainly including futures and options. These instruments derive their value from the price and other related variables of the underlying asset. The assets underlying futures may be a commodity or a financial asset.

Section 2(ac) of Securities Contract Regulation Act (SCRA), 1956 defines Derivative as:

- "A security derived from a debt instrument, share, loan whether secured or unsecured, risk instrument or contract for differences or any other form of security".
- "A contract which derives its value from the prices, or index of prices, of underlying securities".

Thus a futures contract is an agreement between two parties to buy or sell an asset at a certain time in future for a certain price (Hull, 2000).

I. Underlying Asset in a Derivatives Contract

As defined above, the value of a futures instrument depends upon the underlying asset. The underlying asset may assume many forms:

- Shares and share warrants of companies traded on recognized stock exchanges
- Commodities including grain, coffee beans, orange juice, etc.
- Precious metals like gold and silver
- Foreign exchange rates or currencies, interest rates
- Bonds of different types including medium to long term negotiable debt securities issued by governments, companies, etc.
- Short-term securities such as T-bills; and

- Over-the-Counter (OTC)[4] money market products such as loans or deposits.

2. Risks Associated with Derivatives Trading

Risk can be defined as the potential for realizing low returns or even losing money, possibly preventing from meeting important objectives. There are many kinds of risks associated with different investment avenues (Figure 4) broadly divided into two categories: avoidable and unavoidable risk (Shrotriya, 2007). Certain factors affect all types of investments and are beyond the control of investors, known as unavoidable risk. Whereas the other type of risk is avoidable even at the time of investment. Futures are associated with liquidity risk of the market, interest rate risk, inflation risk, political instability risk, and economic risk of the country.

Rewards and risks are always related. It is unrealistic to

FIG. 4

Types of Risks in Futures Market

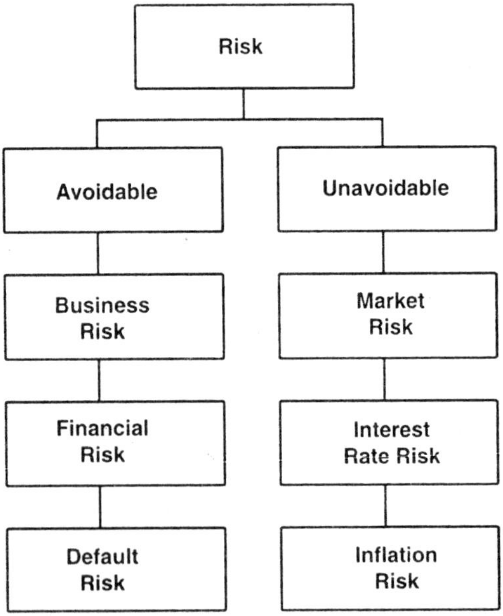

Source : Adapted from Shrotriya, 2007.

expect to be able to earn above-average investment returns without taking above-average risks as well. Futures trading has the reputation of being a highly risky endeavor. It is true that a high percentage of traders eventually lose money. However, futures trading reputation as a highly risky activity is somewhat undeserved. In the words of a renowned psychology expert Mark Douglas, "Most people like to think of themselves as risk takers, but what they really want is a guaranteed outcome with some momentary suspense to make them feel as if the outcome had been in doubt. The momentary suspense adds the thrill factor necessary to keep our lives from getting too boring."

Futures traders should be fully aware of and be comfortable with the risks involved. Managing the risks of trading is a very important part of any trader's success. Although the risks can be managed, it can never be eliminated. Risk in trading is that one cannot always claim to avoid losses by careful planning or brilliant strategy. Some losses are part of the investment process. Many people think the best traders don't lose any money and have only winning trades. This is absolutely not true. The best traders lose a lot of money, but they eventually make even more money over time.

There is no point in trading if one cannot handle the risk involved. While ordinary people tend to take losses personally as a sign of failure, good traders tend to overcome losses in due course of time. The best trading plans at times result in losses because of the amount of randomness in market price action.

3. Participants in Derivatives Market

There are basically three types of participants who trade in futures, mentioned as under:

Hedgers: Hedgers are interested in reducing a risk that they already face (Hull, 2000). They use futures markets to reduce or eliminate the risk associated with the price of an asset. A majority of the participants in futures market belong to this category.

Speculators: A speculator is a trader who enters the futures market in search of profit and, by so doing, willingly accepts increased risk (Robert and James, 2006). Traders transact futures and options contracts to get extra leverage in betting on future movements in the price of an asset. They can increase both the potential gains and potential losses by usage of futures in a speculative venture.

Arbitrageurs: Arbitrage involves locking in a riskless profit by entering simultaneously into transactions in two or more markets. Their behavior is guided by the desire to take advantage of a discrepancy between prices of more or less the same assets or competing assets in different markets (Hull, 2000). For example, if they see the futures price of an asset getting out of line with the cash price, they will take offsetting positions in the two markets to lock in a profit.

4. Applications of Derivatives

There can be different motives for making investments, depending upon the need and circumstances of the individual. The various motives for investing are capital appreciation, income at specific time intervals, and liquidity when required. It also provides a kind of safety and security of life, hedging against inflation and tax implications (Shrotriya, 2007). Some of the applications of financial Futures can be enumerated as follows:

Management of risk: This is the most important function of derivatives. Risk management is not about the elimination of risk rather it is about the management of risk. Derivatives provide a powerful tool for limiting risks that individuals and organizations face in the ordinary conduct of their businesses. Effective use of derivatives can save cost, and it can increase returns for the organizations.

Efficiency in trading: Derivatives allow for free trading of risk components and that leads to improving market efficiency. Traders can use a position (buy/sell) in one or more derivatives products as a substitute for a position in the underlying instruments. This is mainly because of the greater amount of liquidity in the market offered by futures as well as the lower transaction costs associated with trading in derivative as compared to the costs of trading the underlying instrument in cash market.

Speculation: This is not the only use, and probably not the most important use, of financial futures. Financial futures are considered to be risky. If not used properly, these can lead to financial destruction in an organization. However, these instruments act as a powerful instrument for knowledgeable traders to expose them to calculated and well understood risks in search of a reward, in the form of profit.

Price discovery: Another important application of derivatives is the price discovery which means revealing information about future cash market prices through the futures market. Futures markets provide a mechanism by which diverse and scattered opinions of future are collected into one readily discernible number which provides a consensus of knowledgeable thinking.

Price stabilization: Derivative market helps to keep a stabilizing influence on spot prices by reducing the short-term fluctuations. In other words, derivative reduces both peak and depths, simultaneously leading to price stabilization effect in the cash market for underlying asset.

4. CLASSIFICATIONS OF DERIVATIVES

Broadly derivatives can be classified into two categories (Figure 5): Commodity derivatives and financial derivatives. In case of commodity futures, underlying assets can be commodities like wheat, gold, silver, etc., whereas in case of financial futures underlying assets are stocks, currencies, bonds and other interest rate bearing securities, etc. as shown in Figure 5.

I. Forwards

A forward contract is an agreement negotiated between two parties for the delivery of a physical asset (e.g. oil or gold) at a certain time in future, for a certain price fixed at the inception of the contract (Robert and James, 2006). It is the simplest form of derivative contract mostly entered by individuals in day-to-day's life.

Forward contract is a cash market transaction in which delivery of the instrument is deferred until the contract has been made. Although the delivery is made in the future, the price is determined on the initial trade date. One of the parties to a forward contract assumes a long position (buyer) and

FIG. 5
Basic Classification of Derivatives

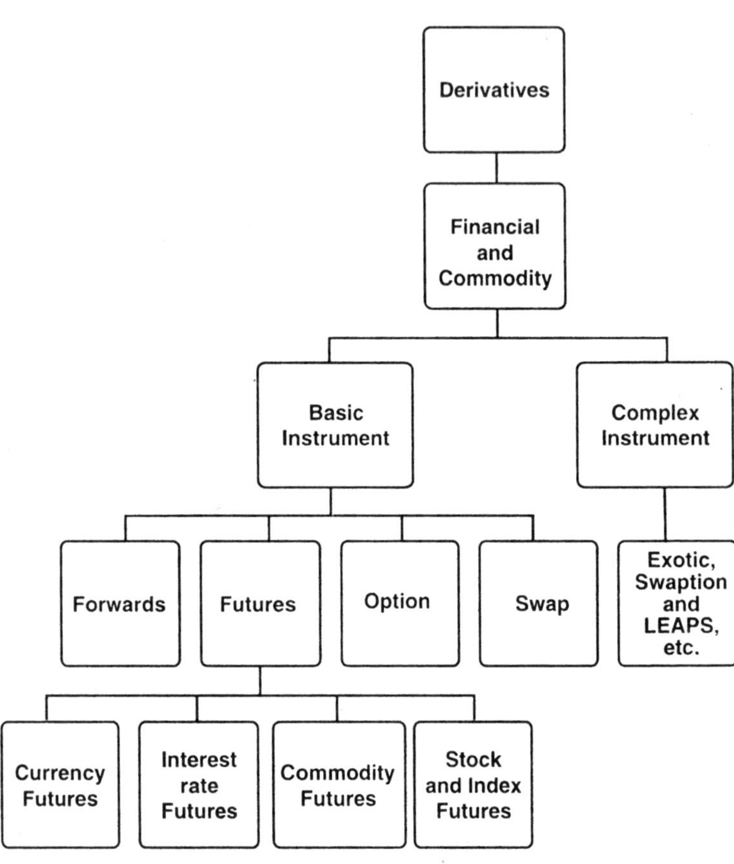

Source : Developed by the researcher (*Italic* shows the area of interest of the study).

agrees to buy the underlying asset at a certain future date for a certain price. The other party to the contract known as seller assumes a short position and agrees to sell the asset on the same date for the same price. The specified price is referred to as the delivery price. The contract terms like delivery price and quantity are mutually agreed upon by the parties to the contract.

No margins are generally payable by any of the parties to the other. Forwards contracts are traded over-the-counter and not on a trading exchange like futures contract. Lack of liquidity and counter-party default risks are the main drawbacks of a forward contract.

2. Futures

Futures contract is an agreement between two parties to buy or sell an asset at a certain time in the future for a certain price (Hull, 2000). Futures is a standardized forward contact to buy (long) or sell (short) the underlying asset at a specified price at a specified future date through a specified exchange. Futures contracts are traded on exchanges that work as a buyer or seller for the counterparty. Exchange sets the standardized terms in term of quality, quantity, price quotation, date and delivery place (in case of commodity). The features of a futures contract may be specified as follows:

- These are traded on an organized exchange like LIFFE,[5] NSE, BSE, CBOT,[6] etc.
- These involve standardized contract terms viz. the underlying asset, lot size, the time of maturity, etc.
- These are associated with a clearing house to ensure smooth functioning of the market.
- There are margin requirements and daily settlement (marking to market) to act as further safeguard against default risk.
- These provide for supervision and monitoring of contract by a regulatory authority.
- Almost ninety percent future contracts are settled via cash settlement instead of actual delivery of underlying asset.

Futures contracts being traded on organized exchanges impart liquidity to the transaction. The Clearing house, being the counter party to both sides of a transaction, provides a mechanism that guarantees the honouring of the contract and ensuring a very low level of default (Hirani, 2007).

Following are the important types of financial futures contract:

- Stock Index Futures,
- Individual Stock Futures,
- Currency Futures, and
- Interest Rate Futures bearing securities like Bonds, T-Bill Futures.

3. Options

In case of futures contract, both parties are under obligation to perform their respective obligations out of a contract. But an options contract as the name suggests, is in some sense, an optional contract. An option is the right, but not the obligation, to buy or sell something at a stated date at a stated price. A "call option" gives one the right to buy; a "put option" gives one the right to sell. Options are the standardized financial contract that allows the buyer (holder) of the option, i.e. the right at the cost of option premium, not the obligation, to buy (call options) or sell (put options) a specified asset at a set price on or before a specified date through exchanges.

4. Swaps

A swap can be defined as a barter or exchange. It is a contract whereby parties agree to exchange obligations that each of them have under their respective underlying contracts or we can say, a swap is an agreement between two or more parties to exchange stream of cash flows over a period of time in the future. The parties that agree to the swap are known as counter parties. The two commonly used swaps are: (i) Interest rate swaps which entail swapping only the interest-related cash flows between the parties in the same currency, and (ii) Currency swaps: These entail swapping both principal and interest between the parties, with the cash flows in one direction being in a different currency than the cash flows in the opposite direction.

5. HISTORIES OF FUTURES MARKETS IN INDIA

Futures markets in India have been in existence in one form or the other for a long time. In the area of commodities, the Bombay Cotton Trade Association started futures trading way back in 1875. In 1952, the Government of India banned cash settlement and options trading. Futures trading shifted to informal forwards markets. In recent years, government policy has shifted in favour of an increased role of market-based pricing and less suspicious futures trading. The first step towards introduction of financial futures trading in India was the promulgation of the Securities Laws (Amendment) Ordinance, 1995. It provided for withdrawal of prohibition on options in securities. The last decade, beginning the year 2000, saw lifting of ban on futures trading in many commodities. Around the same period, national electronic commodity exchanges were also set-up. Table 1 gives a chronology of introduction of derivatives in India.

TABLE I

Indian Futures Market and its Developments

Date	*Progress*
December 14, 1995	NSE asked SEBI for permission to trade index futures.
November 18, 1996	SEBI set-up L.C. Gupta Committee to draft a policy framework for index futures.
May 11, 1998	L.C. Gupta Committee submitted report.
July 7, 1999	RBI gave permission for OTC forward rate agreements (FRAs) and interest rate swaps.
May 24, 2000	SIMEX chose Nifty for trading futures and options on an Indian index.
May 25, 2000	SEBI gave permission to NSE and BSE to do index futures trading.
June 9, 2000	Trading of BSE Sensex futures commenced at BSE.
June 12, 2000	Trading of Nifty futures commenced at NSE.
August 31, 2000	Trading of futures and options on Nifty to commence at SIMEX.
June 4, 2001	Trading of Equity Index Options at NSE.
July 2, 2001	Trading of Stock Options at NSE.
November 9, 2002	Trading of Single Stock futures at BSE.
	June 23, 2003 Trading of Interest Rate Futures at NSE.
September 13, 2004	Weekly Options at BSE.
January 1, 2008	Trading of Chhota (Mini) Sensex at BSE.
January 1, 2008	Trading of Mini Index Futures and Options at NSE.
August 29, 2008	Trading of Currency Futures at NSE.
October 2, 2008	Trading of Currency Futures at BSE.

Source : Compiled from BSE and NSE.

Futures trading commenced in India in June 2000 after Securities and Exchange Board of India SEBI granted the final approval of this effect in May 2001 on the recommendation of L.C. Gupta committee.[7] SEBI permitted the derivative segments of two stock exchanges, NSE and BSE, and their clearing house/corporation to commence trading and settlement in approved futures contracts. Initially, SEBI approved trading in index futures contracts based on various stock market indices such as, S&P CNX, Nifty and Sensex. Subsequently, index-based trading was permitted in options as well as individual securities.

The trading in BSE Sensex options commenced on June 4, 2001 and the trading in options on individual securities commenced in July 2001. Futures contracts on individual stocks were launched in November 2001. The Futures trading on NSE commenced with S&P CNX Nifty Index futures on June 12, 2000. The trading in index options commenced on June 4, 2001 and trading in options on individual securities commenced on July 2, 2001. Single stock futures were launched on November 9, 2001. The index futures and options contract on NSE are based on S&P CNX. In June 2003, NSE introduced Interest Rate Futures which were subsequently banned due to pricing issue.

6. REGULATIONS OF FUTURES TRADING IN INDIA

The regulatory framework in India is based on the L.C. Gupta Committee Report, and the J.R. Varma Committee Report.[8] It is mostly consistent with the IOSCO[9] principles and addresses the common concerns of investor protection, market efficiency and integrity and financial integrity. The L.C. Gupta Committee Report provides a perspective on division of regulatory responsibility between the exchange and the SEBI. It recommends that SEBI's role should be restricted to approving rules, byelaws and regulations of a futures exchange also to approving the proposed futures contracts before commencement of their trading.

It emphasizes the supervisory and advisory role of SEBI with a view to permitting desirable flexibility, maximizing regulatory effectiveness and minimizing regulatory cost. Regulatory requirements for authorization of Futures brokers/

dealers include relating to capital adequacy, net worth, certification requirement and initial registration with SEBI. It also suggests establishment of a separate clearing corporation, maximum exposure limits, mark to market margins, margin collection from clients and segregation of clients' funds, regulation of sales practice and accounting and disclosure requirements for futures trading. The J.R. Verma committee suggests a methodology for risk containment measures for index-based futures and options, stock options and single stock futures. The risk containment measures include calculation of margins, position limits, exposure limits and reporting and disclosure.

7. DERIVATIVES PRODUCTS TRADED IN INDIA

India has many stock markets among them National Stock Exchange (NSE), and Bombay Stock Exchange (BSE) are the most famous markets not only in India but also in the world. Lots of derivative products are being traded in both the markets.

I. Derivatives Products Traded in Segment of BSE

The BSE created history on June 9, 2000 when it launched trading in Sensex-based futures contract for the first time. It

TABLE 2

Products Traded in Derivatives Segment of the BSE

Sl. No.	*Product Traded with underlying asset*	*Introduction Date*
1.	Index Futures-Sensex	June 9, 2000
2.	Index Options-Sensex	June 1, 2001
3.	Stock Option on 109 Stocks	July 9, 2001
4.	Stock Futures on 109 Stocks	November 9, 2002
5.	Weekly Option on 4 Stocks	September 13, 2004
6.	Chhota (mini) SENSEX	January 1, 2008
7.	Futures and Options on Sector-wise indices namely BSE TECK, BSE FMCG, BSE Metal, BSE Bankex and BSE Oil and Gas.	N.A
8.	Currency Futures on US Dollar Rupee	October 1, 2008

Source : Compiled from BSE website: www.bseindia.com

was followed by trading in index options on June 1, 2001; in stock options and single stock futures (31 stocks) on July 9, 2001 and November 9, 2002, respectively.

2. Derivatives Products Traded in Segment of NSE

Table 3 presents a description of the types of products traded at futures and options segment of NSE. NSE started trading in index futures, based on popular SandP CNX Index, on June 12, 2000 as its first derivatives product.

TABLE 3
Products Traded in Futures and Options Segment of NSE

1.	Index Futures-SandP CNX Nifty	June 12, 2000
2.	Index Options-SandP CNX Nifty	June 4, 2001
3.	Stock Option on 233 Stocks	July 2, 2001
4.	Stock Futures on 233	November 9, 2001
5.	Interest Rate Futures-T-Bills and 10 years' Bond	June 23, 2003
6.	CNX IT Futures and Options	August 29, 2003
7.	Bank Nifty Futures and Options	June 13, 2005
8.	CNX Nifty Junior Futures and Options	June 1, 2007
9.	CNX 100 Futures and Options	June 1, 2007
10.	Nifty Midcap 50 Futures and Options	October 5, 2007
11.	Mini Index Futures and Options-SandP CNX Nifty index	January 1, 2008
12.	Long Term Option contracts on SandP CNX Nifty Index	March 3, 2008
13.	Currency Futures on US Dollar Rupee	August 29, 2008
14.	S&P CNX Defty Futures and Options	December 10, 2008

Source : Compiled from NSE website.

8. GROWTH OF DERIVATIVES MARKET IN INDIA

The futures and options segment of NSE witnessed huge increase in volumes during 2009-10 and continued to achieve a commendable place on the international front. Globally NSE (National Stock Exchange of India) ranked in the fifth position in terms of futures and options traded in 2010. Among the top ten equity index futures and options, the Indian S&P CNX Nifty Index Options comes in fourth position whereas SandP CNX Nifty Index Futures in ninth rank.

FIG. 6

Business Growth of Futures and Options

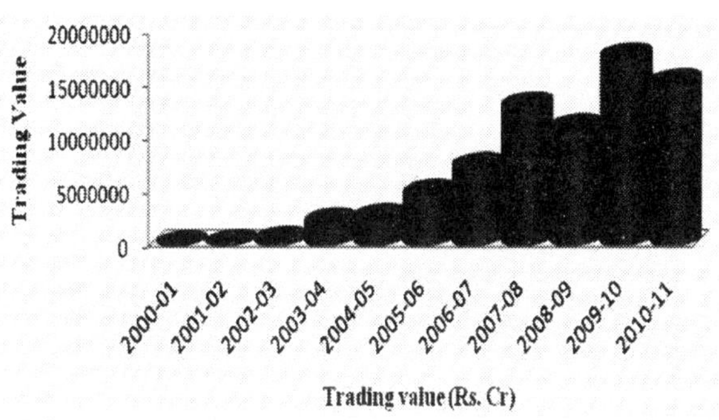

Source : Developed by the researcher based on nseindia.com

The futures trading in India commenced on June 2000 with futures trading on SandP CNX Nifty Index, and Sensex Index. Subsequently, the product base has been increasing. The derivatives trading system in India provides a fully automated screen-based trading for all kinds of derivative products available on stock exchange on a nationwide basis. It supports an anonymous order driven market, which operates on a strict price/time priority. It provides tremendous flexibility to users in terms of kinds of orders that can be placed on the system.

Equity derivatives market in India has registered an "explosive growth" (Figure 6) and is expected to continue the same in the years to come. Introduced in 2000, financial derivatives market in India has shown a remarkable growth both in terms of volumes and numbers of traded contracts.

Among all the products traded on NSE in futures and options (FandO) segment, single stock futures also known as equity futures, are most popular in terms of volumes and number of contract traded, followed by index futures with turnover shares of 52 percent and 31 percent, respectively (Figure 7). In case of BSE, index futures outperform stock futures.

FIG. 7

Product-wise Turnover of Futures and Options during 2009-10

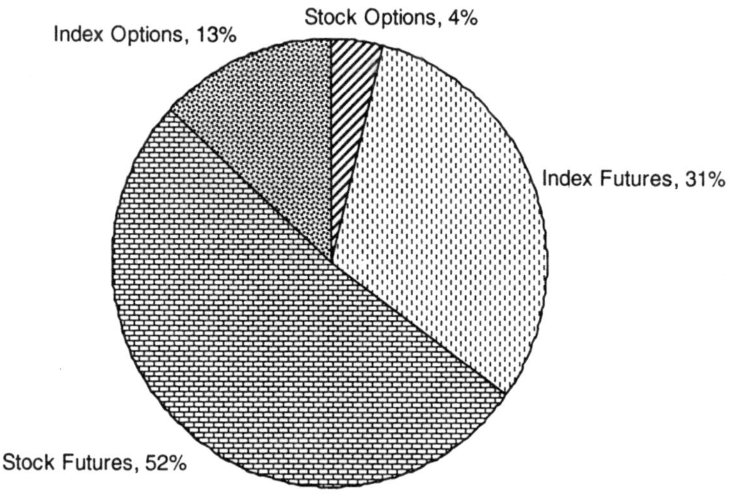

Source : Developed by Researcher based on NSE Fact Book 2010.

Despite encouraging growth and developments, industry analysts feel that the Futures market has not realized its full potential in terms of growth and trading yet. Analysts point out that the equity derivative markets on the BSE and NSE has been limited to only four products—index futures, index options and individual stock futures and options, which in turn, are limited to certain select stocks only. Although recently NSE and BSE has added more products in their derivatives segment (Weekly Options, Currency futures, Mini Index, etc.) but still it is far less than the depth and variety of products prevailing across many developed capital markets. Successful development of futures markets must be built on a foundation of solid product design, strong regulations, and sound market infrastructure (Fratzscher, 2006).

9. INDIAN FUTURES MARKET *VERSUS* GLOBAL FUTURES MARKET

India's equity derivatives market is significant in size and dominates the global trading in equity futures. Equity derivatives markets are less developed in other Asian countries, even ones where cash market activity is strong (Purfield *et al.*, 2006). Variation in derivatives markets development relate mainly to differences in the operational and legal infrastructure (Fratzscher, 2006). The Futures Industry Association (FIA)[10] annual survey 2010 conducted by Acworth found that global futures and options industry has returned to rapid growth as per the 2009 leveling. Year 2010 showed the total number of contracts traded on derivatives exchanges around the world reaching 22.3 billion, which is 25.6% higher than 2009.

TABLE 4

Growth of Global Derivatives in Term of Volume

	Jan.-Dec. 2009	*Jan.-Dec. 2010*	*% Change*
Futures	8,188,016,317	11,182,528,178	36.6%
Options	9,556,587,701	11,112,719,271	16.3%
Total	17,744,604,018	22,295,247,449	25.6%

Volume-wise the global futures and options grew by 36.6% and 16.3% respectively (Table 4), and equity indices improved to 16.2%, at the same time individual equities also showed upturn of 12.5% (Table 5).

The FIA survey (Table 6) showed in the year 2010 National Stock Exchange of India and Multi-Commodity Exchange of India (includes MCX-SX) achieved 5th and 9th rank among the top ten derivatives exchanges worldwide.

TABLE 5

Growth of Global Derivatives Category-wise

Category	*Jan.-Dec. 2009*	*Jan.-Dec. 2010*	*% Change*
Equity Indices	6,382,027,655	7,413,788,422	16.2%
Individual Equities	5,588,884,611	6,285,494,200	12.5%

The FIA survey also showed that globally NSE (National Stock Exchange of India) ranked in the fifth position in terms of futures and options traded in 2010. Among the top ten equity index futures and options, the Indian S&P CNX Nifty Index Options comes in fourth position whereas S&P CNX Nifty Index Futures in ninth rank (Table 7).

TABLE 6

Top 10 Derivatives Exchanges Worldwide

Rank	*Exchange*	*Jan.-Dec. 2009*	*Jan.-Dec. 2010*	*% Change*
1	Korea Exchange	3,102,891,777	3,748,861,401	20.8%
2	CME Group (includes CBOT and Nymex)	2,589,555,745	3,080,492,118	19.0%
3	Eurex (includes ISE)	2,647,406,849	2,642,092,726	-0.2%
4	NYSE Euronext (includes U.S. and EU markets)	1,729,965,293	2,154,742,282	24.6%
5	National Stock Exchange of India	918,507,122	1,615,788,910	75.9%
6	BM and F Bovespa	920,375,712	1,422,103,993	54.5%
7	CBOE Group (includes CFE and C2)	1,135,920,178	1,123,505,008	-1.1%
8	Nasdaq OMX (includes U.S. and Nordic markets)	815,545,867	1,099,437,223	34.8%
9	Multi-Commodity Exchange of India (includes MCX-SX)	385,447,281	1,081,813,643	180.7%
10	Russian Trading Systems Stock Exchange	474,440,043	623,992,363	31.5%

Ranked by Number of Futures and Options traded and/or cleared in 2010.

In 2010, FIA surveyed the well known 78 exchanges of the world and found that Indian market falls in the top ten most powerful ones. The data amply establish Indian market to be much stronger than before and better than many others in comparison.

TABLE 7
Top 10 Equity Index Futures and Options Worldwide

Rank	*Contract*	*Jan.-Dec. 2009*	*Jan.-Dec. 2010*	*% Change*
1	Kospi 200 Options, KRX	2,920,990,655	3,525,898,562	20.7%
2	E-mini SandP 500 Index Futures, CME	56,314,143	555,328,670	-0.2%
3	SPDR SandP 500 ETF Options	347,697,659	456,863,881	31.4%
4	SandP CNX Nifty Index Options, NSE India	321,265,217	529,773,463	64.9%
5	Euro Stoxx 50 Futures, Eurex	333,407,299	372,229,766	11.6%
6	Euro Stoxx 50 Index Options, Eurex	300,208,574	284,707,318	-5.2%
7	RTS Index Futures, RTS	150,019,917	224,696,733	49.8%
8	SandP 500 Index Options, CBOE	154,869,646	175,291,508	13.2%
9	SandP CNX Nifty Index Futures, NSE India	195,759,414	156,351,505	-20.1%
10	Nikkei 225 Mini Futures, OSE	104,738,309	125,113,769	19.5%

Ranked by Number of Contracts traded and/or cleared in 2010.
Source : http://www.futur uresindustry.org/volume-.asp

10. SUMMARY AND CONCLUDING REMARKS

The financial industry across the world has been redefined and revolutionized by the advancement of derivatives. Derivatives are risk management tools that help in effective management of risk by various stakeholders. It provide an opportunity to transfer risk, from the one who wishes to avoid it; to one, who wishes to accept it. India's experience with the launch of equity futures has been extremely encouraging and successful. The futures turnover on the NSE has surpassed the equity market turnover. Significantly, its growth in the recent years has surpassed the growth of its counterpart globally.

India is one of the most successful developing countries in terms of a vibrant market for exchange-traded derivatives. This reiterates the strengths of the modern development of India's securities markets, which are based on nationwide market access, anonymous safe and secure electronic trading, and a predominantly retail market. There is an increasing sense that the derivatives market is playing a major role in shaping price discovery. Factors like increased volatility in financial asset prices; growing integration of national financial markets with international markets; development of more sophisticated risk management tools; wider choices of risk management strategies to economic agents and innovations in financial engineering, have been driving the growth of financial futures worldwide and have also fuelled the growth of futures here, in India.

Notes and References

1. Institutional investors are organizations which pool large sums of money and invest those sums in securities, real property and other investment assets.
2. Retail investors purchase small amount of securities for him/herself, as opposed to an institutional investor. Retail investors are also called individual investor or small investor.
3. Proprietary investment consists of trading carried out by brokerage houses on their own behalf.
4. Over-the-counter (OTC) or off-exchange trading is to trade financial instruments such as stocks, bonds, commodities or derivatives directly between two parties. It is contrasted with exchange trading, which occurs via facilities constructed for the purpose of trading (i.e. *exchanges*), such as futures exchanges or stock exchanges.
5. The London International Financial Futures and Options Exchange (LIFFE, pronounced 'life') is a futures exchange based in London.
6. The Chicago Board of Trade (CBOT), established in 1848, is the world's oldest futures and options exchange.

7. SEBI appointed L.C. Gupta Committee on 18th November 1996 to develop appropriate regulatory framework for the derivatives trading and to recommend suggestive bye-laws for Regulation and Control of Trading and Settlement of Derivatives Contracts.
8. The SEBI Board while approving the introduction of index futures trading put up the setting up of a group to recommend measures for risk containment in the derivative market in India. Accordingly, SEBI constituted a group in June, 1998: with Prof. J.R. Varma, as Chairman.
9. International Organization of Securities Commission (IOSCO) is an international organization that brings together the regulators of the world's securities and futures markets.
10. FIA: The Futures Industry Association is the leading trade organization for the futures, options and OTC cleared derivatives markets. It is the only association representative of all organizations that have an interest in the listed derivatives markets.

References

Bodla, B.S., and Jindal, K. (2008). Equity Derivatives in India: Growth Pattern and Trading Volume Effects. *The Icfai Journal of Derivatives Markets*, Vol. V, No. 1, 62-82.

Fratzscher, O. (2006). Emerging Derivative Markets in Asia. *EAP Flagship on Asian Financial Market Development* (Washington: World Bank).

Hentschel, L., and Kothari, S.P. (2000). Are Corporations Reducing or taking Risks with Derivatives? Massachusetts Institute of Technology, *Working Paper* (July).

Hull, J.C. (2000). Options, Futures, and Other Derivatives. Prentice-Hall, Inc., Upper Saddle River, New Jersey 07458, U.S.A.

Kant, R. (2008). Securities Trading Frauds in Banking and Financial Industry. *Treasury Management*, The Icfai University Press, May, 45-47.

Mckenzie, M.D., Timothy, J.B., and Arobert, W.F. (2000). New Insight into the Impact of the Introduction of Futures Trading on Spot Price Volatility. *Working Paper Series*, The Australian National University.

Purfield, C., Oura, H., Krama, C., and Jobst, A. (2006). Asian Equity Markets: Growth, Opportunities, and Challenges. *IMF Working Paper*, Asia and Pacific Department and Monetary and Capital Markets Department.

Rinalini, P.K., and Kakati, M. (2007). Impact of Futures and Options trading on Index Stocks' Systematic Risk, Correlation Structure, and Volatility. *The Journal of Applied Finance*, Vol. 13, No. 8, 5-19.

Robert, W.K., and James, A.O. (2006). Understanding Futures Markets, Sixth Edition. Blackwell Publishing, 350, Main Street, Malden, MA 02148-5020, USA.

Shrotriya, V. (2007). Insights into Personal Investment Management. *Portfolio Organizer*, The Icfai University Press, February, 46-52.

Tofano, P. and Haushalter (1996). Who Manages Risk? An Empirical Examination of Risk Management Practices in the Gold Mining Industry. *Journal of Finance*, 51(4), 1097-1137.

CHAPTER

4

Mutual Fund and the Response of Small Investors

The Indian Context

AMITAVA BASU

ABSTRACT

Mutual fund has a long and successful history in developed financial market, like the United States, but in India it came into force only in 1964, when the UTI was set-up with twin objectives of mobilizing household saving and investing the funds in the capital market for industrial growth. Mutual fund is very much beneficial for the small investors as they have limited resources, lack of professional advice, lack of information and patience to take independent investment decision on their own. Mutual fund is most suitable investment option for them as it offers an opportunity to invest in a diversified way, and professionally managed portfolio of securities at a relatively low cost.

Of late, Indian Capital Market has witnessed an upsurge due to exceedingly strong performance by the Indian corporate sector and substantial rise in investment of FIIs, backed by more than 8% GDP growth rate with an increase in Indian foreign exchange reserves. Nothing seems to be working against the market. All these create a positive background for investing in mutual fund. But in India mutual funds are yet to emerge as a significant investment vehicle for the small investors. A very insignificant portion of the household saving is invested in the capital market, including mutual fund. It has high potential, suitable for small investors, who still however, are not very willing towards investing here. This paper offers an insight into the reasons that are responsible for this reluctance.

Keywords: Security market, Small investors, household savings, market uncertainty, Potentiality.

INTRODUCTION

Mutual fund has a long and successful history in a developed financial market, like the United States, but in India it came into force only in 1964, when UTI was set-up with twin objectives of mobilizing household saving and investing the funds in the capital market for industrial growth. Mutual Fund can be defined as a collective fund or a diverse holding of savings and funds from a number of investors who share a basic common financial objective. This accumulated fund is then invested in different types of securities, like shares, bonds, debentures, etc. in such a diverse way that the risk of investment gets reduced. Here units are issued to the investors in proportion of the money invested by them. The income earned through these investments and the capital appreciation realized is shared by its unit holders in proportion to the number of units held by them. Thus, a Mutual Fund is the most suitable investment option for the common people (small investors) as it offers an opportunity of diversification, professionally managed portfolio of securities at a relatively low cost. The added advantages are that Mutual funds provide easy liquidity, maintain transparency by disclosing regular information about 'NAV' per unit, asset under management and assets allocation. Investors can easily find a fund that matches their specific asset and risk allocation strategy.

TABLE 1

Trend in Introduction of Mutual Fund Schemes (1999 as base year)

Year	2000	2001	2002	2003	2004	2005	2006	2007	2008	2009	2010
(1)	*(2)*	*(3)*	*(4)*	*(5)*	*(6)*	*(7)*	*(8)*	*(9)*	*(10)*	*(11)*	*(12)*
No. of Schemes	277	394	417	406	403	451	592	756	956	1001	882
Trend	100	142.24	150.54	146.57	145.49	162.82	213.72	272.92	345.13	361.37	318.41

Source : AMFI.

In India, the history of Mutual Fund can broadly be divided into three phases. The first phase (1964-87) was a monopoly of Unit Trust of India, regulated and administered by RBI. However, in 1978 the control of UTI was transferred from RBI to IDBI. In this phase number of schemes was limited, as UTI was the sole organization. In the second phase (1987-93) public sector banks, LICI, GIC entered into the Indian Mutual Fund market. At the end of 1993, the MF industry had assets under management of Rs. 47,004 crores with 160 schemes. In the third phase (1993-2003) private sector was allowed to enter the Mutual Fund market in 1993. In this phase the MF industry developed while offering a wide variety of schemes. Another significant development of this phase was an enactment of MF regulation and after that the industry started functioning under SEBI. The number of mutual fund houses went on increasing, with many foreign mutual funds setting up in India and also the industry witnessed several mergers and acquisitions. Here we have shown (Table 1 and Graph 1) the recent trend of total number of schemes of Mutual Fund industry.

GRAPH I

Trend in Introduction of MF Schemes

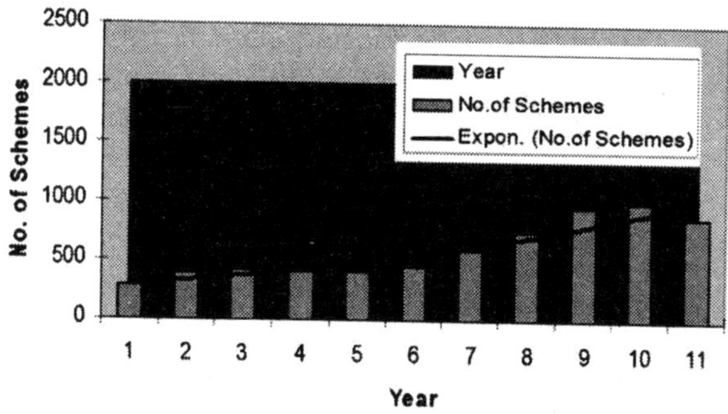

The above data reveal increasing trend in introducing number of schemes by the Mutual fund industry except for the years 2003 and 2004. The cause of this decrease was the UTI debacle. The last four years (2005-08) showed a rapid growth in

TABLE 2

Trend in Investment in Mutual Funds (2000 as base year)

Year	*2000*	*2001*	*2002*	*2003*	*2004*	*2005*	*2006*	*2007*	*2008*	*2009*	*2010*
(1)	*(2)*	*(3)*	*(4)*	*(5)*	*(6)*	*(7)*	*(8)*	*(9)*	*(10)*	*(11)*	*(12)*
AUM	90586.87	100594.2	109299.4	79464	139616.3	149554	231862	326388	505152	417302	613979
Trend	100	111.05	120.66	87.72	154.12	165.09	255.96	360.30	557.64	460.66	677.78

Source : AMFI.

introduction of new schemes due to steady upward trend in the Indian stock market. Here, we have also shown (Table 2 and Graph 2) the trend in investment in Mutual fund with the increase in number of schemes.

GRAPH 2

Trend in Investment in MF

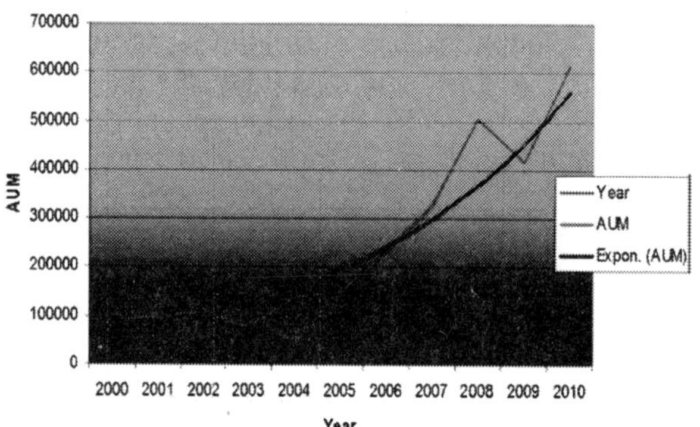

The same results are seen in case of investment also. Before the UTI debacle, it was the most popular Mutual Fund and at the end of Jan. 2003 it was way ahead of other Mutual Fund companies with Rs. 44,541 Crores of assets under its management. How the debacle influenced the investment is shown in the given data. However, things were back to normal by the year 2004 and we see a steady increasing trend again in investment. If we compare the position of Indian mutual fund industry with other developed market economies (Tables 3 and 4) in terms of introduction of mutual fund schemes and AUM, it is revealed that their market is saturated. On the other hand, Indian market shows huge growth potentiality.

At present, MF companies offer a variety of (882 schemes as on 31/03/10) of schemes in accordance with the age, financial position, risk tolerance and return expectations of investors. Different schemes cater to the different needs of the investors. An investor looking for growth over long-term and

TABLE 3

Trend in introduction of Schemes (2000 as base year)

Year	*USA*	*FRANCE*	*UK*	*JAPAN*	*INDIA*
2000	100	100	100	100	100
2001	104.67	109.72	109.15	81.10	142.24
2002	106.60	116.77	108.10	83.25	150.54
2003	105.81	119.38	110.44	78.92	146.57
2004	104.30	121.36	104.57	75.99	145.49
2005	103.21	121.46	105.69	74.10	162.82
2006	102.36	119.15	103.83	76.66	213.72
2007	104.22	124.28	117.61	79.94	272.92
2008	102.99	126.60	127.13	87.02	345.13
2009	102.96	127.49	146.54	96.78	361.37

Source : Handbook on Statistic on the Indian Security Market, Published by SEBI, 2009.

TABLE 4

Trend in Investment in Mutual Funds (2000 as base year)

Year	*USA*	*FRANCE*	*UK*	*JAPAN*	*INDIA*
2000	100.00	100	100	100	100
2001	101.73	110.03	96.22	85.92626	111.05
2002	·101.88	108.72	84.41	68.4049	120.66
2003	93.34	128.81	77.00	60.30627	87.72
2004	108.30	175.03	105.68	69.45731	154.12
2005	118.41	208.94	131.32	79.45508	165.09
2006	130.07	207.68	145.82	93.49421	255.96
2007	151.85	269.65	201.27	115.1429	360.30
2008	175.27	1217.70	239.20	142.0179	557.64
2009	140.24	242.49	140.45	114.4355	460.66

Source : Handbook on Statistic on the Indian Security Market, Published by SEBI, 2009.

expecting higher return even at the cost of high risk can opt for growth schemes of Mutual Fund. These schemes are suitable for the young investors. An investor looking for a regular and steady income can select income scheme of Mutual Fund. These schemes are specially meant for the retired persons or who need some supplemental earning. Mutual Fund companies also offer some schemes for the investors who are looking for a combination of income and moderate growth. Mutual Fund companies' offers money market liquid schemes for providing easy liquidity for such investors who want to invest for a very short period or need money as and when demanded. Taxes saving schemes (ELSS) are also offered by the Mutual Fund companies for the investors seeking tax rebate. Many other schemes are also available in the market, framed by the Mutual Fund companies as per the requirement of different types of investors.

In this backdrop, this paper highlights on few aspects:

(i) Why the small investors/first-timers should opt for mutual fund rather than direct investment in stock market.
(ii) Potential of mutual fund industry in India.
(iii) Dominance of corporate sector in Indian mutual fund industry.
(iv) Reasons of small investors' reluctance to participate in capital market.
(v) Remedies and suggestions to encourage and mobilize Indian household savings in Indian capital market.

Mutual fund is very much beneficial for the small investors as they have limited resources, lack of professional advice, lack of information and patience to take independent investment decision on their own. Individual investors get a plenty of choices regarding investment. This makes them confused and perplexed, as they can't decide, which schemes would be the most suitable for them. While investing in capital market small investors should take mutual fund route as they can invest with small amounts, get the benefits of diversification, get tax benefits and to manage their portfolio professionally. In taking investment decision small investors should keep the following basic points in mind:

- Needs and financial goal of investment.
- Present source of income and its future continuity.
- Term and period of investment.
- The degree of risk that can be afforded.
- Expected return corresponding to the risk category.

Of late, Indian capital Market has witnessed an upsurge due to an exceedingly strong performance by the Indian corporate sector and substantial rise in investment of FII, backed by more than 8% GDP growth rate with an increase in Indian foreign exchange reserves. Nothing seems to be working against the market. All these create a positive background for investing in mutual funds. An expanding range of products that cater to different needs, as well as emerging opportunities like global investment funds and real estate funds, will keep the industry buoyant in the years ahead. Frost and Sullivan projects that the Indian asset-management industry will grow by more than 20 percent over the next five years.

"The Indian asset management industry is witnessing rapid growth as a result of an economic boom, increase in personal financial assets, entry of foreign asset management companies, favorable stock markets and aggressive marketing by mutual funds". Frost and Sullivan research manager, said. "Even though the value of assets under management has risen rapidly, the relatively low penetration rate of mutual funds greatly contributes to industry opportunities."

According to the study, the Indian asset management industry is still in the nascent stages of growth when compared to developed countries. For example, in the United States, assets managed by mutual funds represented 78.6 percent of the country's gross domestic product at the end of 2006, whereas in India they accounted for a meager 6.6 percent. This notable difference indicates the enormous market potential for mutual fund industry in India. In the United States, mutual funds manage about 20 percent of total household financial assets whereas Indian mutual funds only managed 3.6 percent between 2005 and 2006. Mutual fund has a high potential to mobilize huge source of Indian household savings but are yet to emerge as an asset class of any significance for the small investors. Household savings is showing an increasing trend in India. At present it is more than 24% of GDP, which is quite impressive in comparison to the international standard.

TABLE 3

Household Savings as a Percentage of GDP

Year	*1990-91*	*91-92 to 1996-97*	*1997-98 to 2002-03*	*2003-04 to 2006-07*	*2007-08*
Household Savings as a % of GDP	18.4	16.8	20.8	23.8	24.3

Source : Reserve Bank of India, Annual Report, 2009.

But in India mutual funds are yet to emerge as a significant investment vehicle for the small investors. In India the small investors mainly consider three things while taking investment decision that is Return, Liquidity and Security. If we highlight on investment pattern of small investors, it clearly indicates that fixed income-bearing instruments are the most preferred assets for them. Investments made by households have characteristically been conservative and poorly diversified. Roughly 54% of the total savings went into physical assets and the remaining is invested in the financial instruments. Major share of financial instrument savings goes to banking deposit and social security sector. Here, we have shown graphical representation (Graph 3) of investment pattern of household sector.

It is revealed that a very insignificant portion of the total household savings is invested in the capital market. Mutual funds get much more popularity in a developed financial market likes USA. In USA nearly every second household owns mutual fund. At the end of March 2006, in the USA alone there were 8002 mutual funds with total assets over 427 lakh crores. Significantly, people in USA have 47% of their household financial assets in mutual funds and they hold about 90% of

GRAPH 3

Distribution of Household Financial Savings

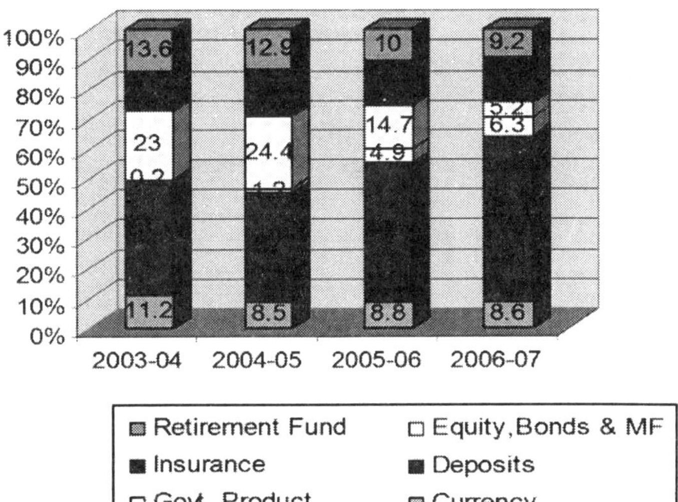

Source : CSO.

total mutual fund assets. Mutual funds have become very large in the USA with small investors' money. They play an important role in mobilizing household savings. In India the problem lies in excessive dominance of corporate/institutions. In USA corporate sectors hold only 10% of the net assets value of mutual funds whereas in India their share as high as 51%. In contrast, only 5% of the Indian household saving is invested in the capital market, including mutual fund. Here, we have shown the unit holding pattern of Indian mutual fund industry, which revealed that 96.1% of the total investors accounts are from individual but only 42.83% of total mutual fund assets are held by them. Whereas 2.24% of the total investors accounts are from corporate/institutions but their share is 51.01% of the net assets value.

If we categorically analyze the different schemes of mutual funds, it has clearly proved the dominance of corporate sectors in Indian mutual fund market. Here, we have shown

GRAPH 4

Unit Holding Pattern of Indian MF Industry

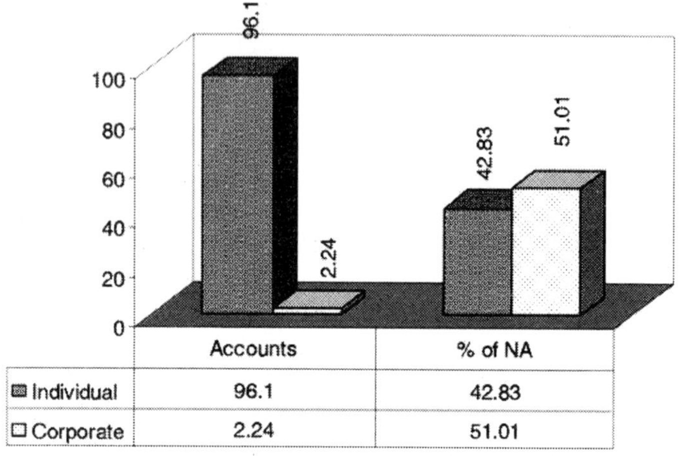

Source : SEBI.

data (Table 6) related to different schemes to understand their nature and preference of investors.

TABLE 6

Year	*Total Sales Proceed from all Schemes*	*Sales of Liquid and money market Scheme*	*Redemption of Liquid and money market Scheme*	*As a % of total investment*	*Reed. as a % of Total sales*
2003	314206	195047	190042	62.08	97.43
2004	587480	375646	351069	63.94	93.46
2005	821958	638594	628247	77.69	98.38
2006	1057126	836859	832654	79.16	99.50
2007	1800257	1626790	1621805	90.36	99.69
2008	4337042	3432738	3417761	79.15	99.56
2009	5261429	4187977	4191576	79.60	100.09
2010	9976364	7044818	7056891	70.62	100.17

Year	*Sales of Growth Fund Scheme*	*Redemption of Growth Fund Schemes*	*Reed. as a % of Sales of Growth Fund Scheme*	*Total Sales Proceed from all Schemes*	*As a % Total Sales Proceed from all Schemes*
2003	4618	3917	84.82	314206	1.47
2004	26642	18958	71.16	587480	4.53
2005	37079	29432	79.38	821958	4.51
2006	82086	50450	61.46	1057126	7.77
2007	89682	65930	73.52	1800257	4.98
2008	119838	79056	65.97	4337042	2.76
2009	29481	28425	96.42	5261429	0.56
2010	61114	60519	99.03	9976364	0.61
Average			78.97		3.40

Source : Annual Reports Published by AMFI.

The above data reveal that on an average only 3.4% of the total investment is invested in the Growth fund whereas 75.32% of the fund goes to the Liquid/Money market scheme. Mainly investors from the corporate sectors are interested in these types of schemes. If we analyse the nature of investment of both the schemes it shows that redemption rate of liquid and money market schemes is very high (average 98.54%) whereas incase of growth fund it is 78.97%. So, on the one hand, the huge investment in liquid and money market schemes and on the other hand very high redemption rate proves the dominance of corporate sectors in our mutual fund industry. Corporate sectors have invested their funds for a short period and use mutual funds as trustee of their fund. They park their surplus fund in mutual fund liquid/money market schemes and wait for any profitable investment avenues that will crop up in the mean time and at the same time their objectives of maintaining liquidity, preservation of capital, earning moderate income is fulfilled. On the contrary, by selling their share at a time, they can create instability in the market. On the other hand, mutual fund companies prefer corporate as their bulk investments help to huge rise in company's assets under management with minimum effort and lower transaction cost resulting in better ranking in the industry.

A country, where only 6.3% (2006-07) of household savings go into the stock markets for investment, definitely needs much greater participation from the small investors and this percentage is insignificant compared to similar percentage for US of 60%. Now if we throw light on the reluctance of participation of small investors in Indian capital market, it is seen that volatility and uncertainty of the market discourages them most to enter in the market. Volatility by its very nature, can affect the investor financially and emotionally. If we analyze the data of early 90s, we see that as high as 23.3% (1990-91) of household savings was invested in the stock market. At that time, investment in UTI was only 13.3% and mutual fund other than UTI was 3.1%. But the scenario totally changed in the mid-90s and the Ketan Parekh (KP) scam in early 2000, shook the confidence of the investors to invest in the stock market. As a result of these scams, the investment in the stock market dropped to 0.2% in 2003-04. The same scenario was prevailing in case of UTI also. Before the UTI debacle, it was the most popular and trusted mutual fund among the mutual funds companies in India and household investment dropped from 13.3% (1990-91) to –0.7 in 2004-05. Despite the sustained rally, the rising bank deposits and small savings are proof that the wounds of the scams since the early 1990s are still green. Even through mutual funds, participation has been minimal. The market is still dominated by the FIIs and the elite class. So this is one of the most important reasons of reluctance of small investors to invest in the stock market.

Investment is a specialised job requiring professional expertise and knowledge. The small investors, however, lack this and thus perceive stock market as risky. They stick to their own timing, which most of the time does not go with their capital, cash flows and objectives. Since they acquire surplus money every month, they invest this surplus money which they want to increase over the time and yet do not want to risk their capital. Some await market correction before investing which is not a sagacious step because one should keep staying in the market. Some try their own strategy and have a mixed fare of success and failure. Without proper Information retail people buy mostly on rumors and without any proper financial research or practical knowledge of how to avoid unnecessary risks in investment.

Despite the huge potential, the report warns that the rural sector's limited participation greatly restrains the industry's growth. Mutual funds remain out of the reach of a majority of the rural population due to poor distribution, lack of investor awareness and limited banking facilities. The technological innovations and conveniences offered by the asset management industry cater largely to the urban investors. Due to the poor penetration of the Internet, mobile phones and ATMs in rural areas, mutual fund investments are not within the easy reach of the rural investor.

GRAPH 5

Branch Penetration

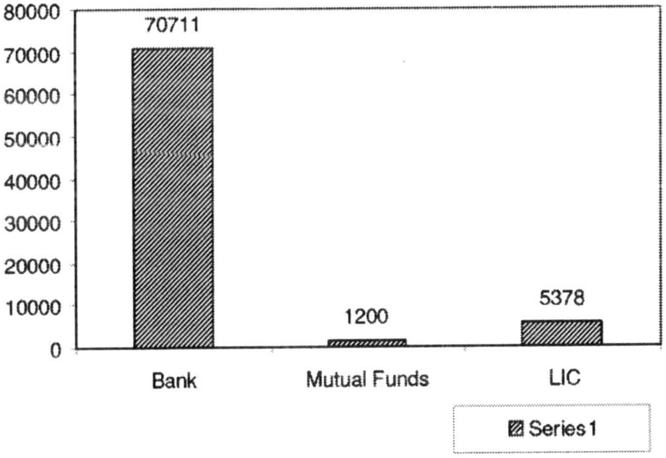

Source : Macquarie Research, RBI, Company Website.

The Graphs (5 and 6) depict that the mutual funds companies do not have adequate distribution network to capture the market in rural areas and Graph 7 also proves that the top ten cities of India account for around 90% of the industry AUM (Assets under Management). Thus, it becomes

GRAPH 6

Agents (000)

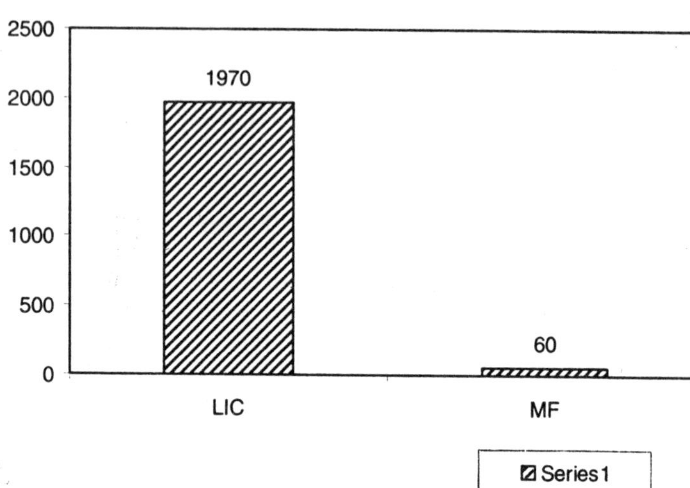

Source : Macquarie Research, RBI, Company Website.

GRAPH 7

City-wise Share of AUM of Indian MF Industry

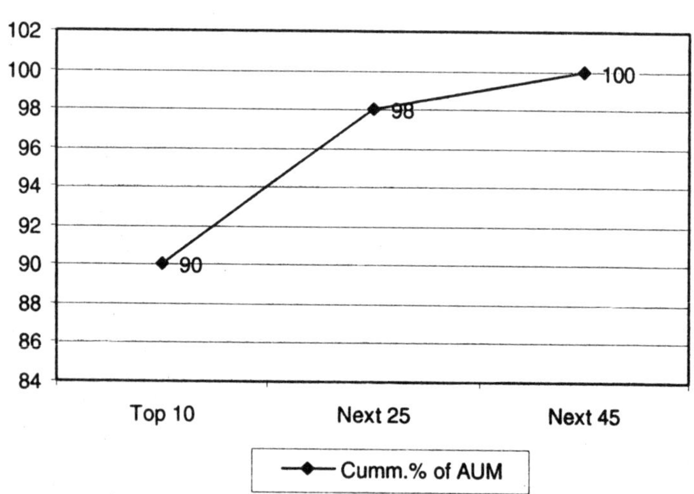

Source : Transfer Agent database (CAMS).

evident that penetration of mutual fund companies is still restricted to urban areas only.

In order to make the Indian stock market a benchmark for the rest of the world, to mobilize huge source of household savings and encourage them to participate in the market at a greater percentage. Several initiatives have been taken by the SEBI in the recent past. In the first place, SEBI-registered investors' associations educate investors. Training programmes for educating investors are started so that they (investors) become aware of the functioning of the equity market. For this purpose SEBI has decided to set-up an Investor Protection and Education Fund (IPEF). The main aim of the fund is to protect the interest of the investors and create awareness among them. The fund would be used in conducting education programmes through print and electronic media. Seminars and symposiums will be organised with the help of funds. The fund would finance conducting research and development programmes. In this way investors can understand the basics of both fundamental and technical issues. Proper education can help them understand the impact of global and domestic factors like inflation and interest rate movement in the market.

Secondly, SEBI has also decided to slash the cost of investing in mutual funds schemes. This can be particularly beneficial for retail investors because it is easier and safer for the first-timer to invest in mutual fund schemes rather than directly invest in equities. It is expected that this move will lure the retail investors in small towns and rural areas as well, to mutual fund investment.

So, it is high time that the mutual fund companies think how to mobilize the huge unutilized source of household savings to increase stability and lessen the dependence on FIIs. Thus, in present scenario Fund houses have to be more receptive to the needs of small investors by charging them less, educating them, being more transparent and investor-friendly and responding to their grievances on priority and should not only concentrate in urban areas but try to expand their network in the remote areas of the country as well and undertake strategic initiative to minimize operational, systemic and structural risks.

References

Prithvi Haldea, 2005, "The small investor has been edged out of the primary market systematically"; Article 1/Indian Express-Express Money, 4th July.

Sen Pronab, Bahel, Nikhil, 2003, "Developing the Indian Debt Capital Markets: Small Investor Perspectives", Perspective Planning Division, Panning Commission Government of India, July 2003.

Barua, K. Samir and Varma, R. Jayanth, 1993, "Securities Scam: Genesis, Mechanics and Impact", *Vikalpa*, January-March 1993, 18(1), 3-12.

Fama, E., 1970, "Efficient Capital Markets: A Review of Theory and Empirical Work", *Journal of Finance*, 25(2), pp. 383-417.

AIG Investments, 2007, "Critical Issues to take the Industry Forward", September, 2007.

AMFI Updates, Vol. VI, Issue II, July-September, 2006.

Central Statistical Organization, Gross Financial Savings of Household Sector.

Triphaty, Nalini Pravha, 1996, "Mutual fund In India: A Financial Service in Capital Market, *Finance India*, Vol. X, No. 1, March, pp. 85-91.

N. Kumar, Nikhil, 2007, "How To Mitigate Volatility?" Goa Institute of Management.

Sai Prasan, "Sebi and Mutual Funds : All set for the Next Level", *The Finance Express*, Feb. 14, 2008.

Shashikant, Uma, 2007, "Retail Tucked In", *Outlook Money*, Feb. 1, 2007.

CHAPTER

E-Government Implementation Challenges in India and its Role in Sustainable Development

ANAND NAYYAR

E-Government basically means the use of Information and Communication Technologies (ICTs) to improve the activities of various government agencies. India's position in E-Readiness is very low as compared to other countries of the world. Various challenges are surrounding the implementation of E-Government in India like Low-Literacy, Low per capita income and limited financial resources. In this Research Paper, A Conceptual framework is proposed for the Effective Implementation of E-Government in India. The Conceptual Framework proposed can be validated in Real Life Situation.

I. INTRODUCTION

E-Government refers to the delivery of national or local

government information and services via Internet or digital means to citizens or businesses or other government agencies. It is basically defined as the use of Information Technology to provide citizen and organizations with more convenient access to government information and services to provide delivery of public services to citizens, business partners and persons working in Public sector. In other words, we can define E-Government as the use of Information and Communication Technologies (ICTs) to improve the activities of public sector organizations. E-Government, nowadays, plays a very significant role in the development of nation. It has brought revolution in the governance of the government. According to Economists Intelligence Unit, E-readiness index of India is very low. So the implementation of E-Government is very challenging. It is because of the low level of literacy, low per capita income and insufficient infrastructure for the implementation of E-Government.

II. COMPONENTS OF INDIAN E-GOVERNMENT PROGRAM

In the recent years lots of initiative has been taken to implement E-Government in the country at National, State or District level. Some of the implementations were highly successful and some were unsuccessful. The National E-Government program is conducted to effectively implement the E-Government in India. The components of E-Government Program of India are as follow:

1. *Awareness and Communication*: The success of entire E-Government program depends on the awareness about the program. Therefore, the Government of India disseminates the information about the E-Government plans.
2. *Capacity Building*: The capacity building component takes into account that different states are at different levels of readiness for E-Governance and have different levels of aspiration. The role of capacity building team is at the program level to provide leadership and vision including policy formulation,

frameworks preparation, progress monitoring and capacity management.

3. *Assessment*: The Government of India is investing a significant part of its scarce resources in E-Government projects. So it is very essential that a robust assessment strategy is devised for the existing E-Government projects.
4. *Infrastructure and Technical*: This cell provides support to the Department of Information Technology in implementing projects and components of E-Government.
5. *Monitoring and Evaluation*: The Program Management, Monitoring and Evaluation Unit of the Program Management Unit for National E-Government programme develop a comprehensive MIS at programme level and track the physical and financial progress of various projects.
6. *Common Services Centre*: Common Services Center (CSC) scheme is the most prominent component of E-Government. The scope of support includes Identification of core components of CSC Scheme; Frame problem agendas related with application software, legal instruments, and essential backend for CSC, etc.
7. *Project and Financial Appraisal*: The cell identity resources to provide assistance in project development and implementation to various implementing agencies.
8. *Research and Development*: The E-Governance RandD team provides consultancy and research inputs in the area of E-Governance Technical Standards including interoperability standards e-Government Enterprise architecture frameworks, Information Security, etc.

III. INDIA'S POSITION ON E-READINESS

E-Readiness is defined as the ability to use Information and Communication Technologies (ICT) to develop one's economy and to foster one's welfare. Every year, Economist Intelligence Unit produces a ranking of E-Readiness across countries based on six parameters: Connectivity and Technology Infrastructure, business environment, social and cultural environment, legal environment, government policy and vision and consumer and business adoption. In 2008, E-Readiness rankings, Global E-Readiness improved for the fourth year in a row, from 6.2 in 2007 to 6.4 in 2008. Denmark getting 5th Place from 1st Place, USA now ranks 1st , 2nd Position goes to Hong Kong, Sweden 3rd and Australia 4th. In 2009 E-Readiness ranking, Global E-Readiness fell partly due to fall in the global economy in the later part of 2008. According to the latest E-Readiness report India is now at 58th Position with a readiness score of 4.17.

TABLE I

Economist Intelliegent Unit E-Readiness Rankings in 2009 of various Countries

Rank	*Country*	*E-Readiness Score (out of 10) 2009*
1	Denmark	8.87
2	Sweden	8.67
3	Netherlands	8.64
4	Norway	8.62
5	U.S.A.	8.60
6	Australia	8.45
7	Singapore	8.35
8	Hong Kong	8.33
9	Canada	8.33
10	Finland	8.30

Source : http://www.en.wikipedia.or/wiki/E-Readiness.

IV. IMPLEMENTATION OF E-GOVERNMENT IN INDIA—CHALLENGES

Implementation of E-Government has changed the way of living of people in many countries. But the implementation of E-Government in India is very difficult because of its developing property. The Government agencies finds a lot of difficulties in the smooth implementation of E-Government in India because of factors like low literacy, low per capita income, insufficient infrastructure and limited financial resource.

1. Low Literacy

Literacy may be defined as the ability to read and write with understanding in any language. Any formal education or minimum educational standard is not necessary to be considered literate. According to United Nations Development Programme Report 2009 Georgia is the only country with 100% Literacy rate followed by Cuba, Estonia and Latavia with equal percentage of 99.8%. India ranked 149 with literacy rate of 66%.

TABLE 2

Literacy Rate of Various Countries

Rank	*Country Name*	*Literacy Rate*
1	Georgia	100.0
2	Cuba, Estonia, Latvia	99.8
5	Barbados, Slovenia, Lithuania, Ukraine, Armenia	99.7
10	Kazakhstan, Tajikistan, Azerbaijan, Russia	99.5

Source : http://www.en.wikipedia.org/wiki/list_of_countries_by_literacy_rate.

2. Low Per Capita Income

Per Capita Income means how much an individual receives if we talk of monetary terms of the Yearly Income generated in the country. Per Capita Income is reported in Units of currency per year. Globally according to the calculation of National Average Per Capita Income using PPP method, Luxembourg has highest per capita income of 54,430 with India at 143rd Place with 2880.

3. Limited Financial Resource

The Gross Domestic Product (GDP) is one of the measures of National Income and output for a given country's economy.

TABLE 3

National Average Per Capita Income of Selected Countries

Rank	*Country*	*Per Capita Income in U.S $*
1	Luxembourg	54,430
2	Bermuda	36,000
3	United States	37,500
4	Norway	37,300
5	Liechtenstein	25,000
6	Channel Islands	N/A
7	Switzerland	32,030
8	Denmark	31,210
9	Ireland	30,450
10	Iceland	30,140
143	India	2,880

Source : http://www.sucess-and-culture.net/articles/percapitaincome.html).

GDP is defined as the total market value of all final goods and services produced within the country in a given period of time.

TABLE 4

GDP of Selected Countries in 2010 According to IMF

Rank	*Country*	*GDP (Millions of USD)*
1	United States	14,624,184
2	People's Republic of China	5,745,133
3	Japan	5,390,897
4	Germany	3,305,898
11	India	1,430,020
20	Belgium	461,331
35	UAE	239,650
40	Egypt	216,830

Source : http://en.wikipedia.org/wiki/List_of_countries_by_GDP_(nominal)

GDP of a country is the measure of its financial strength. According to the List by International Monetary Fund, U.S.A. has highest Per Capita Income with 14,624,184 followed by People's Republic of China with 5,745,133 and India at 11th position with 1,430,020.

V. STEPS FOR THE SUCCESSFUL IMPLEMENTATION OF E-GOVERNMENT IN INDIA

On the basis of the above study and seeing different facts and figures of the E-Readiness as well as its challenges a Conceptual Framework is designed for the effective implementation of E-Government in India. It is divided into following five stages:

1. Vision for E-Government Implementation

In the first stage the vision for the effective implementation of E-Government has to be determined. In this level it is planned to what extend the E-Government can be implemented.

2. Assessment of E-Readiness

To fulfil the vision of E-Readiness of India a proper assessment has to be undertaken. It is compared with respect to other countries. The E-Readiness reveals the position of India with respect to the other countries.

3. Overcoming Challenges of E-Government

In the assessment process the challenges for effective implementation of E-Government will be exposed. These challenges are low literacy levels, low per capita income and limited financial resource in India. The challenges should be overcome for the effective implementation of E-Government.

4. Developing the Environment for E-Government

The positive environment needs to be developed to meet the vision of E-Government implementation. This environment is internal environment and external environment.

5. Implementation of E-Government

After the above steps effective implementation, the E-Government should be finally implemented. This is the final step of the Conceptual Framework for the effective implementation of E-Government in India.

The above steps are properly summarized in a conceptual framework which is shown in the following figure.

FIG. I

A Conceptual Framework for E-Government Implementation in India

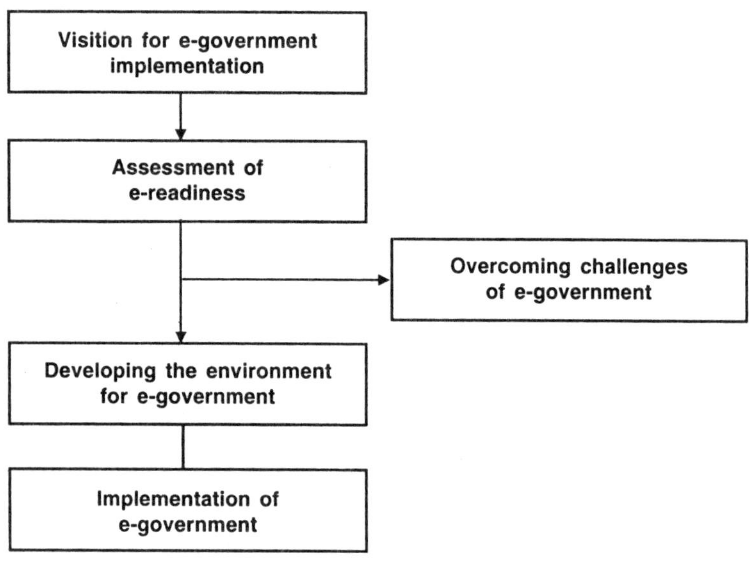

VI. CONCLUSION

According to the Economist Intelligence Unit, the E-Readiness index of India is very low. Various challenges are shrouding India for effective E-Government Implementation like low literacy, low per capita income and Limited Financial Resource. A vision is required to implement E-Government in India. To meet the challenges, an environment needs to be developed for the effective E-Government implementation in India. A Conceptual Framework is developed for the effective implementation of E-Government in India. This conceptual framework can be further validated in the real life situation.

References

Palvia, S.C.J., and Sharma, S.S. (2007); E-Government and E-Governance: Definitions/Domain Framework and Status around the World, Foundation of e-government, ICEG, 2007, pp. 1-12

Bedi, K., Singh, P.J. and Srivastava, S. (2001); Government net: new governance opportunities for India, New Delhi: Sage.

http://en.wikipedia.org/wiki/E-readiness.

http://en.wikipedia.org/wiki/List_of_countries_by_literacy_rate.

http://www.success-and-culture.net/articles/percapitaincome.shtml.

http://en.wikipedia.org/wiki/List_of_countries_by_GDP_(nominal).

CHAPTER

6

Sustaining Micro Financing Through Re-Engineering and Synergy

S.S. BHUSHANAM

ABSTRACT

The objective of micro financing has to be to support poor to access a range of quality financial services that include savings, insurance, and growth/development-related projects, to help them out of poverty. There is no dearth for numerous schemes/programs by various government/private/autonomous institutions to serve the concerns and necessities of the poor and the needy through micro financing. But there exist a very big gap between the expected results and actual outcomes. In this paper attempt has been made to address the objective through reinforcement of management of micro finance institutions by management re-engineering. The approach suggested here is to maximize the practical application of management practices more realistically which will lead to synergy in the field of the subject under focus. The synergy is expected to happen through enhancing productivity at all levels of the system and creating value added services to the lowest level of activity and beneficiary. The vital pre requisites in working towards increasing the effectiveness of various programs are: programs integration and adapting project management methodologies.

Keywords: synergy, re-engineering, human resource, training, MIS,

1. MICRO FINANCING SYSTEMS AND CHALLENGES

Micro finance majorly appears to meet the immediate necessities, a credit service to poor clients. But microcredit is one of provisions under a broad category of services of microfinance.

Challenges to micro finance services with comparison to banks: Banks do not provide financial services to clients with no cash income. Banks incur substantial costs to manage a client account. Poor people have no assets that can be secured by a bank as security. Because of these difficulties, when poor people often rely on moneylender, whose interest rates can be very high, but services of moneylenders are convenient and fast, and they can be very flexible when borrowers run into problems.

2. RURAL DEVELOPMENT

Rural development in general has to include the actions and initiatives taken to improve the standard of living in non-urban neighborhoods, countryside, and remote villages. Economic activities have to relate to production of food and raw materials. Rural development actions largely have to aim at the social and economic development of the areas. These programs usually include the local authorities, regional development agencies, NGOs, governments or international development organizations. But local populations can also bring about their initiatives for development.

3. TRANSFORMING THE RURAL NON-FARM ECONOMY

Rural development also has to rely on activities other than farming for their income. Nonfarm work accounts for between one-third and one-half of rural incomes in the developing world. In recent years, accelerating globalization, increasing competition from large businesses, expanding urban markets for rural goods and services, and greater availability of information and communication technology have combined to expose rural nonfarm businesses to new opportunities as well as new risks. It is important to address key questions about the role of public intervention in the rural nonfarm economy and how the rural poor can participate in and navigate the rapid transition underway in rural areas.

4. SCHEMES AND MEASURES FOR RURAL DEVELOPMENT

An illustrative list of schemes that are being practiced for rural development programs in some of the other nations in the world is presented as under. The authorities and experts may consider for their suitable adaptation in our local regions.

I. Schemes

Environmental Stewardship: Scheme provides funding to farmers who deliver effective environmental management on their land.

Countryside Stewardship Scheme: Payments to farmers to enhance and conserve landscapes, their wildlife and history and to help people to enjoy them.

Environmentally Sensitive Areas Scheme: Encourage farmers to adopt agricultural practices which would safeguard and enhance high landscape, wildlife or historic value.

Farm Woodland Premium Scheme: Incentives to farmers to convert non-productive land to woodland.

Organic Farming Scheme: Converting from conventional to organic farming methods.

Rural Enterprise Scheme: Assistance for projects that help to develop more sustainable, economies and helping farmers adapt to changing markets and develop new business opportunities.

Vocational Training Scheme: Activities that contribute to an improvement in the occupational skill and competence of farmers.

Processing and Marketing Scheme: Improving the processing and marketing of agricultural products.

2. Measures

Measures for provision of: Advisory services to farmers and forest holders; more and better basic services for the economy and the rural population. Training in support of measures; support for skills acquisition and animation with a view to preparing and implementing a local development strategy

Measures for support for : The setting up of farm management, farm relief and farm advisory services; adding value to agricultural and forestry products: investment in infrastructure related to the development and adaptation of agriculture and forestry.; farming in Less Favored Areas; for the management of existing woods and forests; non-productive investments in forestry measures; the creation and development of micro-enterprises; Encouragement for tourism activities; village renewal and development.

5. COMPREHENSIVE DEVELOPMENTAL SUPPORT AND TRAINING

For the sake of illustration some of the institutions that are already in the similar activity are included here. This is with the view that such of those services have to be integrated and coordinated together to maximize the benefits and to enable them translated into wealth creation and value addition to the targets.

1. Agricultural Development and Training Society (ADATS)

Projects for agricultural development and training Society: ADATS is a comprehensive rural development organization working in the fields of Community, adult literacy, health, and support to legal issues

2. National Institute of Rural Development (NIRD)

To examine the factors contributing to the improvement of economic and social well-being in rural areas; on a sustainable basis with focus on the rural poor and the other disadvantaged groups through research.

3. Andhra Pradesh Academy of Rural Development (APARD)

An apex training institute for capacity building of rural development officers and panchayat raj officials; focus on research that helps to offer consulting services in rural development.

4. District Rural Development Agencies (DRDA)

District-level development execution and monitoring agencies. Substantial sums of rural development funds of government of India are transferred and routed through them under various centrally sponsored schemes.

5. Synergy through Science and Technology

The theme of Science and Technology brings out rightly the need and approach to be organized towards accomplishment of desired effective results to the betterment and prosperity of rural India. A list of relevant items and aspects being considered by researchers, scientists and authorities is presented as under: Non-farm occupation in rural India; Rural development strategies for poverty alleviation in India; Status and condition use of modern implements of farm machinery and hand tools; upgradation of the segment of unorganized sector workers: rural artisans; India; rural sanitation; Technologies for rural development and Inclusive Growth in India rural shelter.

6. INFRASTRUCTURE PROJECTS

The primary objective of the projects has to be to improve the living standards of communities that participate by increasing their access to infrastructure services; such of the projects are to include: the building and/or repair of roads;

health clinics; schools; footbridges; electrical resources; potable water resources; irrigation and drainage systems. Approaches of support services required for infrastructure projects include the following: capacity building services; direct training programs; cascading mode of training; research and consulting services; education services:

7. RURAL MARKETING : CHALLENGES, OPPORTUNITIES AND STRATEGIES

"The future lies with those companies who see the poor as their customers".

—C.K. Prahalad

1. Rural Markets

The Indian rural market today accounts for only about seven per cent of the total share. Marketers need to understand the social dynamics and attitude variations within each village and derive a pattern looking at the challenges and the opportunities which rural markets offer to the marketers. It can be said that the future is very promising for those who can understand the dynamics of rural markets and exploit them to their best advantage.

2. Rural Products

Rural products of India are unique, innovative and have good utility and values. Large number of these rural products (like handicraft items, food products, embroidery, clothes and other products) sustains a significant segment of the population in the rural areas. Several attributes of rural products can be identified, for which, it has a demand in the market. Out of the lots, 'ethnic origin' and 'indigenous design and appearance' are two traits of rural products, attracting a premium in the market.

3. Opportunities

The Indian rural market has a huge demand base and offers great opportunities to marketers. Two-thirds of Indian consumers live in rural areas and almost half of the national income is generated here. Infrastructure is improving rapidly; Majority of villages is being electrified; rural telephone density has increased and number of "pucca" houses is also increasing gradually.

4. Quality and Logistic Issues

Non-uniformity of rural products and lack of its quality control measures has been creating a negative demand. Besides, the small sized and dispersed production units of these rural products hinder realization of the economies of scale in marketing and result in high transaction costs per unit of output. Niche-based products have no local market. Products in local use are also not marketed horizontally; they often first travel down to market through a long chain of intermediaries and then up to more difficult locations in the rural areas. In the process, the people in rural areas suffer from both low prices as producers and high prices as consumers. In this conflict, rural products lose its equilibrium and the supply side becomes exponentially high. Because of this hazard, rural entrepreneurs face acute economic loss and rural markets become stagnant.

5. Need for Building Sustainable Market Linkages for Rural Products

Therefore, there is an emergent need for building sustainable market linkages for rural products, so that, it can be connected to larger markets and farmers can get a sustainable livelihood. While rural products are forced to increasingly become part of global supply chains, these products need to adapt themselves, not only according to the changing tastes of the national market, but also according to changes in tastes in the international market. Therefore, a process is essential to explore the market linkages and capacity building through a bottom up approach and continuous dialogue with stakeholders of rural enterprise. This process should ensure the participation of rural people as consumers and producers in the globalization mechanism, with better livelihoods and global access to markets. The real challenge of building a sustainable market linkage starts here.

8. RURAL ARTISANS NEED SUPPORT IN THE ERA OF GLOBAL MARKETING

The major challenges to rural artisans are: Technology-Skill; Marketing-Infrastructure-Finance-Policy support-Availability of appropriate Information

1. Reasons for Problems Faced by Unorganized Sector of Artisans

Lack of Skills; Less exposure to Information and Technology; Lack of Formal Training; Absence of non-farm policy; Marketing support; Non-competitive products; Unable to thrive competition; Application of traditional left over technologies

2. Some Insights from the Perspective of Rural Artisans

Neglect by state and central governments; non-coverage under agricultural relief programs; non-involvement in rural developmental programs; lack of skill improvement and technology upgradation; lack of specialized markets; non-existence of infrastructural facilities; non-availability of quality raw materials; weak financial power; inability to get bank loans; poor access to information; lack of linkages with different developmental institutions

3. Causes for Failure of Rural Development Programs

Non-involvement of rural artisans in the developmental programs: it is the most important reason behind non-achievement of desired goals of rural developmental programs. Most of the technologies remain confined to RandD institutions; RandD is conducted as per convenience of researchers and not as per the need of rural artisans.

9. SYNERGY

A synergy is where different entities cooperate advantageously for a final outcome. If used in a business application it means that teamwork of several agencies will produce an overall better result than if each agency was working toward the same goal individually. It is the working together of two things to produce an effect greater than the sum of their individual effects. Synergism, in the context micro financing for rural uplift, may be understood as two or more agents working together to produce a result not obtainable by any of the agents independently. It is a combined action; the combined healthy action of every organ of a particular system; However, the concept of groups' cohesion needs to be considered and addressed carefully. Groups' cohesion is that property which is inferred from the number and strength of mutual positive attitudes among the groups.

I. Synergy through an Integrated Project Management Approach

It is suggested to adopt discipline of project management approach of planning, organizing, securing and managing resources to bring about the successful completion of specific goals and objectives particularly under uncertainties; such an integrated management of micro finance system is expected to result in achieving optimization and synergy.

10. REENGINEERING OF MICRO FINANCING SYSTEMS

Business process re-engineering (BPR) is the analysis and design of workflows and processes within an organization to achieve a defined business outcome. The cross-functional team is to re-engineer separate functional tasks into complete cross-functional processes. Management information systems developments aim to integrate a wide number of business functions which include human resource management systems and customer relationship management. Business process re-engineering is business process redesign, business transformation, or business process change management. It help organizations fundamentally rethink how they do their work in order to dramatically improve customer service, cut operational costs, and achieve effective development. Business Process Re-engineering is basically the fundamental re-thinking and radical re-design, made to an organization's existing resources. It is more than just business improvising. It is an approach for redesigning the way work is done to better support the organization's mission and reduce costs.

In the context of sustaining effectiveness reengineering, the processes of strategies for various objectives, planning, MIS, human resource management and training related functions of micro financing system are suggested to be focused to start with.

II. OBJECTIVES AND STRATEGIES FOR MANAGEMENT

Selected lists of suggested specific objectives and schemes that can be considered for planning and implementation for micro finance systems are presented below.

1. Specific Objectives and Schemes

Holistic programs of self-uplift for the rural communities; To harness human resources and enable the poor to transform their lives through programs driven by themselves; Critical healthcare issues that are inextricably intertwined with the rural India's poverty; illiteracy and gender discrimination, all of which hinted at the formidable walls of social and economic disparities to be overcome; holistic and development-oriented, focusing first on the empowerment of women; various training programs that tackled hard-hitting issues like healthcare and nutrition, micro-banking and income generation; Support groups that encourage education and trade skills development.

2. Programs for Counseling and Support Groups

Programs to address through informal legal counseling and victim support groups: about eradication of alcoholism, as alcoholism promotes violence; Learn about available trade skills and services they can learn in order to create a livelihood for themselves and better opportunities in, and for, their communities; Vocational training in diverse activities, including: agriculture, dairy, petty shops, food products, fabrics (weaving, sewing, knitting, and embroidery), traditional painting and bamboo products; Ensuring self-reliance, building operational management, and mainstreaming the entrepreneurs into the local market; Natural resource management training.

12. SPECIAL ORGANIZATIONAL REQUIREMENTS TO BE ADDRESSED

The obstacles and challenges in building a sound commercial microfinance industry are discussed here.

1. The Obstacles and Challenges

Inappropriate subsidy characterized by continued subsidization of the industry; Poor regulation and supervision of formal financial system; Operation of most microfinance institutions as nonprofit organizations; not permitting financial institutions to mobilize client savings; Limited management capacity to successfully manage a commercial financial intermediary; Institutional inefficiencies in terms of high operational costs; Need for more dissemination and adoption of rural, agricultural microfinance methodologies; Unable to innovations to face challenges in risk management in rural finance

2. Challenges of Risk Management in Micro Financing

Rural finance is about managing risk; Lenders can effectively pool and aggregate risk held by a large number of borrowers if the risk they face is largely independent; A major advantage of microfinance entities is their ability to pool risk; Correlated (associated) risk cannot be pooled. Small rural finance entities are simply not capable of pooling and managing correlated risk on their own. Agriculture remains a dominant activity in many rural economies of the poorest nations in the world: Risks in agriculture are correlated; Bad fortunes through price decline or natural disasters cause many households to suffer; Insurance markets lack in most developing and emerging economies, and rarely do local insurance markets emerge to address correlated risk problems. There are numerous challenges in developing financial markets to manage risk in developing countries.

13. HUMAN RESOURCE MANAGEMENT FOR MICRO FINANCE

1. Building Efficient Human Resources (HR)

The microfinance sector essentially require to focus on HR needs and covered issues of HR challenges; how management courses can help and capacity building of HR to increase financial literacy of clients; lakh personnel are needed in coming years in the microfinance sector; The microfinance insights state: they lack strategic thinkers with experience in microfinance; lack strategic thinkers on capital markets and experience; essential need identified is for management course on microfinance to generate micro finance managers; Need of training and proper motivation for the existing officers; Develop HR motivation strategies that are to be adopted; identify need for customized HR training programs for microfinance institutions; The staff incentive schemes need to be properly designed.

2. Special Training Needs to be Considered

Bring together different stake holders; Agree on some basic minimum competency required for micro finance; Technical support and training; Develop network institutions of HR skills and services; Mainstream Educational Institutions offering Micro finance Courses; Skills on appraisals, fund management, managing groups, capacity building; For poor people: identify, set-up and manage their livelihood activities.

3. Challenges of HRM

Challenges may be discussed under following subheads: Recruitment; Training; Capacity Building; Benefits; Incentive Management; Performance Appraisal; Career Building; Grievance redress policies; Retention; Local composition of caste/religion; Exposure visits to best practices MFIs; Incentives may be designed as per the requirement of MFI and in reference to context; Continuous mentoring.

14. MANAGEMENT INFORMATION SYSTEMS (MIS) FOR MICROFINANCE

An MIS for microfinance must have the following characteristics: Cost effectiveness; Functionality and flexibility; Reliability; Simple to use; Scalability; Integration

1. Benefits of Computerized MIS

A major advantage of MIS is that it provides easy access to accurate and up-to-date information. For example, loan officers get information on loans that need follow-up, branch managers can monitor daily progress of the branch, and senior management can get a full picture of the portfolio performance and quality. Detailed information is captured on customers and their activities that can then be used to assess client business to assess impact. Better controlled and with minimum opportunity for errors facilitates better understanding, setting priorities, objectives and strategy; Overview of the organization's performance, efficiency and effectiveness of business; Flexibility to structure products and services to the needs of its target group. Efficiency and productivity of staff is increased; MIS lowers transaction cost, increases productivity; Integration and consolidation

2. Challenges and Obstacles to be Reviewed and Addressed

MIS can play an important role in making microfinance institutions more effective. But majority are unable to take up MIS as a strategy and implement suitably; the reasons include the following; Lack of organizational and human potential; Absence of suitable MIS applications; Risk and failure of the existing MIS; Diversity of geography and language in rural areas as hurdles; Unavailability of vendors to implement and support MIS; High cost of IT solutions for MFIs; Lack of commitment of senior management within MFIs; Lack of awareness about benefits of IT.

15. CONCLUSION

It has been found through several researches that many

people from the poor community have the talent to organize business of different nature. They only need the financial back-up to prove themselves. At the same time, if these people are provided with the financial assistance the economic condition of the society is also bound to change. With these, the concept and scope of micro finance has assumed a new aspect altogether. Microfinance should have its special focus on customer orientation and management, and microfinance institutions must provide customer-demanded products and services targeted to achieve social goals and sustainable development

References

Ali Ahmad, CIO—The First Microfinance Bank Ltd.—Article on MIS for Microfinance.

Bauchspies, Science, Technology, Society: A Sociological Approach—Wiley-Blackwell, Benjamin Blanchard. System Engineering Management, John Wiley.

Chinmaya Organization for Rural Development.

David, I. Cleland, Roland Gareis, Global Project Management Hand Book, McGraw Hill.

David Buchanan, Andrezej Huczynski. Organizational Behavior, Pentice Hall.

Firpo, J. (2005), Championing Scale in Microfinance: Technology's Role in Delivering Accessible Financial Services to the Poor.

Paul, C. Dinsmore, "The Right Project Done the Right Way, John Wiley.

Rao, M. (2004), Microfinance and ICTs: Exploring Mutual Benefits and Synergy, Science and Technology, 2008, Thematic Report.

CHAPTER

7

BSE and Sectoral Indices

A Comparative Study

CHETNA PARMAR AND CA MITUAL PARMAR

ABSTRACT

The global economic meltdown has influenced all the sectors of the Indian capital market and economy. Its impact is more noticeable on the Indian capital market and the sectoral indices. The indices are declining and the markets are following the same trend. The BSE SENSEX has been the worst strike among the Indian stock market indices. The other sectoral indices are also following the SENSEX until a revival in the last quarter of 2008. Because of the declining trends in the capital markets, the investors are in a dilemma whether their investments will be safe or not. Even though the situation has stabilized a little bit now on 2009, still there is an ambiguity among the investors about the performance of the indices. In this backdrop, an attempt was made to study the performance of the sectoral indices in comparison with SENSEX on Bull period and Bear Period. The author has taken the data of the last three financial years which parts of bull period and bear period, the studied the correlation co efficient to establish the relationship between the selected sectoral indices and BSE. Seven leading sectoral indices were taken for the analysis, which have a significant impact on the total economic situation of last three years of the country.

Keywords: SENSEX, Indices, Free float Market Capitalization, FMCG, BOLT, Free float Factor.

INTRODUCTION

Indian financial market has been going through a fascinating change and it opened up excellent business and investment opportunities in the financial sector, much growing financial service sector and public are more aware about financial products. The growth and evolution of the financial market led to the development of well structured capital market with attractive investment opportunities for the individual investors. The development of capital market have led to the development of regulatory bodies which amend new law for financial service provided as per the requirement of the market, also development of various sub-market which called as indices, indices were provide authentic information to investors. Financial regulation and innovations have changed the whole structure and functioning of the financial markets of many industrialized countries since 1990s. Initially, the stock market index was formed and later on the sectoral indices developed and these are comprehensively providing the necessary information to the investors to invest their funds for productive utilization of the country. Understanding the importance of the stock market indices, a study has been initialized to establish a relationship between the leading stock market index of the country, the SENSEX and seven significant sectoral indices, which are of prime importance to the overall performance of the economy. The relation of SENSEX with these indices has been computed with the help of the statistical tool; correlation co-efficient. Further, the study has been taken the financial year April 2008 to March 2009, as this has been the period which has witnessed the impact of global financial crisis, than after on April 2009 to March 2010 first quarter has been recover of the market, on 2010 to 2011 has considering again bull market.

BOMBAY STOCK EXCHANGE

The Bombay Stock Exchange is the first and leading stock exchange in India, which obtained permanent recognition in 1956 from the Government of India the Securities Contract Act, 1956. BSE's pivotal and pre-eminent role in the development of the Indian capital market is widely recognized throughout the country, BSE provides an efficient and transparent market for trading in equity, debt instruments and derivatives. It has a nation-wide reach with its mark in more than 359 cities and town of India. BSE has always been on par with the international standards. Keeping in view the larger interests of the investors, the systems and processes are designed to safeguard market integrity and enhance transparency in operations. BSE is the first exchange in India and the second in the world to obtain ISO 9001:2000 certifications. It is also the first exchange in the country and second in the world to receive information security management system standard BS 7799-2-2002 certification for it's On-Line Trading System popularly known among the market as BOLT.

SENSEX

The BSE's index, SENSEX is India's first stock market that enjoys a specific identify and is tracked worldwide. It is an index of leading 30 stocks representing 12 major sectors. The SENSEX is constructed on a "free-float" methodology, and is sensitive to market sentiments and market realities. Apart from the SENSEX, BSE offers 21 indices, including 12 sectoral indices. The SENSEX is the guide to all the investors of the country. In one way it regulates the inflow and outflow of funds into the companies listed in the exchange.

FRAME OF FREE-FLOAT METHODOLOGY

SENSEX is calculating using the "Free-Float Market Capitalization" Methodology, wherein, the level of index at any point of time reflects the free-float market value of 30 components stocks relative to a base period. The full market civilization of a company is determined by multiplying the price of its stock by the number of shares issued by the company. This market capitalization is further multiplied by the free float factor to determine the free float market capitalization. Initially the index calculation was based on full market capitalizations, later on to give more realistic version of the trading activities, the free-float methodology has been adopted by the stock exchange.

RESEARCH DESIGN

Scope of the Study

The study would cover the pattern SENSEX selected seven indices. It's included nine to ten major sectors on SENSEX. Within the time frame from 2008 to 2010, which is further take into consider all the months.

Objectives

(1) A study the impact on portfolio construction and diversification of portfolio from selected sectors.
(2) To compare the performance of selected individual indices.
(3) To analyze the performance of the indices during Bear Run period and Bull Run period.
(4) To guide the investor regarding diversify in the portfolio.

Hypotheses

H_0: There is not significance difference on performance of correlation co-efficient between SENSEX and Indices
H_0: There is significance difference on performance of correlation co-efficient between SENSEX and Indices

DATA COLLECTION

The present study is of analytical nature and accordingly,

the use is made secondary data collected from SENSEX and other information collected from business news paper, websites and magazines. Indices data have been collected from SENSEX website only.

Samples Size

Seven leading sectoral indices were taken for the analysis, which have a significant impact on the total economic situation of last three years of the country. Sectroal were included as BANKTX, FMCG, IT, METAL, POWER, PSU, REALLTY.

Data Collection Method

This study is mainly based on secondary data. All the data of seven Sectroal indices have been collected on website of National Stock Exchange. Also refers some others website which again part of secondary sources.

FUNDAMENTAL TECHNIQUES

1. Mean

Average value of sample, other words said that average represented all the samples.

2. Correlation Coefficient

A broad class of statistical relationships between two or more random variables or observed data values :

$$r = \frac{n(\Sigma xy) - (\Sigma x)(\Sigma y)}{[n\Sigma x^2 - (\Sigma x)^2][n\Sigma y)^2]}$$

All the indices were presently working with a free float methodology of calculation only even though some of them were initially lunched with full market capitalization methodology. The following table shows a comprehensive picture of the specifications of indices selected for the analysis. Table shows that SENSEX was highly fluctuation throughout the year; upper limits had been crossed 17287.31 while lower limit had reached to 8891.61. Comparative analysis of seven sectoral indices lowest fluctuation shows on Fast Moving Consumer Goods indices.

Index Specification

Index	*Base Period*	*Base Index Value*	*Date of Launch*	*Method of Calculation*
(1)	*(2)*	*(3)*	*(4)*	*(5)*
BSE BANKEX	01 January, 2002	1000	23 June, 2003	Free-float market capitalization
BSE FMCG	01 February, 1999	1000	09 August, 1999	Launched on full market capitalization method and effective August 23, 2004, calculation method shifted to free-float market capitalization
BSE IT	01 February, 1999	1000	09 August, 1999	Launched on full market capitalization method and effective August 23, 2004, calculation method shifted to free-float market capitalization
BSE Metal	01 February, 1999	1000	23 August, 2004	Free-float market capitalization
BSE Oil and Gas	01 February, 1999	1000	23 August, 2004	Free-float market capitalization
BSE Power Index	03 January, 2005	1000	09 November, 2007	Free-float market capitalization
BSE Realty	2005	1000	09 July, 2007	Free-float market capitalization

Source : bseindia.com.

TABLE I

April 2008 to March 2009/Values of BSE-Sensex and Sectoral Indices

SENSEX	*BANKTX*	*FMCG*	*IT*	*METAL*	*POWER*	*PUS*	*REALITY*
(1)	*(2)*	*(3)*	*(4)*	*(5)*	*(6)*	*(7)*	*(8)*
15644.44	8819.68	2,461.38	4,261.93	16,114.40	3,189.81	8,081.53	8505.49
17287.31	7714.59	2,427.76	4,643.79	16,914.63	3,338.81	7,079.66	7008.66
16415.57	5915.98	2,080.33	4,019.82	13,207.30	2,936.24	5,666.42	4543.47
13461.6	6516.41	2,139.18	3,689.57	12,912.61	2,252.39	6,706.14	5079.01
14355.75	7009.69	2,215.60	3,966.75	12,348.02	2,574.27	6,747.07	4995.25
14564.53	6478.85	2,160.76	3,095.08	8,992.06	2,604.11	6,246.03	3508.77
12860.43	5011.24	1,799.83	2,861.94	5,367.60	2,260.27	4,564.92	1978.24
9788.06	4645.4	1,936.60	2,558.94	4,383.38	1,583.37	4,585.83	1561.01
9092.72	5454.54	1,987.38	2,227.96	5,214.35	1,631.69	5,279.61	2274.13
9647.31	4900.06	2,032.69	2,236.51	5,100.14	1,829.31	5,115.61	1668.08
9424.24	4240.1	2,043.26	2,096.17	4,690.97	1,792.32	4,984.99	1413.19
8891.61	4490.97	2,036.24	2,285.68	5,795.07	1,751.75	5,230.17	1560.83

Source : bseindia.com.

TABLE 2

April 2009 to March 10/Values of BSE—Sensex and Sectoral Indices

SENSEX	BANKTX	FMCG	IT	METAL	POWER	PUS	REALITY
(1)	(2)	(3)	(4)	(5)	(6)	(7)	(8)
11403.25	5685.22	2,095.00	2,563.35	6,885.81	2112.76	5,863.56	2,130.41
14625.25	8258.43	2,096.64	2,997.55	10,878.42	2881.36	8,427.44	3,819.89
14493.84	8211.48	2,262.69	3,287.20	10,830.90	2842.34	7,922.57	3,207.19
15670.31	8465.76	2,738.15	3.962.12	12,395.26	2970.46	8,365.69	3,908.77
15666.64	8344.62	2,553.52	4,172.52	12,382.92	2991.94	8,382.38	4,413.59
17126.84	9855.6	2,575.82	4,570.91	14,176.62	3076.05	8,909.15	4,509.66
15896.28	9336.16	2,808.97	4,425.52	13,940.17	2914.62	8,400.20	3,827.13
16926.22	10042.46	2,872.10	4,757.27	16,292.03	2979.44	9,139.38	3,660.45
17464.81	10030.8	2,791.55	5,186.35	17,399.22	3188.55	9,531.73	3,855.78
16357.96	9654.09	2,725.38	4,977.71	15,962.05	3061.52	9,473.93	3,500.22
16429.55	9828.68	2,662.05	5,173.99	16,401.52	2961.56	9,214.28	3,236.69
17527.77	10652.35	2,831.12	5,237.50	17,973.81	3085.72	9,038.27	3,273.56

Source : bseindia.com.

As analysis of 2008-09, which researcher has knew that more fluctuation on reality sector. On comparison on 2009-10 SENSEX was crossed 17527.77 upper points while lower point was 11403.25. So that actual variation on SENSEX 6500 points on 2009-10. It was observed that the BANKTX 5000 points was fluctuation. Metal shows highest fluctuation. Power indices were evidence for stable. Comparison to 2008-09 reality sector has been enlarges, IT indices were also growing. Power sector indices were stable and slowly growing.

Table 3 indicates the performance SENSEX and its indices on 2010-11, which researcher knew that market should growing very fast and at the same selected sectors faced high fluctuations due to the flow of foreign institutional investor's investment. On comparison on 2010-11 SENSEX was reached its peak level at 20509.09 upper points while lower point was 16944.63. So that actual variation on SENSEX 5000 points which is comparative less than 2009-10. It was observed that the BANKTX well performance and propose less fluctuation. An FMCG index was extremely steady. IT, METAL, POWER, PUS indices was also much stable, just reality sectors shows down turn.

All other indices were similarly treated with the same equation to ascertain the relationship on BSE SENSEX and its indices. The following table signifies the correlation co-efficient of the selected indices from last three years.

By practical observed the trends in the correlation co efficient, it should be said that all indices were showing a high range of positive correlation on 2008-09. All indices has been near to 0.90 that indicates SENSEX provided good return than indices also provided good return. Table also shows comparison 2009-10 that only reality sector was not well positive correlation with SENSEX while all other sector performance was equally good. On 2010-11 shows positive as well as negative correlation among indices. BANKTX, FMCG, IT having positive correlation, and METAL, PUS shows 60% per cent having positive relation, Power and Reality sector just 0.02 to 0.05 positive correlation co efficient which is very less.

This confirms the fact that the movement of the leading index of the country influences all the indices. So the investors

TABLE 3

2010-11/Values of BSE—Sensex and Sectoral Indices

SENSEX	BANKTX	FMCG	IT	METAL	POWER	PUS	REALITY
(1)	(2)	(3)	(4)	(5)	(6)	(7)	(8)
17,558.71	11,155.07	2,877.76	5,357.83	17,664.76	3,170.61	9,113.05	3,491.18
16,944.63	10,656.56	2,980.55	5,174.70	15,146.67	3,032.63	9,133.94	3,097.92
17,700.90	10,765.03	3,230.23	5,319.21	14,704.25	3,150.10	9,508.65	3,196.82
17,868.29	11,539.55	3,229.86	5.474.84	15,399.81	3,110.24	9,576.60	3,372.93
17,971.12	12,190.64	3,385.07	5,375.62	14,977.50	3,033.05	9,641.33	3,331.76
20,069.12	14,025.04	3,719.54	5,947.07	16,864.91	3,235.14	10,279.56	3,726.86
20,032.34	14,016.21	3,605.10	5,992.77	16,681.58	3,118.16	10,139.97	3,635.12
19,521.25	13,618.77	3,582.71	6,094.00	15,626.11	2,891.48	9,291.00	2,925.40
20,509.09	13,379.73	3,684.12	6,824.82	17,595.86	2,988.56	9,460.63	2,856.22
18,327.76	12,064.01	3,366.20	6,371.10	16,115.67	2,744.20	8,706.88	2,228.72
17,823.40	11,840.34	3,432.42	6,106.81	15,348.81	2,523.29	8,380.61	1,981.65
19,445.22	13,299.77	3,596.10	6,548.10	16,161.39	2,712.11	8,960.08	2,337.01

Source : bseindia.com.

TABLE 4

Sl. No.	Sectoral Indices 2008-09/10/11	Correlation Co-Efficient with BSE Sensex		
		2008-09	2009-10	2010-11
1.	BANKTX	0.96	0.97	0.94
2.	FMCG	0.88	0.82	0.89
3.	IT	0.95	0.90	0.76
4.	METAL	0.98	0.94	0.57
5.	POWER	0.98	0.94	0.05
6.	PUS	0.95	0.94	0.47
7.	REALITY	0.98	0.63	0.098

Source : Correlation Co-efficient from the Tables 1, 2, 3.

GRAPH I

Correlation of Co-efficient from Last Three Years

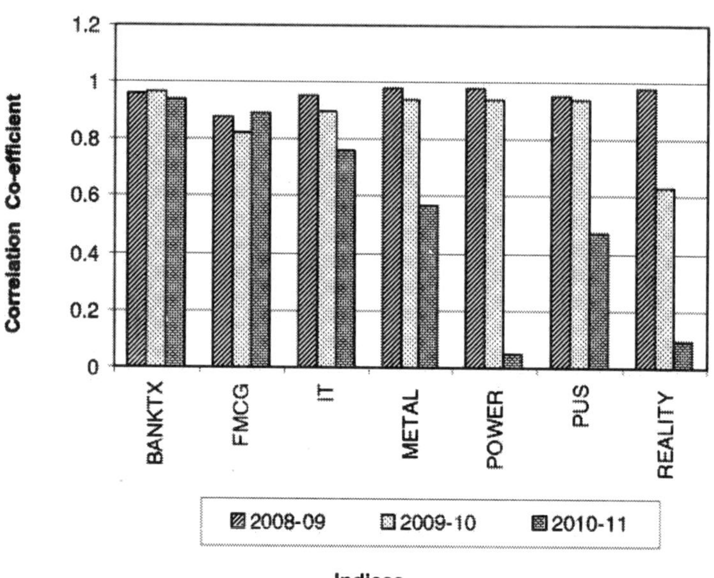

can follow the leading index for their investment in various sectors. When the time of portfolio construction allocation of the fund is very significant role included indices performance

Calculation of Co-efficient of Correlation

2008-09

SENSEX/X	Y BANKTX	(X-X)	(Y-Y)	X2	Y2	X*Y
(1)	(2)	(3)	(4)	(5)	(6)	(7)
17,287.31	8,819.68	5,162.51	2,886.55	26651509.5	8332170.903	14901843.24
16,415.57	7,714.59	4,290.77	1,781.46	18410707.19	3173599.732	7643835.124
13,461.60	5,915.98	1,336.80	-17.15	1787034.24	294.1225	-22926.12
14,355.75	6,516.41	2,230.95	583.28	4977137.903	340215.5584	1301268.516
14,564.53	7,009.69	2,439.73	1,076.56	5952282.473	1158981.434	2626515.729
12,860.43	6,478.85	735.63	545.72	541151.4969	297810.3184	401448.0036
9,788.06	5,011.24	-2,336.74	-921.89	5460353.828	849881.1721	2154217.239
9,092.72	4,645.40	-3,032.08	-1,287.73	9193509.126	1658248.553	3904500.378
9,647.31	5,454.54	-2,477.49	-478.59	6137956.7	229048.3881	1185701.939
9,424.24	4,900.06	-2,700.56	-1,033.07	7293024.314	1067233.625	2789867.519
8,891.61	4,240.10	-3,233.19	-1,693.03	10453517.58	2866350.581	5473887.666
9,708.50	4,490.97	-2,416.30	-1,442.16	5838505.69	2079825.466	3484691.208
145,497.63	71,197.51	0.03	-0.05	102696690	22053659.85	45844850.44
12,124.80	5,933.13	0.00	0.00	10133.93754	4696.132435	47590312.77
						0.963323159

and the life stage of that particular industry also play vital role for the positive return compared to the market return.

CONCLUSION

Financial planning is an essential on allocation of the savings and one has to do with maximum plan to success of the positive return on investments either by the individual investors or institutional investors. The investors also well known about time of buying and selling and enough knowledge about selection of financial instrument with time horizon. Than after investors will make good strategic for return, investors also having knowledge about bull and bear market.

The present study emphasizes the fact that the stock markets are very sensitive to the market affecting factors and the leading indices will always move on associate with SENSEX. Industry lifecycle, stage of leading sectors also affected the indices return. Investors has to take into consideration both the fundamental part of the company like profitability, past records, corporate governance, chief executives, along with a close watch of the coming and going markets which called efficient market reaction. Investors need to continuous monitoring of the markets instead of depending on individual perceptions; one can rely upon the stock market indices, as these provide authentic and unbiased information on the performance of the market. Researchers conclude that best option of selection of any scrip first go the detail analysis of fundamental and market analysis of the investment opportunities.

REFERENCES

The Financial Express, Hyderabad, 23rd March, 2009

The Economic Times, 7th January, 2009.

Deccan Chronicle, 13th Dec, 2009.

The Hindu, 16th October, 2009.

Venkatech Ganesh, "Rediscovering India", *Business World*, 20th July, 2009.

Preethi Singh, "Investment Management", Himalaya Publishing House, 2006.

V.K. Bulla, "Investment Management", Fifth Edition.
S.P. Gupta, "Statistical Methods", 11th Edition.

Website

www.bseindia.com
www.moneycontrol.com
www.prudentchannel.com

CHAPTER

An Application of Z-Score Model

A Study of Reliance Industries Limited

ELIZA SHARMA

ABSTRACT

Finance is the backbone of any company. Financial distress is a situation where a firm's operating cash flows is not sufficient to satisfy current obligations and the firm is forced to take corrective actions. A firm in financial distress may also face bankruptcy or liquidation to meet its liabilities. This paper aims to measure the financial health of Reliance Industries Ltd. by using the Solvency Ratio test and Z-Score Model (Altman's 1968) from the year 2000 to 2010. An attempt has been made in the present study to have an insight into the examination of financial health of the organization. The result clearly indicates that the solvency position of the company is healthy. The Z-Score analysis also shows that except the year 2008-09, the company is in healthy zone. Only in the year 2008-09 the company was in distress zone and we can assign the Global Crisis for the cause of this financial distress.

INTRODUCTION

Finance is a significant facet of every business. Both excessive as well as inadequate finance position are dangerous from the business point of view. The performance of any company can be judged by its financial statements, which throws light on the operational efficiency and financial position of the company. It is necessary to bench mark the efficiency of utilization of capital and assets, return to shareholders as well as predicting financial distress. The prediction and prevention of financial distress is one of the major factors, which will help to avoid bankruptcy.

REVIEW OF LITERATURE

Anup Chowdhury and Suborna Barua (2009) investigated the financial attributes of Z category shares companies using Z-score analysis and found that 90 percent of those companies are suffering with financial problems. Krishna Chaitanya (2005) used Z model to measure the financial fitness of IDBI and concluded that IDBI is likely to become insolvent in the years to come. Bagchi, S.K. (2004) analyzed about practical implication of accounting ratios in risk evaluation and concluded that accounting ratios are still dominant factors in the matter of credit risk evaluation. Mansur A. Mulla (2002) made a study in textile mill with the help of Z-score model for evaluating the financial health with five weighted financial ratios. L.C. Gupta (1999) attempted a refinement of Beaver's method with the objective of predicting the business failure. Keeping in view the significance of measurement of financial distress with Z-Score model, an attempt has been made to measure the financial distress of one the renowned company of India that is Reliance Industries Ltd.

OBJECTIVES

The objectives of this study are as follows:

- To analyze the financial performance of the company through solvency ratios.

- To measure the financial distress of the company with Altman's Z-Score model.

RESEARCH METHODOLOGY

The study is concerned with Reliance Industries Ltd. The study is based on the secondary data, which has been collected from the financial statements of Reliance Industries Ltd. for the years 2000-01 to 2009-10. Ratio Analysis which is one of the reliable tools for the analysis of financial statements has been used on the collected data, solvency ratios has been calculated to check the solvency position of the company. Z-Score model is used to check in which zone the company is in, Distress (Bankruptcy), Grey (Healthy) Or Safe (Too Healthy).

ABOUT THE COMPANY

The Reliance Group, founded by Dhirubhai H. Ambani, is India's largest private sector enterprise, with businesses in the energy and materials value chain. Group's annual revenues are in excess of US $ 44 billion. The flagship company, *Reliance Industries Limited,* is a Fortune Global 500 company and is the largest private sector company in India. Backward vertical integration has been the cornerstone of the evolution and growth of Reliance. Starting with textiles in the late seventies, Reliance pursued a strategy of backward vertical integration—in polyester, fiber intermediates, plastics, petrochemicals, petroleum refining and oil and gas exploration and production—to be fully integrated along the materials and energy value chain. The Group's activities span exploration and production of oil and gas, petroleum refining and marketing, petrochemicals (polyester, fiber intermediates, plastics and chemicals), textiles, retail and special economic zones. Reliance enjoys global leadership in its businesses, being the largest polyester yarn and fibre producer in the world and among the top five to ten producers in the world in major petrochemical products.

Major Group Companies are Reliance Industries Limited (including main subsidiary Reliance Retail Limited) and *Reliance Industrial Infrastructure Limited.*

Solvency Test

The detection of the firm's operating and financial difficulties is a subject which has been particularly amenable to analyze with the financial ratios. To detect the sign of looming bankruptcy, analysts calculate the following ratios:

1. *Working capital to Total Assets*: This ratio expresses the liquidity position of the company towards the total capitalization. Working Capital is defined as the difference between the current assets and current liabilities.
2. *Retained Earning to Total Assets*: This ratio indicates the amount of assets which have been financed through retention of profits. Retained Earnings is the part of profit which has not been distributed to the shareholders as dividend but retained by the company to utilize it in some future opportunities.
3. *Earning Before Interest and Taxes to Total Assets*: This ratio indicates the earning power of the company, or the productivity of the firm's assets.
4. *Equity to Total Assets*: This ratio indicates the long-term solvency of the firm. This measure shows how much assets of an enterprise can decline in value before the liabilities exceed the assets and the concern becomes insolvent.

TABLE I

Solvency Ratios

YEAR	WC/TA	RE/TA	EBIT/TA	EQ/TA	SA/TA
2009-10	0.09	0.02	0.09	0.69	0.80
2008-09	0.08	0.02	0.08	0.63	0.60
2007-08	0.13	0.03	0.16	0.69	0.93
2006-07	0.10	0.02	0.13	0.70	1.01
2005-06	0.09	0.03	0.12	0.69	0.96
2004-05	0.14	0.11	0.13	0.68	0.91
2003-04	0.14	0.08	0.11	0.62	0.79
2002-03	0.19	0.05	0.10	0.61	0.79
2001-02	0.21	0.05	0.10	0.60	0.80
2000-01	0.14	0.07	0.13	0.59	0.77
Mean	0.13	0.05	0.12	0.65	0.84

WC = Working Capital, TA = Total Assets, RE = Retained Earning
EBIT = Earning Before Interest and Tax, EQ = Equity, SA = Sales.

5. *Sales to Total Assets*: This ratio indicates the sales generating capacity of the company's assets and measure of management's capacity to deal with competitive conditions.

FIG. 1

Working Capital to Total Assets Ratio

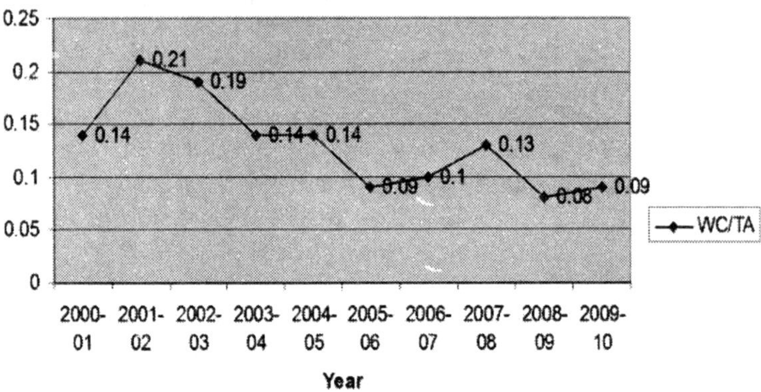

Interpretation: It may be seen from the Figure 1 that the working capital of the company fluctuates during the study period. It is varied from 0.08 in the year 2008-09 to 0.21 in the year 2000-01, showing efficient mobilization of working capital during the study period.

FIG. 2

Retained Earning to Total Assets Ratio

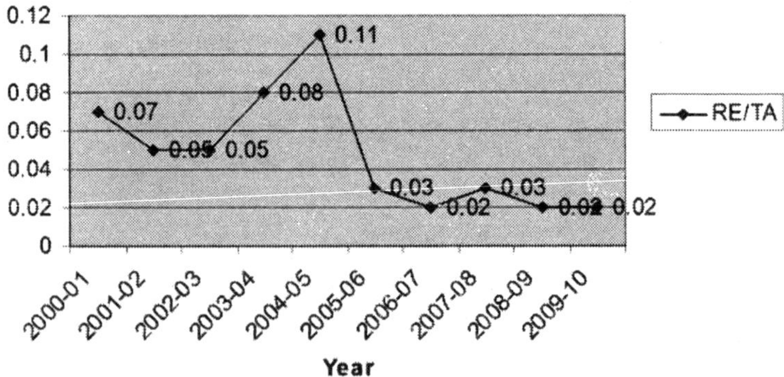

Interpretation: It can be seen from the Figure 2 that the retained earning to total asset has varied from 0.02 in the year 2005-06 to 0.11 in the year 2004-05 which shows that the company depends more on the external debt rather than financing capital expenditures from the retained earning.

FIG. 3

Earning before Interest and Tax to Total Assets Ratio

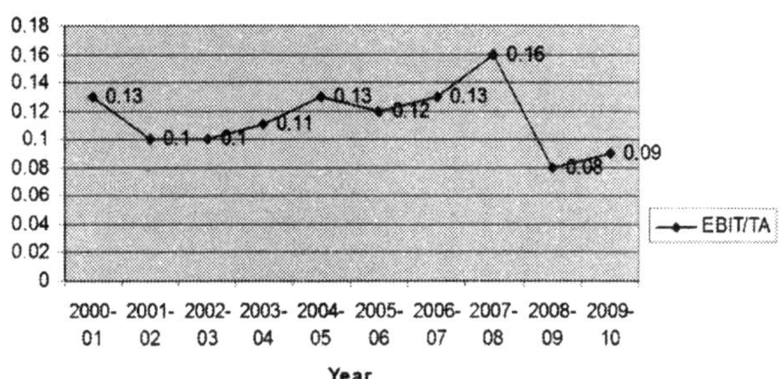

Interpretation: It can be seen from the Figure 3 that the EBIT is fluctuating every year during the study period, ranging between 0.08 to 0.16 which shows that the company is in a position to meet it's financial obligations like interest and tax payments.

FIG. 4

Equity to Total Assets Ratio

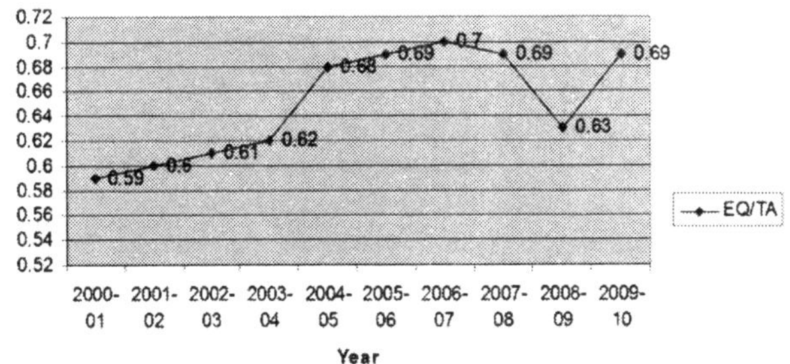

Interpretation: It can be seen from the figure 4 that the Equity of the company is varying between 0.59 to 0.70 during the study period which shows the interest of the shareholders are high due to healthy position of the company.

FIG. 5
Sales to Total Assets Ratio

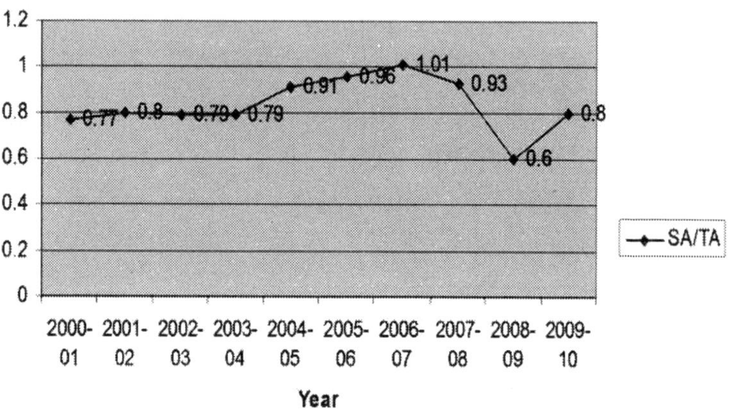

Interpretation: It can be seen from the Figure 5 that the Sales of the company is ranging between 0.60 to 1.01 during the study period which shows that the sales of the company is high in compare to total assets invested by the company in the year 2006-07 even this ratio was 1.01 which shows the highest sales during study period.

TABLE 2
Mean Values of the Solvency Ratios

Ratio	*WC/TA*	*RE/TA*	*EBIT/TA*	*EQ/TA*	*SA/TA*
Mean	0.13	0.05	0.12	0.65	0.84

Z-Score Analysis

Altman's Z-Score Test: For the purpose of knowing the financial health of the company this study uses 'Z'-Score model, which captures the predictive viability of a company's

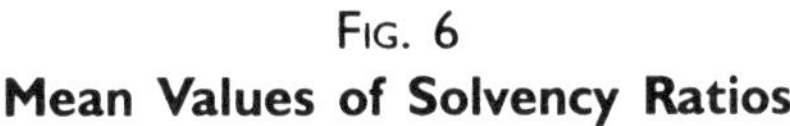

FIG. 6
Mean Values of Solvency Ratios

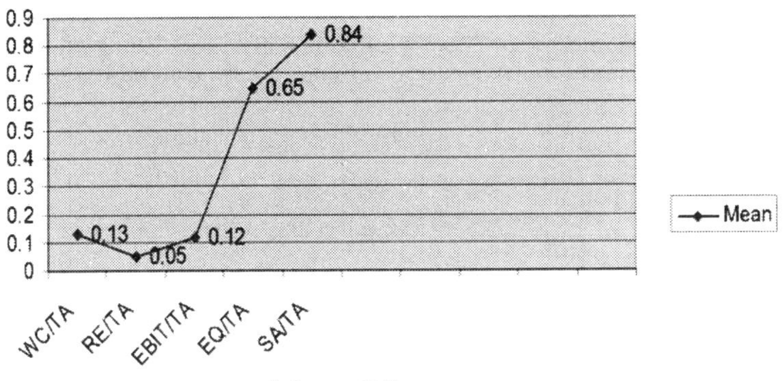

financial health by using a combination of financial ratios that ultimately predicts a score, which are used to determine the financial health of the company.

$$Z = 0.717 \times 1 + 0.847 \times 2 + 3.107 \times 3 + 0.42 \times 4 + 0.998 \times 5$$

Where:

Z = Discriminant function score of a firm
X1 = Working Capital to Total Assets
X2 = Retained Earnings to Total Assets
X3 = Earning Before Interest and Tax to Total Assets
X4 = Equity to Total Assets
X5 = Sales to Total Assets

Test

Z<1.23 indicates Distress (Bankruptcy) Zone
Z> 1.23 and Z< 2.9 indicates the Grey (Healthy) Zone
Z>2.9 indicates the Safe (Too Healthy) Zone.

TABLE 3

YEAR	2009-10	2008-09	2007-08	2006-07	2005-06
Z Score	1.45	1.19	1.84	1.81	1.72
YEAR	2004-05	2003-04	2002-03	2001-02	2000-01
Z Score	1.79	1.55	1.54	1.56	1.59

Z-Score Values

Figure 7 represents the trend of Z-Score of Reliance Industries Ltd. from the year 2000-01 to 2009-10.

FIG. 7
Z-Score Values

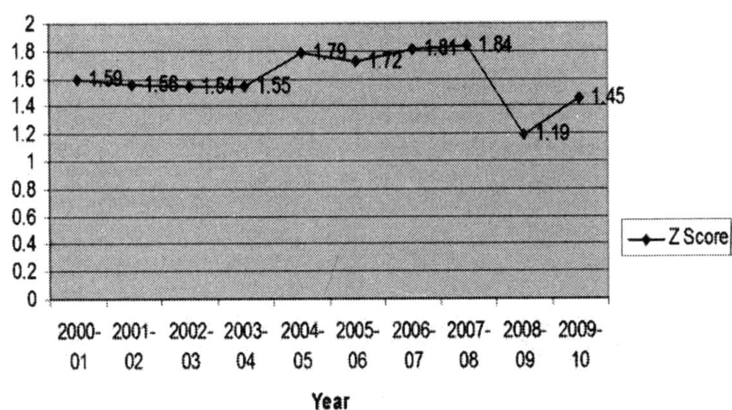

Interpretation: The Z-score analysis was applied to evaluate the general trend in the financial health of the Reliance Industries Ltd. by using solvency ratios. It is clear from the figure 7 that the company's Z-score is in Grey Zone for the study period except the year 2008-09 which has the lowest Z-Score 1.19 that is below 1.23 means in this year the financial health of the company was poor and it was in financial distress. Except the year 2008-09 the Z-score of the company was between 1.23 to 2.9 that means it was in Grey Zone. As far as the mean value of Z-Score is concerned it is 1.61, this also shows that the company is in Grey Zone.

CONCLUSION

As per the Altman guidelines, the financial health of the sample units were tested through Z-Score, and finally it was concluded that the financial health of Reliance Industries Ltd. was healthy. From the analysis, it is clear that the solvency position of the company is healthy.

REFERENCES

Altman, E.I. (1968), "Financial Ratios, Discriminant Analysis and the Prediction of Corporate Bankruptcy", *Journal of Finance,* 23(4): 589-609.

Anup Chowdhury and Suborna Barua (2009), "Rationalities of Z category Shares in Dhaka Stock Exchange: Are they in Financial Distress Risk?", *BRAC University Journal,* Vol. VI, No. 1, 2009, 45-58.

Bagchi, S.K. (2004), "Accounting Ratios for Risk Evaluation", *The Management Accountant,* July, Vol. 39, No. 7, 571-73.

Gupta, L.C. (1999), "Return Indian Equity Shares Reviewed in ICFAI", *Journal of Applied Finance,* Vol. 6, No. 4, October 1999.

Krishna, Chaitanya V. (2005), "Measuring Financial Distress of IDBI using Altman Z-score model", *ICFAI University Journal of Bank Management,* ICFAI Press, Vol. 10(3), 7-17.

Mansur, A. Mulla, "Use of Z-score Analysis for evaluation of Financial Health of Textile Mills—A Case Study", *Abhigyan,* Vol. XIX, No. 4, Jan.-March 2002. 37-41.

CHAPTER

Forecasting Exchange Rate

A Case Study of Short-term Exchange Rate between INR and US Dollar

ABHISHEK KUMAR CHINTU AND ONKAR NATH MISHRA

ABSTRACT

The most important function of the forex market is to determine the exchange rate of the concerned currency in various other currencies. A reliable forecast of future spot rates provides essentially an informational input for the management of foreign exchange exposure and other financial decisions. In this project an analysis of the short-term exchange rate between the INR and USD has been carried out. The analysis pertains for the exchange rate of the month of September (2010). The techniques of forecasting exchange rate namely, exponential regression and moving average models have been employed to generate the forecast. The research attempts to test the weak form of Efficient Market Hypothesis (EMH). It also attempts to examine whether the technical analysis can aid the chartists to beat the market or not.

Keywords: Exchange rate forecasting, exponential regression, moving average, EMH hypothesis, forecast accuracy

INTRODUCTION

A foreign exchange market, often abbreviated as forex market is the market where one currency (foreign currency) is bought and sold against another currency (domestic or home currency). The most important function of the forex market is to determine the exchange rate of the concerned currency in various other currencies. The genesis of forex market is traced to the need for foreign currency to facilitate international trade, foreign investment, and borrowing and lending to foreigners.

The equilibrium exchange rate is determined in the same way as the price of any other good is determined in economics ie. by demand and supply forces. The exchange rate in this sense is nothing but the price of one currency in terms of other currency. There are various factors which create the demand for foreign currency which when equated with the supply of the same determines the equilibrium exchange rate.

A reliable forecast of future spot rates provides essentially an informational input for the management of foreign exchange exposure and other financial decisions. Exchange rate forecasts are necessary to evaluate the foreign denominated cash flows involved in international transactions. Thus, exchange rate forecasting is very important to evaluate the benefits and risks attached to the international business environment. It must be noted that the need to forecast exchange rate has come into picture when the countries have opted for floating exchange.

A forecast represents an expectation about a future value or values of a variable. Exchange rate forecasting refers to the entire process of estimating the future exchange rate. It is an act of predicting the exchange rate well in advance for the purpose of financial decision-making as for instance working capital management, foreign exchange exposure management, and international capital budgeting decisions. The exchange rate forecasting is more an art rather than science. The forecasting of exchange rate is not a cake walk either for the economist or for the financial analysts. No technique and even technological development in the form of sophisticated software till now has proved to yield robust results.

LITERATURE REVIEW

In the international finance literature, various theoretical models are available to analyze exchange rate determination and behaviour. The dominant model was the flexible-price monetary model that has been analyzed in many early studies like Frenkel (1976), Mussa (1976, 1979), Frenkel and Johnson (1978), and more recently by Vitek (2005), Nwafor (2006), Molodtsova and Papell, (2007). Following this, the sticky price or overshooting model by Dornbusch (1976, 1980) evolved, which has been tested, amongst others, by Alquist and Chinn (2008) and Zita and Gupta (2007). The portfolio balance model also developed alongside, which allowed for imperfect substitutability between domestic and foreign assets, and considered wealth effects of current account imbalances.

Examination of the empirical literature suggests that there is no consensus among economists on the appropriate monetary model that explains exchange rates well. It is also observed that the in-sample predictive performance of monetary models was good in the years following the breakdown of the Bretton Woods system (see e.g. Bilson, 1978, Frankel, 1979), but their performance collapsed in the 1980s.

Studies by MacDonald and Taylor (1991, 1993, 1994), Choudhry and Lawler (1997), Diamandis, Georgoutsos and Kouretas (1998), Mark and Sul (2001) attribute monetary models to be long-run equilibrium phenomena. Empirical literature (e.g.: Chinn and Meese 1995, Taylor, 1995, Neely and Sarno 2002, Sarno and Taylor, 2002) suggests that over short horizons of one to three years, monetary fundamentals generally do not predict changes in the spot rate. However, over longer horizons of four to five years, fundamentals do provide some predictive power for some currencies (Kim and Mo, 1994, Mark, 1995, Chinn and Meese, 1995).

Furthermore, with the growing development of foreign exchange markets and a rise in the trading volume in these markets, the micro-level dynamics in foreign exchange markets increasingly became important in determining exchange rates.

Agents in the foreign exchange market have access to private information about fundamentals or liquidity, which is reflected in the buying/selling transactions they undertake, that are termed as order flows (Medeiros, 2005, Bjonnes and Rime, 2003). Microstructure theory evolved in order to capture the micro level dynamics in the foreign exchange market (Evans and Lyons, 2001, 2007). An extensive survey of literature on theoretical and empirical findings is available in Dornbusch (1990), Frankel and Rose (1995), Taylor (1995), Cuthbertson (1996), Sarno and Taylor (2002), Gandolfo (2006) and Schmidt (2006).

The microstructure theory of exchange rates provides an alternative view to the determination of exchange rates. Unlike macroeconomic models that are based on public information, micro-based models suggest that some agents may have access to private information about fundamentals or liquidity that can be exploited in the short-run. In microeconomic models of asset prices, transactions play a causal role in price determination (Evans and Lyons, 2001, 2007). The microstructure theory of exchange rates gained popularity since the late 1990s when it was empirically tested that information in order flows drive exchange rates (Evans and Lyons, 1999, Luo, 2001, Medeiros, 2005). Evans and Lyons (2007) quantify the effect of news on exchange rates and observe that two-thirds of the effect of macro news on exchange rates is transmitted via order flow. Bjonnes and Rime (2003) find that private information plays an important role in the foreign exchange market and has a permanent effect on exchange rates.

A large body of empirical literature, reviewed by Frankel and Rose (1995) and Meese (1990), focuses on whether existing theoretical and econometric models of exchange rate determination represent good descriptions of the empirical data. Nevertheless, the literature has not converged on a particular class of models capable of challenging the Meese and Rogoff (1983) result that structural macro-models cannot out-perform a naïve random-walk. Most of the studies conclude that monetary fundamentals such as the GDP differential, the inflation differential, the relative money growth, and the short-term interest rate differential have negligible out of sample predictive power at least over short time horizons

Nevertheless, despite the use of a variety of models over the last half a decade or so, forecasting the exchange rates has remained a challenge for both academicians as well as market participants.

Most of the studies conclude that monetary fundamentals such as the GDP differential, the inflation differential, the relative money growth, and the short-term interest rate differential have negligible out of sample predictive power at least over short time horizons. However, there is some evidence that with longer time horizons the forecasting accuracy of fundamentals based exchange rate models improves (see e.g. Mark (1995) and Cheung *et al.* (2003), In a recent study, Sarno and Taylor (2002) analyse how to optimally select the correct number of fundamentals to be used in computing the best forecasting model in each period. They show that ex-ante it is not possible to implement a procedure that is able to account for the frequent shifts occurring in the weight each fundamental has in driving exchange rate dynamics. Although fundamentals do not appear to help in forecasting short-run exchange rate returns, the existence of links between exchange rates and fundamentals in the short-run is stated in the important work of Andersen, *et al.* (2003). They found, using real time data, that macroeconomic announcement surprises produce quick jumps in the conditional mean of .the US dollar exchange rates from January 1992 to December 1998. Andersen *et al.* (2007) and Faust, *et al.* (2007) confirm this result for the euro-dollar exchange rate.

A great deal of research work has been undertaken by experts on financial markets and economists on both Random Walk and Efficient Market Hypothesis. Literature available depicts studies concerning developed and emerging markets. Some important work has been done by Thomas (1995), Basu and Morey (1998), Nath (2001). Nath and Reddy (2002), covering Indian stock market returns but very little work has been done to study the long memory of exchange rate in India.

The present study contributes to the ongoing debate regarding the possibility of correctly forecasting future exchange rate movements. The forecast which we are interested in this paper has been described as immediate forecast (Moosa, p. 15). The econometric evidence resulting from this kind of study can suggest which model should be adopted in order to achieve a better forecasting performance. The present study contributes to the ongoing debate regarding the possibility of correctly forecasting future exchange rate movements. The econometric evidence resulting from this kind of study can suggest which model should be adopted in order to achieve a better forecasting performance.

RESEARCH OBJECTIVES

This study is aimed to achieve the following objectives:

1. To test the Efficient Market Hypothesis (EMH) in the Indian foreign exchange market, particularly for the exchange rate between INR and USD.
2. To find out whether the foreign exchange rate between INR and USD is really determined in a random fashion.
3. To have a comparative study of the accuracy of the forecasting techniques of exponential smoothing *verses* exponential estimation.
4. To have knowledge about the main features of short-term exchange rate determination for the concerned currencies.
5. To know the extent to which abnormal profits can be reaped in the forex market by using various derivative instruments for hedging and speculating.

RESEARCH METHODOLOGY

The research methodology adopted in this paper can be explained under following heads:

RESEARCH DESIGN

A time series design has been adopted for this study. It entails the collection of data about a phenomenon at different point of time in order to ascertain the behaviour of the concerned variable over a period of time. The data can be collected either annually, monthly, weekly or daily as the case may be and as the need may arise.

Time series analysis is an integral part of financial analysis. The topic is interesting and useful, with applications to the prediction of interest rates, foreign currency risk, stock market volatility, and the like. Since the spot exchange rate between any pair of currencies are determined daily depending on the forces of demand and supply for the currencies concerned, the data about the exchange rate between the INR and USD have been recorded daily.

In this paper, we will forecast a future value of the exchange rate, St+T. The expectation is constructed using an information set selected by the forecaster. The information set should be available at time t. The notation used for forecasts of St+T is:

$$Et[St+T]$$

where Et[.] represent an expectation taken at time t.

Each forecast has an associated forecasting error, et+1. We will define the forecasting error as:

$$et+1= St+1 - Et[St+1]$$

The forecasting error will be used to judge the quality of the forecasts. A typical metric used for this purpose is the Mean Square Error or MSE. The MSE is defined as:

$$MSE = [(et+1)2 + (et+2)2 + (et+3)2 + ... + (et+T)2]/T$$

where T is the number of forecasts. We will say that the higher the MSE, the less accurate the forecasting model. Thus, we shall employ MSE as the criteria to judge the accuracy of forecasting model in our paper.

Sampling Frame

Sample size—This study is a small sample study. The sample size is thirty. As we know for a sample to be small its size must not exceed thirty. However, at the same time it must be taken into account that all the results deduced from the small sample of size usually more than twenty-five hold true for the large sample as well. Hence, without compromising with the quality of the results, same can be arrived at with much ease.

Sampling period—The forecasting of exchange rate has been done for the entire month of September 2010. The actual exchange rate starting from Sept. 01 to Sept. 30 was taken and forecast was generated for each corresponding day. The month of September was chosen using simple random sampling.

Data Resource

The data can be classified as quantitative data and qualitative data. Quantitative data are measurements in which numbers are used directly to represent the characteristics of something. Since they are recorded directly with numbers, they are in a form that lends itself to statistical analysis. Qualitative data represent descriptions of things that are made without assigning numbers directly.

For the purpose of this study, secondary data has been utilised. The exchange rate between the INR and USD has been taken from the official website of the International Monetary Fund (IMF).

HYPOTHESIS

In this research project we shall test the following hypothesis:

1. The short-term exchange rate is randomly determined.
2. The foreign exchange rate market exhibits weak form of market efficiency.
3. Today's exchange rate is a function of yesterday's exchange rate plus an error term.
4. Technical analysis is able to predict the future exchange rate.

DATA ANALYSIS AND EMPIRICAL FINDINGS

We can have a fair good idea about the given time series

by employing certain measures of central tendency and measures of dispersion. These two measures are also the very basis of other sophisticated measures and statistical analysis.

(a) Measures of Central Tendency

The measures of central tendency of any given data set are the single most important measures. They tell us what the time series is on an average. The mean, median and mode and standard error of mean is shown in the Table 1.

TABLE 1

Measures of central tendency	*Mean*	*Median*	*Mode*	*SE (mean)*	*95% fiducial limits of mean*
	45.94570	46.24001	46.82863	0.1245	46.188 – 45.70

From the above central measures it is clear that there is little difference among the three most important measures of central tendency. The series is therefore normally distributed.

(b) Measures of Dispersion

The measures of dispersion are the second most important measure. They measure the variation in the given series around its central values and thus enable us to detect the nature of distribution. They are shown in the Table 2.

TABLE 2

Measures of dispersion	*SD*	*SE* (σ)	*VAR*	*Range*	*CoV*	*Skewness*
	0.68246	0.12459	0.46575	2.42053	1.48530	–1.29374

The scatter plot of the chosen time series is depicted in Figure 1.

From the following scatter diagram it is clear that the Rupee has depreciated *vis-a-vis* dollar in the month of September. The thick line reprents the regression line of exchange rate which we shall be estimated using the exponential regression.

FIG. 1
Rate

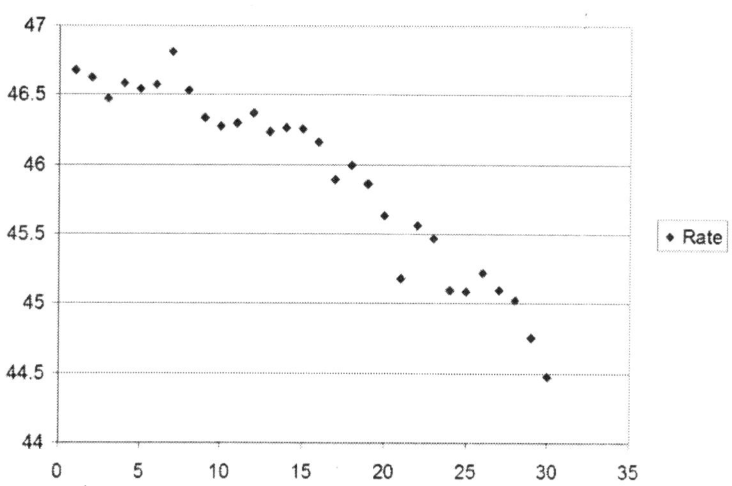

Testing the Randomness of Exchange Rate

It is extremely important in time series of exchange rate to know whether the series is a result of chance or not. If it is so then the forecasting of exchange rate is a futile exercise.

In this case we proceed as follow:

H_0 = The given series is random
H_A = The given series is not random

Since the number of observation is equal to 30, it can be fairly approximated by the normal distribution as given below:

$$Z = R - \mu/\sigma$$

For the given series

$$R = 15$$

$$\mu = \frac{2 \times 10 \times 19 + 1}{10 + 19}$$

$$= 14.10344$$

$\sigma = (380 \times 351/841 \times 28)^{1/2}$
$= 2.37995$

Putting the values in the formula for Z, we have:

$Z_{cal} = 15 - 14.\ 10344/2.37995$
$= 0.\ 3767$

Since $Z_{cal} < Z_{tab}$ at 5% level of significance null hypothesis is accepted, meaning thereby the series is random.

Developing the Forecast for the given series

In order to develop a forecast for the original series we shall employ the techniques of exponential regression and exponential smoothing also known as the moving average method.

Exponential regression: The rate of change can be best captured using exponential curve. Consequently, we fit the following equation:

$$Y = a\ b^x$$

In logarithmic form we can express it as

$$\log Y = \log a + x \log b$$

where

$\log Y$ = dependent variable
$\log a$ = vertical intercept
b = slope co efficient

The estimated equation is

$$\log Y = 1.66176 - 0.01171\ X$$

The summary statistics for the estimated series is presented in the Table 3.

TABLE 3

Measures of Central Tendency	*FRCST 1*
Mean	47.69282
Median	46.52158
Mode	44.17909
Measures of dispersion	
SD	11.088
SE (σ)	1.43145
VAR	122.943
CoV	23.24878
RANGE	37.3073
Measures of forecast accuracy	
MAD	8.9105
MSE	113.393
DWS	0.0202

From the analysis of the above table it is clear that the exponential regression generates a very poor forecast of the exchange rate. The important findings are summarized below:

- Though the measures of central tendencies are quite close to their original counterparts the variation is extremely high as is evident from very high values of variance, range and coefficient of variation.
- The forecast is extremely poor as MSE and MAD both are exceptionally high.
- The forecast errors are positively auto-correlated.

Moving average model: This model is conceptualized as follow:

$$F_{t+1} = \alpha\ Y_t + \beta\ F_t$$

where

F_{t+1}= forecast of the time series for period t+1

F_t = forecast of the time series for period t
Y_t = actual value of the time series in period t
α = smoothing constant
$\beta = 1 - \alpha \ (\alpha + \beta = 1)$

The value of α which minimises the Mean Square Error and thus gives the most accurate forecast is computed by trial and error. By comparing the errors for different values of alpha we see that it is least for alpha = 0.8 and beta = 0.2.

The values have been calculated in the manner as shown below:

F_1 will have no forecast as it is the initial value or the actual itself will be the forecasted value.

$$
\begin{aligned}
F_2 &= \alpha Y_1 + (1 - \alpha) F_1 &&= 0.8\ (46.67427) + 0.2\ (46.67427) \\
&= \alpha Y_1 + (1 - \alpha) Y_1 &&= 1 \times 46.67427 \\
&= Y_1 &&= 47.67427 \\
F_3 &= \alpha Y_2 + (1 - \alpha) F_2 &&= 0.8\ (46.62638) + 0.2\ (46.67427) \\
&= \alpha Y_2 + (1 - \alpha) Y_1 &&= 37.30110 + 9.33485 \\
&= Y_2 &&= 46.63595
\end{aligned}
$$

Similarly, all other values have been calculated

F_4 = ...

....

F_{30} = ...

In the following table we have summarised the various measures for the estimated series using moving average model:

TABLE 4

Measures of central tendency	*FRCST 2*
Mean	46.01513
Median	46.25496
Mode	46.73462
Measures of dispersion	
S D	0.6122

SE (ó)	0.08038
VAR	0.374780
CoV	1.330431
RANGE	2.0011
Measures of forecast accuracy	
MAD	0.20105
MSE	0.08192
DWS	2.0904

Important findings from the above table are listed below:

- The moving average model generates excellent forecast for the concerned period. This is reinforced by the small figures of measures of forecast error. Both MSE as well as MAD are quite low.
- The Value of DWS is almost equal to 2 thereby indicating no auto-correlation.
- The forecasted series has little variation as indicated by low values of various measures of dispersion.

IMPLICATIONS AND LIMITATIONS

Exchange rate forecasting may be short-term forecasting or long term forecasting. Former is needed for short-term operations such as money market operations, financing working capital requirements etc. This forecast is required for daily trading in the foreign exchange market for daily operations. It is of significant importance as most of exchange traded derivative products in currency segment are marked to market on a daily basis.

Managing exchange rate has become a daunting exercise for central banks. There has been currency crises that has wiped out economic wealth for many. For many countries, the actual benefits of currency depreciation are less impressive than what conventional wisdom predicts in terms of boosting export competitiveness to raising aggregate economic output. The above findings have some major implications which are explained below:

- The first and most important implication is related to the relevance of technical analysis. We know that the chartists use the historical exchange rate data to study the trends in exchange rate and thus, forecast the future exchange rate. Since the forex market has weak form efficiency, the forecast generated by it may be doubtful. The study refutes the presence of any trend in the exchange rate useful enough to predict the future exchange rate.
- Secondly, it also implies that it is not possible to consistently outperform the market. Since the successive exchange rate changes show no autocorrelation, it is impossible to beat the market.
- Last but not the least, it has some important lessons for the the central banks as well who participate in the forex market to contain volatility in the forex exchange rate.

CONCLUSION

In the preceding section, we have tested the various aspects of the short-term exchange rate determination for a specific pair of currency namely Indian rupee and US dollar. We have tried to investigate the extent to which our hypothesis is supported by the empirical results. In order to facilitate the comparison of both forecasting techniques the summary table is given below:

TABLE 5

	FRCST 1	*FRCST 2*	*ORIGINAL SERIES*
Measures of Central Tendency			
Mean	47.69282	46.01513	45.94570
Median	46.52158	46.25496	46.24001
Mode	44.17909	46.73462	46.82863
Measures of Dispersion			
SD	11.088	0.6122	0.68246

SE (ó)	1.43145	0.08038	0.124599
VAR	122.943	0.374780	0.46575
CoV	23.24878	1.330431	1.48530
SKW	0.31689	-1.17525	-1.29374
RANGE	37.3073	2.0011	2.42053
Measures of Forecast Accuracy			
MAD	8.9105	0.20105	—
MSE	113.393	0.08192	—
DWS	0.0202	2.0904	—

From the analysis of the results presented in the above table, we find that:

- The Efficient Market Hypothesis (EMH) is validated from our study. There exists ample evidence for the presence of weak form of market efficiency in the Indian foreign exchange market. All the past information is reflected in the present exchange rate.
- The forecast generated by the exponential regression are very poor. It either underestimates or over-estimates the future exchange rate.
- The moving average method gives quite close estimates as evidenced by low values of dispersion as well as MAD and MSE.
- The historical exchange rate contains no information sufficient enough to predict the future exchange rate.
- The exchange rates move in a random fashion. This limits the use of charting techniques for forecasting the exchange rate and making use of it for derivating trading in the foreign exchange market.

These findings lead to the conclusion that forex market is informationally efficient. Therefore, the technical analysis is of no use in predicting the future exchange rate. These findings and conclusions have significant implications for the currency derivative markets and the central banks interventions in the forex market to check excessive fluctuations in the spot exchange rate as well future exchange rate.

Direction for Future Research

As we have mentioned elsewhere in this report that this study suffers from the limitations of traditional time series analysis, without going into the detailed discussion of the same we can say that the present study supplements and not supplants the existing literature on forecasting exchange rate.

Further studies can be carried out:

- For a longer time horizon to validate the robustness of the results
- The various expectations may be incorporated in the model to perform a comparative study.
- The other forms of EMH specifically speaking the semi-strong and strong form may be tested.

References

Alquist, R. and M. Chinn (2008), "Conventional and Unconventional Approaches to Exchange Rate Modelling and Assessment," *International Journal of Finance and Economics.*

Basu and Morey: Stock Market Prices in India after Economic Liberalization, *EPW*, February 14, 1998.

Bilson, J.F.O. (1978), "The Monetary Approach to the Exchange Rate: Some Empirical Evidence," Staff Papers, International Monetary Fund, 25, 48-75.

Bjønnes, G.H. and D. Rime (2003), "Dealer Behavior and Trading Systems in Foreign Exchange Markets," Norges Bank, Working Paper, Research Department, November.

Choudhry, T. and P. Lawler (1997), "The Monetary Model of Exchange Rates: Evidence from the Canadian Float of the 1950s," *Journal of Macroeconomics*, 19, 349-62.

Cheung, Y., 1995, "A Search for Long Memory in International Stock.

Market Returns", *Journal of International Money and Finance*, 14, pp. 597-615. Chinn M.D. and R.A. Meese (1995), "Banking on Currency Forecasts: How Predictable is Change in Money?" *Journal of International Economics*, 38, 161-78.

Cuthbertson, K. (1996), "Quantitative Financial Economics: Stocks, Bonds and Foreign Exchange," John Wiley and Sons, Chichester.

Diamandis, P.F., D.A. Georgoutsos and G.P. Kouretas (1998), "The Monetary Approach to the Exchange Rate: Long-Run Relationships, Identification and Temporal Stability," *Journal of Macroeconomics*, 20, 741-66.

Dornbusch, R., 1976a, Expectations and exchange rate dynamics, *Journal of Political Economy,* 84, 1161-76.

Dornbusch, R., 1976b, The theory of flexible exchange rate regimes and macroeconomic policy, in: J. Frenkel and H. Jhonson, eds. The economics of exchange rates (Addison-Wesley, reading).

Dornbusch, R. (1980), "Exchange Rate Economics: Where Do We Stand?" *Brookings Papers on Economic Activity,* 1, 143-85.

Dornbusch, R. (1990), "Real Exchange Rates and Macroeconomics: A Selective Survey," NBER Working Paper 2775, *National Bureau of Economic Research.*

Evans, M.D.D. and R.K. Lyons (1999), "Order Flow and Exchange Rate Dynamics," NBER, August.

Frenkel, J., 1976, A monetary approach to the exchange rate: Doctrinal aspects and empirical evidence, *Scandinavian Journal of Economics,* 78, 200-24.

Frenkel, J., The mystery of multiplying marks: A modification of the monetary model, *Review of Economics and Statistics,* 64, 515-19.

Frenkel, J., Tests of monetary and portfolio balance models of exchange rate determination, in: J. Bilson and R. Marston, eds., Exchange rate Theory and Practice (University of Chicago Press).

Frenkel and Clements K, 1980, Exchange Rates, money, and relative prices: The dollar pound in the 1920s, *Journal of international Economics,* 10, 249-62.

Frankel, J.A. and A.K. Rose (1995), "Empirical Research on Nominal Exchange Rates", in G. Grossman and K. Rogoff (eds.), Handbook of International Economics, Vol. III, Elsevier Science, 1689-1729.

Frenkel, J.A. and H.A. Johnson (eds.) (1978), "The Economics of Exchange Rates: Selected Studies," Addison-Wesley.

Gandolfo, G. (2006), "International Finance and Open Economy Macroeconomics", Springer.

Luo, J. (2001), "Market Conditions, Order Flow and Exchange Rate Determination", Financial Market Group, Department of Accounting and Finance, London School of Economics.

MacDonald, R. and M.P. Taylor (1991), "Exchange Rates, Policy Convergence, and the European Monetary System," *Review of Economics and Statistics,* 73, 553-58.

MacDonald, R. and M.P. Taylor (1992), "Exchange Rate Behavior under Alternative Exchange Rate Arrangements", Mimeo, International Monetary Fund.

MacDonald, R. and M.P. Taylor (1993), "The Monetary Approach to the Exchange Rate: Rational Expectations, Long-run Equilibrium and Forecasting," IMF Working Paper WP/92/34. Mark 1995.

MacDonald, R. and M.P. Taylor (1994), "The Monetary Model of the Exchange Rate: Long-run Relationships, Short-run Dynamics and How to Beat a Random Walk," *Journal of International Money and Finance*, 13, 276-90. Marleand Sal (2001).

Mark, N.C. (1995), "Exchange Rate and Fundamentals: Evidence of Long Horizon Predictability," *American Economic Review*, 85, 201-18.

Mark, N.C. and D. Sul (2001), "Nominal Exchange Rates and Monetary Fundamentals: Evidence from a Small Post Bretton Woods Panel," *Journal of International Economics*, 53, 29-52

Meese Richard A. and Rogoff, K. (1983a), "Empirical Exchange Rate Models of the Seventies : Do they fit out in sample?" *Journal of International Economics*, 14, pp. 3-24.

Meese, R.A. (1990), "Currency Fluctuations in the Post-Bretton Woods Era", *Journal of Economic Perspectives*, 4, 117-34.

Meese, R.A. (2001), "Why Order Flow Explains Exchange Rates," NBER, November.

Meese, R.A. (2007), "How is Macro News Transmitted to Exchange Rates?" NBER, May 2007.

Medeiros, O.R. de (2005), "Order Flow and Exchange Rate Dynamics in Brazil", Universidade de Brasília, Brazil, manuscript.

Molodtsova, T. and D.H. Papell (2007), "Out-of-Sample Exchange Rate Predictability with Taylor Rule Fundamentals," University of Houston, manuscript.

Mussa, M. (1976), "The Exchange Rate, The Balance of Payments and Monetary and Fiscal Policy Under a Regime of Controlled Floating," *Scandinavian Journal of Economics*, 78, pp. 229-48.

Mussa, M. (1979), "Empirical Regularities in the Behaviour of Exchange Rates and Theories of the Forward Exchange Market", Carnegie-Rochester Conference Series on Public Policy, 11, pp. 9-57.

Mussa, M. (1990), Exchange rates in theory and in reality, Essays in International Finance No. 179 (Princeton University, Princeton, NJ)

Moosa, Imad A., Forecasting Exchange Rate, 1999, McGraw Hill Companies, New York

Neely, C.J. and L. Sarno (2002), "How Well Do Monetary Fundamentals Forecast Exchange Rates?" *Federal Reserve Bank of St. Louis Review*, 84, 51-74.

Nath, Golak C. and and Reddy Dr. Y.V., Long Memory in Rupee Dollar Exchange Rate: An Empirical Study 2002.

Nath, G.C. and Reddy, Y.V., "Efficient Market Hypothesis and Indian Stock Market—A case study for India", *Udyog Pragati*, October-December 2002.

Nath, G.C., 2001, "Long Memory and Indian Stock Market—An Empirical Evidence", UTIICM Conference Paper, 2001.

Nwafor, F.C. (2006), "The Naira-Dollar Exchange Rate Determination: A Monetary Perspective," *International Research Journal of Finance and Economics*, 5.

Reitz, S. (2002), "Central Bank Intervention and Exchange Rate Expectations—Evidence from the Daily DM/US-Dollar Exchange Rate," Discussion paper 17/02, Economic Research Centre of the Deutsche Bundesbank.

Sarno, L. and M. Taylor (2001) "Official Intervention in the Foreign Exchange Market: Is it Effective and, if so, How Does it Work?" *Journal of Economic Literature*, 39, 839-68.

Sarno, L. and M. Taylor (2002), "The Economics of Exchange Rates," Cambridge University Press, Sarno and Valente, 2005.

Schmidt, R. (2006) "The Behavioural Economics of Foreign Exchange Markets," European University Studies, Series V, Economics and Management, Peter Lang.

Taylor, M.P. (1995), "The Economics of Exchange Rates," *Journal of Economic Literature*, 33, 13-47.

Thomas (1995), Heteroskedasticity Models on the BSE.

Vitek, F. (2005), "The Exchange Rate Forecasting Puzzle", manuscript, University of British Columbia.

Zita, S. and R. Gupta (2007), "Modelling and Forecasting the Metical-Rand Exchange Rate," University of Pretoria Working Paper: 2007-02.

CHAPTER

10

The Changing Structure of Trade and Investment and its Impacts on the Globalisation of Indian Economy

FOZIA AND NAHID

ABSTRACT

The structure of international trade related to the rise of international capital mobility and trade in intermediate goods, the theoretically harmonious world of comparative advantage gives way to the competitive struggle of absolute advantages and relatives desirability of a location for the production of a part of the production process. The globalization of production comprises both international trade and Foreign Direct Investment. It comes with great promise of a new phase of export growth from developing countries, whose addition in the process open new market. The changing structure of trade and investment create the possibilities for harmonizing economic policies between countries seeking to build closer economic relation, the objective is to eliminate and regulatory "Trade Frictions" restricting expansion of international trade and foreign investment from within countries rather than at their border. These frictions take many standards, Foreign Direct Investment policies and professionally licensing systems. In creation of trade, expansion of country total imports on entering into bilateral, leading to an improvement in economic welfare as high cost domestic output is replaced by lower cost output.

Keywords: International Trade, Foreign Direct Investment, Globalisation.

INTRODUCTION

Globalization is characterized by global productivity, profits, raise in standards of living, maintaining social equality, bringing in far more effective and efficient government and market driven economic system by optimum utilization of resources. The changing structure of trade and investment is the result of globalisation of Indian economy. The reallocation of resources has been by far constructive towards building a more integrated socio-cost efficient economic system. This has been observed to be a natural by-product of the increasing inter-dependence of national economies. The impact has been furthered with several developing countries emerging strongly as global economic force having re-organized production process with changes in nature and location of development and finance. This has been a clear indication of the benefits of globalization, global partnership and regional integration. The global village has witnessed a tremendous flow of trade, capital, and services as a resultant of the globalization and trade liberalization process. The challenges of globalization today; the resultant volatility in the international financial markets; emergence of e-finance and capital flows. Changes in international economic governance have to keep pace with the growth of international interdependence. The role of IMF, World Bank, ADB, EBRD, other international agencies and the central banks demands them to be more alert and develop means to face the challenges of a dynamic changing financial scenario interlocking trade and transfers. The world economy at the turn of the century has influenced the process of globalization, global partnership and capital flows as a portfolio of global socio-economic enrichment. The re-allocation of good and services without the movement of labour; emergence of developing countries like India and China as an exporter of goods and services and also as a provider of the largest consumer base for world trade; weakening of dollar and improvement of terms of trade have been some of the remarkable trends in world investment.

OVERVIEW OF WORLD TRENDS IN TRADE AND INVESTMENT

I. International Trade

International trade is exchange of capital, raw materials, goods, and services across international borders or territories. In most countries, it represents a significant share of gross domestic product (GDP).

Industrialization, advanced transportation, globalization, multinational corporations, and outsourcing are all on the international trade system. Increasing international trade is crucial to the continuance of globalization. Without international trade, nations would be limited to the goods and services produced within their own borders.

International trade uses a variety of currencies, the most important of which are held as foreign reserves by governments and central banks. Here the percentage of global cumulative reserves held for each currency between 1995 and 2005 are shown: the US dollar is the most sought-after currency, with the Euro in strong demand as well. World trade in 2009 was dominated by the worst financial and economic crisis in decades. China, Brazil and India saw exports drop by between a fifth and a third in the second half of 2008, but countries not belonging to the top 20 developing countries were hit even harder. Trade and GDP growth have started to pick up again, but some economists fear a "double-dip" recession. If unemployment continues to grow, it may become harder for governments to resist protectionist pressures. In terms of the WTO negotiations, the crisis cuts both ways. Governments are preoccupied with more immediate concerns. But the crisis has shattered the sense that protectionism was unthinkable, making a trade deal seem more valuable.

Regulation of International Trade

Traditionally trade was regulated through bilateral treaties between two nations. For centuries under the belief in mercantilism most nations had high tariffs and many restrictions on international trade. In the years since the Second World War, controversial multilateral treaties like the General Agreement on Tariffs and Trade (GATT) and World Trade Organization have attempted to promote free trade while creating a globally regulated trade structure.

Free trade is usually most strongly supported by the most economically powerful nations. The Netherlands and the United Kingdom were both strong advocates of free trade when they were economically dominant, today the United States, the United Kingdom, Australia and Japan are its greatest proponents. However, many other countries (such as India, China and Russia) are increasingly becoming advocates of free trade as they become more economically powerful themselves. As tariff levels fall there is also an increasing willingness to negotiate non-tariff measures, including foreign direct investment, procurement and trade facilitation. The latter looks at the transaction cost associated with meeting trade and customs procedures.

During recessions there is often strong domestic pressure to increase tariffs to protect domestic industries. This occurred around the world during the Great Depression. Many economists have attempted to portray tariffs as the underlining reason behind the collapse in world trade that many believe seriously deepened the depression.

The regulation of international trade is done through the World Trade Organization at the global level, and through several other regional arrangements such as MERCOSUR in South America, the North American Free Trade Agreement (NAFTA) between the United States, Canada and Mexico, and the European Union between 27 independent states. Refer to international trade.

Importance of International Trade

In some sense most economists share the common belief that the net effect of globalisation is that the economic significance of national boundaries has deteriorated. As a result, firms have significantly increased their international trade of goods and services, as well as the value and distribution of their portfolio of assets. This is achieved by introducing more stages of production, in order to capitalise on opportunities for specialisation or by seeking new investment opportunities.

Risk in International Trade

Companies doing business across international borders face many of the same risks as would normally be evident in strictly domestic transactions. For example :

(i) Buyer insolvency (purchaser cannot pay);
(ii) Non-acceptance (buyer rejects goods as different from the agreed upon specifications);
(iii) Credit risk (allowing the buyer to take possession of goods prior to payment);
(iv) Regulatory risk (e.g., a change in rules that prevents the transaction);
(v) Intervention (governmental action to prevent a transaction being completed);
(vi) Political risk (change in leadership interfering with transactions or prices); and
(vii) War and other uncontrollable events.

2. Investment

Foreign direct investment (FDI) or foreign investment refers to long-term participation by country A into country B. It usually involves participation in management, joint-venture, transfer of technology and expertise. There are two types of FDI: inward foreign direct investment and outward foreign direct investment, resulting in a net FDI inflow (positive or negative) and "stock of foreign direct investment", which is the cumulative number for a given period. Direct investment excludes investment through purchase of shares.

Foreign direct investment (FDI) is a major catalyst for development and the integration of developing countries in the global economy

Foreign direct investment recognised as a powerful engine to bring major benefits to countries and regions, in terms of enhanced financing, export capacity, growth, employment, skills and technology transfer

Host country policies toward attracting FDI and benefiting from foreign corporate presence are largely equivalent to policies for mobilising domestic resources for productive investment. They include improvements of the general macroeconomic and institutional frameworks; creation of a regulatory environment that is transparent and non-discriminatory and, hence, conducive to inward FDI; and upgrading of infrastructure, technology and human competencies to the level where the full potential benefits of foreign corporate presence can be realised.

The policy adjustment needed to attract and maximise the benefits of FDI for development needs to be undertaken by investment host countries, home countries also share a responsibility in helping developing countries improve the investment environment, build capacities and maximise the benefits of FDI for development. This can be achieved, for instance, by pursuing policies of openness to trade, exploiting synergies between FDI and official development assistance, promoting the goal of sustainable development in international business operations, encouraging public-private partnership particularly for infrastructure investments, curbing the supply side of bribery and corruption in international business operations, supporting institutional and human capacity building, and supporting participation of developing countries in multilateral forum.

Business governance also matters. The business sector is part of the solution and has the potential to be a strong partner in an investment strategy for growth and sustainable development.

According to a report by the United Nations Conference on Trade and Development (UNCTAD), "a number of developing countries have emerged as significant sources of foreign direct investment (FDI) in other developing countries, and their investments are now considered a new and important source of capital and production know-how, especially for host countries in developing regions

I. Domestic Investment

(i) Hotel and Tourism: FDI in Hotel and Tourism Sector in India

100% FDI is permissible in the sector on the automatic route.

The term hotels include restaurants, beach resorts, and other tourist complexes providing accommodation and/or catering and food facilities to tourists. Tourism-related industry include travel agencies, tour operating agencies and tourist transport operating agencies, units providing facilities for cultural, adventure and wildlife experience to tourists, surface, air and water transport facilities to tourists, leisure, entertainment, amusement, sports, and health units for tourists and Convention/Seminar units and organizations.

(ii) Telecommunication: FDI in Telecommunication Sector

(i) In basic, cellular, value-added services and global mobile personal communications by satellite, FDI is limited to 49% subject to licensing and security requirements and adherence by the companies (who are investing and the companies in which investment is being made) to the license conditions for foreign equity cap and lock-in period for transfer and addition of equity and other license provisions.

(ii) ISPs with gateways, radio-paging and end-to-end bandwidth, FDI is permitted up to 74% with FDI, beyond 49% requiring Government approval. These services would be subject to licensing and security requirements.

(iii) No equity cap is applicable to manufacturing activities

(iii) Trading : FDI in Trading Companies in India

Trading is permitted under automatic route with FDI up to 51% provided it is primarily export activities, and the undertaking is an export house/trading house/super trading house/star trading house. However, under the FIPB route:

(i) 100% FDI is permitted in case of trading companies for the following activities:
(ii) exports;
(iii) bulk imports with ex-port/ex-bonded warehouse sales;
(iv) cash and carry wholesale trading;
(v) Other import of goods or services provided at least 75% is for procurement and sale of goods and services among the companies of the same group and not for third party use or onward transfer/ distribution/sales.

India will be third largest FDI Recipient in 2010-12

"If the situation continues to improve, India is likely to be among the most promising investor-home countries in 2010-12 as well as the third highest economy for FDI in 2010-12," UNCTAD says in its World Investment Report, 2010.

India remained in the list of top ten countries in 2009 to have the highest FDIs in the world. In 2009, the country received FDI worth $34.6 billion, while the outward FDI was $14.9 billion, the report.

The global FDI flow began to bottom out in the later half of 2009 and has shown a modest recovery in the first half of 2010 with South Asia being the first to bounce back from the recent downturn.

Increasing intra-regional FDI has become an effective vehicle for industrial upgrading in the South Asia region, providing opportunities to countries at different stages of development

The outward flow of FDI from the region, which had declined, is likely to recover riding on cross border mergers and acquisitions (M and As). "FDI outflows are expected to rebound in 2010, sustained by MandA opportunities associated with Indian and Chinese firms' persistent pursuit of natural resources and markets," it says. Besides, UNCTAD said recent forecasts suggest that the global economy has exited recession and returned to growth. The world economy is expected to grow by 3 per cent in 2010.

2. *Global Investment*

Global foreign direct investment (FDI) witnessed a modest, but uneven recovery in the first half of 2010. This sparks some cautious optimism for FDI prospects in the short run and for a full recovery further on. Most regions are expected to see a rebound in FDI flows in 2010. The evolving nature and role of FDI varies among regions. Africa is witnessing the rise of new sources of FDI. Industrial upgrading through FDI in Asia is spreading to more industries and more countries. Latin American transactional corporations (TNCs) are going global. Foreign banks play a stabilizing role in South-East Europe, but their large scale presence also raises potential concerns. High levels of unemployment in developed countries triggered concerns about the impact of outward investment on employment at home. Overcoming barriers for attracting FDI remains a key challenge for small, vulnerable and weak economies. Overseas development assistance (ODA) can act as a catalyst for boosting the role of FDI in least developed countries (LDCs). For landlocked developing countries (LLDCs) to succeed in attracting FDI they need to shift their strategy to focus on distance to markets rather than distance to ports. Focusing on key niche sectors is crucial if small islands developing States (SIDS) are to succeed in attracting FDI.

(i) Foreign Direct Investments in Malaysia

The economic policies of the government encourage foreign direct investments in Malaysia. The stock of foreign direct investment at home in Malaysia is $86.43 billion and at abroad is $70.7 billion. Malaysia ranks 24th in the ease-of-doing-business index according to the World Bank.

The Future of Malaysian Economy

The GDP per capita of Malaysia is $ 14,800 which is decent as compared to the other developing countries and is one of the highest in South East Asia. In 2008, 70% of Malaysian population lived in urban areas. With the life expectancy of 72 years at birth and an 88.7% literacy rate,

Malaysia enjoys a good standard of living. Kuala Lumpur is rated as an alpha world city.

In June 2010, Malaysian Prime Minister Nazib will introduce the 10th Malaysia Plan. The economic reforms in the 10th Malaysia Plan are expected to attract foreign direct investments. Seeing the current economic developments and the role of Malaysia in world economics, it can be predicted that the economy will grow further with the foreign direct investments and its growing manufacturing sector. Malaysia is a member of Asia Pacific Economic Co-operation (APEC), Association of South East Nations (ASEAN) and World Trade Organization (WTO).

(ii) Foreign Direct Investment in the United States

The United States is the world's largest recipient of FDI. More than $325.3 billion in FDI flowed into the United States in 2008, which is a 37 percent increase from 2007. The $2.1 trillion stock of FDI in the United States at the end of 2008 is the equivalent of approximately 16 percent of U.S. gross domestic product (GDP).

Benefits of FDI in America: In the last 6 years, over 4000 new projects and 630,000 new jobs have been created by foreign companies, resulting in close to $ 314 billion in investment. Unarguably, US affiliates of foreign companies have a history of paying higher wages than US corporations. Foreign companies have in the past supported an annual US payroll of $364 billion with an average annual compensation of $68,000 per employee.

Increased US exports through the use of multinational distribution networks. FDI has resulted in 30% of jobs for Americans in the manufacturing sector, which accounts for 12% of all manufacturing jobs in the US.

(iii) Foreign Direct Investment in China

FDI in China has been one of the major successes of the past 3 decades. Starting from a baseline of less than $19 billion just 20 years ago, FDI in China has grown to over $300 billion in the first 10 years. China has continued its massive growth and is the leader among all developing nations in terms of FDI. Even though there was a slight dip in FDI in 2009 as a result of the global slowdown, 2010 has again seen investments increase. The Chinese continue to steamroll with expectations that economic growth will be 10% this year.

(iv) Foreign Direct Investment in India

A recent UNCTAD survey projected India as the second most important FDI destination (after China) for transnational corporations during 2010-12. As per the data, the sectors which attracted higher inflows were services, telecommunication, construction activities and computer software and hardware. Mauritius, Singapore, the US and the UK were among the leading sources of FDI. FDI for 2009-10 at USD 25.88 billion was lower by five per cent from USD 27.33 billion in the previous fiscal. Foreign direct investment in August dipped by about 60 per cent to USD 1.33 billion, the lowest in 2010 fiscal, industry department data released showed.

(v) Foreign Direct Investment and the Developing World

Foreign investment can be a significant driver of development in poor nations. It provides an inflow of foreign capital and funds, in addition to an increase in the transfer of skills, technology, and job opportunities. Many of the East Asian tigers such as China, South Korea, Malaysia, and Singapore benefited from investment abroad.

CHANGING STRUCTURE OF TRADE AND INVESTMENT IN INDIA

1. Trade in India

The table showed that oil export of India registered a growth of 7.5 per cent during 2008-09 to 2009-10. The non-oil export of India registered a decline of -0.7 per cent during 2008-09 to 2009-10. During 2008-09 to 2009-10, India's total exports at 840755 crore to 845123 crore posted a growth of 0.5 per cent.

The table showed that oil Import of India registered a decline of -2.0 per cent during 2008-09 to 2009-10. The non-oil import of India also registered a decline of -1.0 per cent during 2008-09 to 2009-10. During 2008-09 to 2009-10, India's total

Foreign Trade (Annual)

Crore

Years	*2003-04*	*2004-05*	*2005-06*	*2006-07*	*2007-08*	*2008-09*	*2009-10*	*%change*
(1)	*(2)*	*(3)*	*(4)*	*(5)*	*(6)*	*(7)*	*(8)*	*(9)*
Export								
Oil	16397	31404	51533	84520	114192	123398	132616	7.5
Non-Oil	276969	343935	404885	487259	541672	717357	712509	-0.7
Aggregate	293367	375340	456418	571779	655864	840755	845125	0.5
Import								
Oil	94520	134094	194640	258572	320655	419968	411579	-2.0
Non-Oil	264588	366971	465769	581935	691657	954468	944890	-1.0
Aggregate	359108	501065	660409	840506	1012312	1374436	1356469	-1.3
Trade Balance								
Oil	-78123	-102690	-143107	-174052	-206463	-296570	-278963	
Non-Oil	12382	-23035	-60884	-94675	-149985	-237111	-232381	
Aggregate	-65741	-125725	-203991	-268727	-356448	-533680	-511343	

Source : *RBI Bulletin* (Date of Publish : Dec. 2009, 2010).

imports at 1374436 crore to 1356469 crore posted a decline of -1.3 per cent.

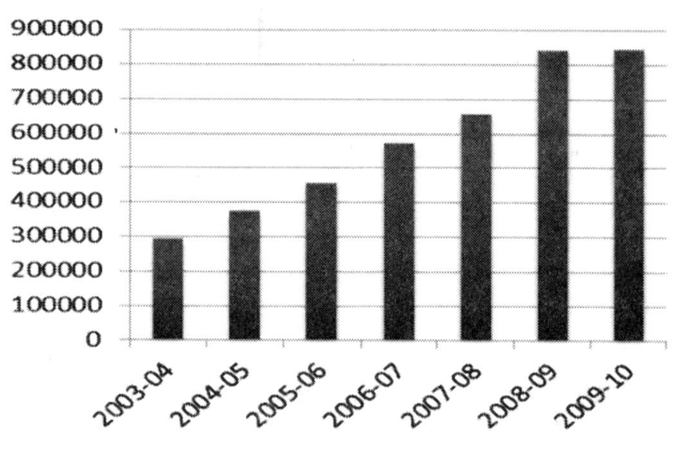

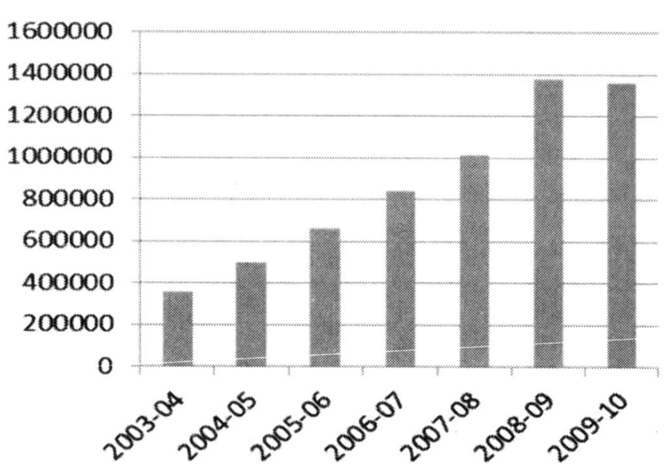

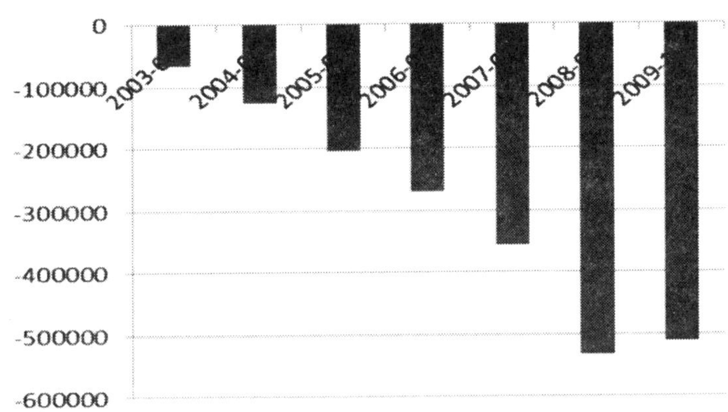

In the table, the total trade balance showed a decline of -65741 crore in 2003-04, -125725 crore in 2004-05, -203991 crore in 2005-06, -268727 crore in 2006-07,-356448 crore in 2007-08, -533680 crore in 2008-09 and -511343 crore in 2009-10.

In the last seven years our total exports witnessed robust growth to reach a level of 845125 crore in 2009-10 from 293367 crore in 2003-04, and during 2008-09 to 2009-10 showed a growth of 0.5 per cent. In the last six total import witnessed robust growth to reach a level of 1356469 crore in 2009-10 from 359108 crore in 2003-04, and during 2008-09 to 2009-10 showed a decline of -1.3 of per cent.

FOREIGN DIRECT INVESTMENT IN INDIA

India has been ranked at the third place in global foreign direct investments in 2009 and will continue to remain among the top five attractive destinations for international investors during 2010-11. The 2009 survey of the Japan Bank for International Cooperation released in November 2009, conducted among Japanese investors continues to rank India as the second most promising country for overseas business operations after China. A report released in February 2010 by Leeds University Business School, commissioned by UK Trade and Investment (UKTI), ranks India among the top three countries where British companies can do better business during 2012-14. According to Ernst and Young's 2010 European Attractiveness Survey, India is ranked as the 4th most attractive foreign direct investment (FDI) destination in 2010. However, it is ranked the 2nd most attractive destination following China in the next three years. Moreover, according to the Asian Investment Intentions survey released by the Asia Pacific Foundation in Canada, more and more Canadian firms are now focusing on India as an investment destination. From 8 per cent in 2005, the percentage of Canadian companies showing interest in India has gone up to 13.4 per cent in 2010.

India attracted FDI equity inflows of US $ 2,214 million in April 2010. The cumulative amount of FDI equity inflows from August 1991 to April 2010 stood at US $ 134,642 million. The services sector comprising financial and non-financial services attracted 21 per cent of the total FDI equity inflow into India, with FDI worth US $ 4.4 billion during April-March 2009-10, while construction activities including roadways and highways attracted second largest amount of FDI worth US $ 2.9 billion during the same period. Property and real estate was the third highest sector attracting FDI worth US $ 2.8 billion followed by telecommunications, which garnered US $ 2.5 billion during the financial year 2009-10. The automobile industry received FDI worth US $ 1.2 billion while power attracted FDI worth US$ 1.4 billion during April-March 2009-10.

In April 2010, the telecommunication sector attracted the highest amount of FDI worth US $ 430 million, followed by services sector at US $ 355 million and computer hardware and software at US $ 172 million, according to data released by DIPP. During the financial year 2009-10, Mauritius has led investors into India with US $ 10.4 billion worth of FDI comprising 43 per cent of the total FDI equity inflows into the country. The FDI equity inflows in Mauritius is followed by Singapore at US $ 2.4 billion and the US with US $ 2 billion. During April 2010, Mauritius invested US $ 568 million in India, followed by Singapore which invested US $ 434 million and Japan that invested US $ 327 million

FDI Equity Inflow

Financial year	*Amount of Foreign Direct Investment Inflow (including advance)*	
March-April	*US $ Million*	*% change*
2005-06	5546	—
2006-07	15726	184
2007-08*	24581	56
2008-09*	27331	11
2009-10**	25888	-5.2

Notes : (i) Including amount remitted through RBI's—NRI Schemes, stock swapped and advances pending for issue of shares).

(ii) FEDAI (Foreign Exchange Dealers Association of India) conversion rate from rupees to US dollar applied, on the basis of monthly average rate provided by RBI (DEAP), Mumbai.

(iii) *Includes Stock Swap of Shares US $ 3.2 billion for the year 2006-07 and US $ 5.0 Billion for the year 2007- 08.

(iv) Variation in equity inflows reported in above Table II-A and II-B for 2006-07 is due to difference in reporting of inflows through Stock Swap by RBI in the monthly report to DIPP and monthly RBI bulletin.

(v) **Includes US $ 40 million as Stock swapped during July 2009.

Source : RBI in the monthly report to DIPP and monthly RBI bulletin.

The table showed that Foreign direct investment equity inflow of India registered a growth of 184 per cent during 2005-06 to 2006-07, during 2006-07 to 2007-08 the amount of foreign direct investment inflow of India registered a growth of 56 per cent, during 2007-08 to 2008-09 the amount of foreign direct investment inflow of India registered a growth of 11 per cent and during 2008-09 to 2009-10 the amount of foreign direct investment inflow of India registered a decline of -5.2 per cent.

The table showed, during 2005-06 to 2006-07, India's foreign direct investment inflow at 5546 US $ million to 15726 posted a growth of 184 per cent. During 2006-07 to 2007-08, India's foreign direct investment inflow at 15726 US $ million to 24581 posted a growth of 56 per cent. During 2007-08 to

2008-09, India's foreign direct investment inflow at 24581 US $ million to 27331 posted a growth of 11 per cent. During 2008-09 to 2009-10, India's foreign direct investment inflow at 22331 US $ million to 25888 posted a growth of -5.2 per cent.

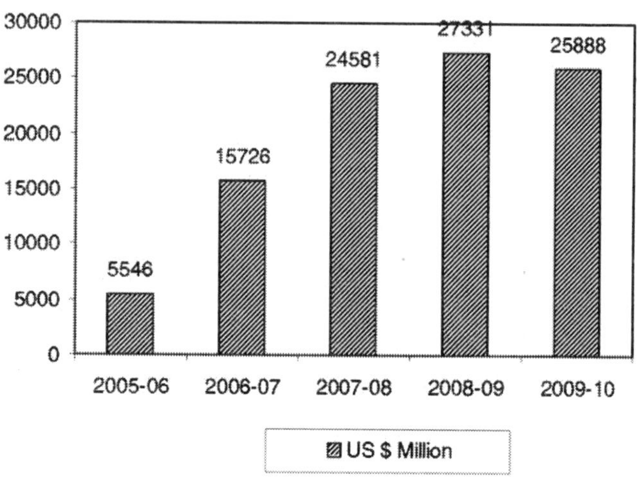

CONCLUSION

This structural change in trade is the result of the emergence of global production systems, whereby parts and components of a good are produced in different locations around the globe. While intermediate goods trade constitutes a rising share of world trade. As a result, firms have significantly increased their international trade of goods and services, as well as the value and distribution of their portfolio of assets. The changing structure of trade and investment create benefit to whole country such as global productivity, profits, rise in standards of living, maintaining social equality, optimum utilization of resources, flow of trade, capital flows, and service; emergence of e-finance and the growth of international interdependence. Foreign investment is a significant driver of development in poor nations. It provides an inflow of foreign capital and funds, in addition to an increase in the transfer of skills, technology, and job opportunities. A number of developing countries have emerged as significant sources of foreign direct investment (FDI) in other developing countries, and their investments are now considered a new and important source of capital and production know-how, especially for host countries in developing regions. The changing structure of trade and investment is also benefits to know the growth and decline in the percentage of the trade and investment.

References

Arndt, S. (1997), "Globalization and the Open Economy", in *North American Journal of Economics and Finance*, 8(1), 71-79.

Agosin, M. and R. Mayer (2000), "Foreign investment in developing countries: Does it crowd in domestic investment? Discussion Papers No. 159. Geneva: UNCTAD, May.

Aggarwal, Aman, *et al.*, (2006) "The Changing Structure Of World Investment, Trade, Capital Flows and Its Impact of Global Integration and Regional Cooperation."

Brooks Douglas H., Emma Xiaoqin Fan, and Lea R. Sumulong (2003), "Foreign Direct Investment: Trends, TRIMs and WTO Negotiations", *Asian Development Review*, Vol. 20, No. 1, 2003, Asian Development Bank, pp. 1-33.

Dunning, J. (2000), "The eclectic paradigm as an envelope for economic and business theories of MNE Activity", in *International Business Review*, 9, 163-90.

Dunkley Graham (2000), the Free Trade Adventure: The WTO, the Uruguay and Globalism—A Critique, Zed Books, London.

Head Keith and John Ries, (2004), "Regionalism within Multilateralism: The WTO Trade Policy Review of Canada", *The World Economy*, Vol. 27, No. 9, September, pp. 1377-1400.

Matsushita Mitsuo, (2004) "Governance of International Trade under WTO Agreements—Relationships between WTO Agreements and Other Trade Agreements", *Journal of World Trade*, Volume 38, Number 2, April, pp. 183-211.

Nagesh Kumar, (2001), "WTO Regime, Host Country Policies and Global Patterns of MNE Activity: Recent Quantitative Studies and India's Strategic Response", *Economic and Political Weekly*, Vol. 46, Nos. 6-12, January.

Nath Kamal, (2004), "WTO Framework A Major Victory", *The Hindu Business Line*, 2 August.

Rao, M.B. (2003), World Trade Organization and India, Vikas Publishing House, New Delhi.

Myneni, (2005). World Trade Organization, India Law House, New Delhi.

UNCTAD (2006). World Investment Report, 2006: FDI from Developing and Transition Economies: Implications for Development, New York: United Nations.

CHAPTER

11

Sustainable Development of Secondary School Students in Relation to Gender and Religion

TABINDA IQBAL

ABSTRACT

Sustainable development has defined by the brundland commission as "development that meets the needs of the present without compromising the ability of future generations to meet their own needs". The investigator has tried to "study the sustainable development of secondary school students in relation to gender", the sample of the study consists of 300 male and female secondary school students of Aligarh (one of the district of western UP). A scale for assessing sustainable development prepared by Bharti Varshney (M.Ed. students department of Education A.M.U. Aligarh) was used for data collection, t-test when applied on data, revealed that there is no significant difference in the male and female of secondary school students towards sustainable development.

Keywords: Sustainable development, gender, awareness, environment, secondary school.

INTRODUCTION

"Sustainable development" has most commonly used in specific reference to the sustainability of ecosystems. Different countries have been adopting the term sustainable development for their own specific purpose also. This has brought sustainability to the forefront of public consciousness and is seen by many as being a natural progression in human evaluation as we develop the thought and means to sustain our own existence on earth. For example, the Australian government has incorporated the term "economically sustainable development as an official aim of policy, although environmental groups feel some principles are missing and there is still a long way to go in practice. The environment is much more than ecology and biodiversity. It also includes the human environment, including social, cultural, economic, political and information components all included in environmentally sustainable development. Sustainability has become a complex term that can be applied to almost every fact of life on earth particularly the many different units of biological organization, such as wetlands, prairies and forests and is expressed in human organization concepts, such as; eco-villages eco-municipalities, sustainable cities and human activities and disciplines, architecture and renewable energy.

In other words the goal of sustainability is to minimize resource use per unit of product or money spent and to maximize the output per unit of resource input or money spent.

It is not just about pollution weather change or environmental issues; it is about the relationship between all aspects of ecological and human life. Therefore, "human beings are at the centre of concern for sustainable development".

The dictionary meaning of sustainability is "the amount of degree to which the earth's resource may be exploited without deleterious effects" (The Chambers Dictionary).

STATEMENT OF THE PROBLEM

The investigator has tried to study, of sustainable development of secondary school students in relation to gender".

REVIEW LITERATURE

Environment studies drew public attention worldwide after the Stockholm conference in 1972. Researches on issues related to environment and number of workshops, seminars and conferences were organized under the leadership of governmental and non-governmental agencies. The earlier works were mainly done on environmental awareness and attitude towards environmental education.

The principal functions of environmental education as indicated by seminars and conferences held in different countries (Kuwait, Bangkok, Europe), Bogotá UNEP-AAU (1978) UNESCO (1980), Cappuro (1979) Morris (1976), and Harvey (1977) were to develop awareness and sensitivity to total environment and its allied problem, to provide knowledge about the environment; to develop attitude, social values and strong feeling to concern for the environment to develop skills to solve environmental problems.

Zafar Saba (2002) made an attempt to see the effect of academic discipline, gender, intelligence and socioeconomic status on environmental awareness of pupils. The research study was conducted on 400 students out of which 200 were girls and 200 were boys. It is evident from the result that academic discipline has a long effect on environmental awareness of pupils. The girls' students of science stream exhibited highest degree of environmental awareness than the boys in the same stream. This may be done to the influence of subject on gender. Thus, we see that study of science has a direct influence on pupils awareness towards their environment. It has been noticed that intelligence does not contribute significantly to the environmental awareness in all the discipline accept social science girls. It has also noticed that economic status of students too has no significant effect on their environmental awareness.

OBJECTIVES

(1) To study the effect of gender (male and female) of secondary school students towards sustainable development.
(2) To study the effect of religion (Muslims and Non-Muslims) of secondary school students towards sustainable development.

HYPOTHESES

(1) There will be no significant difference between male and female secondary school students towards sustainable development.
(2) There will be no significant difference between Muslims and Non-Muslims secondary school students towards sustainable development.

Sample

A sample study was conducted with 300 male and female of secondary school students.

Results and Findings

TABLE I

Comparison of Male and Female Secondary School Students Towards Sustainable Development (Total Sample 300)

Groups	*Mean*	*SD*	*t-value*	*Remark*
Males	94.28	13.80	1.16	Not significant
Females	96.26	15.83		

The mean score for males sample (N = 164) is 94.28, SD = 13.80 and for females sample (136) mean is 96.26, SD = 15.83, and SED = 1.078. The calculated t-value is 1.16 which is not significant. Hence the null hypothesis stands accepted.

The reason of not significant difference between male and female secondary school students may be due to the fact that the students taken as samples are studying in the same institutions which are co-educational and the same teachers are there to teach everyone in irrespective of sex. The school environment is same and cultural differences are also not there. Students get their education from same teacher, therefore, the behavior of male and female secondary school students have no shown any variation.

TABLE 2

Comparison of Muslims and Non-Muslims Secondary School Students towards Sustainable Development (Total Sample 300)

Groups	*Mean*	*SD*	*t-value*	*Remark*
Muslims	69.8	6.8	0.394	Not significant
Non-muslims	70.2	6.3		

The Mean score for Muslims sample is 69.8, SD = 6.8 and for Non Muslims sample Mean is 70.2, SD = 6.3, the calculated t-value is 0.394, which is not significant. Hence the null hypothesis stands accepted.

The above result leads to interpret that religion hardly makes a difference on pupil's behavior towards sustainable development. Both the communities are studying in the school of same standard with similar values and culture; and in the school they are taught about environmental protection and conservation. Therefore, students of both communities exhibit almost same behaviour towards sustainable development. Here it can further be said that schools are playing significant role in moulding the behaviour of pupils in right direction towards sustainable development.

CONCLUSION

The findings of present investigation have been summarized according to the objectives of the present study as follows:

Objective 1

To study the effect of gender (male and female) of secondary school students towards sustainable development.

On comparing the male and female of secondary school students towards sustainable development, no significant difference was observed.

Objective 2

To study the effect of religion (Muslims and Non-Muslims) of secondary school students towards sustainable development.

On comparing the Muslims and Non-Muslims secondary school students towards sustainable development, no notable difference in the behaviour of students was found.

Suggestions

As started earlier, the present investigation has selected a study of sustainable development of secondary school students in relation to gender as the main variable of study. The present study may serve as a threshold for further studies considering different aspects related to the problem.

The investigator would like to submit her humble suggestions, in the light of her experiences and the results of the present study.

1. While analyzing the sustainable development of secondary school students in relation to gender, many other variables like parental education, personality, family background and certain other demographic factors, etc. were outside the purview of the present investigation. Therefore, the investigator suggests that future researches in this area may take into account mentioned variables which are not touched in the present study.
2. In this study, the investigator has selected secondary school students as sample. The investigator suggests that the future researcher in this area many include students of other levels of education also like senior secondary and college level, etc.

3. While conducting the study, it has noticed by the investigator that studies on sustainable development were few. To study the male and female of secondary school students regarding sustainable development may prove to be worthwhile for future researchers.
4. There was no suitable tool available for studying the environment behavior of secondary school students. So the investigator herself has constructed the desired scale which may certain sampling error, statistical error, and other limitations like not covering all the issues related to sustainable development.

Any further researcher therefore must take into account these factors.

References

Aburonia, H. (2004), Sustainability in Housing from a Socio-cultural Perspectives in Libya 5th International Post-graduate Research Conference, April 14th, 15th.

Akram, M. (2007), Environmental Concern and Sustainable Development: Various Perspectives, *University News*, 45(44) p. 94.

Activities, U.S. (2005), UNESCO International Science, Technology and Environmental Education. Connect 31, 10 (1-2).

Bringulio, L. (2003), The Usefulness of Sustainability Indicators. Symposium Sustainability Indicators for Malta.

Basheer, K. (2007), Development and Environmental Concern. *University News*, 45(44).

Darryl, I., R.J. Macer (2006), "A Cross Cultural Introduction to Bioethics", Eubious Ethics Institute, p. 63.

Dash, D. and Satapathy, M.K. (2007), Education for Sustainable Development: Role of College and Teacher Training Institutions, *University News*, (49), p. 2.

Grainger, A. (2005), Sustainable Development and International Relations, Exploring Sustainable Development, London: Earth Scan Pub. Ltd.

NCERT (2005), National Curriculum Framework, 2005, New Delhi, NCERT.

Zafar Saba (2002), Environmental Awareness among Senior Secondary Schools in Relation to their Gender, Academic Stream, Intelligence and Socio-economic Background, Department of Education, AMU, Aligarh.

Website

http://www.ibe.unesco .org .../
http://en. Wikipedia.org/wiki/sustainability.
http://www. Un-documents, net/weed-ocf.htm.

CHAPTER

12

SHG-Bank Linkage Programme in India

HARI BABU BATHINI AND RAGHU KATRAGADDA

ABSTRACT

The formal financial institutions in India have ventured into microfinance in a massive way by adopting the SHG-Bank Linkage Programme model. The present paper makes an attempt to review the performance of the programme in different states of India and across three major institutions—commercial banks, cooperatives, and the regional rural banks. The study also presents vital information about the leading NGOs with major credit linkages in Indian states. The SHG-Bank Linkage Programme is a major plank of the strategy for delivering financial services to the poor in a sustainable manner. The search for such alternatives started with internal introspection regarding the innovations which the poor had been traditionally making, to meet their financial services needs. It was observed that the poor tended to come together in a variety of informal ways for pooling their savings and dispensing small and unsecured loans at varying costs to group members on the basis of need.

This study attempts to review the spread of credit linkages between self-help groups (SHGs) and banks across credit delivery models adapted by the Reserve Bank of India (RBI) and the National Bank for Agriculture and Rural Development (NABARD). It further examines the spread of credit linkages across different regions and states of India. It also reviews the participation of commercial banks, regional rural banks, and cooperatives in the SHG-Bank Linkage Programme across different states in India.

INTRODUCTION

In India, the adaptation of the new microfinance approach by rural financial institutions assumed the form of the "Self-Help Group-Bank Linkage Program". After an initial pilot study the RBI set-up a working group on non-governmental organizations (NGOs) and SHGs. The working group made recommendations for internalization of the SHG concept as a potential intervention tool in the area of banking with the poor. The RBI was quick to accept the recommendations and advised the banks to consider mainstreaming lending to SHGs as part of their rural credit operations. Under the SHG-bank linkage program, NGOs and banks interact with the poor, especially women, to form small homogenous groups. These small groups are encouraged to meet frequently and collect small thrift amounts from their members and are taught simple accounting methods to enable them to maintain their accounts. Although individually these poor could never have enough savings to open a bank account, the pooled savings enable them to open a formal bank account in the name of the group. This is the first step in establishing links with the formal banking system. Groups then, meet often and use the pooled thrift to impart small loans to members for meeting their small emergent needs. This saves them from usurious debt traps and thus begins their empowerment through group dynamics, decision-making, and funds management. Gradually the pooled thrift grows and soon they are ready to receive external funds in multiples of their group savings. Bank loans enable the group members to undertake income generating activities.

Through the SHG-bank linkage programme the RBI and NABARD have tried to promote relationship banking, i.e., improving the existing relationship between the poor and bankers with the social intermediation of NGOs. The Indian model is predominantly a "Linkage Model", which draws upon the strengths of various partners: NGOs, who are best in mobilizing the poor and building their capacities, and bankers, whose financial strength is financing. As compared to other countries where parallel model of lending to the poor is predominant, the Indian linkage model tries to use the existing formal financial network to increase the outreach to the poor, while ensuring the necessary flexibility of operations for both bankers and the poor. Various credit delivery innovations such as Grameen Bank Replications, NGO networking, credit unions, and SHG federations have been encouraged by NABARD for increasing the outreach. It has also instituted a Micro Credit Innovations Department for planning, propagating, and facilitating the microfinance movement.

REVIEW OF SHG-BANK LINKAGE PROGRAMME IN INDIA

Review of Models

In India, three types of SHG models have emerged:

1. *Bank-SHG-Members*: The bank itself acts as a self-help group promoting institution (SHPI).
2. *Bank-Facilitating Agency-SHG-Members*: Facilitating agencies like NGOs, government agencies, or other community-based organizations form groups.
3. *Bank-NGO-MFI-SHG-Members*: NGOs act both as facilitators and microfinance intermediaries. First they promote groups, nurture them, and train them, and then they approach banks for bulk loans for lending to the SHGs.

The second model, where SHGs were formed and nurtured by the NGOs, was more popular among the bankers. Banks opened saving accounts and then provided credit directly to the SHGs, while NGOs acted as facilitators. This

Models of SHG Linkages

Model	SHGs		Bank Loans	
	No. of Linkages	Percentage of Total	Amount (Rs. in millions)	Percentage of Total
1	13561	14	339.79	18
2	65636	70	1339.95	69
3	15448	16	250.10	13

approach has been widely accepted by the practitioners partly because of the large scale participation of state government through development agencies like the District Rural Development Agency (DRDA), District Women Development

Distribution of SHG Credit Links by State

States	Population Distribution	Population below poverty line	SHG Linkages
Andhra Pradesh	7.90	15.77	42.26
Uttar Pradesh	16.4	31.15	11.29
Tamil Nadu	6.60	21.12	12.10
Karnataka	5.30	20.04	9.24
Kerala	3.40	12.72	4.84
Maharashtra	9.30	25.02	4.32
Orissa	3.74	42.50	3.54
West Bengal	8.04	27.02	2.96
Gujarat	4.88	14.07	2.62
Madhya Pradesh	7.80	37.43	2.01
Rajasthan	5.19	15.28	1.69
Bihar	10.20	42.60	1.66
Rest of States/UT	9.58	17.39	1.47

Notes : The figures are in percentiles. The rest of the states and union territories (UT) include Hamachal Pradesh, Haryana, Punjab, Jammu and Kashmir, Assam, Meghalaya, Tripura, Sikkim, Manipur, UT of Andaman and Nicobar Islands, Goa, and UT of Pondicherry.

Agency (DWDA), and some of the centrally sponsored social sector missions, and also because of special initiatives of NABARD.

Sixteen percent of the SHGs were credit linked under the third model where NGOs acted as facilitators as well as microfinance intermediaries. Under this model, NGOs formed SHG federations and then facilitated them to assume the role of MFIs. This model is expected to gain wider recognition with smaller banks venturing into large scale financing of SHGs. Under the first model SHG linkages were facilitated through NABARD's policy of converting regional rural banks (RRBs) into self-help promoting institutions (SHPIs).

ANALYSIS BY STATE

During the past few years, India has tried several credit models to alleviate poverty, some of which were formulated without considering spatial dimensions. Land is a factor that is far more complex with its socio-cultural factors and typology that creates imbalances in the market and the socioeconomic growth of the people. Of the aspects that affect the success of the program, very important are its suitability and adaptability among practitioners as well as the poor living in that region.

The programme since its initiation has shown severe spatial preferences. It has been predominant in certain states, namely, Andhra Pradesh, Uttar Pradesh, Tamil Nadu, and Karnataka. These four states accounted for two-thirds of the SHG credit linkages, with Andhra Pradesh alone accounting for 40%. Of these four states, only Uttar Pradesh had a higher poverty ratio (31.15%) than the national average of 26.1%. Some of the factors identified for the outstanding performance of Andhra Pradesh in the SHG-bank linkage programme were the following:

(a) Forty percent of the SHGs that were credit linked under Development of Women and Children in Rural Areas (DWCRA) were concentrated in Andhra Pradesh alone.

(b) 2700 groups were promoted in that state under a special project sponsored by United Nations

Development Programme called South Asia Poverty Alleviation Program.

(c) The credit movement in the south led to the evolution of community based development finance institutions, which were composed of SHGs promoted by NGOs or by district rural development agencies.

(d) District collectors, NABARD district development managers, and lead bank managers profoundly supported the SHG-bank linkage programme in the state.

(e) Leading NGOs in the microfinance sector in India, like Mysore Resettlement and Development Agency (MYRADA), Society for Helping Awaking Rural Poor through Education (SHARE) and Bharatiya Samruddhi Investments Consulting Services Ltd. (BASIX), were also working in Andhra Pradesh.

Uttar Pradesh is one of the densely populated states with a high incidence of poverty. Among all the states of India, the Human Development Index is lowest in Uttar Pradesh. Credit links here were facilitated by Uttar Pradesh Land Development Corporation, which is implementing a World Bank–aided Land Development Programme with the component of organizing the rural poor as SHGs. CASPOR Ltd. and the Grameen Project of Oriental Bank of Commerce have also supported a number of SHG credit links in Uttar Pradesh. The other two states, Karnataka and Tamil Nadu, in south India were supported by large sized NGOs like MYRADA and SHARE. As these NGOs had greater creditability it enabled them to leverage bank finance easily. Moreover, as the micro finance movement had "originated" in South India, the awareness and acceptability of the programme was relatively higher. Kerala, Maharashtra, Orissa, West Bengal, Gujarat, Madhya Pradesh, Rajasthan, and Bihar together had 23.6% of SHG linkages while the remaining states and union territories had only 1.47%.

Rajasthan, Meghalaya, Orissa, Bihar, West Bengal, Madhya Pradesh, and Gujarat have been identified by NABARD for having higher potential of increasing SHG outreach. In general, the lower credit linkages in some of these states can be explained by a lack of concentrated efforts by banks; the inability of banks to identify NGOs with savings and credit groups; a lack of motivation among bankers; a lack of large sized NGOs with previous background working with SHGs; and the unsuitability of the approach to the region.

CONCLUSION

Microfinance has emerged as a vital approach to meet the heterogeneous needs of the poor. In India, microfinance in the formal sector has assumed the form of SHG-bank linkage program. Through this program, the Reserve Bank of India and NABARD have tried to promote relationship banking, i.e., "Improving the existing relationship between the poor and the bankers with the social intermediation of the NGOs". The SHG-bank linkage programme in India is rapidly expanding its outreach under the pioneering initiative of NABARD, the monitoring and supervision of RBI, and the promotional policies of the government of India. At the grassroot level the programme is being implemented by the commercial banks, cooperatives, and regional rural banks, with government agencies like DRDA/DWDA acting as facilitators. As of March 2011, 314,775 SHGs were credit linked, with the majority of them being fostered in the years since the Global Micro Credit Summit in Washington. With an average membership of twenty members per SHG, the programme has catered to 4.295 million poor households.

REFERENCES

Baydas, M.M., Graham, D.H., and Valenzuela, L. (1997, August). Commercial Banks in Micro finance: New Actors in the Micro finance World. Micro-Enterprise Best Practices.

Binswanger, H. and Khandekar, S. (1995). The Impact of Formal Finance on Rural Economy of India. *Journal of Development Studies*, 32(2), 234-65.

Self-Help Groups: A Keystone of Micro finance in India—Women Empowerment and Social Security, C.S. Reddy and Sandeep Manak.

Micro Finance in India: A Critique, Rajashri Gosh.

Micro Finance Industry: Some Changes and Continuity: Nimal A. Fernando.

Scaling-up Micro finance for India's Rural Poor, Priya Basu and Pradeep Srivastava.

CHAPTER

13

Micro Financing Through CBIGA and Rural Women Empowerment

A Case Study

JYOTI KUMARI

ABSTRACT

Women empowerment is a process of awareness and capacity building leading to participation, to greater decision-making power and control and to transformative action. A study was undertaken on different aspects of rural women empowerment, i.e. educational, economic, personal, social and psychological empowerment. The study was conducted to know the empowerment among rural women through CBIGA [Community Based Income Generating Activity—A kind of micro financings] which has been provided by Informal Women Education Centre, Banasthali Vidyapeeth in Tonk district of Rajasthan state in India. 12 rural women from different villages of selected districts formed the target group / case for the study. The design used in the study was the Multiple Case Study Design for the purpose of exploring the phenomenon under study through the use of a replication strategy. A semi-structured interview and observation were used to collect the information and required data through personal interview with these rural women and supervisor. The data was analyzed by using qualitative data analysis techniques. The findings of the study concluded that high empowerment of beneficiary rural women could take place in personal, educational, economic, social and psychological walk of life through micro financing or CBIGA.

Keywords : CBIGA—Community Based Income Generating Activities.

INTRODUCTION

> *"Just as a bird cannot fly with its one wing only, a nation cannot march forward if the women are left behind. India has a tradition of women playing important role in the advancement of civilization".*
>
> —Swami Vivekananda

At the threshold of 21st century today, the issue of women in development has been debated and their role in different fields of production accepted and appreciated. All the nations today are attempting to correct the blames, wrong orientations and misconceptions regarding women's capabilities and potential in order to bring the women into the mainstream of development. As a result of the deliberation in the various international conferences during and after the *International Women's Decade (1975-85),* policies have been formulated for integrating women into national programmes by making a shift from the welfare and beneficiary approach to an approach the partnership or total participation in development.

As *Mahatma Gandhi,* the father of the Indian nation firmly believed, women's productive abilities and attitudes are essential forces that need to be allowed full and free play for human development with justice and dignity. But, unfortunately, women who constitute half the world's population are often caught in a deprivation trap of powerlessness, vulnerability, physical weakness, poverty and marginalization (Figure 1).

FIG. 1

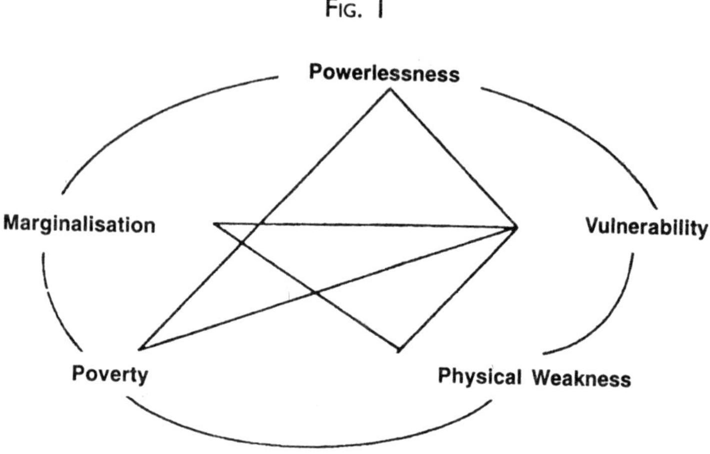

Technology especially ICTs are emerging as a powerful tool for women empowerment in a developing country like India, but as Eva Rathgeber clearly stated, "the key issue is that the technologies should be adapted to suit women rather than that women should be asked to adapt technology". Indian women who are handicapped by social customs, traditions and social evils, need special attention so that they can play their full and proper role in national life.

A woman is the nucleus around whom the family, the society and the whole community moves. The development of the whole community can not be separated or viewed in isolation from the development of women. Their contribution to their homes and their work outside the home had made them powerful and indispensable agents of our society for bringing about social change and development of new technology.

The declaration of the year *1975* as *International Women's Year,* the decade *1975-85* as *International Women's Decade* by *United Nation* and the *World Conference on Women* in *September 1995* in *Beijing, China* have become powerful agenda for empowerment of women. Policies and programmes have been focused to enhance the status of rural women which is an index of civilization and growth of a society.

India is a country with total population of 1,02,70,15,247, where the no. of females for 1000 males is 933, as per the Census 2001. It is an important fact that no society will progress satisfactorily unless women, who constitute almost half of their population are given equal opportunities. The late Indian Prime Minister Pandit Jawahar Lal Nehru, a great visionary and the architect of modern India, always felt that the development of women should be given top priority in the pattern of progress in the economic development of the country. According to him, "one of the truest measures of the nation's development is the state of its women". So, there is a greater need for bringing women into the mainstream of development of India. Where they can be successful in all fields if they are given the opportunity.

The women folk can easily be considered as backbone of any nation and better half of the men in almost all spheres of community development of which India is not an exception. Rural women who constitute 50% of total rural population, play an active role in all spheres of economic life and contribute richly towards income and employment to the rural sector in general and rural women in particular. These are the women who need and deserve poverty alleviation programmes and education more than any other.

RATIONAL OF THE STUDY

> *"You can tell the condition of a nation by looking at the status of its women".*
>
> —Jawaharlal Nehru

Emphatic words by one of our country's premier leaders. The statement stresses the role women have to play in a society. India is currently witnessing a revolution of sorts in economy and the technological sectors, yet even 60 years after independence, women's liberation seems a distant dream. As a country with more than 70% of its population residing in rural areas, it is worthwhile to examine the condition of women in our villages. A closer look at them reveals a striking paradox for a country poised to take the leap to become superpower in the not-so-distant future. Women are pillars on which the family unit stands but rural women present a picture of abject poverty and exploitation both inside and outside the home. Hence, empowerment of women has far reaching changes. It will affect not just the current generation of women but also the ones to come, for in woman lies the potential for the betterment of her children and her society and ultimately the country.

According to *World Bank (2004)* the main key services fail poor people in access, quantity and quality. This necessitates a set of development targets known as *Millennium Development Goals (MDG)*. These call for halving of the global, poverty and broad improvements in human development by *2015*. The *Millennium Declaration* adopted by *UN in 2000* underscored the urgency of ensuring that the benefits of new technologies, specially *Information and Communication Technologies (ICTs)* are made available to all. One resource that liberates people from poverty and empowers them is knowledge. It is also now well understood that any attempt to improve the quality of life of people in developing countries would be incomplete without progress towards the empowerment of women.

Women cannot be ignored while devising various policies for rural and socio-economic development. So, giving women equal opportunities is very much required. Women's empowerment is obviously essential for raising their socio-economic status in the society and recently women's empowerment has acquired an important place in government policy, non-government advocacy and academic research.

Very few studies are available related to empowerment of women and the contributing factors for it. This study will be of immense help for policy-makers and women development programs initiators to improve the present running programs and also to plan the future programs most effectively.

STATEMENT OF THE PROBLEM

Micro Financing through Community-based Income Generating Activities [CBIGA] and Rural Women Empowerment—*A Case Study*.

OBJECTIVES

(1) To study the various community-based income generating activities owned by rural women of Informal Women Education Centre.

(2) To study the role of community-based income generating activities in the overall empowerment of rural women with reference to their—

(a) Personal empowerment

(b) Educational empowerment

(c) Economic empowerment

(d) Social empowerment

(e) Psychological empowerment

(3) To study the role of community-based income generating activities in providing micro finance to the rural women.

VARIABLES

Women Empowerment—Women empowerment is a process by which women gain control over resources (income, knowledge, information, technology, skill and training), challenge the ideology of patriarchy and participate in leadership, decision-making process, enhance the self-image of women , to become active participants in the process of change and to develop the skills to asset themselves.

Community Based Income Generating Activities—CBIGA are considered as those activities which has been provided by Informal Women Education Centre and helps the rural women in generating income within the sphere of their community.

Micro finance—Micro finance is the provision of financial services such as loans, savings, insurance and training to people living in poverty. It is a broad category of services, which includes micro credit and micro credit is provision of credit services to poor clients.

METHODOLOGY

Method—Case Study Method

According to nature of research problem researcher has

used the Case Study Method to investigate the contemporary phenomenon within its real-life context with the help of multiple sources of evidence.

Design—Multiple Case Study Design

While much case study focuses on a single case , often chosen because of its unique characteristics, the multiple case study design will allow the researcher to explore the phenomenon under study through the use of a replication strategy. According to this, if all or most of the cases provide similar results, there can be substantial support for the development of a preliminary theory that will describe the phenomenon [Eisenhardt, 1989].

Sampling—Purposive Sampling and Random Sampling

The researcher has used the Purposive Sampling Technique in the selection of centre [case] for the study.

In the selection of rural women [multiple cases] working in these centres in different community-based income generating activities the researcher has used the Random Sampling Technique to reduce the biases of the multiple cases selection in the study.

Case—For the present study the Case Design was the following:

Sl. No.	*Name of Case*	*No. of Multiple Cases*
1.	Informal Women Education Centre* Banasthali Vidyapeeth	28

Tools

(1) Personal Profile Performa—Self-constructed
(2) Interview Schedule (Face-to-face)—Self-constructed
(3) Observation

Analysis Procedure—Qualitative Data Analysis

According to the nature of data collected with the help of selected tools, the researcher has used Qualitative Data Analysis as data analysis procedure.

RESULTS OR FINDINGS

The different activities which comes under Khadi and Village Industries are owned by rural women as community-based income generating activities.

The CBIGA under Informal Women Education Centre played a significant role in the empowerment of rural women with reference to their:

Personal Empowerment

These CBIGA helped the rural women to improve their personal profile. It made them to be aware about their self.

Educational Empowerment

With reference to educational empowerment these CBIGA helped a lot to the rural women. As it made education according to their need. It made significant impact on their own educational level as well as their children education. It also helped in improvement of educational level of whole family.

Economic Empowerment

As Informal Women Education Centre provides the work and money for their work to rural women through CBIGA. It helped these rural women to earn income while getting educated and monthly income helped them in getting empowered economically also. This income helped them to improve their living standard, economic condition of these rural women and their family. It also helped them to start thinking about the utilization of their earned money as now they were able to earn and they had their own money to spend.

Social Empowerment

The CBIGA helped the rural women to come out from their home and to become an active part of social system. After joining the IWEC and CBIGA these women were able to share their knowledge, problems and also their ideas. It made them confident and gave them a voice and social status to speak in the society and in their houses for themselves and also for the others. Thus, it empowered them socially.

Psychological Empowerment

These CBIGA and Informal Women Education also helped the rural women to empower psychologically. It helped in improving thinking, decision-making power, achievement motivation, confidence level, self-reliance and attitude towards life, education, children, family and self.

The CBIGA has been found a better kind of micro financing which provide not only the finance as daily wages to rural women but also make them confident and self reliant. Its directing their life in right direction and also helping them in deciding their own path of success.

POTENTIAL CONTRIBUTION OF THE STUDY

1. The study will provide valuable information to the government and non-government agencies about the extent of rural women empowerment and education through community-based income generating activities.
2. It will be of immense help for policy-makers and women development program initiators to plan the future program most effectively.
3. It will be helpful in knowing the success, failure and impact of Informal Women Education Centre.
4. The study will help in introducing CBIGA as a new kind of micro financing which is more effective.

References

Agrawal, Meenu and Shabana Nelasco, 'Empowerment of Rural Women in India', Kanishka Publication, New Delhi: 2009.

Dhavamani, P., 'Empowerment of Rural Women Through SHGs in Sattur Taluk of Virudhunagar District, College Sadhna, *Journal for Bloomers of Research*, Vol. 2, No. 2: Feb. 2010.

Jerinabi, U. and S. Santhiyavalli, 'Empowerment of Women through Convergence Technology', *Delhi Business Review*, Vol. 2, No. 2: July-December 2001.

K. Robert Yin, 'Case Study Research-Design and Methods', Sage Publication, London, New Delhi: 1987.

Kumari, Sujata, Vandana Kaushik and Neeta Lodha, 'Problems Faced by Rural Women Entrepreneurs of Rajasthan', *Stud. Home Commu. Science,* 4(2): 2010.

P., Sudarshan Pillai and K.P. Saraswathy Amna, 'Women Small Business Owners in India', International Handbook of Women and Small Business Entrepreneurship. (206-208).

Suguna, B., 'Empowerment of Rural Women Through SHGs', Discovery Publishing House Pvt. Ltd., New Delhi: 2010.

Suresh, K. and Others, 'Micro Finance and Empowerment of Rural Women—A Case Study of Dairy Enterprise', *Karnataka Journal of Agriculture Science* (831-834), 22(4): 2009.

G.U., Bharathamma, 'Empowerment of Rural Women Throuogh IGA in Gadag District on Northern Karnataka: 2005, http://etd.uasd.edu/ft/th8424. pdf

Handy, Femida and Meenaz Kassam, 'Women's Empowerment in Rural India,' Paper presented at ISTR Conference, Toranto, Cannada: 2004, http://www.istr.org/conference/toranto/workingpapers/handy.femida.pdf

Jain, Suman, 'ICTs and Women's Empowerment: Some Case Studies from India'.

'National Policy for the Empowerment of Women: 2001, http://www.nic.in/empwomen.htm

'Status of India's Rural Women', Pub. 2007, Updated 2 Jan. 2011<http://www.shvoong.com/humanities/1652424-status-india-rural-women/

CHAPTER

14

Micro Finance through SHG

A Way for Sustainable Development

LAXMI RANI DUBEY, MASSOUMEH NASROLLAH ZADEH, ARPITA KOTNALA AND DEVENDRA KUMAR MEENA

ABSTRACT

The Self Help Group (SHG)-Bank Linkage Programme, in the past eighteen years, has become a well known tool for bankers, developmental agencies and even for corporate houses. SHGs, in many ways, have gone beyond the means of delivering the financial services as a channel and turned out to be focal point for purveying various services to the poor. The programme, over a period, has become the common vehicle in the development process, converging important development programmes. With the small beginning as Pilot Programme launched by NABARD by linking 255 SHGs with banks in 1992, the programme has reached to linking of 69.5 lakh saving-linked SHGs and 48.5 lakh credit-linked SHGs and thus about 9.7 crore households are covered under the programme, envisaging synthesis of formal financial system and informal sector. NABARD has been bringing out the consolidated document annually for various data related to the Micro finance. In spite of these good efforts there are certain issues needs to be resolved in long-run, which can be successfully done through the recommendation being highlighted in the paper. Micro finance is the vehicle which can be utilized to make sustainable development in the India through alleviating poverty in rural India.

INTRODUCTION

Micro finance sector has traversed a long journey from micro savings to micro credit and then to micro enterprises and now entered the field of micro insurance, micro remittance and micro pension. This gradual and evolutionary growth process has given a great opportunity to the rural poor in India to attain reasonable economic, social and cultural empowerment, leading to better living standard and quality of life for participating households. Financial institutions in the country continued to play a leading role in the micro finance programme for nearly two decades now. They have joined hands proactively with informal delivery channels to give micro finance sector the necessary momentum. During the current year too, micro finance has registered an impressive expansion at the grass-root level. The bank operating, presently, in the formal financial system comprises Public Sector CBs (27), Private Sector CBs (22), RRBs (82), State Cooperative Banks (31) and District Central Cooperative Banks (370). Most of the banks participating in the process of micro finance have reported the progress made under the programme. In addition, the information relating to bulk lending provided by Banks and Financial Institutions to Micro Finance Institutions (MFIs) for on lending to groups and individuals have also been provided. Based on these data and information, this paper attempts an assessment of progress on varied dimensions of the micro finance sector. NABARD has been instrumental in facilitating various activities under micro finance sector, involving all possible partners at the ground level in the field. NABARD has been encouraging voluntary agencies, bankers, socially spirited individuals, other formal and informal entities and also government functionaries to promote and nurture SHGs. The focus in this direction has been on training and capacity building of partners, promotional grant assistance to Self Help Promoting Institutions (SHPIs), Revolving Fund Assistance (RFA) to MFIs, equity/capital support to MFIs to supplement their financial resources and provision of 100 per cent refinance against bank loans provided by various banks for micro finance activities.

DEFINITION OF MICRO FINANCE

Micro finance is defined as the provision of thrift, credit and other financial services and products in very small amounts to the poor for enabling them to raise income levels and improve their standards of living.

> *Micro finance refers to the entire range of financial services available such as savings and insurance, production and investment credit, housing finance for the poor and includes skill up gradation and entrepreneurial development that would enable them to overcome poverty.*
>
> —Dr. K.G. Karmaker

> *Micro finance provides credit support in small doses along with training and other related services to people who are resource poor but who are able to undertake economic activities.*
>
> —Dr. K.G. Karmaker

Micro finance provides credit support in small doses along with training and other related services to people who are resource poor but who are able to undertake economic activity.

NEED FOR MICRO FINANCE

Lack of collateral among the poor taxes credit away from them towards those better off and the land use poor are sidelined. The importance of collateral arises from the gaps in information that banks have to work with. Robinson has put it well: "since the credit-worthiness of potential rural borrowers cannot be adequately evaluated by an institution and since the use of credit by borrower cannot be adequately evaluated by an institution, and the combined effect may produce a greater likelihood of default and may, therefore, results in the lender seeking compensation in the form of higher interest rate, ultimately they end up lending to well-to-do. When there is no collateral, the information in credit still takes place in informal market; small sums of money are loaned for short duration of time, running at zero interest rates for personal relations to rates as high as 200% being charged by professional money lenders which are exploitative in nature. Also mutual knowledge and threat of losing face in the community becomes the substitute for collateral. This innovation of combining both the attributes is called the group lending, also well known as Grameen bank model. Also this is based on the hypothesis that the credit on reasonable terms can bring about significant reduction in the poverty.

MICRO FINANCE INSTITUTIONAL STRUCTURE

Mainstream Micro finance Institutional Structure: This includes NABARD, SIDBI, HDFC, other commercial, regional banks, co-operative credit societies, etc.

Alternative Micro finance Institutional Structure: It includes NGO's alternative MFI's, specifically organized as co-operatives (such as SEWA (Self Employed Women Association), Mutually-Aided Co-operative Thrift and Credit Societies (MACTS) in A.P. and non-banking finance companies, such as BASIX, CFTS, etc.

Basic services provided by Micro finance Institutional Structure.

Savings (Compulsory and optional).

Consumption credit, production credit, housing credit, housing loans and investment credit.

Insurance or risk fund services.

Micro finance through SHG.

Micro finance by non-formal financial organizations were already started well before formal institute.

GRAMEEN BANK MODEL OF MICRO FINANCE

To bridge the gap between formal and informal systems, Mohammad Yunus started a research project in Bangladesh in 1979 and established Grameen bank in 1983. Grameen bank group (GBG) model is alternative to SHG's although in smaller numbers. The group are much smaller, i.e., of five members to start with thrift, the groups are affinity groups. Affinity may be kinship/caste/occupation. They have frequent weekly meetings. The savings habit is inculcated in groups with compulsory saving component linked to average size of loan.

The Grameen bank follows a credit plus approach wherein members take an oath to adhere to 14 decisions which includes decisions as sending children to school, use of clean toilets, not accepting dowry, etc.

The individual savings is deposited in the bank, and members get loan directly from the bank. The GBG only helps bank in screening the borrowers and also assuring repayment. 0.5% of the loan amount is deducted to develop a group fund. It is negligible to at least 2% per months of rate of interest.

ROLE OF WOMEN IN MICRO FINANCE

In the present context of poverty in India, the position of women has been particularly vulnerable. Besides being subjected to poverty around them, women are subjected to gender specific abuse including violence. As a result, women are denied to basic rights to food, shelter, health, life and security. Female Infanticide has become common in many parts of the country.

Otero has identified some reasons for inaccessibility of credit to women:

1. Women are small borrower and can be easily excluded from participating in programs that require a minimum size of loan which is beyond their capacity to absorb usefully.
2. Women have the smallest and the transaction costs of administrating small loan often discourages institutions from lending to smallest businesses.

3. Women tend to have less experience in competing application forms and can be dissuaded from seeking credit if the procedures are too complicated.
4. Women are less likely to meet collateral regulations, especially when collateral is the form of land.

In the book in 'Grameen Bank' Fuglesang and Chandler feed that:

> "In the Grammen Bank's experience women use their earnings for the family in terms of permanent housing, clothing, nutrition, education, which will add up to health welfare and development. For men increased earnings may go well to the family but it also has the strong tendency to disappear in the houses and other forms of personally gratifying consumption."

It is also well known fact that women are first victims in case of any financial crisis in the family. In this context, financing of women for self-employment not only strengthens the family income but also empowers the position of women in the family if not in the society. From a pure banking point of view, women have proven to have risk taking ability; they exhibit a greater social reliability and sense of accountability.

RASTRIYA MAHILA KOSH (RMK)

Government of India decided to set-up a National Credit Fund for women (RMK) in 1993. As the name suggests, it is dedicated for women, specifically to providing poor women with micro-credit. The KOSH endeavors to be client friendly and less formal than banking institutes, with simple lending procedures and minimal documentation. The objective is to simplify the transaction from borrower perspective, without compromising the quality of loan application. Loans are distributed through intermediate micro-credit organizations (IMOs) or the Self-Help Promotion Institutes (SHPIs). These SHPIs, in turn lend to SHGs. The interest structure as already state, the RMK lends at 8% p.a. to SHPIs which, in turn, charge

12% p.a. to SHGs and SHG is allowed to fix what each member will pay subject to ceiling of 18% p.a.

TASK FORCE FOR MICRO FINANCE

These are different structure and organization of Micro finance as they are operating under diverse legal framework and have been adopting varied approaches; it is increasingly being felt that a suitable national policy framework is essential for any orderly development of the micro finance sector.

It was in the above backdrop that the women's World Banking (WWB), New York in association with friend of WWB, Ahmadabad, organized a high level policy forum on "Building India's leadership in Micro finance on 6th November, 1988, the forum was addressed by Governor of RBI and other senior bank officials and prominent micro finance practitioners. The forum suggested that a high-powered Task force on Micro Finance may be constituted by NABARD to arrive at a conceptual policy framework for sustainable growth of micro finance in the country.

Accordingly, a Task force was constituted by NABARD under chairmanship of Shri Y.C. Nanda, Managing Director, and NABARD.

The terms of reference of task force were as under:

- To work out a conceptual framework for a national policy for microfinance.
- To examine and suggest organizational and regulatory framework for bringing the operations of micro finance institutions to main stream.
- To suggest a framework for inter-institutional co-ordination and the roles and responsibilities of the self-regulating organizations.
- To examine and suggest ways and means for an appropriate mechanism for emerging micro finance institutions.

SAVINGS OF SHGS WITH BANKS

As on 31 March 2010, a total of 69.53 lakh SHGs were

having saving bank accounts with the banking sector with outstanding savings of 6198.71 crore as against 61.21 lakh SHGs with savings of 5545.62 crore as on 31 March 2009, thereby showing a growth rate of 13.6 per cent and 11.8 per cent, respectively. Thus, more than 97 million poor households were associated with banking agencies under SHG-Bank Linkage Programme. As on 31 March 2010, the CBs lead with savings accounts of 40.53 lakh SHGs (58.3%) with savings amount of 3673.89 crore (59.3%) followed by RRBs having savings bank accounts of 18.21 lakh SHGs (26.2%) with savings amount of 1299.37 crore (21.0%) and Cooperative Banks having savings bank accounts of 10.79 lakh SHGs (15.5%) with savings amount of 1225.44 crore (19.8%). The share under SGSY was 16.94 lakh SHGs with savings of 1,292.62 crore forming 24.4 per cent of the total SHGs having savings accounts with the banks and 20.8 per cent of their total savings amount.

RECOMMENDATIONS

The major recommendations of Task force can be divided into four broad heads:

1. Mainstreaming of micro finance institutes and other structures.
2. Regulation and supervision of micro finance institutes (MFIs).
3. Organizational aspects relating to MFIs.
4. Capacity building of MFIs, Banks, SHGs, etc.

The National Policy for Micro Finance

Envisioned by the Task force, the National Policy for MF seeks to achieve the following mission in the medium term:

> "Five years, hence we are looking for a process change leading to empowerment of 75 lakh poor households, and most particularly of the women from these households, through strong and viable people's structures like SHGs and MFIs, which draws strength and support from the opportunity for both poor and banks."

ISSUES TO BE RESOLVED UPSCALING OF THE PROGRAMME

The Self-Help Group Bank linkage programme and facing problems of up scaling as there is lack of credible non-governmental organizations and the other agencies for social intermediation is limiting the speed of programme.

CAPACITY BUILDING

Capacity building of various partners in programme is gigantic task. The enormity of programme warrants not only NABARD but also other agencies which could also include donor agencies to collaborate for capacity building.

SUSTAINABILITY OF SHGS

The sustainability of SHGs depends to a great extent on quality of SHG, which is in turn dependent on the case and attention given by SHPI in formation stage. It has been observed that there has been a tendency at field level to hasten the process of group formation of SHGs to achieve targets which affects the sustainability of SHGs in long-run.

ATTITUDE OF FORMAL INSTITUTES

The bankers at grass-root level still view this programme as a social development programme and do not in general treat SHGs as business proposition.

IMPACT OF GOVERNMENT PROGRAMME WITH SUBSIDY COMPONENT

These programme are affecting the sustainability of SHGs. The members have the tendency to join such schemes where subsidy is available, thus disintegrating the SHGs and dampening the effect on SHG bank linkage programme.

SUGGESTIONS FOR FUTURE IMPROVEMENTS

Need for Computerization of Micro Finance Operations

Normally accounts of SHGs members at villages are tracked with handwritten sheets and pass books. Much of time is devoted to manually updating the records; little time is spent on discussion on economic and social aspects. Introduction of Smart-card into micro-credit programme will save lot of variable time spent in tracking accounts.

The members can carry out the smart-card that electronically holds members information and records of transaction, the members can update the transaction through hand-held computers (HHC) brought by facilitator which has information downloaded from computers in bank branches in the village and at the end of the day the facilitator downloads information from HHC to the Branch computer.

PRE-EXISTING GROUPS (PEGS) SHOULD BE USED FOR UPSCALING THE PROGRAMME AND REDUCING UNEVEN GROWTH

The concept of group activity is not new to rural India; historically there have been groups in our villages like Chit Fund groups, particularly in South India, are already operating with objectives of taking advantage of pooled contributions. There are also other affinity groups performing common economic activity. These groups should be identified and should be converted to SHGs linking them with bank, especially in states with high poverty rate.

PROPER CARE TO BE TAKEN DURING FORMULATION OF SHGS

As the sustainability of SHGs depends on care and attention given by SMPI at formulation stage, due care should be taken to select the group and see to it that it should be homogenous as far as possible in name of achieving target should not be in hurry during group formulation.

ATTITUDE OF FORMAL INSTITUTION TO BE CHANGED

As the poor are also bankable and micro finance programme is fast spreading it should be considered as business proposition.

MICRO FINANCE MOVEMENT SHOULD BE GENDER NEUTRAL

Micro finance movement as focused should disproportionately more attention on the financing of women, although a great majority of women require credit support. It is tough going for male-headed poor households as well unless and until more and more men are also brought under micro finance, there would be gender imbalance and upscaling and mainstreaming will remain virtually incomplete.

THE RECOMMENDATIONS OF TASK FORCE SHOULD BE SUCCESSFULLY IMPLEMENTED

If the recommendations of task force on micro finance are properly implemented, there would be a lot of improvement in micro finance operation and will become most sustainable in long-run.

CONCLUSION

It can be summed-up that micro-financing through informal group has benefit such as :

> Saving mobilized by poor, access to required amount of appropriate credit by poor, matching the demand and supply of credit structure and opening new market for FIs, reduction in transaction cost for both lender and borrower, tremendous, improvement in recovery, heralding a new realization of subsidy use and corruption use credit, remarkable empowerment of poor women.

This is found that even the poor people are bankable

profitably through micro finance and will improve the opportunity for investment by poor. Simultaneously, the poor will improve their savings potential, credit-handling capacity and access to financial institutions, inculcate entrepreneurial skill, develop an urge for investment and also increase the risk taking attitude through SHGs. There is still a way out of the grinding cycle of poverty that crushes the poor, the availability of microcredit through SHG system is an important channel for credit availability and poverty alleviation through self-help efforts and without any subsidy.

References

Sarangi, U.C., Task Force on Credit Related Issues of Farmers, Published by Ministry of agriculture, Government of india, June 2010.

Status of Micro Finance in India, Published by Micro Credit Innovation Department of NABARD, (2009-10).

Synghal, Sudharshan, Taking Micro-credit to Women.

Financing Agriculture, April-June, 2002.

Wadhwa, C., Banking-NGO Collaboration for Better Rural Lending to Poor. Financing Agriculture, April-June, 2002.

Dasgupta, Working and impact of rural self-help groups and other forms of micro-financing.' *Indian Journal of Agriculture Economics,* July-Sept., 2001.

Dadhich, C.L., Micro Finance—A Panacea for Poverty Alleviation. *Indian Journal of Agricultural Economics,* July-Sept., 2001.

Karmaker, K.G., Micro Financing Revisited, *Financing Agriculture.* April-June, 2002.

Patel, A.R., Baria, B.G., Micro finance Operations : Performance and Issues. *Financing Agriculture,* April-June, 2002.

CHAPTER

15

Prospects of Green Banking in India

MAANSI KATARIA

ABSTRACT

Climate change is no more an environmental concern. As banks also form a part of the society, banks are also responsible for protecting the environment. To fulfil this responsibility banks need to take green initiatives towards substantial reduction of carbon emission. Green banking as a term covers several different areas, but in general refers to how environmentally friendly your bank is, and how much their policies are committed to green and ethical issues. The undergone study tries to explore the need of green banking in the Indian banking industry. It also illustrates few international initiatives been taken world-wide to protect the environment. This paper investigates the various levels of green banking at which the Indian banks can operate. The study also suggests some products that can be adopted by the Indian banks for promoting green initiatives.

Keywords: Carbon footprint, Credit risk, Green Mortgages, Online banking, United Nations Environment Programme

INTRODUCTION

Climate change is the most subtle issue in today's scenario. Across the globe there have been continuous endeavors to measure and mitigate the risk of climate change caused by human activity. Many countries in the world over have made commitments necessary to mitigate climate change. India also has committed to cut its domestic carbon intensity by 20-25 percent from 2005 levels, by the year 2010. As socially responsible corporate citizens (SRCC), Indian banks too have a major role and responsibility in supplementing government efforts towards substantial reduction in carbon emission.

The word 'green' in green banking includes all those activities that results in reduction of harmful impact on the environment. From consumer point of view it can be in the form of recycling of bottles, cans, paper etc., reusing of bags, refilling of water bottles etc, or by reducing emissions, pollutants, water use and so on.

Green banking is an emerging term in India. It includes clump of areas from bank. Under this a bank takes into account environment friendly measures to how and also where their money is invested. The term green banking sometimes also referred to as ethical banking. An ethical bank operates with the aim of protecting the environment. But green banking is much broader concept than ethical banking. A green bank is a bank that promotes environmental and social responsibility but operates as a traditional community bank and provides excellent services to investors and clients.[1]

Bankers are the important professional group who has interaction with the other groups of people and also with general masses. They can adopt different green activities within their in-house environment and also can initiate the protection of the air pollution, water pollution by their clients. Bankers can finance the green projects, which are environmental friendly and discourage the projects that damage the environment. The banking sector is one of the major sources of financial institutions that provide lending facilities to many industrial projects such as cement, chemicals, power, textiles, etc., which cause maximum carbon emission. Thus, the banking sector can play a central role in developing the economy and also in protecting the environment.

Despite of the fact that banks are environmental friendly and do not impact the environment severely by its internal activities, but still the external activities does effect the environment. The external activities involve the activities being performed by the bank customers that can harm the environment.

NEED OF GREEN BANKING

Green banking is very important in mitigating the following risks involved in the banking sector:

1. Legal Risk

Like all other business organizations, banks too face legal risk if they do not comply with the required environment rules and regulations. Banks may also face risk from direct lending if they take the possession of pollution causing assets.

2. Credit Risk

With the adverse change in climate conditions, there are direct as well as indirect costs that banks are facing now days. It has been observed that due to global warming, there have been extreme weather conditions that affect the economic assets financed by the banks and thus leasing to high occurrence of credit default. Banks also face indirect risk when they lend to the companies whose businesses are adversely affected because of the changes in environmental regulations.

3. Reputation Risk

Being a part of the society, banks are also susceptible to reputation risk. With the advancement and awareness of environment, banks also have to take care of their activities so that they do not damage the environment whether directly or indirectly.[2]

GLOBAL FRAMEWORKS ON CLIMATE CHANGE FOR THE FINANCIAL SECTOR

Several initiatives have been taken world-wide to support the climate change. There are many initiatives that provide guidance for the finance sector in tackling a range of environmental, social and governance (ESG) issues and few that specifically focus on climate change. Some of these international initiatives are listed below:

1. UNEP Finance Initiative

UNEP Finance initiative is a part of the United Nations Environment Programme. It is a strategic public-private partnership between UNEP and the global financial sector. UNEP Finance Initiative works with more than 180 banks, insurers and investment firms and a number of partner organizations to understand he impacts of environmental, social and governance issues on financial performance and sustainable development. It consists of a broad range of financial institutions in a constructive dialogue about the nexus between economic development, environmental protection and sustainable development.

2. The Climate Principles

The Climate Principles provides a fully comprehensive and voluntary framework to guide the finance sector in tackling the challenge of climate change. They provide them direction on managing climate change. Adopting the Climate Principles by any institution means they are committed for the following:

(a) Minimizing operational carbon footprint.

(b) Engaging with customers, suppliers and wider society to seek opportunities for a low carbon economy.

(c) Developing products and services that enable customers to manage climate change-related risks and business opportunities.

(d) Make business decisions that will reduce climate change-related risks.

(e) Support the development of sound energy and climate change policy.

3. The Equator Principles

The Equator principles provide a set of financial industry benchmarks for determining, assessing and managing social and environmental risk in project financing. Equator Principles Financial Institutions (EPFIs) commit to not providing loans to projects where the borrower will not or is unable to comply with their respective social and environmental policies and procedures that implement the EPs.

4. United Nations Principles for Responsible Investments

UN Principles for Responsible Investment provides a set of voluntary ESG principles that investors should take into account of due to the potential affect they can have on the performance of investment portfolios. Currently, around 728 organizations globally have signed the principles. The organizations that have signed the Principles are demonstrating senior level support for sustainable development.

GREEN BANKING *V.* ONLINE BANKING

One of the easiest way by which the bank can go green is to start providing the online services to its customers. The benefits of using online banking comprises of reduction in paper usage, less mail and less movements to branch offices, increase in the bank's profitability, etc. Through online banking, banks can lower their own costs that result from bulk usage of paper and mailing fees as more and more customers start using online banking.

According to a recent study by Javelin Strategy and Research held at US, bank customers loved this idea. 43% of customers polled said they would rather do business with a bank that seems more "green". It's true that monthly paper statements do have a great impact. If every household in the US were able to switch to paperless billing, this would save an estimated 16.5 million trees per year or about 46,000 acres.

A bank can do much more to help the environment than by just promoting online banking. To protect the environment, a green bank can reduce its carbon footprint by building more efficient branches, implementing energy-efficient operational procedures, offering transportation services to its employees promoting sustainable banking and so on. Banks can also promote green banking by providing support to eco-friendly groups and also by spreading the advantages of being green through e-pamphlets, websites, etc.

LEVELS OF GREEN BANKING

Level 1 : Unfolded Corporate Activities

At this level, banks sponsor 'green' events and undertake public relation activities that are not directly related to the core business activities of the company or a firm. Large number of banks in India has been at this level of green for a long time.

Level 2 : Quarantined Business Projects or Practices

Banks now days develop separate products or activities that they add to their conventional banking portfolio. Banks under the umbrella of green products build isolated projects and activities for promoting the green initiatives that helps in protecting the environment. For example, banks offer various green products like green credit card, green mortgages, etc.

Level 3 : Systemic Business Practices

At this level, the green principles and practices underline most of the bank's products and processes. The focus of every bank is to protect the environment in addition to its core business. Every bank designs its activities to support the impact of their functioning on four levels, i.e., people/place, processes, principles and purpose.

Level 4 : Strategic Ecosystem Innovation

Green banking doesn't denote only the activities to be carried out by the banks. The success of green and social transformation requires participation from the larger system a bank and its clients. Strategic ecosystem innovation broadens the focus of bank's activities to include more activities by the banks in surplus to the daily functioning of the banks.

Level 5 : Intentional Eco-system Innovation

The difference between Level 4 (Strategic) and Level 5 (Intentional) is that level 4 is driven by a strategic response to external challenges, while level 5 is driven by the primacy of purpose (social and green impact). At this level, a socially responsible and green bank is a hybrid company which exists with a purpose to bring new innovative products that can improve the level of the whole eco-system.

VEHICLES TO ADOPT GREEN BANKING

Indian banks can adopt green banking as one of the tool for sustainable banking. Some of the green banking strategies that can be adopted by banks are:

1. Green Banking Financial Products

To promote green banking, Indian banks need to develop new and innovative green financial products. These products should aim at reducing the carbon emissions. Banks can provide their customers with an option to invest in environment-friendly projects and can also conduct environmental audits of the financed projects. Banks can also include green guidelines in their credit policies raise the number of customers with green loan portfolio.

2. Green Mortgages

Banks can also offer to its customers green mortgages. There are two variants of green mortgages: the Energy Improvement Mortgage and the Energy Efficient Mortgage. The energy improvement mortgages are for those customers that replace or improve their home or building with energy efficient devices like solar panels, etc. On the other hand, the energy efficient mortgages provide loans to customers that construct their buildings or homes with energy efficient stuff.

3. Carbon Credit Business

Indian banks can also work under the Kyoto protocol to protect the environment. Under the umbrella of Clean Development Mechanism (CDM) banks can set-up dedicated carbon credit cells to capture a major share of the carbon credit business.

4. Abatement of Carbon Footprint

Carbon footprint illustrates the impact of our activities on the environment. It depicts the amount of green house gas produced by us in our daily life while burning the fossil fuels for electricity, heating, transportation, etc. Indian banks can reduce their carbon-footprint by adopting the following measures:

(a) Paperless Banking

With the advancement in technology, more and more banks branches are getting computerized which provides ample scope to banks to practice paperless banking. Banks should encourage their customers to switch over to electronic transactions and popularize e-statements.

(b) Encourage Mass Transportation System

To save fuel banks can also start providing their employees with mass transportation system. With this initiative a huge amount of fuel can be saved and also results in controlling the pollution level.

(c) Green Deposits

Banks can offer higher rates on certificate of deposits, savings account and also on money market accounts if customers choose to conduct their banking activities online.

5. Green Credit Cards

Banks can also accompany its customers with green credit card facility. With a green credit card, the cardholders can earn rewards or points which can be redeemed as a contribution to charitable organizations that works with a mission to protect the environment. Banks can offer attractive incentives for its customers who use their green credit card for luxurious purchases.

CONCLUSION

It has been found that existing studies mostly agree on the fact that banking institutions interact with the environment basically in two ways: directly, through their "day-to-day" operational activities and indirectly, through the products and services they offer. Therefore, banks should play a pro-active role to take environmental aspect as a part of their lending principle. They should only lend to the industries that carry out their operations without generating any pollution. Green banking is not a new term in today's global scenario as banks are taking a number of initiatives to protect the environment. Countries like USA, Canada, and Netherland etc. have already taken steps towards green banking. Some Indian banks have also started green initiatives but still there is lot more to be done. Green banking also helps a bank to minimize and control various types of risks like credit risk, legal risk and reputation risk.

NOTES AND REFERENCES

1. Mamun Rashid, 'Green Banking', *The Financial Express*, Vol. 18, No. 182, Regd No Da 1589, Dhaka, Tuesday, May 10, 2011.
2. Pravakar Sahoo and Bibhu Prasad Nayak, *"Green Banking in India"*, *Indian Economic Journal*, 125/2008.

REFERENCES

Mr. Mridul Dharwal and Mr. Ankur Agarwal, 'Green Banking: An Innovative Initiative for Sustainable Development'.

Mamun Rashid, 'Green Banking', *The Financial Express*, Vol. 18, No. 182, Regd. No. Da 1589, Dhaka, Tuesday, May 10, 2011.

Dr. Katrin Kaeufer, 'Banking as a Vehicle for Socio-economic Development and Change: Case Studies of Socially Responsible and Green Banks, Jan. 2010.

Pravakar Sahoo and Bibhu Prasad Nayak, 'Green Banking in India', *Indian Economic Journal*, 125/2008.

www.scribd.com/38662765-Green-Banking.pdf

http://green.wikia.com/wiki/Green_Banking.

Climate Change and Finance in India: Banking on the Low Carbon Economy, May 2010.

CHAPTER

16

Foreign Direct Investment in Indian Retail Sector

Strategic Issues and Implication

MUSHTAQ AHMAD

ABSTRACT

Indian retail industry is one of the sunrise sectors with huge growth potential. According to the Investment Commission of India, the retail sector is expected to grow almost three times its current levels to $ 660 billion by 2015. However, in spite of the recent developments in retailing and its immense contribution to the economy, retailing continues to be the least evolved industries and the growth of organised retailing in India has been much slower as compared to rest of the world. Undoubtedly, this dismal situation of the retail sector, despite the ongoing wave of incessant liberalization and globalization, stems from the absence of an FDI encouraging policy in the Indian retail sector. In this context, the present paper attempts to analyse the strategic issues concerning the influx of foreign direct investment in the Indian retail industry. Moreover, with the latest move of the government to allow FDI in the multibrand retailing sector, the paper analyzes the reason why foreign retailers are interested in India, the strategies they are adopting to enter India and their prospects in India. The findings of the study point out that FDI in retail would undoubtedly enable India Inc to integrate its economy with that of the global economy. Thus, as a matter of fact FDI in the buzzing Indian retail sector should not just be freely allowed but should be significantly encouraged. In this paper we highlighten the strategic issues and implication of FDI in Indian Retail Sector.

Keywords : FDI, Retail Sector, Issues and Implication in India.

INTRODUCTION

The Indian retail industry is the fifth largest in the world. Comprising of organized and unorganized sectors, retail industry is one of the fastest growing industries in India, especially over the last few years. With growing market demand, the industry is expected to grow at a pace of 25-30% annually. The Indian retail industry is expected to grow from Rs. 35,000 crore in 2004-05 to Rs. 109,000 crore by the year 2010. The Indian retail industry is the most promising emerging market for investment. In 2007, the retail trade in India had a share of 8-10% in the GDP (Gross Domestic Product) of the country. In 2009, it rose to 12%. It is also expected to reach 22% by 2010 (Kearney, A.T). According to the Investment Commission of India, the retail sector is expected to grow almost three times its current levels to $ 660 billion by 2015. It is expected that India will be among the top 5 retail markets then. The organized sector is expected to grow to $ 100 bn and account for 12-15% of retail sales by 2015 (Singhal 1999). However, in late 1990's the retail sector has witnessed a level of transformation. Though initially, the retail industry in India was mostly unorganized, however with the change of tastes and preferences of the consumers, the industry is getting more popular these days and getting organized as well. As the retail market place changes shape and competition increases, the potential for improving retail productivity and cutting costs is likely to decrease. Therefore, it is important for retailers to secure a distinctive position in the market place based on values, relationships or experience. Also, as the organised retail space in India continues to grow, it is likely to see a number of initiatives in the near future. Companies are likely to combine expansion with innovative measures as they look to ensure profitability in difficult times. One such initiative includes assessing the prospects of foreign players in this sector through foreign direct investment.

The arrival of FDI in India was witnessed during the end of 1990's when the Indian national government announced a number of reforms which aimed at helping in the process of liberalization and deregulation of the Indian economy. Since its inception there has been a remarkable surge in the FDI inflows in the country. The total amount of FDI in India came to around US $ 42.3 billion in 2001, in 2002 this figure stood at US$ 54.1 billion, in 2003 this figure came to US $ 75.4 billion, and in 2004 this figure increased to US $ 113 billion. This shows that the flow of foreign direct investment in India has grown at a very fast pace over the last few years (http://business.mapsofindia.com). According to the latest data released by Department of Policy and Promotion (DIPP) the FDI inflow during 2008-09 (from April 2008 to March 2009) stood at approx. US $ 27.3 billion. It is interesting to note here that as per an UNCTAD study India achieved a substantial 85.1 per cent increase in FDI flows in calendar year 2008—the highest increase across all countries—even as global flows declined by 14.5 per cent (UNCTAD, 2008). Moreover, FDI for all the permissible items/activities can be brought in through the Automatic Route under powers delegated to the Reserve Bank of India (RBI), and for the remaining items/activities through Government approval, which is accorded on the recommendation of the Foreign Investment Promotion Board (FIPB). In recent years the destination sectors in FDI have became more varied. FDI inflows have shifted from infrastructure, natural resources and export driven manufacturing to other areas such as retailing, tourism, construction and off shore services. Despite all the advantages that come along foreign investment in any sector of the economy, it is to be noted that FDI in India is not liberally allowed in all sectors including the retail sector, where FDI is either absolutely forbidden on the grounds of national interest, or, other sectors where the existing and notified sectoral policy does not permit FDI beyond a ceiling (http://dipp.nic.in/manual/manual_0403.pdf). In this context, the present paper attempts to analyse the strategic issues concerning the influx of foreign direct investment in the Indian retail industry.

GROWTH DRIVERS IN INDIA FOR RETAIL SECTOR

The retail industry in India is currently growing at a great pace and is expected to go up to US$ 833 billion by the year 2013. It is further expected to reach US$ 1.3 trillion by the year 2018 at a CAGR of 10%. As the country has got a high growth rate, the consumer spending has also gone up and is also expected to go up further in the future. The key factors that drive growth in retail industry are young demographic profile, increasing consumer aspirations, growing middle class incomes and improving demand from rural markets. Also, rising incomes and improvements in infrastructure are enlarging consumer markets and accelerating the convergence of consumer tastes. Liberalization of the Indian economy, increase in spending per capita income and the advent of dual income families also help in the growth of retail sector.

MAJOR ATTRACTIONS FOR GLOBAL RETAILERS IN INDIA

Retailing is being perceived as a beginner and as an attractive commercial business for organized business, i.e. the pure retailer is starting to emerge now. Indian organized retail industry is one of the sunrise sectors with huge growth potential. Total retail market in India stood at USD 350 billion in 2007-08 and is estimated to attain USD 573 billion by 2012-13. Organised retail industry accounts for only 5.5% of total retail industry and is expected to reach 10% by 2012 (http://business.rediff.com). A.T. Kearney, the well-known international management consultancy, recently identified India as the 'second most attractive retail destination' globally from among thirty emergent markets. It has made India the cause of a good deal of excitement and the cynosure of many foreign investors' eyes. With a contribution of an overwhelming 14% to the national GDP and employing 7% of the total workforce (only agriculture employs more) in the country, the retail industry is definitely one of the pillars of the Indian economy. Foreign companies' attraction to India is the billion-plus population. Also, there are huge employment opportunities in retail sector in India. India's retail industry is the second largest sector, after agriculture, which provides employment. According to Associated Chambers of Commerce and Industry of India (ASSOCHAM), the retail sector will create 50,000 jobs in the next few years. As per the US Census Bureau, the young population in India is likely to constitute 53 per cent of the total population by 2020 and 46.5 per cent of the population by 2050 much higher than countries like the US, the UK, Germany, China, etc. India's demographic scenario is likely to change favourably, and therefore, will most certainly drive retail sales growth, especially in the organised retail segment. Even though organised retailers have a far lesser reach in India than in other developed countries, the first-mover advantage of some retail players will contribute to the sector's growth. India in such a scenario presents some major attractions to foreign retailers. There is a huge, huge industry with no large players. Some Indian large players have entered just recently like Reliance, Trent. Moreover, India can support significant players averaging $ 1 bn. in Grocery and $ 0.3-0.5 bn. in apparel within next ten years. The transition will open multiple opportunities for companies and investors. In addition to these, improved living standards and continuing economic growth, friendly business environment, growing spending power and increasing number of conscious customers aspiring to own quality and branded products in India are also attracting to global retailers to enter in Indian market.

CHALLENGES OF RETAILING IN INDIA

In India the retailing industry has a long way to go and to become a truly flourishing industry, retailing needs to cross various hurdles. The first challenge facing the organized retail sector is the competition from unorganized sector. Needless to say, the Indian retail sector is overwhelmingly swarmed by the unorganized retailing with the dominance of small and medium enterprises in contradiction to the presence of few giant corporate retailing outlets. The tax structure in India favors small retail business. Organized retail sector has to pay huge taxes, which is negligible for small retail business. Thus, the cost of business operations is very high in India. Developed supply chain and integrated IT management is absent in retail sector. This lack of adequate infrastructure facilities, lack of trained work force and low skill level for retailing management further makes the sector quite complex. Also, the intrinsic complexity of retailing-rapid price changes, threat of product obsolescence, low margins, high cost of real estate and dissimilarity in consumer groups are the other challenges that the retail sector in India is facing. While in some sectors the restrictions imposed by the government are comprehensible; the restrictions imposed in few others, including the retail sector, are utterly baseless and are acting as shackles in the progressive development of that particular sector and eventually the overall development of the Indian Inc. The scenario is kind of depressing and unappealing, since despite the ongoing wave of incessant liberalization and globalization, the Indian retail sector is still aloof from progressive and ostentatious development. This dismal situation of the retail sector undoubtedly stems from the absence of an FDI encouraging policy in the Indian retail sector.

CHALLENGES FOR GLOBAL RETAILERS IN INDIAN RETAIL SECTOR

History has witnessed that the concern of allowing unrestrained FDI flows in the retail sector has never been free from controversies and simultaneously has been an issue for unsuccessful deliberation ever since the advent of FDI in India. Where on one hand there has been a strong outcry for the unrestricted flow of FDI in the retail trading by an overwhelming number of both domestic as well as foreign corporate retail giants; to the contrary, the critics of unrestrained FDI have always fiercely retorted by highlighting the adverse impact, the FDI in the retail trading will have on the unorganized retail trade, which is the source of employment to an enormous amount of the population of India. The antagonists of FDI in retail sector oppose the same on various grounds, like, that the entry of large global retailers such as Wal-Mart would kill local shops and millions of jobs, since the unorganized retail sector employs an enormous percentage of Indian population after the agriculture sector; secondly, that the global retailers would conspire and exercise monopolistic power to raise prices and monopolistic (big buying) power to reduce the prices received by the supply.

IMPACT AND ROLE OF FDI IN INDIAN RETAIL SECTOR

In the fierce battle between the advocators and antagonist of unrestrained FDI flows in the Indian retail sector, the interests of the consumers have been blatantly and utterly disregarded. Therefore, one of the arguments which inevitably need to be considered and addressed while deliberating upon the captioned issue is the interests of consumers at large in relation to the interests of retailers. Interestingly, in contradiction to the recommendations of the Parliamentary Committee's report, the Economic Survey, 2008-09 raised hopes of all those looking for a favourable response of the government on the subject. While, the Economic Survey has made a strong case for opening up the FDI for multi-brand retail, it has recommended a gradual opening of the sector. Improving the investment environment would require FDI in multi-format retail, starting with food retailing. Initially the FDI could be allowed subject to the setting up a modern logistics system, perhaps jointly with other organised retailers.

Thus, FDI in retailing is favoured on a number of grounds. The global retailers have advanced management know how in merchandising and inventory management and have adopted new technologies which can significantly improve productivity and efficiency in retailing. The entry of large low-cost retailers and adoption of integrated supply chain management by them is likely to lower down the prices. Also FDI in retailing can easily assure the quality of product, better shopping experience and customer services. They promote the linkage of local suppliers, farmers and manufacturers, no doubt only those who can meet the quality and safety standards, to global market and this will ensure a reliable and profitable market to these local players. As multinational players are spreading their operation, regional players are also developing their supply chain differentiating their strategies and improving their operations to counter the size of international players. This all will encourage the investment and employment in supply chain management. Moreover, joint ventures would ease capital constraints of existing organised retailers and FDI would lead to development of different retail formats and modernization of the sector. Therefore, FDI in retail would undoubtedly enable India Inc to integrate its economy with that of the global economy. FDI will help to overcome both—the lack of experience in organized retailing as well as lack of trained manpower. FDI in retail would reduce cost of intermediation and entail setting up of integrated supply chains that would minimize wastage, give producers a better price and benefit both producers and consumers.

CONCLUSIONS

Amidst today's time of fierce competition and a quest to achieve and enhance a substantial level of economic and social development; each and every nation is trying to liberalize its economic policies in order to attract investments from not only, domestic players, but also from magnates all across the globe. Consequently, people with generous reserves of funds, all around the globe, are expanding their wings and seeking opportunities of investing in different spheres of this lucrative market. India too is not oblivious to the rapid developments taking place in the global market and has emerged as one of the prime destinations for the investment of funds from an impressive number of foreign investors.

References

India Retail Biz, Allowing FDI in retail will enlarge scope, bring fresh capital, and increase competition, say industry leaders, Welcoming Survey, available at last visited 26th April, 2009, Accessed from http://www.indiaretailbiz.com/blog/2009/07/02.

Indian Retail Biz, Economic Survey recommends opening of retail to foreign investment (FDI); suggests making beginning with 'food' segment, Accessed from http://www.indiaretailbiz.com/blog/2009/07/02.

Singhal, Arvind, 2009, Indian Retail: The road ahead, Retail biz, available at www.etretailbiz.com, last visited 14th Oct. 2010.

Role of FDI in Retail Sector, *The Economic Times 2009*, Accessed from http://economictimes.indiatimes.com.

Retail Indai Article of *The Times of India*, Accessed from http://timesofindia.indiatimes.com.

UNCTAD 2008, 'Assessing the impact of the current financial and economic crisis on global FDI flows'. Foreign Direct Investment In Indian Retail Sector—Strategic Issues and Implication.

CHAPTER

17

Recent Trends in FDI and Its Impact on Growth and Development of India

NAHID AND FOZIA

ABSTRACT

FDI or Foreign Direct Investment is a form of investment that earns interest in enterprises which functions outside the domestic territory of investor. The economy of India is the eleventh largest economy in the world in PPP terms. India is a preferred destination of foreign direct investments. This paper attempts to study recent trends in FDI and its impact on growth and development of Indian economy and challenges faced by FDI in India. The paper findings show that there is a positive correlation between FDI and domestic investment. FDI also has a positive interaction with human capital, sound macro-economic policies and stability of institutions, thus, it contributes towards the enhancement of economic growth and development.

Keywords: Foreign Direct Investment, Indian Economy, Investment, Development.

INTRODUCTION

The economy of India is the eleventh largest economy in the world by nominal GDP and the fourth largest by purchasing power parity (PPP). As the fourth-largest economy in the world in PPP terms, India is a preferred destination for foreign direct investments (FDI). India has strength in telecommunication, information technology and other significant areas such as auto-components, chemicals, apparels, pharmaceuticals and jewellery. Despite a surge in foreign investments, rigid FDI policies resulted in a significant hindrance. However, due to some positive economic reforms aimed at deregulating the economy and stimulating foreign investment, India has positioned itself as one of the front-runners of the rapidly growing Asia Pacific Region. FDI eludes definition owing to the presence of many authorities such as organization for Economic Co-operation and Development (OCED), International Monetary Fund, (IMF), International Bank for Reconstruction and Development (IBRD) and United Nations Conference on Trade and Development (UNCTAD). The role of the foreign direct investment (FDI) has been widely recognized as a growth-enhancing factor in the developing countries. The effects of FDI in the host economy are normally believed to be increase in the employment, increase in productivity, and increase in exports and, of course, increased pace of transfer of technology. This article analyzes the role of foreign direct investment and trade in promoting economic growth across selected developing countries and the interaction among FDI, trade, and economic growth. We examine data from 66 developing countries over the last three decades. Our results suggest that FDI, trade, human capital, and domestic investment are important sources of economic growth for developing countries. We find a strong positive interaction between FDI and trade in advancing economic growth. Our results also show that FDI stimulates domestic investment. A number of changes were approved on the FDI policy to remove the caps in most sectors. Industrial policy reforms have substantially reduced industrial licensing requirements, removed restrictions on expansion and facilitated easy access to foreign technology and foreign direct investment FDI. The impact of FDI on growth, or rather the lack, is not found to be dependent on stock of human capital. Some of the regressions used suggest that FDI is only growth enhancing in countries with low educational attainment. FDI remains significantly and positively linked with growth when controlling for inflation or government size, but FDI becomes insignificant when controlled for trade openness, black market premium or financial development. This paper revisits the FDI and economic growth relationship by examining the role FDI inflows play in promoting growth in the main economic sectors, namely, primary, manufacturing, and services. Often-mentioned benefits, such as transfers of technology and management know-how, introduction of new processes, and employee training tend to relate to the manufacturing sector rather than the agriculture or mining sectors. Most developing countries now consider FDI as an important source of development, but its economic effects are almost impossible to either predict or measure with precision. However, many empirical studies have shown significant role of FDI in economic growth of host developing countries, through its contribution in human resources development, technological transfer, capital formation and international trades. As a result, most developing countries recognize the potential value of FDI and have liberalized their investment regimes and engaged in investment promotion activities to attract various countries. India could become a major destination for FDI, one of the largest in the developing world. Inward and outward FDI stocks as a percentage of gross domestic products in the selected countries in Asia is depicted in. The role of foreign direct investment (FDI) has been widely recognized as a growth-enhancing factor in developing countries. FDI enables investment receiving countries to achieve investment levels beyond their own domestic saving. It has been a matter of great concern for many economists that how FDI affects economic growth of the host country. In a closed economy, with no access to foreign saving, investment is financed solely from domestic savings. Most developing countries now consider FDI as an important source of development, but its economic effects are almost impossible to either predict or measure with precision. However, many empirical studies have shown significant role of FDI in economic growth of host developing countries through its contribution in human resources development, technological transfer, capital formation and international trade. Foreign direct investment (FDI) has become a major source of capital flows in many developing nations. The study of the impacts, causes, and economic relationships of FDI has gained in popularity in the last decade. There is substantial agreement that FDI can contribute to economic growth and can result in technology transfers to developing countries. There is no doubt that foreign direct investment (FDI) is an important aspect of the recent wave of globalization. FDI provides much needed resources to developing countries such as capital, technology, managerial skills, entrepreneurial ability, brands, and access to markets. These are essential for developing countries to industrialize, develop, and create jobs attacking the poverty situation in their countries. Through FDI, foreign investors benefit from utilizing their assets and resources efficiently, while FDI networks.

OVERVIEW

Foreign Direct Investment or FDI is the process whereby residents of one country (the source country) acquires ownership of assets for the purpose of controlling the production, distribution, and other activities of a firm in another country (the host country). The international monetary fund's balance of payment manual defines FDI as an investment that is made to acquire a lasting interest in an enterprise operating in an economy other than that of the investor.

In India, Foreign Direct Investment Policy allows for investment only in case of the following form of investments:

- Through financial alliance
- Through joint schemes and technical alliance

- Through private placements or preferential allotments
- Though capital markets, via Euro issues

Foreign Direct Investment in India is not allowed under the following industrial sectors:

- Arms and ammunition
- Atomic Energy
- Coal and lignite
- Rail Transport
- Mining, chrome, gypsum, sulfur, gold, diamonds, copper, zinc

FDI In India Across Different Sectors Hotel and Tourism Hotels include restaurants, beach resorts and business ventures providing accommodation and food facilities to tourist. Tourism would include travel agencies, tour operators, transport facilities, leisure, entertainment, amusement sports and health, 100 per cent FDI is permitted for this sector through the automatic route.

Trading

For trading companies 100 per cent FDI is allowed for :

- Exports
- Bulk Imports
- Cash and Carry wholesale trading

Up to 100 per cent equity is allowed in the following sectors :

- Export Trading Companies
- Hotels and Tourism-related Projects
- Hospitals, Diagnostic Centers
- Shipping
- Deep Sea Fishing
- Oil Exploration
- Power
- Housing and Real Estate Development

- Highways, Bridges and Ports
- Sick Industrial Units
- Industries Requiring Compulsory Licensing
- Manganese, chrome, gypsum, sulfur, gold, diamonds, copper, zinc

A number of projects have been announced in areas such as electricity generation, distribution and transmission, as well as the development of roads and highways, with opportunities for Investment in India. Government of India recognizes the key role of Foreign Direct Investment (FDI) in economic development not only as an addition to domestic capital but also as an important source of technology and global best practices. The Government of India has put in place a liberal and transparent FDI policy.

FDI up to 100% is allowed under the automatic route in most sectors/activities. FDI policy in India is reckoned to be among the most liberal in emerging economies. FDI Policy permits FDI up to 100% from foreign/NRI investor without prior approval in most of the sectors including the services sector under automatic route. FDI in sectors/activities under automatic route does not require any prior approval either by the Government or the RBI.

- India is now the third most favored destination for Foreign Direct Investment (FDI), behind China and the USA, according to an AT Kearney survey that tracked investor confidence among global executives to determine their order of preferences.
- India's share of global FDI flows raised from 1.8 per cent in 1996 to 2.2 per cent in 1997.
- FDI in India in 1997-98 was lower at U.S. $ 5,025 million compared to U.S. $ 6,008 million in 1996-97 because of a decline in portfolio investment. Although foreign direct investment (FDI) increased by 18.6 per cent from U.S.$ 2,696 million in 1996-97 to U.S.$ 3,197 million in 1997-98
- International developments continue to affect capital flows into India in 1998-99 as well.

Mauritius, as in the previous two years, was the dominant source of FDI inflows in 1997-98. U.S.A. and S. Korea were, respectively, the second and third large sources of FDI. Over the years, FDI inflow in the country is increasing. However, India has tremendous potential for absorbing greater flow of FDI in the coming years. Serious efforts are being made to attract greater inflow of FDI in the country by taking several actions both on policy and implementation front. Since the last publication of the Manual in November 2002, Foreign Investment Promotion Board has been shifted to Department of Economic Affairs, Ministry of Finance and Company Affairs.

RECENT TRENDS IN FDI

India is the third most attractive foreign direct investment destination in the world, behind China as number one and the United States as number two. In 2008, India was ranked number two but slipped to the number three spot given the economic downturn and the surge of investments by Chinese and Indian firms acquiring American companies. According to India's Department of Industrial Policy and Promotion, despite the global recession and liquidity crunch, the Indian economy recorded an 11 percent increase in FDI in 2008-09, with sectors like chemicals and telecommunication experiencing robust growth of 227 percent and 103 percent respectively. Foreign Direct Investments (FDI) in the real estate sector in India would contribute towards making the sector more organized. Besides increasing professionalism in the sector, it would bring in advanced technology and help in the creation of healthy and competitive market environment for both domestic and foreign investors. India is poised as the most favorite FDI destination in South East Asia, outpacing China. With the opening up of different sectors to add to its economic growth, India's FDI inflow in the first half of this fiscal is an upwards of Rs. 11,460 crore. India has witnessed significant rise in foreign direct investment inflows in January 2010 as compared to December 2009. According to the latest data released by Department of Industrial Policy and Promotion (DIPP), January 2010 witnessed inflows of US $ 2,042 million as compared to US $ 1,542 million in the month of December 2009. The Indian

Rapid FDI Growth in India from 2000-04 to 2010

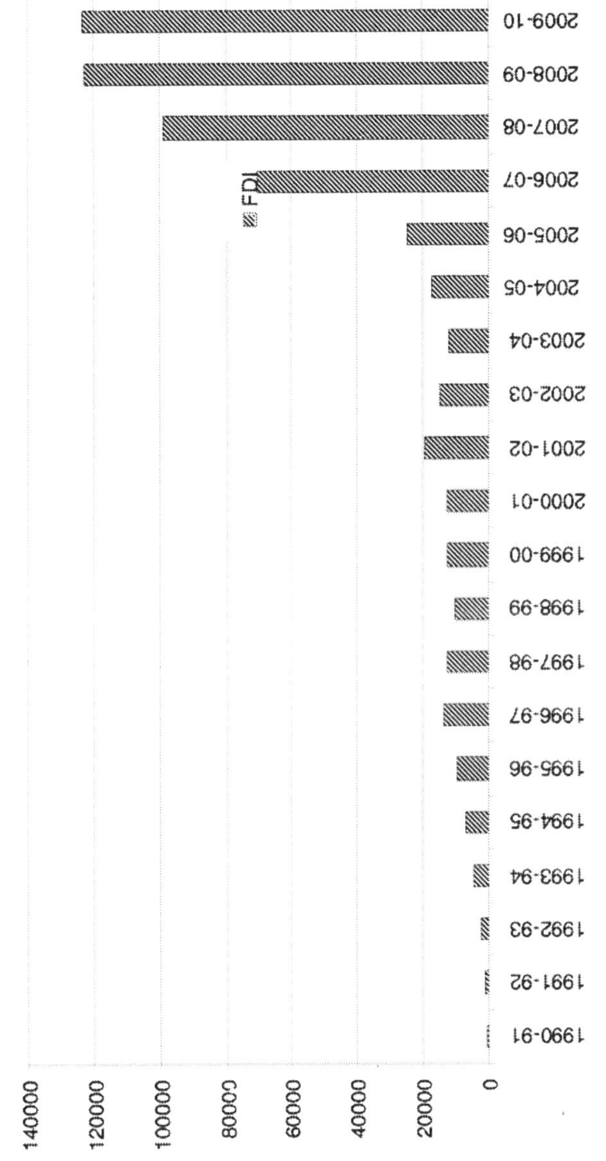

www.dipp.nic.in (Department of Industrial Promotion and Policy).

diaspora has sustained considerable faith in the investment dynamics of the economy. As per the latest FDI estimates released by Department of Industrial Policy and Promotion, the Non-Resident Indians (NRIs) have provided FDI inflows worth about US $ 41.78 million (Rs. 1,948.03 million) in the month of December 2009 through the automatic route, almost 2.71 per cent of the total FDI inflows in the same month. Total NRI FDI inflows through the period April-December 2009-10 stood at US $ 320.05 million (Rs. 15,325.77 million), which is about 1.53 per cent of the total FDI inflows in the said period, according to the latest SIA Newsletter published by the Department of Industrial Policy and Promotion. Global FDI inflows grew for the third consecutive year in 2006, reaching over US $ 1.23 trillion, according to the latest estimates by the UNCTAD.(3) This performance was impressive, with FDI inflows rising by 34.3% in 2006 compared to 28.9% in 2005, and rising to US $ 1.23 trillion from US $ 916.3 billion in 2005 .At the same time, the data for 2004 was revised upward from a previously reported US $ 695 billion, to US $ 710.8 billion reflecting an upward adjustment to inflows to the U.S. and Euro zone countries. The latter adjustment means that global FDI has began to recover a year earlier than initially reported (i.e., in 2004 rather than in 2005) after declining each year during 2001-03. With this very strong performance, global FDI inflows in 2006 fell just short of the peak of US $ 1.4 trillion in 2000. EME inflows of US $ 461.9 billion for 2006 are just slightly below the previous pinnacle of US $ 481.9 billion achieved in 1999. However, since the rate of growth of FDI inflows to developed countries was significantly stronger than that to EMEs in both 2005 and 2006, the latter's share of total global inflows declined to 38% in 2006, down from 44% in 2005 and a peak of 48% in 2004. There are other potential benefits to host countries from encouraging capital inflows:

(i) Foreign firms bring superior technology. The extent of benefits to host countries depends on whether the technology spreads freely to existing firms.

(ii) Foreign investment increases competition in the host economy. The entry of a new firm in a non-tradable sector increases the industry output and reduces the domestic price, leading to a net improvement in welfare.

(iii) Foreign investment typically results in increased domestic investment. In an analysis of panel data for 58 developing countries, Bosworth and Collins (1999) find that about half of each dollar of capital inflow translates into an increase in domestic investment. Their findings suggest a foreign resource transfer equal to 53-69 percent of the inflow of financial capital. The remainder is diverted into reserve accumulation or capital outflows. However, when the capital inflows take the form of FDI, their results suggest a near one-for-one relationship between the FDI and domestic investment.

(iv) Foreign investment gives advantages in terms of export market access arising from economies of scale in marketing of foreign firms or from their ability to gain market access abroad. Besides their contributions through joint ventures, foreign firms can serve as catalysts for other domestic exporters. In an empirical analysis, the probability a domestic plant will export was found to be positively correlated with proximity to multinational firms. One implication is that governments may encourage potential exporters to locate near each other by creating export processing zones, conferring special benefits such as duty-free imports of inputs, subsidized infrastructure, or tax holidays, to help reduce costs for domestic firms of breaking into foreign markets. Export processing zones are a useful transitional device in the absence of broad-based reform, but may introduce spatial distortions when governments locate the zones in inappropriate places.

(v) Foreign investment can aid in bridging a host country foreign exchange gap. Two gaps may exist in the economy: insufficient saving to support capital accumulation to achieve a given growth target; and insufficient foreign exchange to transform domestic to foreign resources. If investment requires imported inputs, then domestic saving may not guarantee

> growth if the saving cannot be converted to foreign exchange to acquire imports. Capital inflows help ensure that foreign exchange will be available to purchase imports for investment.

Total NRI FDI inflows through the period April-December 2009-10 stood at US $ 320.05 million. In the years since the bursting of the housing bubble, the personal saving rate has trended up from around 1% to around 6%, while the ratio of household debt to disposable income has dropped from 130% to 118%. Changes over time in the availability of credit to households can explain 90% of the variance of the saving rate since the mid-1960s, including the recent uptrend, according to a simple empirical model. According to India's Department of Industrial Policy and Promotion, despite the global recession and liquidity crunch, the Indian economy recorded an 11 percent increase in FDI in 2008-09, with sectors like chemicals and telecommunication experiencing robust growth of 227 percent and 103 percent respectively. India has witnessed significant rise in foreign direct investment inflows in January 2010 as compared to December 2009. According to the latest data released by Department of Industrial Policy and Promotion (DIPP), January 2010 witnessed inflows of US $ 2,042 million as compared to US $ 1,542 million in the month of December 2009. The Indian Diaspora has sustained considerable faith in the investment dynamics of the economy. As per the latest FDI estimates released by Department of Industrial Policy and Promotion, the Non-Resident Indians (NRIs) have provided FDI inflows worth about US $ 41.78 million (Rs. 1,948.03 million) in the month of December 2009 through the automatic route, almost 2.71 pe cent of the total FDI inflows in the same month. The states of Karnataka and Gujarat are now preparing for major events to be held for attracting investments into the State for different investment sectors. These states are extending all cooperation to investors through their Global Investor Meet in June 2010 and Golden Jubilee celebrations starting May, respectively. These events are expected to garner major inflows from investors; both domestic as well as overseas Conventional wisdom has it that Foreign Direct Investment (FDI) flows to India have not been commensurate with her economic potential and performance. India has only very emerged as a destination for FDI since the pre-reform years were marked with a sharp antipathy toward foreign capital unless under certain conditions. With FDI becoming a significant component of investment only, accounting practices in India lagged behind international norms. This paper, however, identifies the quality of FDI as more important than its quantity. Work has argued that high Chinese FDI might well be concealing difficulties. The paper argues that raising investment is more important than just raising the FDI component of such investment. Most of the developing and least developed countries worldwide equally participated in the process of direct investment activities.

- FDI inflows to Latin American and Caribbean region increased by 11 percent on an average in comparison to previous year.
- In African region FDI inflows made a record in the year 2006.
- Flow of FDI to South, East and South East Asia and Oceania maintained an upward trend.
- Both Turkey and oil rich Gulf States continued to attract maximum FDI inflows.
- United States Economy, being world's largest economy also attracted larger FDI inflows from Euro Zone and Japan.

Foreign direct investment flows declined sharply in 2001 and continued their decline in 2002, decreasing further by 27 per cent. In 2002, the volume of FDI inflows reached about US$ 534 billion, which contrasts with US$ 735 billion in 2001, and is equivalent to a third of the US$ 1,492 .billion peak in 2000). A major factor behind this decline is the slowdown in the world economy, which has reduced world demand and accentuated and accelerated the global restructuring process of major MNEs in sectors characterized by excess capacity. The decline in FDI in 2001 also reflects the aftermath of the 11 September 2001 incident. The decline in 2001 was mainly concentrated in developed countries as a result of a considerable drop in cross-border mergers and acquisitions (M&As). FDI inflows to developed countries decreased by 59 per cent, compared with 14 per cent in developing economies. In 2002, similar trends continued with a major decline in developed countries and a smaller decline in developing countries. FDI in 2001 was higher than that in 1998, after which dramatic increases. Now-a-days, virtually all countries are actively seeking to attract FDI, because of the expected favorable effect on income generation from capital inflows, advanced technology, management skills and market know-how. It would be useful to review the key determinants and factors of FDI based on the theories of international investment factors associated with the extent and pattern of FDI in developing host countries: attractiveness of the economic conditions in host countries. The review of host country determinants is closely linked with the role of national policies and especially the liberalization of policies, a key factor in globalization, as FDI determinants. Location-specific determinants have a crucial influence on a host country's inflow of FDI. FDI reached to $ 174 billion and $ 100 billion in services sector accounting for 64 percent and 96 percent of their FDI stocks, respectively. In Singapore, financial services—foreign investment holding companies—attracted $ 98 billion of FDI flows, 36 percent of FDI stock in the country. In Hong Kong, China. On the other hand, manufacturing continues to be the dominant sector in other Asian developing countries-China, Malaysia, Taiwan and Thailand, even if services FDI has increased over the years. In China, manufacturing sector that received an aggregate of $ 240 billion FDI between 1997 and 2004 accounts 66 percent of the FDI flows.

There are a number of popular misconceptions about FDI:

- FDI does not necessarily imply control of the enterprise, since only a 10 percent ownership is required to establish a direct investment relationship.
- FDI does not constitute a "10 percent ownership" or more) by a group of "unrelated" investors domiciled in the same foreign country—FDI involves only one investor or a "related group" of investors in one or more countries.

With the integration of international capital average of 13

percent a year during 1990–97.1 Driven by large cross-border mergers and acquisitions (M&A), these inflows increased by an average of nearly 50 percent a year during 1998–2000, reaching a record $ 1.5 trillion in 2000. Inflows declined to $ 729 billion in 2001, mostly as a result of the sharp drop in cross-border M&A among the industrial countries, coinciding with the correction in world equity markets. Worldwide, the value of cross-border M&A declined from the record $1.1 trillion in 2000 to about $ 600 billion in 2001. The industrial countries have long dominated the FDI inflows and outflows and accounted for 94 percent of outflows and over 70 percent of inflows in 2001. Inflows of FDI to developing countries grew by an average of 23 percent a year during 1990-2000. In 2001, these inflows declined by 13 percent to $ 215 billion, largely reflecting reduced inflows into Hong Kong Special Administrative Region, Brazil, and Argentina.

ROLE OF FDI IN GROWTH AND DEVELOPMENT

Foreign Direct Investment (FDI) has emerged as the most important source of external resource flows to developing countries over the 1990s and has become a significant part of capital formation in the developing countries despite their share in global distribution of FDI continuing to remain small or even declining. The effects of FDI in the host economy are normally believed to be increase in the employment, increase in productivity, and increase in exports and, of course, increased pace of transfer of technology. The foreign direct investment (FDI) has been widely recognized as a growth-enhancing factor in the developing countries. FDI in ASEAN countries suggests clearly that foreign firms have played a leading role in successful export-oriented development strategies. At the same time, however, there is general consensus that the presence of foreign investors has not always contributed greatly to indigenous capabilities. The potential advantages of the FDI on the host economy are it facilitates the use and exploitation of local raw-materials, it introduces modern techniques of management and marketing, it eases the access to new technologies. Foreign inflows could be used for financing current account deficits, finance flows in form of FDI do not generate repayment of principal and interests, it increases the stock of human capital. While few would disagree strongly with this assessment, the question still remains of what host countries could have done differently and what should be done now. Because attracting foreign investors has now become more important than ever as a policy priority, it may be an opportune moment to reassess policy approaches to inward investment in order to improve the linkages with the local economy in the future. Many of the policies adopted in the ASEAN towards foreign investors are designed, implicitly or explicitly, to develop indigenous capabilities. These include any or all of the following requirements, local joint venture partners, divestiture of foreign control after a certain period of time, local content levels which force investors to purchase a high share of inputs locally, expatriate personnel limits, including on the board of directors, and compulsory licensing and other forms of mandatory technology transfers. The ASEAN countries have adopted most of these strategies at different points in time. As we have tried to show throughout this paper, empirical research on the contribution of FDI to the growth process of developing economies remains ambiguous. The emerging FDI literature stipulates that the relationship between FDI and growth is highly heterogeneous across countries. Economic development is an all-encompassing concept. It centers on economic and social progress, but also entails many different aspects that are not easily quantified, such as political freedom, social justice, and environmental soundness. Without a doubt, all these matters combine to contribute to an overall high standard of living. However, empirical evidence has amply demonstrated that all these varied elements of economic development correlate with economic growth.

THE CONTRIBUTION OF FDI TO CAPITAL FORMATION

As already mentioned FDI does not necessarily lead to fixed investment but represents one way to finance it. Accordingly, the relation of FDI to Gross Fixed Capital Formation should not be interpreted as the share which foreign investors contributed to building capital stocks but it must be understood as an indicator of how important foreign investors are in financing fixed investment. Even bearing in mind this caveat the ratio is difficult to interpret. Firstly, FDI may represent investment in the financial sector that does not lead to the formation of fixed capital. Striking as the rise in the importance of FDI may seem in host countries' resource flows, FDI is only part of the total financing by foreign investors in host countries. At the same time that foreign companies mobilize resources within their own corporate systems, their affiliates can also raise funds through bonds, loans, and equity issuances. To the extent that these sources are in the international capital markets, they increase the total inflows of foreign financial resources for development. Indeed, as data for United States transnational corporations suggest, the flows of external resources to host countries due to the presence of foreign enterprises often double FDI flow alone.

IMPACT OF FDI ON SKILL AND TECHNOLOGY

FDI may play an important role in closing the technology gap between the ACs and the EU if it is associated with a transfer of skills and technology. Whereas technology flows are analyzed in quite a number of studies, we will come to them later, flows of skills are often neglected in the analyses of the role of multinational enterprises in development. One exception is the 1999 World Investment Report, where a summary can be found of the discussion of how FDI might influence skills in the recipient countries). It shows that the interaction of FDI and skills is rather complex. Investors might be interested in undertaking some form of training, "at the minimum to ensure that technologies in use are deployed efficiently". Nigeria needs to strive more in order to attract FDI because of its acknowledged advantages of transferring technology and as a tool of economic development. The obvious benefits the country stands to gain as a result are summarized as follows:

- Facilitating Technology Spillover
- Encouraging Innovation

- Allowing Technology Adoption
- Developing Local Human Capital.

FDI AND REGION DEVELOPMENT

Recognizing the importance of FDI in the foreign investors will also have an important impact on regional cohesion. For most countries, no information on the location of foreign investment by regions is available. Detailed data are provided by Hungary, Lithuania, and Latvia, the two latter being admittedly two of the smaller countries analyzed, so that regional effects are not typical for all ACs. For Poland, only a regional breakdown of the most regions can improve their attraction of FDI. Analyzing the location pattern of FDI across European regions, we find a number of significant regional attraction factors, good infrastructure and accessibility; a highly educated regional workforce and a high level of spending on R&D attract FDI.

REGIONAL POLICY FACTORS FOR FDI

A highly educated regional workforce (skill effect) :

- A high level of spending on RandD (innovation effect)
- Strong regional clusters (industry specialization effect)
- Penetration of new technologies (ICT effect)
- Infrastructure and accessibility (access effect)
- A well-functioning investment promotion agency
- Regional economic strategies
- FDI incentives

FOREIGN TRADE INDICATORS

Export

India bans the export of such products as wildlife products, certain wood products, and chemical wood pulp. In addition, India places special restrictions on the export of some sensitive products. In 2009, in order to fight against the financial crisis, the Indian government adopted a series of policies to promote exports, including several economic stimulus packages, foreign trade supplementary policy 2009, and "foreign trade policy, 2009-2014", etc. In addition, the India Government also issued corresponding export administration measures Exports during August, 2010 were valued at US $ 16644 million (Rs. 77509 crore) which was 22.5 per cent higher in Dollar terms (18.0 per cent higher in Rupee terms) than the level of US $ 13586 million (Rs. 65670 crore) during August, 2009. Cumulative value of exports for the period April-August 2010 was US $ 85273 million (Rs. 392811 crore) as against US $ 66326 million (Rs. 322424 crore) registering a growth of 28.6 per cent in Dollar terms and 21.8 per cent in Rupee terms over the same period last year. India's exports during October, 2010 were valued at US $ 17960 million (Rs. 79763 crore) which was 21.3 per cent higher in Dollar terms (15.3 per cent higher in Rupee terms) than the level of US $ 14806 million (Rs. 69175 crore) during October 2009. Cumulative value of exports for the period April-October 2010 was US $ 121394 million (Rs. 556162 crore) as against US $ 95756 million (Rs. 462437 crore) registering a growth of 26.8 per cent in Dollar terms and 20.3 per cent in Rupee terms over the same period last year.

Import

The Ministry of Commerce and Industry of India is the major government body administering import and export. India has a complicated administration system for its imports, which fall into four major categories: (1) unrestricted imports, for which only the filling of a form of "Open General License" is required; (2) prohibited imports, such as wildlife products, ivories, animal stomach lining, and animal oil and fat; (3) restricted imports, for which a special license issued by the Directorate General of Foreign Trade (DGFT) is needed, including certain chemical and poultry products; and (4) exclusive imports, i.e., products that can be imported only by state-owned companies at a time and in a quantity as approved by the Cabinet, including petroleum products, some drugs and some bulk grains. Imports during August 2010 were valued at US $ 29679 million (Rs. 138211 crore) representing a growth of 32.2 per cent in Dollar terms (27.4 per cent in Rupee terms) over the level of imports valued at US $ 22449 million (Rs. 108506 crore) in August 2009. Cumulative value of imports for the period April-August, 2010 was US $ 141894 million (Rs. 653828 crore) as against US $ 106605 million (Rs. 518024 crore) registering a growth of 33.1 per cent in Dollar terms and 26.2 per cent in Rupee terms over the same period last year. India's imports during October, 2010 were valued at US $ 27689 million (Rs. 122970 crore) representing a growth of 6.8 per cent in Dollar terms (1.5 per cent in Rupee terms) over the level of imports valued at US $ 25936 million (Rs. 121175 crore) in October, 2009. Cumulative value of imports for the period April-October, 2010 was US $ 194167 million (Rs. 889827 crore) as against US $ 154067 million (Rs. 743470 crore) registering a growth of 26.0 per cent in Dollar terms and 19.7 per cent in Rupee terms over the same period last years. Oil imports during October, 2010 were valued at US $ 8410 million which was 0.3 per cent higher than oil imports valued at US $ 8389 million in the corresponding period last year. Oil imports during April-October 2010 were valued at US$ 57125 million which was 24.6 per cent higher than the oil imports of US $ 45865 million in the corresponding period last year.

CONCLUSION

The economy of India is the eleventh largest economy in the world by nominal GDP and the fourth largest by purchasing power parity (PPP). As the fourth-largest economy in the world in PPP terms, India is a preferred destination for foreign direct investments (FDI). FDI remains significantly and positively linked with growth when controlling for inflation or government size, but FDI becomes insignificant when controlled for trade openness, black market premium or financial development. This paper revisits the FDI and economic growth relationship by examining the role FDI inflows play in promoting growth in the main economic sectors, namely primary, manufacturing, and services. Foreign Direct Investment or FDI is the process whereby residents of one country (the source country) acquires ownership of assets for the purpose of controlling the production, distribution, and other activities of a firm in another country. The key role of Foreign Direct Investment (FDI) in economic development not only as an addition to domestic capital but also as an important source of technology and global best practices. The Government of India has put in place a liberal and transparent FDI policy. Foreign Direct Investments (FDI) in the real estate sector in India would contribute towards making the sector more organized. Besides increasing professionalism in the sector, it would bring in advanced technology and help in the creation of healthy and competitive market environment for both domestic and foreign investors. Foreign Direct Investment (FDI) has emerged as the most important source of external resource flows to developing countries over the 1990s and has become a significant part of capital formation in the developing countries despite their share in global distribution of FDI continuing to remain small or even declining. The effects of FDI in the host economy are normally believed to be increase in the employment, increase in productivity, and increase in exports and, of course, increased pace of transfer of technology. The foreign direct investment (FDI) has been widely recognized as a growth-enhancing factor in the developing countries. The FDI in ASEAN countries presented above suggests clearly that foreign firms have played a leading role in successful export-oriented development strategies. Most developing countries now consider FDI as an important source of development, but its economic effects are almost impossible to either predict or measure with precision. However, many empirical studies have shown significant role of FDI in economic growth of host developing countries through its contribution in human resources development, technological transfer, capital formation and international trade. Foreign direct investment (FDI) has become a major source of capital flows in many developing nations.

References

Alfaro, Laura, (2003). FDI and Growth: Does the sector matter?

Atique, Zeeshan, Mohsin Husnain Ahmed, Usman Azhar, The Impact of FDI on Economic Growth Under Foreign Trade Regimes: A Case Study of Pakistan.

Ayadi, Sunday Folorunso, FDI and Economic Growth in Nigeria.

Blomstorm, Magnus, (2006), Study on FDI and Regional Development, Final Report.

Brooke, H. Douglas (2003), Emma Xiaogin Fan, Lea Rsumulory, Foreign Direct Investment in Developing Asia: Trends, Effects, and likely Issues for the forthcoming WTO Negotiations".

Essen (2001), The Impact of trade and FDI on Concession (preparation of the second concession report).

Falki Nuzhat, Impact of FDI on Economic Growth in Pakistan.

Foreign Market Access Report, 2010.

Hout, Henri, Bezuiden (2008), Wim Naude, FDI and Trade in Southern African Development Community.

Jayachandra, G., A. Seilan (2010), *International Research Journal of Finance and Economics*.

Kohpaiboon, Archanun: Trade Regime and FDI-Growth Nexus: A Case Study of Thailand.

Makki, S., Shiva, Impact of FDI and Trade on Economic Growth.

Patterson, Neil (2004), Marie Montanjees, John Motala, Foreign Direct Investment (Trends, Data, Availability, Concepts and Recording Practices).

Press release on India's Foreign Trade 2010. Ministry of Commerce Industry.

Sun, Xiaolun (2002), FDI and Economic Development What. Do the States Need to Do?.

Thomsen Stophen, 1999/1, Southeast Asia: The Role of FDI Policies in Development.

Wasantha, P.P.A., Athukorala, The Impact of FDI for Economic Growth : A Case Study in Srilanka.

Wu, Xiadong (2001), Impact of FDI on Relative Return to skill.

www.mbaknol.com

www.papers.ssrn.com

CHAPTER

18

The Mirage of Foreign Direct Investment in Higher Education

NANDITA MAJUMDAR

INTRODUCTION

Food, clothing and shelter are considered as the basic needs of a human being. Education became the fourth necessity for man along with the basic needs. Education has gained its own place with the pace of time in every society. It indeed proved to be a powerful tool to combat the cut-throat competition that man faces in every juncture of life. India is always a learning hub of many cultures, epics, Vedas and so on. Still there was a need to understand the importance of education in human life in India.

The education sector in India is one of the most important sectors, as it holds the key to social and economic development of the country. The Indian government formulated the National Policy on Education in 1986 and modified it in 1992. The major objectives of the policy are to empower women, correct the regional and social imbalances that are there in the country, and also to ensure the development of the minorities of India. Later on many organizations and quality assurance certification institutes were developed to improve the quality of education in India. Some of them were the introduction of UGC, AICTE, NAAC, ISO Certification, etc. As per the current Union Budget allocation of 2011-12, an amount of Rs. 52,057 crore is set aside for the education.

Education institutions in India have witnessed dramatically rapid growth, by doubling the number of universities since 1990-91 and the enrolments being more than double at the expense of quality, decreased flexibility in the course design, poor combination of knowledge and increasing rate of unavailability of laboratories, journals, field work, etc. An average Indian graduate is poorly compared with their equivalent in other developed or for those matter even developing countries. This led to both the ends of the quality, on one hand it enhanced the quality of education by providing standards matching international universities and on the other hand it led to poor first hand information of the country and its economic structure they are living in.

FDI Inflows to Education sector in India are expected to increase, as many foreign educational institutions have submitted proposals to make investments in the sector. FDI Inflows to Education sector in India are expected to come from Egmont Imaginations which has submitted a proposal to establish 200 play schools in the country. Further FDI Inflows to Education sector in India are expected to come from major American universities such as, Georgia Institute of Technology, Yale, and Standford, as they are eager to establish greenfield campuses in the country.

INDIAN SCENARIO OF HIGHER EDUCATION

India is the third largest higher education system in the world after China and the USA. In terms of the number of institutions India is the largest higher education system in the world with 19,227 institutions (602 universities and 18,625 colleges), of these, there are 63 unaided deemed universities with enrolment of 60,000 students, and 7650 unaided private colleges with enrolment of 31,50,000 students. Even with such a huge system in place, higher education in India is in a miserable condition. This poses a severe constraint on the supply of qualified manpower. Even after six decades of independence, higher education is not accessible to the poorest groups of the population. Hardly seven or eight per cent of the population in the age group of 17-23 years is enrolled in the institutions of higher education. This obliviously had shifted the interest of the parents and students to private education and foreign universities.

Financial constraints with exploding enrolments and very high demand from primary and secondary education are considered to be a big drawback for the higher education system. The growth rate of government institutions in the last five years has been around 5 per cent against the private sector's 75 per cent. The sources of funding for these institutions were expected from government, non-government sectors and other sources, such as Voluntary donation, endowments, etc. The sources which could potentially provide approximately 20 per cent of the funds is currently funding barely 3per cent of the cost of education.

BASIS OF FDI IN HIGHER EDUCATION

The implications of FDI into higher education is not a simple question as it has its bearing not only in the higher education, but also on the education sector and more broadly on the whole process of creation of knowledge.

The policy of FDI in education services is through involuntarily route. In the lack of any policy in this sector, foreign capital may flow in or out by means of offshore foreign institutions' campus or through the tie-ups with the private partner in India. There is also no edge for foreign capital investment in education services. Since the foreign education providers are coming in free-for-all manner, an unregulated inflow of foreign capital particularly in education sector is a cause of great concern. It is now felt that FDI in education must be guided by certain norms and direction, as it is an insightful sector and its implications should be tested before any FDI policy.

Foreign education institutions should be permitted in with policies to guarantee the incentive for good institutions and disincentives for sub-standard institutions to coming to India, and all conventions that apply to domestic institutions should also be appropriate to foreign institutions.

KEY ARGUMENTS

- If international educational institutions come to India, then students would be able to get foreign education in India, cheaper.
- The seats are limited in the Indian educational institutions and so foreign direct investment in the educational sector would result in more opportunities for the Indian students.
- The Indian students will get libraries and labs that are of world class standards.
- The setting up of international educational institutions in India will attract students from the neighboring countries to come and study in those institutions in India and this will help the country to become an important destination for education.
- It will enable the Indian students to come in touch with the best professors from across the globe. And avail world class research facilities
- FDI in education will also lead to higher number of Indian students getting jobs in internationally acclaimed companies.
- It will attract the topmost universities across the world to set-up their branches in the country.

THE MIRAGE OF FDI

The next major challenge that arises here is whether the FDI can solve the financial challenges and provide qualitative higher education?

This question is a debatable one; many experts opined that FDI in education sector is going to create miracles whereas a part of the experts said that it is nothing but a mirage. The opinions differed from academicians, educational experts and political parties. The pros and cons of FDI in higher education were seen both in micro as well as the macro-level.

The future scenario in the education sector, after the General Agreement on Trade in Services (GATS) became operational, is highly uncertain. Prof Sudhanshu Bhushan, Senior Fellow, National Institute for Educational Planning and Administration [NIEPA], in a FICCI background paper, pointed out that, "The most important challenge is not just to guarantee the expansion of education, but also to improve its quality and link education to society's needs and development goals."

The first challenge or differed opinion points on, whether FDI meant to invest really in higher education institution in India. The answer is NO; it is observed that one of the foreign institutions has invested any money in this country in the last 10 years but offered around 150 foreign programmes. A foreign investor is interested in selling his educational products such as courseware, some of which are copyrighted offering what are called "twinning programmes" or are "franchising" their degree programmes. Here the Motive seems to be only commercial. In the beginning Indian higher education sector felt that the twinning programmes, that is programmes that offer part of the study in India and the other part of the study in foreign institutions is a gift in disguise. Later it was realized that it is just a trick to attract the institutions and students.

The Association of Indian Universities thus has laid down guidelines for twinning arrangement to ensure genuine partnerships and protect consumers, these guidelines are often violated. Degrees awarded under such programmes are not recognised in India.There are also instances of false marketing of foreign programmes, wherein institutions claim to have resources that they don't really possess or give employment guarantees when there's no international equivalence of degrees. At times, students in twinning programmes have not been able to obtain visas to study abroad at the foreign partner's campus.

In all this issues the main targets are the students with lots of dreams to be big. The students who enroll in such institutions are left with no choice. Therefore, they settle for some B or C grade foreign universities. The next argument is related to the quality provided by the foreign institutions. It is believed that foreign institutions can bring quality programs with high standards. Besides, updated curriculum, teaching-learning processes, evaluation of processes may be internalized within educational institution in India. It may also reap the benefits of improved managerial and organizational skills to run the institutions. It is also argued that FDI could promote competitiveness in the education system as a whole. But it is observed that quality is maintained only in certain specific sectors, where FDI takes place, whereas in mass education sector the spillover effect of quality may not take place. In fact, it might lead to dualism in education. Another issue related to FDI in higher education is that, it is drawing as a source of investment or a source by which foreign currency can get into the country, which leads to profit motive. The traditional concept of education considered to be non-tradable is changing. It is the government's responsibility to provide education facilities to its citizens. India has seen a drastic fall in the allocation of funds for higher education step-by-step. To raise the participation rate for 7 percent to 10 percent targeted by the end of Tenth Plan is also an uphill task in view of impending financial shortage. It may be argued that FDI may be used as a source of investment at least in some selected sectors, but not in higher education.

CONCLUSION

As business week once stated that 'unlike China, India's significant cheap labour is not a pool of factory workers, but a huge crop of scientists'. Globalisation has made the world very small place to live in; therefore, we cannot deny the truth of the competition related to quality and quantity in case of skilled labour in the market. FDI is just a chance to enhance the potential upbringing of the competition in the labour market. Though 100 percent FDI seems to be a mirage in the hottest desert, still it can leap a thousand trees and a pond of water with a little effort in investing the foreign money in the institutions.

India can follow the guidelines of China related to FDI. In China, the entry of foreign institutions is by invitation only and the conditions under which the foreign educational provider can come to China include:

1. Foreign institutions must partner with Chinese institutions.
2. Partnerships must not seek profit as their objective.
3. No less than half the members of the governing body of the institution must be Chinese citizens.
4. The post of president or the equivalent must be held by a Chinese citizen residing in China.
5. The basic language of instruction should be Chinese
6. Tuition fees may not be raised without approval.

In Malaysia also, foreign institutions can enter only by invitation from the Ministry of Education. Such an institution has to establish a Malaysian company with majority Malaysian ownership and has to be registered with the government. Permission for each course is required. Courses should be accredited and approved in the home country and recognized by an appropriate professional association in Malaysia. In Singapore also, foreign institutions can enter by invitation and only elite universities are invited. Their collaboration with local partner is permitted, but they cannot use terms like university, college and academy. Applications for setting up higher education institutions are considered on a case-to-case basis. All countries of the world impose at least some restrictions in relation foreign educational providers. Barriers are most extensive for commercial presence in educational services. Authorities must study the system of regulation and accreditation of Educational institutions in foreign countries. Our own accreditation system and laws for foreign institutions must be developed taking into account the treatment given to them in their respective countries.

India must also frame such guidelines to the foreign investors. As citizens of India, we have to ensure that the government takes care of public interests and act to protect public services like education from the predatory elements that preach the ideology of the marketplace as the solution to every issue. The approach of the government is focusing on short-term market concerns. The immediate need is to plug the gap between opportunities in industry and the availability of matching skills. The future of higher education services will also be shaped by domestic factors, including the domestic regulatory framework and the state of the domestic education system in terms of quantity, quality, costs, infrastructure and finances.

The major aspect needed here is the adequate infrastructure and more effective registration and certification system. This would prevent unapproved institutions from partnering, protect and inform consumers, enable good quality foreign institutions to enter the Indian market.

References

Anandakrishnan, M., 2006, "FDI and False Hopes", *Frontline*, Vol. 23, No. 23.

Konkan Sharma, "FDI in Higher Education: Aspirations and Reality", *Mainstream*, Vol. XLV, No. 25.

Navdeep Kumar, FDI in higher education in India: Issues and Concerns, *Political Economy Journal of India*, July-December, 2009.

Pawan Agrawal, "Higher Education and the Labour Market in India", ICRIER, New Delhi.

Vijender Sharma, Indian Higher Education: Commodification and Foreign Direct Investment, *The Marxist*, Vol. XXIII, No. 2, April to June, 2007.

Vishwanathan, S., "FDI and False Hopes", *Frontline*, December 1, 2006.

CHAPTER

19

Need of Financial Inclusion for Poverty Alleviation and GDP Growth

RAMESH KUMAR MIRYALA

ABSTRACT

Since last three decades the major objective of policy-makers is to remove poverty from India. Many programmes and policies were started at the grass-root level. But results were not very encouraging. After liberalization India's GDP growth witnessed an encouraging change. It was hoped that it will be a solution for the problem. But due to some basic reasons at grass-root level, results were not very overwhelming. It has also been realized by the policy-makers that increase in GDP alone is not the solution of the deep rooted problem of poverty. Growth is necessary but not sufficient for the poverty eradication. Inclusive growth can be a solution for poverty removal. In the 1990s government of India started many programmes which were specially made for enhancing the income level of the poor masses. Consequently, all the major initiatives of government - in agricultural and rural development, in industry and urban development, in infrastructure and services, in education and health care—sought to promote 'inclusive growth'. It is apparent from the study that Inclusive growth is necessary for sustainable development and equitable distribution of wealth and prosperity. The success of poverty alleviation programmes can be achieved in real sense, when common man is also a part of growth.

INTRODUCTION

India is the largest democracy in the world, something to be very proud of, but, does this democracy really offer the average Indian the choice that it ought to? Rapid economic growth over the past decade in India was the main driver of poverty reduction, but; poor face multiple deprivations due to the interaction of economic, political and social processes. Beyond the lack of income, the multidimensional concept of poverty refers to disadvantages that those afflicted are subjected to when trying to access productive resources such as land, credit and services (e.g. health and education), to vulnerability and powerlessness as well as social exclusion. A 10 percentage points drop in poverty levels, other things being equal, can increase economic growth by one percent and reduce investment by up to eight percent of GDP.[1] This is so because the poor are in no position to engage in many of the profitable activities that stimulate investment and growth, thus creating a vicious circle in which low growth results in high poverty and high poverty, in turn, results in low growth.

DEFINITION OF THE POVERTY

The international poverty line has been recalibrated at $ 1.25 a day, using new data on purchasing power parties; earlier it was merely $ 1 a day. As per the World Bank report the new data change our view of poverty in the world, there are more people—extremely poor people and the incidence of poverty reaches farther into middle-income countries. By the new measurements 1.4 billion people are living in extreme poverty more than one quarter of the population of developing countries.[2] Human Development Index (HDI) is probably the most widely recognized and used composite measure embodying other welfare dimensions (i.e., on health and education) apart from income. Starting in 1998, UNDP also began releasing estimates of a Human Poverty Index, a measure closely related to the HDI.[3] India was the first country in the world to define poverty as the total per capita expenditure of the lowest expenditure class, which consumed 2400 kcal/day in rural and 2100 kcal/day in urban areas and attempt to provide comprehensive package of essential goods and services to people below the poverty line category. A recent World Bank study estimates that about 47 percent of children below 3 years in India are undernourished. Persisting malnutrition has a severally debilitating effect on human development and this has serious implications for economic growth in general.

INCIDENCE OF POVERTY

Nearly one-fourth of India's population is below poverty line. In terms of incidence of poverty measured in India on the basis of consumption expenditure, there is a definite improvement over the years, both in rural and urban areas. There is about 7 to 8 percentage points decline in poverty ratio in 2004-05 over 1993-94 and improvement being more predominant in the rural areas.

There are several factors affect the extent and depth of poverty and hunger; some of them have overwhelming impacts under the Indian setting. An effective water policy and institutional support is needed to ensure judicious and equitable allocation, distribution and exploitation of water and land resources. Table 1 shows that with the increase of farm size poverty in rural areas decreases. Similarly, Table 2 shows the positive impact of rainwater on poverty alleviation. Because good farm size and good rain water ensures good production. Farmers those who are leaving in rural areas but have no land are suffering from hunger and poverty which is clear from the tables. Incidence of poverty and hunger is very severe in this segment of the society.

TABLE 1

Incidence of Hunger and Poverty by Farm Size in Rural India

Land Class	*Percentage of Population*	
	Hungry	*Poor*
Landless	49	54
<0.5 ha	32	38
0.5-1 ha	24	27
1.0-2 ha	17	19
2.0-4 ha	12	14
>4 ha	12	13

Source : IARI-FAO/RAP study (2001) based on 50th NSS Round (1993-94).

TABLE 2

Impact of Irrigation on Alleviation of Hunger and Poverty in India

Irrigated area (%)	*Percentage of Population*	
	Hungry	*Poor*
Rainfed	33	35
<20	20	22
20-50	22	23
50-80	18	24
>80	19	26

Source : IARI-FAO/RAP study (2001) based on 50th NSS Round (1993-94).

Literacy has a very high impact on poverty alleviation as well as on hunger reduction (Table 3). The illiterate people, whether urban or rural, are the most poor and malnourished. In urban areas the impact of literacy on poverty is the highest. Education, even above primary level, is extremely effective in reducing both poverty and hunger. Therefore, the education policy of the country must be geared to remove illiteracy as soon as possible.

TABLE 3

Impact of Literacy on Alleviation of Hunger and Poverty in India

Above Primary Level	26	18	20	33
Graduate and Technical	14	8	7	4

Source : IARI-FAO/RAP study (2001) based on 50th NSS Round (1993-94).

TABLE 4

Relative Performance of Fifteen Major States in Poverty Reduction Over Three Decades

(States have been Sorted According to the Poverty Ratio as Reported by the Planning Commission in the Order of Higher to Lower Value)

States with poverty ratio above national average	States with poverty ratio below national average
1973-74 (54.88%—All India)	
Orissa, West Bengal, Bihar, Madhya Pradesh, Kerala, Uttar Pradesh, Tamilnadu	Karnataka, Maharashtra, Assam, Andhra Pradesh, Gujarat, Punjab, Rajasthan, Haryana
1983-84 (44.48%—All India)	
Orissa, Bihar, West Bengal, Tamilnadu, Madhya Pradesh, Uttar Pradesh	Maharashtra, Assam, Kerala, Karnataka, Rajasthan, Gujarat, Andhra Pradesh, Punjab, Haryana
1993-94 (35.97%—All India)	
Bihar, Orissa, Madhya Pradesh, Assam, Uttar Pradesh, Maharashtra	West Bengal, Tamilnadu, Karnataka, Rajasthan, Kerala, Haryana, Gujarat, Andhra Pradesh, Punjab
2004-05 (27.5%—All India)	
Orissa, Bihar, Madhya Pradesh, Uttar Pradesh, Maharashtra	Karnataka, West Bengal, Tamilnadu, Rajasthan, Assam, Gujarat, Andhra Pradesh, Kerala, Haryana, Punjab

Source : Planning Commission (2002) and Planning Commission (2007).

The states (Table 6) could be grouped into four categories on the basis of poverty ratio in the initial year (1973-74), the rate of decline in poverty over three decades, 1973-74 to 2004-05, and other characteristics, like, size of the state, income and population.

GROWTH-POVERTY LINKAGE

Poverty reduction is one of the major objectives of economic growth. Economists recognize that even when there is robust economic growth poverty reduction may not always be fully achieved. Economic growth is necessary but not sufficient when it comes to poverty reduction. We cannot preclude the role of economic growth in creating necessary resources for social development, but, at the same time, complementary social and environmental policies are required, too. If poor people do not have access to basic education, how can they take advantage of employment and income opportunities created by economic growth? Poverty is thus a highly complex socio-economic problem that needs to be tackled concurrently in various sectors in order to untangle the Gordian knot of poverty. It is the synergy of combined efforts that produces the most sustainable results.

The relationship between income growth and poverty reduction has been shown to be particularly stronger in developing Asia. In other words, the data suggest that growth has served the poor better in Asia than elsewhere in the developing world. Ferreira and Ravallion (2008), in reviewing the evidence on levels and recent trends in global poverty and income inequality, similarly pointed to the dominant role of Asia in accounting for the bulk of the world's poverty reduction since 1981. Table 5 looks at the 2000-06 period, and derives PEG based on income poverty using the US $ 1.25-a-day yardstick (World Bank 2008). The strongest performers in this more recent period are Indonesia, Pakistan, and PRC, all with elastic poverty reduction responses to economic growth. Malaysia, Thailand, and Vietnam are also strong performers, while Cambodia, India, Mongolia, and the Philippines had the weakest performance.

TABLE 5

Poverty Elasticity of Growth Based on Income Poverty Headcount and Average Annual GDP Growth (%) 2000-06

Country	*Population below US$ 1.25 a day (%), before*	*Population below US$ 1.25 a day (%), after*	*Period*	*GDP Growth in Period*	*PEG*
Indonesia	29.3	21.4	2002-05	16.32	-1.652
Pakistan	35.9	22.6	2002-05	22.65	-1.636
Malaysia	1.9	1.5	1997-04	26.12	-0.806
Thailand	1.9	1.7	2002-04	13.94	-0.755
Vietnam	24.2	21.5	2004-06	17.37	-0.643
Cambodia	48.6	40.2	1994-04	109.48	-0.158
India	49.4	41.6	1994-05	100.67	-0.157
Philippines	22.0	22.6	2003-06	17.68	0.154
Mongolia	15.5	22.4	2000-05	24.00	1.855

Sources : Poverty Data—UNDP Human Development Reports.

GDP GROWTH—ADB KEY INDICATORS OF DEVELOPING ASIAN AND PACIFIC COUNTRIES

Indian Experience

From the inception of the development planning in India the policies of the government have continued to be guided by the firm conviction that rapid economic growth is the prime mover in uplifting the poor by offering them more productive employment and enhancing their income. It was not until the late seventies that the growth rate of the Indian economy actually picked up. The economy grew at the rate of more than 4% per annum in the late seventies, at about 5% during the early eighties and accelerated further since the mid-nineties. Currently, the growth rate is hovering around 8%.

Transformation of the country is quite apparent from the Table 6 which shows the noticeable changes that have occurred in the sectoral composition of output. The share of services in the national income has steadily increased with corresponding fall in the contributions of agriculture and industry over the years.

TABLE 6
Structural Change in GDP (Growth Rate)

	1900-50	*1951-80*	*1980s*	*1990s*	*2000-09*
Agriculture and Allied Activities	—	2.1	4.4	3.2	2.8
Industry	—	5.4	6.4	5.7	6.5
Services	—	4.5	6.3	7.1	9.0
GDP	0.7	3.5	5.6	5.7	7.2
Per Capita Income	0.2	1.1	3.2	3.6	5.4

Source : CSO (2008).

The positive performance seems to be an outcome of reforms encompassing a range of measures that led to transforming spreading over all the sectors of economy. The official estimates for all-India do suggest an inverse relationship between growth and poverty. But does it hold across the states? Table 6 which was consisted on the basis of simple and rank correlation analysis clearly shows the negative relationship between levels of poverty and per capita SDP (State Domestic Product) across the 14 major states in India. Correlation is statistically significant also.

TABLE 7
Correlation Between Growth in Per Capita SDP in Primary Sector and Change in Rural Poverty Level Across Major Indian States (No. of Observations = 13)

Year	*Simple Correlation Coefficient*	*Rank Correlation Coefficient*
1987-88 over 1983	-0.738#	-0.654#
1993-94 over 1987-88	-0.273	-0.375

Statistically significant at 95% confidence level.

This fact is true for the current data also. So, the study shows that there is no significant relationship between the widely believed poverty removal with the improved growth rate, or with the economic reforms. Considering these, the popularly held negative relation between growth and poverty reduction in India, during the last two decades or so, seems suspect.

INCLUSIVE GROWTH : A STRATEGY FOR POVERTY ALLEVIATION

We have realized that growth is necessary for poverty alleviation but not sufficient. Growth has to be inclusive. Growth with equity is the only road to success. It has been globally recognized that high national income growth alone does not address the challenge of employment promotion, poverty reduction and balanced regional development. Nor does growth in itself improve human development. Consequently, all the efforts of government—in agricultural and rural development, in industry and urban development, in infrastructure and services, in education and health care—sought to promote 'inclusive growth'. In India the benefits of economic growth have not equitably reached different parts of our society. Despite the robust economic growth, a large number of groups remain excluded from the opportunities and services provided by the financial sector. Such excluded groups include women, workers of unorganized sector, small and marginal farmers, the self-employed and senior citizens. Sustainable growth and development are not possible unless all the segments of the economy are included. This can be achieved through concerted action between the public and private sector.

Government of India has recognized the importance of inclusive growth. Thus, the Eleventh Plan Document tries to restructure the policies in order to make the growth faster, broad-based and inclusive by reducing the fragmentation of the society. Now, our policies aim at increasing the income and employment opportunities on the one hand and on the other; it tries to finance programmes which are capable of making the growth more inclusive. Inclusive growth is driven by demand side and supply side factors. Banks are playing the role of supply side factors. Demand side factors, such as lower income and/or asset holdings also have a significant effect on financial inclusion. Indian Government and RBI have been focusing to increase the number of bank accounts so that saving habits in this segment of society could be increased.

National Bank for Agriculture and Rural Development (NABARD) in 1992, launched the SHG-bank linkage programme with policy support from the Reserve Bank, to facilitate collective decision making by the poor and provide "door step" banking. In the third period (2005 onwards) financial inclusion has been accepted as a policy objective. The Common Minimum Programme of the (UPA) Government in India has focused on inclusive growth, on making the benefits of growth and income improvements available to all citizens. Microfinance has also been accepted as a tool of economic growth and poverty alleviation which is a part of policy. During the last few years, an increasing number of microfinance investment funds have been set-up with the goal of mobilizing funding for MFIs from foundations, individual and institutional investors and development agencies.

With increasing acceptance of the SHG-based developmental approach there is pressure set on village and block level administrators to achieve targets of forming a certain number of SHGs. Thus, Panchayats are also promoting SHGs in many areas.

Most importantly, in February 2006, Government of India implemented the NREGA (National Rural Employment Guarantee Act). This Act guarantees 100 days of unskilled jobs per rural household. The NREGA is being implemented in 200 most backward districts of 27 states in the country—socio-economically, the most challenging areas in India. Act aims at eradication of extreme poverty and at making villages self-sustaining through productive assets creation. This is meant to regenerate the rural natural resource-base, which in turn will result in sustainable livelihoods for residents. The Act puts Panchayati Raj Institutions at the helm of affairs—beginning with identifying the eligible households to planning the works to be undertaken. The government has referred to it as an "Act of the people, by the people, and for the people". In the context of rural poverty, the NREGA should be seen more as a livelihood-generating programme than a wage-earning scheme. It offers a unique opportunity to turn around rural development and poverty alleviation. For the first time, rural communities have been given not just a development programme, but also a regime of rights. Now question is that how effective are our delivery mechanisms and what are the weaknesses?

CONCLUSION

It is clear from above discussion that growth in GDP alone is not sufficient for poverty alleviation which is the main goal of policy-makers since last three decades. High and sustainable growth are absolute requirements, the fruits of growth must be shared more equally. The benefits of rapid economic growth have to percolate down to the lowest strata of society. A constructive public-private partnership for socially responsible growth is imperative and must occupy a larger space in the future business strategies of India's corporate sector. The Government has recognized the necessity of building capabilities at the local levels for planning, implementation and monitoring of development programmes. The time has now come to act boldly and decisively. For effective delivery system we need transparency in the operation of schemes. There also ought to be greater accountability for politicians and civil servants. The Central Government including the Planning Commission should help poorer states in getting investments for infrastructure and social sector. There is a need to have more devolution of finance, functions and powers to Panchyats to improve accountability and development. The combine and inclusive efforts of all can solve the problem of poverty which is the root cause of all the problems. So the lesson is not to lose sight of the role of the financial inclusion in the economy's growth and development. We are moving in right direction in and accepting the positive role of the state along with private enterprises.

Notes and References

1. Perry *et al.* (2006).
2. (World Bank, 2009).
3. HPI in effect measures deprivation of welfare as measured by the HDI.

References

Majumdar, N.A., 2007: Inclusive Growth: Development Perspectives in Indian Economy, New Delhi: Academic Foundation.

Meier, Gerald M., 2008: Leading Issues in Economic Development, New York: Oxford Uni. Press.

Kelles, Anita, 2003: The Role of ICT in Poverty Reduction, Viitanen.

Habito, Cielito, 2009: Patterns of Inclusive Growth in Developing Asia: Insights from an Enhanced Growth-Poverty Elasticity Analysis, Tokyo: IDBI Working Papers Series, No. 145.

Bandyopadhyay, Kaushik Ranjan, 2007: Poverty Alleviation and Pro-Poor Growth in India, New Delhi: Asian Institute of Transport Development.

CSO, 2009: Government of India, http://www.mospi.gov.in/, New Delhi.

Rao, N.B.: Fostering inclusive growth.

Joseph, Mathew, 2007-08: Financial Inclusion for Inclusive Growth, *Vinimaya*, XXVIII, 13-23.

Chakrabarty, K.C., 10 August, 2009: Banking—Key driver for inclusive growth, Chennai: "Clarity through Debate" series.

Narayan, S., India's Economy: Constraint to Economic Growth, *Asian Journal of Public Affairs,* 1(1), 8-11.

Dieckmann, Rimar, 2007: Microfinance: An Emerging Investment Opportunity, Germany: Deutsche Bank Research.

Chakrabarti, Rajesh, The Indian Microfinance Experience—Accomplishments and Challenges, Gurgaon: Indian Development Foundation.

Eleventh Five Year Plan, 2007-12: Inclusive Growth, I.

Eleventh Five Year Plan, 2007-12: Social Sector, II.

Centre for Science and Environment, An Ecological Act: A backgrounder to the National Rural Employment Guarantee Act (NREGA).

CHAPTER

20

Integration of Sustainability into the Banking Sector

NEETU KWATRA

ABSTRACT

Global warming and climate change are particularly important in the context of sustainable development, especially for developing countries, which tend to be ill-equipped for such changes. According to recent studies on climate change, the majority of Asian companies are "largely oblivious" to the risks posed by climate change issues to their business models and the environment. The contribution of financial institutions including banks to sustainable development is paramount, considering the crucial role they play in financing the economic and developmental activities of the world. In this context, the urgency for banks to act as responsible corporate citizens in the society, especially in a developing country like ours, need be hardly overemphasized. Their activities should reflect their concern for human rights and environment.

Reserve Bank of India feels that, there is general lack of adequate awareness on the issue in India. In this context, the need for sustainable developmental efforts by financial institutions in India assumes urgency and banks, in particular, can help contribute to this effort by playing a meaningful role. RBI in its notification dated 20th November 2007 has advised banks to take note of the issues raised and consider using the same to put in place a suitable and appropriate plan of action towards helping the cause of sustainable development, with the approval of their Boards.

This section focuses on the role of commercial and investment banks in sustainable development. It examines recent trends in banking and sustainable development, innovative banking practices, and events that have shaped the role of the banking sector in sustainable development.

The banks recognize that their role as financiers affords them significant opportunities to promote responsible environmental stewardship and socially responsible development, and thereby minimize their loan risk. The banks are using environmental and social screens developed by the World Bank and the International Finance Corporation for several dozen industry sectors.

In this paper an effort is made to suggest modified procedure for commercial lending by Indian commercial banks to enable them to safeguard their own interests and also help in promoting environmental protection by the industry. Paper explained the need for environmental protection, need for sensitization of branch managers and requested bankers to be aware of funding environment-related projects.

Commercial banks are not the direct generators and dischargers of environmental pollution, but why they should be responsible for lenders' behaviors? In the threats of environmental crisis to human survival and development, to prevent the deterioration of the environment, it has been the focus to solve the environmental pollutions, and the expansion of the environmental legal liability principle and the extension of the undertaking range are effective measures.

Keywords: Banking system, role of banks in economy, banking degree of the economy

INTRODUCTION

The idea of sustainable development grew from numerous environmental movements in earlier decades and was defined in 1987 by the World Commission on Environment and Development (Brundtland Commission 1987) as:

Sustainable Development

Development that meets the needs of the present without compromising the ability of future generations to meet their own needs.. It contains within it two key concepts:

- the concept of needs, in particular the essential needs of the world's poor, to which overriding priority should be given; and
- the idea of limitations imposed by the state of technology and social organization on the environment's ability to meet present and future needs."

All definitions of sustainable development require that we see the world as a system—a system that connects space; and a system that connects time.

When you think of the world as a system over space, you grow to understand that air pollution from North America affects air quality in Asia, and that pesticides sprayed in Argentina could harm fish stocks off the coast of Australia.

And when you think of the world as a system over time, you start to realize that the decisions our grandparents made about how to farm the land continue to affect agricultural practice today; and the economic policies we endorse today will have an impact on urban poverty when our children are adults.

We also understand that quality of life is a system, too. It's good to be physically healthy, but what if you are poor and don't have access to education? It's good to have a secure income, but what if the air in your part of the world is unclean? And it's good to have freedom of religious expression, but what if you can't feed your family?

The concept of sustainable development is rooted is this sort of systems thinking. It helps us understand ourselves and our world. The problems we face are complex and serious—and we can't address them in the same way we created them. But we can address them.

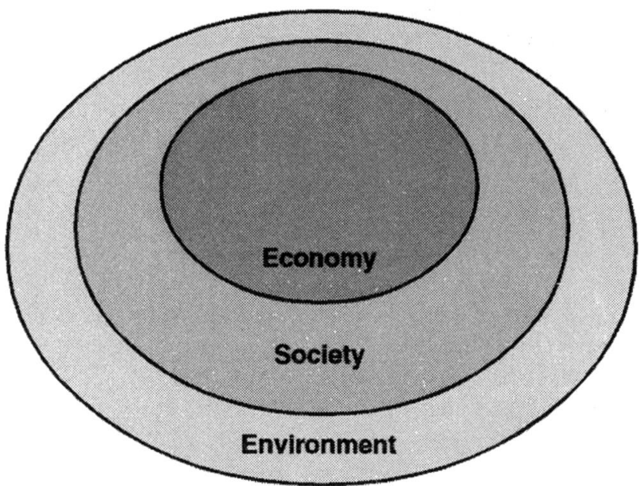

A representation of sustainability showing how both economic and societal values are constrained by environmental limits (2003).

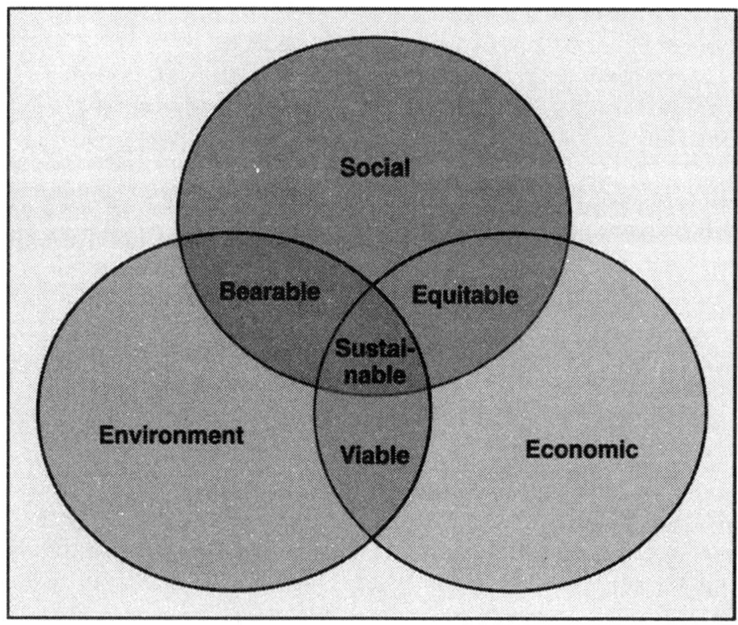

Scheme of sustainable development: at the confluence of three constituent parts. (2006)

WHY BANKS HAS A ROLE

The contribution of financial institutions including banks to sustainable development is paramount, considering the crucial role they play in financing the economic and developmental activities of the world. In this context, the urgency for banks to act as responsible corporate citizens in the society, especially in a developing country like ours, need be hardly overemphasized. Their activities should reflect their concern for human rights and environment.

A lawyer advising a financial institution in any type of financing does not and should not concern himself (unless the client asks him to) with whether the activity being financed will have a beneficial or a deleterious effect on the environment, whether it will be good or bad for the indigenous population, or even whether it is "sustainable" (at least beyond the term of the financing). Rather, the lawyer's role, both in addressing environmental matters and in general, is to identify, assess, and allocate risk.

From this perspective, a project with the potential for significant adverse effects on the environment may be no less desirable than one with little or no identified environmental impacts, so long as the risks in the former case can be effectively allocated entirely to the borrower and the borrower's creditworthiness is sufficient to cover those risks. Likewise, the financial institution itself, unless its board of directors or shareholders have instructed otherwise, will necessarily be guided by what will provide the most financial benefit to it, not by what will provide the most benefit (or least detriment) to the environment.

Nevertheless, lenders and the lawyers who represent them have, in the past decade, been a major force in promoting sustainable development, especially in the less-developed countries. If environmental due diligence and environmental protections in loan documentation are not the product of some moral imperative, then what does motivate lenders and their counsel to emphasize environmental issues in making, and increasingly in policing, their loans or investments? It is the perception that projects with environmental problems may result, directly or indirectly, in adverse economic consequences for the institution. While most lenders historically perceived this concern as less compelling or even absent in less-developed countries, increasingly they understand that environmental issues may have just as serious implications for them in Amazonia as in Amsterdam.

REASON FOR ENVIRONMENTAL, DUE DILIGENCE

There are a number of reasons why financial institutions find it good business practice to evaluate environmental risks carefully before making a loan or investment.

A. Legal Authority to Construct and Operate the Facility

Typically, there will be numerous permits, licenses, and other authorizations, issued by several levels of government authorities, necessary to construct and operate the facility. The lender wants to be sure that all such authorizations have been obtained and, preferably, is no longer subject to judicial challenge. If they have not been obtained, the lender will want to be reasonably certain that there will be no problem obtaining the authorizations before they are legally required for construction or operation. Likewise, the lender wants to know that the facility does or will comply with all applicable environmental laws and implementing regulations.

The lender's lawyers or environmental consultants will look carefully to make sure that the authorizations and statutory and regulatory requirements are consistent with the assumptions upon which the financing decisions are based; i.e., that the facility will be able to operate at a rate and in a manner consistent with the financial projections for at least as long as the term of the loan. The lender's concern here is not only that the borrower can build and operate the project as anticipated, but also that, if the developer defaults and the lender has to take control of the facility, the lender or a third party who might wish to purchase the facility can legally complete its construction or continue to operate it.

B. Impairment of Borrower's Ability to Repay

Even if the facility has legal authorization to operate, it is possible that environmental liabilities could be so great as to impair the borrower's ability to make the payments contemplated in the loan agreement. For less-capitalized companies or non-recourse projects, the costs of cleaning up a single spill or remediating soil and groundwater contamination at a single location could force the company into bankruptcy or force the lenders to accept loan restructuring. Environmental contamination has at times interfered with the continued use of all or part, of a facility; such as when underground tanks or contaminated soil need to be removed from a portion of the property in active use, or when a PCB transformer fire or other indoor contamination has made the facility uninhabitable for an extended period. A severe environmental problem may impair a company's ability to sell consumer products (as happened to Exxon after the Exxon Valdez oil spill) or operate in the community.

Environmental policy can be developed in a number of areas to encourage financial Institutions to Support Sustainable Development

1. Through standardization and improvement of information currently being collected and made available by environmental regulators.
2. Through the development of environmental reporting standards targeted at the financial markets.
3. As part of its involvement in consumer investment protection, requiring financial Institutions to ask investors if they are concerned about how their money is invested environmentally or ethically.
4. Developing, as part of its eco-labeling scheme, a label for environmentally responsible investments.
5. Supporting information dissemination on best practice for financial institutions.
6. The extension of the EMAS scheme to include financial institutions. This would require a greater focus on impacts of products. More formal control through the financial regulatory mechanism is

possible, for instance by making environmental management mandatory, by requiring disclosure of exposure to high risk sectors, by looking at the potential for voluntary investment agreements, and by looking at the role of the European Central Bank. However, they are probably not a priority at present.

The Regulatory Path for Sustainable Development for Banks

An active debt market requires a broad-based and well diversified investor base. Innovation and deregulation have introduced new elements of risk in market operations. Apart from counterparty risk, interest risk, price risk and settlement risk have assumed greater significance and larger proportions. Therefore, issue management techniques, as also secondary market activities like trading, clearing and settlement systems have to be efficiently and prudently organized and regulated. A notable difference between established financial markets and emerging ones is found in the extent to which their legal infrastructure has been developed. Legal regimes develop their laws and regulations to reveal the social, economic and political attributes and aspirations of the society to which they apply. In India, no doubt legal regimes developed suitable laws and regulations, but they were tailored to meet the needs of a planned economy rather than that of a free market. The change in the direction of the economy necessitates reorientation of not only the laws, but also lawyers in this jurisdiction, who may have little or no experience of the new legal regime and take time to understand the issues they raise. Herein comes the reforms connected with

PUBLIC DEBT ACT, 1944

The Indian debt market can be conveniently classified into three broad categories—Government Securities, Public Sector Units (PSU), Bonds and the Corporate Debt Market. The law relating to Government securities and their management is laid down in the Public Debt Act, 1944. As the Procedures prescribed there are archaic and time-consuming, the public have been put to inconvenience. In the wake of the tremendous increase in the volume of public debt, the Reserve Bank, agency banks and treasuries were handicapped in improving customer service. A thorough and comprehensive review was undertaken by a Committee appointed by the Reserve Bank of India. This Committee recommended a new legislation, repealing the existing Public Debt Act. The shortcomings noticed are briefly discussed below:

- The proposed legislation, to be called "The Government Securities Act", is intended to redress the woes of individual, small investors, as well as of entities like trusts. The present Act requires a chain of endorsements to be scrutinized to ensure that the successive endorsements through which the last holder derives his title are regular. This involves examination of sale power of all previous holders.
- The Government Securities in the form of promissory notes are not allowed to be issued to trusts under the existing Act. This is causing difficulties to trusts like Provident Funds, etc. which generally acquire G.P. Notes from brokers. This needs to be corrected.
- The existing provisions preclude the claims of legal representatives of deceased sole holders on the basis of any documents other than the probate,

DVP System

Presently, a settlement in securities transactions is recorded through the submission of SGL transfer forms without a direct link with the cash settlement between the buyer and seller, when done outside a DVP system.

A developed DVP system contemplates a synchronies settlement of the transfer of securities with the cash payment. For this purpose, the transfer forms must be modified to include the payment amount. When the electronic system edits the transaction after checking the seller's securities balance, it must also check the buyer's funds account to determine if there are sufficient funds to make payment. If both accounts have a sufficient balance, the transaction will be processed and accounts will be properly updated. If there is an insufficient securities balance for the seller or an insufficient funds balance for the buyer, the transaction will be rejected to be re-entered later. In a DVP system, it is necessary to formulate and establish an overdraft policy to determine the securities processing procedures that will be followed in the book entry system. A daylight overdraft is caused when payments made for securities transfer that have been received by a bank exceed the payments received from securities that have been delivered.

Some central banks are reluctant to permit daylight overdrafts in a securities account, but that by itself, does not solve the problem. In an active market, a dealer may have bought and sold securities in large amounts. If his purchases are processed prior to his sales, he may lack sufficient funds causing transactions to be rejected. This may not enable him to deliver securities and receive payment and may make it impossible for the expected receiver of funds to complete his transactions. A chain of failed transactions could thus gridlock a vibrant market.

Electronic Clearance, Settlement and Depository System

The Nadkarni Committee recognized a need for establishing a secondary market for PSU bonds where transactions can be put through in a transparent manner and reliable market prices of these instruments can emerge. To achieve this purpose, two major recommendations were made, viz. allowing Ready Purchase Operations (REPOS) carried through limited use of Bankers, Receipts (BRs), and establishing, in a phased manner, a centralized agency to operate an ECSD System. Following the submission of the Nadkarni Committee Report, a high level committee on the capital market, consisting of the RBI Governor, Chairman of SEBI and Secretary, Ministry of Finance, Government of India, accepted the need for established ECSD as a precursor to the re-introduction of the Repo facility. However, the interim arrangement suggested for restoration of Repo transactions, based on the use of BRs was not found acceptable. The Depositories Act, 1996 has cleared the decks and set a pace by removing major legal obstacles in the setting up of ECSD mechanism. It is now only a matter of time that a full-fledged ECSD becomes a part of the market mechanism.

Repo Transactions

Although there are different types of repo transactions available in the international repo market, in India the only type of repo prevalent is Buy/Sell back, where agreements are entered into simultaneously for the sale and repurchase of securities at different prices. The repo transactions essentially involve a contract between a holder of securities, who wants to raise funds and an investor (purchaser) for sale of the securities to the purchaser and repurchase of the securities later at a fixed price on a fixed date. The transactions thus involve a forward contract in securities.

Stamp Duty

It is necessary to consider remission in stamp duties on the transfer of debentures since it is a major impediment in active trading and market making in debentures. However, this being a State matter, each State can consider it to boost such market making in their State. It is however desirable if there is uniformity in such stamp duty, with a ceiling after a certain amount.

Securitization of Loan Assets

Securitization of loan assets is a method by which banking and financial institutions can improve their capital adequacy by liquidating risk assets of good quality at a profit. Securitization will become increasingly feasible as interest rates fall. The securitization of loan assets involves the resale of such assets to investors by the primary holders of such assets. Securitization is particularly well developed in the USA, but is also becoming attractive in Europe. Securitization is typically provided without recourse to the primary asset holder, which implies that the subsequent holder of the asset takes a risk on the repayment principal and interest on the original loan. Good quality loan assets are readily securitisable; however, it is also possible to "bundle" assets of varying quality and securities such bundles.

Role of Banks in Economic Development

A proper financial sector is of special importance for the economic growth of developing and underdeveloped countries.

The commercial banking sector which forms one of the backbones of the financial sector should be well organized and efficient for the growth dynamics of a growing economy. No under-developed country can progress without first setting up a sound system of commercial banking. The importance of a sound system of commercial banking for a developing country may be depicted as follows:

Capital Formation

The rate of saving is generally low in an underdeveloped economy due to the existence of deep-rooted poverty among the people. Even the potential savings of the country cannot be realized due to lack of adequate banking facilities in the country. To mobilize dormant savings and to make them available to the entrepreneurs for productive purposes, the development of a sound system of commercial banking is essential for a developing economy.

Monetization

An underdeveloped economy is characterized by the existence of a large non-monetized sector, particularly, in the backward and inaccessible areas of the country. The existence of this non-monetized sector is a hindrance in the economic development of the country. The banks, by opening branches in rural and backward areas, can promote the process of monetization in the economy.

Innovations

Innovations are an essential prerequisite for economic progress. These innovations are mostly financed by bank credit in the developed countries. But the entrepreneurs in underdeveloped countries cannot bring about these innovations for lack of bank credit in an adequate measure. The banks should, therefore, pay special attention to the financing of business innovations by providing adequate and cheap credit to entrepreneurs.

Finance for Priority Sectors

The commercial banks in underdeveloped countries generally hesitate in extending financial accommodation to such sectors as agriculture and small scale industries, on account of the risks involved therein. They mostly extend credit to trade and commerce where the risk involved is far less. But for the development of these countries it is essential that the banks take risk in extending credit facilities to the priority sectors, such as agriculture and small scale industries.

Provision for Medium and Long-term Finance

The commercial banks in underdeveloped countries invariably give loans and advances for a short period of time. They generally hesitate to extend medium and long-term loans to businessmen. As is well-known, the new business need medium and long-term loans for their proper establishment. The commercial banks should, therefore, change their policies in favor of granting medium and long-term accommodation to business and industry.

Social Responsibilities of the Indian Banking Sector: There are few measures to be adopted by banks for their social perspective for maintaining sustainable development

1. In the Annual Policy of the Reserve Bank for 2004-05, the Governor observed: "There has been expansion, greater competition and diversification of ownership of Banks leading to both enhanced efficiency and systemic resilience in the banking Sector. However, there are legitimate concerns in regard to the banking practices that tend to exclude rather than attract vast sections of population, in particular pensioners, Self-employed and those employed in the unorganized sector. While commercial considerations are no doubt important; the banks have been bestowed with several Privileges, especially of seeking public deposits on a highly leveraged basis, and consequently they should be obliged to provide banking services to all segments of the Population, on equitable basis."
2. 'Financial Inclusion' has, since the last 3 years or so, occupied the centre stage and been the theme of many conferences held in India and abroad. In India

high-level Committees have reviewed the state of Financial Inclusion in the country and given their learned views. It needs to be emphasized, however, that 'Financial Inclusion' as a goal was envisioned 40 years ago, in a sense even earlier when Pandit Jawaharlal Nehru made his famous 'tryst with destiny' speech in Parliament and set the tone for the Emergence of an egalitarian society. Major Banks were nationalized in 1969 with the Objective of taking banking to the masses. While it is true that the goal is yet to be achieved one cannot deny the progress made during the period, particularly the policy and institutional framework which have laid the foundation for attainment of Financial Inclusion. We have traversed a long journey since 1969, which has seen the evolution of several policies, models and schemes, successes and failures in our endeavor to attain Financial Inclusion as also inclusive growth.

3. Renewed interest in Financial Inclusion has emanated from the concern that in spite of all the progress made by banks the position of Financial Inclusion in the Country is far from satisfactory. There is a large chunk of the population that remains financially excluded. Financial Exclusion can be thought of in two different ways. One is exclusion from the payments system in the absence of a bank account. The second type of exclusion is from formal credit markets, which drives the excluded towards informal and exploitative markets.
4. The Annual Policy Statement of the Reserve Bank for 2005-06 had stated that:
   - RBI would implement policies to encourage banks, which provide extensive Services while disincentivising those, which are not responsive to the banking needs of the community, including the underprivileged.
   - The nature, scope and cost of services would be monitored to assess whether there was any denial, implicit or explicit, of basic banking services to the common person.

- Banks would be urged to review their existing practices to align them with.

Objective of Financial Inclusion

The Reserve Bank's broad approach to Financial Inclusion is:

- Aim at 'connecting' people with the banking system and not just credit Dispensation.
- Aim at giving people access to the payments system.
- Use multiple channels such as civil service organizations, NGOs, Post Offices, farmers' clubs, panchayats, MFIs, etc. to expand the outreach of banks.
- Adopt a decentralized approach, which is state and region specific and has close involvement and cooperation between the respective State Governments and banks.
- Make use of ICT using biometric smart cards and mobile hand held electronic devices for receipts and disbursement of cash by agents of banks, such as business facilitators/correspondents.
- Portray Financial Inclusion as a viable business model and opportunity.
- Aim at continuous evaluation, sharing of experiences, feedback and improvement.

In consonance with this broad approach, the Reserve Bank has undertaken a Number of measures for attracting the financially excluded population into the structured Financial system, such as asking banks to open no frills accounts with relaxed KYC Norms, offering of modest overdraft facility/ General Credit Card, use of intermediaries to act as agents (BC/BF) for enhancing banks' outreach, drawing up of strategic plans for Development and financial inclusion in the economically less developed regions of the country, use of ICT for enhancing the outreach of banks, adoption of districts for 100 Percent Financial Inclusion, promotion of financial literacy and credit counseling. Guidelines for banks with respect to Priority Sector Lending have been rationalized. With the enactment of the Micro, Small and Medium Enterprises Development Act, 2007, there is now greater attention and focus on coverage of the hitherto neglected micro and small enterprises

It is important, at this juncture, to sound a note of caution. In our quest for Providing access to finance to the unbanked and underserved sectors, we should constantly remind ourselves that we are trying to reach out to a section of our society that is weak and vulnerable. Hence, it is necessary that the systems that we put in place are sound in all respects and are appropriately regulated and supervised. It is important that practices adopted by banks and their charges are perceived as fair and reasonable.

CONCLUSION

In modern sense, banks appeared and consolidated in close connection with the development of commerce and capital accumulation, being a direct consequence of production development and expansion of the entire economy. Playing a significant role in the development of trade, these banks were named commercial banks. In the process of commercial banks' emergence money changers and money lenders played a peculiar role, being the first monetary intermediaries, carrying out trade with money.

Later on, as the economy developed and the volume and structure of exchanges amplified, the place of money changers and money lenders was taken by banks which took over funds from capital holders in order to keep them safely and remunerate their owners with interest. Banks were forming deposits used to provide loans for those in need of capital. In this way, bank deposits were the base of the capital redistribution process as lending sources. Today, the role and place of banks in the economy are closely connected with their attribute of main financial intermediaries in the relation savings-investments. Market economy requires a strong banking system that enables funds redistribution. Nowadays, banking is referred to as a service industry rather than a profession. Therefore, a bank can be associated with a financial service conglomerate able to provide basic financial services and properly function within the economic, political, legal and international environment that determines its profit and expansion opportunities, interest rates, exchange rates and the particular resources a bank needs.

References

Chesbrough, H. Open Innovation, HBS Press, Boston, M.A., 2003.

Cooper, R. Stage Gate Systems: A New Tool for Managing New Products, *Business Horizons*, 33, 1990.

Eppinger, S. and Chitkara, A. The New Practice of Global Product Development, SMR, Summer 2006.

Hansen, M. and Nohria, N. How to Build Collaborative Advantage, SMR, Fall 2004.

Santos, D., Doz, Y. and Williamson, P., Is Your Innovation Process Global?, SMR, Summer 2004.

Teece, D. Profiting from Technological Innovation: Implications for Integration, Licensing, Collaboration and Public Policy, *Research Policy*, 15, 1986.

Remenyi, Joe and Quinones, Benjamin. 2000. Microfinance and Poverty Alleviation: Case studies from Asia and the Pacific. New York, 79, pp. 131-34, 253-63.

Richardson, David C. February, 2000. Unorthodox Microfinance: The Seven Doctrines of Success. *MicroBanking Bulletin*.

Robinson, Marguerite, 2001. The Microfinance Revolution: Sustainable Finance for the Poor.

World Bank, Washington.

Rodenbeck, M. 1998. An Emerging Agenda for Development in the Middle East and North Africa.

CHAPTER

21

Financial Assistance and Incentives to the Senior Citizens of India

With Special Reference to the Senior Citizens of Dholpur in Rajasthan

RAJESH KUMAR SHARMA AND N.K. BANSAL

INTRODUCTION

Senior Citizens are a treasure to our society. They have worked hard all these years for the development of the nation as well as the community. They possess a vast experience in different walks of life. The youth of today can gain from the experience of the senior citizens in taking the nation to greater heights. At this age of their life, they need to be taken care of and made to feel special. Indian Government provides several benefits through its schemes in various sectors of development. With various tax benefits, travel and health care facilities provisioned for them, Indian Government has created reasons for Senior Citizens to feel happy. This corner on Senior Citizens is aimed at providing details on various aspects concerning them.

PARENTS AND SENIOR CITIZENS BILL, 2007

A draft bill in Parliament attempts to mandate the care of elderly citizens in law, and envisions the establishment of tribunals to ensure its functioning. But its definitions and methods leave many questions unanswered. Priya Narayan Parker presents a legislative brief.

DEFINITIONS

- *Senior citizen*: The Bill defines 'senior citizen' as (a) Indian citizens 60 years of age or older, and (b) all parents with children above the age of 18 years. For example, the provisions of this Bill would be applicable to even a 40-year-old parent of a 20-year-old person. This definition differs from that in the National Policy on Older People, which sets the age at 60 years or older.
- *Parent and child*: The Bill defines 'parent' as a biological, adoptive or step mother or father. It defines 'children' as sons, daughters, grandsons and granddaughters. These two definitions do not mirror each other.
- *Relative*: The Bill defines 'relative' as someone who is in possession of or would inherit a senior citizen's property after death. As wills are changeable, it is unclear how one would determine who would inherit the property after death, and therefore who would be obliged to maintain the senior citizen.
- *Normal life*: The Bill states that the obligation of the children or relative to maintain a senior citizen extends to the needs of the senior citizens so that they may lead a 'normal life.' The Bill does not define what consists of a 'normal life.'
- *Organisation*: The Bill clarifies that an 'organisation' that may file an application for maintenance on

behalf of a senior citizen means 'any voluntary organisation registered under the Societies Registration Act, 1860, or any other law for the time being in force'. However, the Societies Registration Act does not define 'voluntary organisation'.

HIGHLIGHTS OF THE BILL

The Maintenance and Welfare of Parents and Senior Citizens Bill, 2007 seeks to make it a legal obligation for children and heirs to provide maintenance to senior citizens. It also permits state governments to establish old age homes in every district.

- Senior citizens who are unable to maintain themselves shall have the right to apply to a maintenance tribunal seeking a monthly allowance from their children or heirs.
- State governments may set-up maintenance tribunals in every sub-division to decide the level of maintenance. Appellate tribunals may be established at the district level.
- State governments shall set the maximum monthly maintenance allowance. The Bill caps the maximum monthly allowance at Rs. 10,000 per month.
- Punishment for not paying the required monthly allowance shall be Rs. 5,000 or up to three months imprisonment or both.

It is indeed notable that according to the Bill, the definition of senior citizen includes both Indian citizens aged over 60 years, and all parents irrespective of age, but the Bill does not address the needs of senior citizens who do not have children or property. Relatives are obliged to provide maintenance to childless senior citizens. The Bill defines 'relative' as someone who is in possession of or would inherit a senior citizen's property but nothing is said about how one would determine who would inherit the property after death. State governments may establish old age homes and prescribe standards for services provided by them. However, the Bill does not require them to do so.

OTHER FACILITIES TO THE SENIOR CITIZENS

- The state government may establish and maintain at least one old age home per district with a minimum capacity of 150 senior citizens per home. The state government may also prescribe a scheme for the management of such homes. The scheme shall specify standards and services to be provided including those required for medical care and entertainment of residents of these old age homes.
- The state government shall ensure that government hospitals and those funded by the government provide beds for all senior citizens as far as possible. It shall ensure separate queues for senior citizens, expand facilities for treatment of diseases and expand research for chronic elderly diseases and aging. Every district hospital shall also earmark facilities for geriatric patients.
- The state government is responsible for publicising the provisions, as well as ensuring that government officers undergo periodic sensitisations and awareness training on issues relating to the Bill. The district magistrate shall be responsible for implementing the provisions of the Bill.

At present, every country of the world is worried about the maintenance and care of its senior citizens, and the same is true of India where a horrible change in their condition and treatment can be noticed these days. Once a country with full respect to its elders, is now a land of selfish and self-centered members in the families. As in the other countries of the world, in India too, there are several laws that guarantee maintenance and care of the senior citizens and parents. Obviously, these provisions may help the senior citizens to lead a socially-dignified life in the society and to enjoy their old age in a healthy environment. Particularly in the metropolitan cities these provisions may bring new hopes to them.

TABLE I

Laws Regarding Maintenance and Care of Senior Citizens and Parents

Law	*Requirement*	*Maintenance Allowance*
(1)	*(2)*	*(3)*
Constitution of India, Directive Principles, Article 41	The State shall, within the limits of its economic capacity and development, make effective provision for…old age, sickness and disablement, and in other cases of undeserved want.	Not justiciable
Code of Criminal Procedure (Chapter IX, Section 125(1)(2))	Requires persons who have sufficient means to take care of his or her parents if they are unable to take care of themselves.	Rs. 500 per month maximum
Hindu Adoption and Maintenance Act, 1956	Requires Hindu sons and daughters to maintain their elderly parents when parents are unable to maintain themselves	To be determined by court

TABLE 2

International Status of the Senior Citizens

Act	*Purpose/Broad Provisions*
(1)	*(2)*
Sri Lanka: Protection of the Rights of Elders Act, 2000	Establishes National Older Persons' Council; requires children to provide care for their parents and makes provisions for parents to obtain maintenance from children; requires state to provide appropriate residential facilities to destitute elderly without children.
United States: Older Americans Act of 1965	Creates the Administration on Aging within the Department of Health, Education and Welfare; authorises grants to States for community planning, services for elderly, and research and training in the field of aging.
China: Law of the People's Republic of China on Protection of the Rights and Interests of the Elderly, 1996	Places responsibility on families to care for elderly; establishes a state-based old-age insurance system, increases legal protection of elderly with speedy court procedure.
South Africa: Older Persons Act No .13 of 1996	Provides strict controls for registered old-age facilities; makes abuse of the elderly a criminal offence; creates social and cultural community-based services for elderly.
Canada (Saskatchewan and Manitoba): Parents Maintenance Act, 1978 and 1993 respectively	Mandates children to pay maintenance to dependent parents up to $20 per week.

In India, existing schemes for old age pension include the Employees' Provident Fund and the New Pension Scheme, which cover roughly 13% of the working population (10% as government servants and 3% from the formal private sector). In addition, the National Old Age Pension Scheme provides for destitute persons of 65 years and above. Table 4 summarises the schemes for providing for old age security and financial independence in some countries.

OLD-AGE HOMES

The Bill grants state governments permission to establish and maintain old age homes 'as it may deem necessary, in a phased manner,' beginning with 'at least one in each district.' There is no obligation on state governments to establish these homes. The Bill specifies that each old age home should accommodate at least 150 senior citizens. Specifying such details in the Bill reduces the flexibility to cater to differing local conditions and needs. As of 2005, there were 1,018 Old Age Homes in India. Of the 739 homes for which detailed information is available, 427 homes are free of cost, 153 old age homes are on a pay and stay basis, and 146 homes have both free as well as pay and stay facilities. Kerala has 186 old age homes, the most of any state.

TAX BENEFITS

Income tax is a portion of your annual income that is paid to the government at the end of every financial year. This tax money is used to fund various developmental activities, build infrastructure and for defence purposes. The government provides various tax benefits and tax exemptions to certain categories of people such as sportspersons, women and senior citizens. This is done to encourage them to continue earning, investing and providing for themselves. Separate counters are marked for senior citizens at the time of filing Income Tax Returns. Senior citizens who are 65 years and above as on 31st March of the assessment year should be pensioners. They should come personally, if they wish for priority while submitting their Income Tax Returns. Besides, on the spot assessment facility is also provided. Senior citizens are eligible for the various exemptions extended by the government. The government assigns special priority towards senior citizens by providing them tax benefits higher than that of general taxpayers. Read more on Concessions and Facilities given to Senior Citizens .

Source: National Portal Content Management Team, Reviewed on: 29-09-2010.

FINANCIAL PLANNING

Judicious planning of assets not only secures the future, but also provides a good return on investment. Senior citizens should plan and select financial schemes way in advance to receive monetary benefits. These financial schemes and plans are offered by banks, fund houses and financial institutions. Proper planning of available income options leads to better management of expenses. Financial planning allows you to achieve various goals such as buying a new car, paying for health expenses, going on foreign vacations and living a financially secure life after retirement. The process and various steps that lead to the proper management of finances are called financial planning. They may have received money from their voluntary retirement scheme or saved up money over the years from salary and pension. There are many avenues where they can invest this money. This includes stocks, bonds, gold, real estate, Unit Trust of India, mutual funds, fixed deposits and post office schemes. Apart from this, senior citizens may also go for tax-free bonds offered by the Reserve Bank of India. This scheme provides financial security to their lifelong savings. What's more, the interest earned on these tax-free bonds provides a regular source of income. However, selecting the right mix of schemes according to their needs for profit, liquidity and safety can be a daunting task. They may spend time reading up on different schemes available for information before choosing the most suitable one. This can take a lot of time and prove to be quite a hassle. They also have the option of hiring a financial planner. A financial planner is someone who takes an overall view of their financial situation, their commitments and their family responsibilities and evolves the appropriate financial recommendations for them. These planners have exhaustive knowledge about the various financial instruments and tools available. They help them select a portfolio that is just right for them. Financial planners are available at certain financial companies, banks, mutual fund offices and share brokers. Some planners receive commissions from third parties for selling them products that may be unsuitable to their needs.

Source: National Portal Content Management Team, Reviewed on: 21-02-2010

LOANS

Personal loans are helpful when one is in immediate need of financial assistance. Senior citizens are usually denied regular loans because of their inability to show proof of a regular level of income. However, recently, banks have started offering loans to pensioners and older people who can provide collateral in the form of an asset such as a home or land. This loan can be used to meet various expenses such as medical costs, marriage of grand children or paying old age home fees. Loans such as UCO bank's 'UCO Pensioner' and 'UCO Mortgage' are specially created for senior citizens. Other banks that offer special loans for senior citizens are the Bank of Saurashtra, Union Bank of India and the United Bank of India. Some features of loan schemes for senior citizens are the simple procedures, special counters and information centres that are available.

Source: National Portal Content Management Team, Reviewed on 01-12-2010.

RETIREMENT AND PENSION BENEFITS

Retirement and pension benefits are provided to retired government officials to ensure a regular income and a secure future. The provision of such financial benefits results in a feeling of independence and a decent standard of life. As far as retirement benefits are concerned, they usually consist of leave encashment, retirement gratuity and contributed provident fund. Along with these retirement benefits, senior citizens are also entitled to pension benefits that allow them to live a hassle free life after completion of their job tenure. Different types of pension available to senior citizens are superannuation, retiring pension, voluntary retirement pension, compensation pension, compassionate allowance, extraordinary pension and family pension. Superannuation pension is meant for those government officials who retire at the age of 60 years. Voluntary pension is awarded to those who wish to retire three months in advance after completing 20 years of service. Extraordinary pension is another pension scheme that is awarded to those government employees who are disabled or the families of those employees who lose their lives during the tenure of their job.

DEARNESS ALLOWANCE RATES

Dearness Allowance or DA is another benefit provided to senior citizens. The Government announces DA rates twice a year. This allowance is added to the salary or pension of government employees. DA rates are also applicable to senior citizens who have taken complete retirement. Those who go in for reemployment are not eligible to avail dearness allowance. More details on Dearness Allowance are:

- Retirement Benefits
- Pension Payment Schemes
- DR Rates for Pensioners

Source: National Portal Content Management Team, Reviewed on: 01-12-2010.

TAX EXEMPTION ON INTEREST

Senior citizens enjoy additional benefits in terms of saving schemes and interest earned on them. Interest is levied on the amount of money deposited for a particular time period. The rate of interest varies for different durations and is liable to change from year to year. Most banks provide a higher rate of interest to senior citizens than the rate available to the general public. They usually ask for proof of age before opening up such an account. Apart from these benefits, senior citizens also enjoy an annual interest rate of 9 per cent on deposits made by them in post offices, as on March 31, 2007. For information about opening a Post Office Account (External website that opens in a new window), contact the nearest branch in your area. The Reserve Bank of India (External website that opens in a new window) has permitted higher rates of interest on saving schemes of senior citizens. Accordingly, banks have allowed an added interest on fixed deposits for every term as on. Tax is deducted at source for interest on fixed deposits. This makes this form of investment a useful tax free form of income for older people. Other than higher interest rates on deposits, senior citizens also enjoy exemptions on penalty rates for premature withdrawal of term deposits. Fixed deposits are sometimes withdrawn to tide over emergencies like sudden medical expenses and hospitalization. In this case, senior citizens are either exempted completely or charged a meagre percentage rate of their deposits. Some banks like UCO Bank (External website that opens in a new window) provide complete exemption to senior citizens for premature withdrawal of term deposits. Other banks like ICICI Bank (External website that opens in a new window) currently charge around 0.5 to 1.5 per cent penalty depending on the amount of deposit, as on March 31, 2007. For information about current interest rates and other details, one may like to visit the local bank in your vicinity.

Source: National Portal Content Management Team, Reviewed on: 10-06-2010.

Hence, the efforts to make the life of the Indian senior citizens have been made as a result of which it can evidently be seen that many of them find their life easy and comfortable with hardly any dependence on the members of their family. However, it cannot be denied that the emotional needs can be fulfilled and satisfied only with the family members, so the families of them should consider it their liability to take care of the elders. If they are paid respect with this respect, they can be prevented from living on the morsels thrown by others or from going to the old-age homes which can supply them food, clothes and shelter, but which cannot satisfy their emotional needs. As far as the care of the childless senior citizens are concerned, they should be paid respect by all without caring to inherit their property and other valuables. To sum up, the banks and several other funding agencies are there to provide financial assistance and several incentives to the senior citizens so that they are no longer considered unwanted persons or burden to family.

SENIOR CITIZENS IN DHOLPUR DISTRICT— A GLIMPLSE INTO THE METHODOLOGY

Dholpur is one of the districts in Rajasthan. Situated between Agra in Uttar Pradesh and Morena in Madhya Pradesh, it is known for the mixed culture of the three states. The condition of the senior citizens in this district is more or less the same. The study was made on 100 senior citizens 25 each from the four tehsils of the district selected randomly from the different backgrounds. In order to keep the scientific spirit of the work, observation method was used. Both the primary and the secondary data were used for the study. The primary data were collected through the schedule technique, while the secondary data were collected from the newspapers, books, journals and the survey-reports. The study of the senior citizens was made as a part of NSS regular activities. Some of the remarkable aspects of the study can be noticed perusalized through the following tables that make a clear reflection on the various aspects of the senior citizens of Dholpur district in Rajasthan.

TABLE 3

Senior Citizens at the Different Tehsils

Tehsil	*Males*	*Females*	*Total*
Dholpur	17	8	25
Rajakhera	10	15	25
Bari	13	12	25
Baseri	14	11	25
Total	54	46	100

TABLE 4
Literacy Status

Tehsil	*Males*			*Females*			*Total*		
	Literate	*Illiterate*	*Total*	*Literate*	*Illiterate*	*Total*	*Literate*	*Illiterate*	*Total*
(1)	*(2)*	*(3)*	*(4)*	*(5)*	*(6)*	*(7)*	*(8)*	*(9)*	*(10)*
Dholpur	13	4	17	7	1	8	20	5	25
Rajakhera	9	1	10	11	4	15	20	5	25
Bari	8	5	13	9	3	12	17	8	25
Baseri	10	4	14	8	3	11	18	7	25
Total	40	14	54	35	11	46	75	25	100

Table 5
Age Group

Tehsil	*Males*			*Females*			*Total*		
	1960-70	*1970-80*	*Total*	*1960-70*	*1970-80*	*Total*	*1960-70*	*1970-80*	*Total*
(1)	*(2)*	*(3)*	*(4)*	*(5)*	*(6)*	*(7)*	*(8)*	*(9)*	*(10)*
Dholpur	11	6	17	5	3	8	16	9	25
Rajakhera	6	4	10	9	6	15	15	10	25
Bari	10	3	13	7	5	12	17	8	25
Baseri	8	6	14	7	4	11	15	10	25
Total	35	19	54	28	18	46	63	37	100

TABLE 6
Occupational Background

Tehsil	*Males*			*Females*			*Total*		
	Government Sector	*Private Sector*	*Un-employed*	*Government Sector*	*Private Sector*	*Un-employed*	*Government Sector*	*Private Sector*	*Un-employed*
(1)	*(2)*	*(3)*	*(4)*	*(5)*	*(6)*	*(7)*	*(8)*	*(9)*	*(10)*
Dholpur	10	5	2	2	4	2	12	9	4
Rajakhera	7	2	1	6	3	6	13	5	7
Bari	8	3	2	5	1	6	13	4	8
Baseri	9	2	3	4	2	5	13	4	8
Total	34	12	8	17	10	19	51	22	27

TABLE 7

Knowledge of Parents and Senior Citizens Bill, 2007

Tehsil	*Yes*	*No*	*Neutral*	*Ignorant*	*Total*
Dholpur	11	2	6	6	25
Rajakhera	14	4	4	3	25
Bari	9	7	8	1	25
Baseri	11	6	3	5	25
Total	45	19	21	15	100

TABLE 8

Availing Facilities Guaranteed to the Senior Citizens

Tehsil	*Yes*	*No*	*Neutral*	*Ignorant*	*Total*
Dholpur	6	10	6	3	25
Rajakhera	8	11	4	2	25
Bari	4	15	4	2	25
Baseri	14	6	2	3	25
Total	32	42	16	10	100

TABLE 9

Availing Financial Assistance Guaranteed to the Senior Citizens

Tehsil	*Yes*	*No*	*Total*
Dholpur	NIL	25	25
Rajakhera	NIL	25	25
Bari	NIL	25	25
Baseri	NIL	25	25
Total	NIL	100	100

TABLE 10
Point of Satisfaction in the Family

Tehsil	*Yes*	*No*	*Neutral*	*Ignorant*	*Total*
Dholpur	21	1	2	1	25
Rajakhera	19	2	3	1	25
Bari	21	NIL	4	NIL	25
Baseri	18	2	1	4	25
Total	79	5	10	6	100

SUMMING UP

- The condition of the senior citizens of Dholpur District in Rajasthan is more or less the same as in the other cities of India.
- Awareness campaigns need to be run there for the welfare of the senior citizens.
- At least a few of them are the victims of the violence at the hands of their kinsmen, but for the fear of the loss of reputation of the family they donot want to share their agony.
- Most of them are financially dependent on their sons in spite of the fact that they get monthly pension.
- Some of them are familiar with the facilities provided by the government to the senior citizens, but they face problems in availing them.
- In order to link all the senior citizens to the government schemes for the senior citizens, more and more help centres should be opened.
- Mobile medical vans should be sent door-to-door in order to supply medicines to the senior citizens.

INTERVIEWS OF SENIOR CITIZENS OF THE DISTRICT

- Pt. Uma Dutt Sharma, Founder of Pt. U.D. Girls' Degree College, Dholpur
- Mr. Jai Singh Rana, Retired Jailor

- Mrs. Sunita Bhan, Retd. Principal
- Mr. Shyam Babu Sharma, Retd. Teacher
- Mrs. Munni Devi Sharma, Housewife
- Mrs. Farzana Begum, Social Worker
- Mr. Sattar Ahmed, Working taxi driver

References

Senior Citizens *vis-a-vis* the Indian Society By Rama Lingam.

Assistive and Enabling Technology Needs of Elderly People in India: Issues and Initial Results by Prakash Kumar, Dr. Usha Dixit and Dr. V.C. Goyal.

The old age problems and care of senior citizens by N., Suresh K.

Abikusno, Nugroho (2007). Long-term care support and services for older persons: case study of Indonesia.

Raman, A. and Bjorkman, J.W. (2008). Public-Private Partnerships in Health Care in India, Routledge Studies in Development Economics Series.

CHAPTER

22

Do Family and Experience Matter to Access Finance?

A Test on Women Entrepreneurs of Dhaka

M. SAYEED ALAM, SABINA SHARMIN AND OMAR FARUQ

ABSTRACT

Research on women entrepreneurs is mostly available from developed world. The picture of women entrepreneurs from the developing world perspective is scanty. Research on women entrepreneurs is at an exploratory stage in Bangladesh. According to BWCC (Bangladesh Women Chamber of Commerce and Industry) there is lack of field-based data as well as finished information on women entrepreneurs of Bangladesh. A stratified sampling based on three business category strata (boutique, food and others) is used for this study to test relation of two variables (family support and experience) to get institutional support.

From this study of thirty samples it is found that family support will be helpful to get institutional support whereas

experience matter little. This study is concentrated only within Dhaka city and one limited sample so extended areas and more sample size are suggested to generalized the findings
Keywords: Women entrepreneur, Family support, Experience, Institution support

INTRODUCTION

Pine *et. al.* (2010) in their paper said that until the late 1970s, the role of women entrepreneurs was rarely considered (Humbert *et al.*, 2009). Nowadays, however, as Carter and Shaw (2006) noted, research on entrepreneurship is moving from looking at whether gender makes a difference to how it makes a difference. Naser *et al.* (2009) in their paper cited although a number of studies were undertaken to examine factors that influence women entrepreneurs in the developed world (DeLollis, 1997; Christopher, 1998; Goldenberg and Kline, 1999; Inman, 1999; Smith-Hunter, 2003; Smith-Hunter and Englhardt, 2004), a limited number of studies have been undertaken to investigate these factors in the Arab World in general and in the Arab Gulf region in particular (Dechant and Al-Lamky, 2005).

In Bangladesh situation, research on women entrepreneurs is at an exploratory stage. It is evident from the BWCC's (Bangladesh Women Chamber of Commerce and Industry) there is lack of finished information on the situation of women entrepreneurs. There is lack of field based data. Most of the financial institutions, public institutions do not have any gender disaggregated data (BWCC, 2008). Bangladesh Women Chamber of Commerce and Industry (BWCC, 2008) conducted a exploratory study aiming at having an overview of the situation of women entrepreneurs in Bangladesh. The covered issues in this report are socio-demographic profile, types of women owned business and the nature of common barriers. The survey is based on 130 women entrepreneurs from 11 districts (BWCC, 2008).

DEFINITION OF A WOMAN ENTREPRENEUR

An entrepreneur is a person who starts a new business

venture. He/she is a person who can find opportunities and has the ability to develop those opportunities into profit-making businesses (Naser *et. al.*, 2009). Studying women-owned businesses has presented some methodological problems for researchers (Stevenson, 1990). A major difficulty is definition of a woman-owned business (Mattis, 2004). There is no specific definition is available for women entrepreneur in South Asia. Sinha (2005), in her study on "Developing Women Entrepreneurs In South Asia: Issues, Initiatives And Experiences" a preliminary definition set as "women running their own SMEs within the formal sector in South Asia". But because of lack of statistics it is not always possible to concentrate only one formal sector or the differences between formal and the informal sectors is not very clear, or even it is not clear what size of organizations (women entrepreneur) we can consider for analysis.

The National Directory of Woman-Owned Business Firms uses the following criteria to define a woman-owned business (Business Research Services, 2001):

- one or more of the principal owners, or the majority, of shareholders are women;
- as a group, the woman owners or shareholders own at least 51 percent of the business;
- the woman owners or shareholders have dominant control over the business
- and participate in day-to-day operations; and the business is a going concern.

FINANCE AND WOMEN ENTREPRENEURS

Another problem that might confront women entrepreneurs is availability and use of fund. Owing to woman social position and family commitment, it is difficult to obtain the required fund run a business (Naser *et. al.*, 2009). Furthermore, research has shown that it is particularly difficult for women to acquire satisfactory start-up capital (Brush *et al.*, 2000; Shaw *et. al.*, 2000). It has also been suggested the "barriers" to finance might be more acute for female-owned SMEs as there is a perception that financial institutions discriminate against female business owners (Riding and Swift, 1990; Breen *et. al.*, 1995; Brush *et. al.*, 2001).

A. Family and Women Entrepreneurs

Women entrepreneurs might encounter is lack of time needed to run a business. Arab women are responsible for many household chores in addition to raising children. Spending time on household chores and raising children leaves little time for a woman to develop her entrepreneurial knowledge and skills. This also restricts a woman from running a business, visiting banks, attending training courses seminars and conferences, attracting customers or looking for diversified suppliers (Naser *et. al.* 2009). Women may also fear or face prejudice or sexual harassment, and may be restricted in their ability to travel to make contacts. (Sinha, 2005). On this study we proposed first hypothesis :

H_1 : There is no relation between family support and Institution support.

B. Experience and Women Entrepreneurs

According to Nilufer (2001), socio-cultural factors in developing countries influence women's decision to become an entrepreneur. Socio-cultural factors include religious values, ethnic diversity and marital status. Naser *et. al.* 2009 stated in their paper that as it may, the success of any business in the Arab countries depends on the entrepreneur's social position and the network they can create and access. In societies dominated by men, like the Arab Gulf, women entrepreneurs find it difficult to reach men's social positions. Given the nature of women and cultural restrictions on their movements, establishing an effective network and accessing them are not an easy task for women entrepreneurs. Naser *et. al.*, 2009 argument has been documented by previous studies who found that women participation in network is less than men and even the network that they may develop is different than that formed by men (Granovetter, 1985; Aldrich and Zimmer, 1986; Burt, 2000). Based on this literature we can form the following hypothesis :

H_2 : There is a relation between experience and Institution support.

Research Focus : Women have to play dual role while they are in business. At the same time it is learned from the literature that social network for women entrepreneurs are not that strong like male counterpart. In addition to these two variables (dual role and absence of social network) they face third problem that is access to finance is a problem for women. The specific focus of this research is to identify whether family support and experience has any impact and or relation to gain support from the Institution. More specifically if any women entrepreneur has family support whether it is easy for her to gain support from the institution and if any women with experience has advantage to support from the institution. In this paper by institution authors means financial institutions (Banks, Leasing companies, Merchant banking who can provide or issue loans to its clients and all of these institutions, it is not mandatory of these institutions to be listed in the stock markets). A sample of 30 women entrepreneurs constitute the sample of this study.

Boutique alone represents around 70% of the total women entrepreneurs in Bangladesh (Alam, Biswas and Faruqui (2009). It is learn from Faruqui, 2009 that boutique, food business, custom jewelry/flower business are more common business sector for women in Bangladesh. Based on these studies a stratified sampling is used for this study. Three strata called Boutique, Food and others are selected and on the basis of random sampling 30 samples are chosen from the three strata. A structured questionnaire is used to collect the information. And a total of 120 samples are selected and out of this 120 a total of 40 questionnaires were collected and it is found 30 were completely filled up.

RESEARCH METHODOLOGY

Result

A. Reliability Analyses

The reliability of the scales is satisfactory, as the majority of them have alpha coefficients above 0.6 (Table 1). According to Cronbach, 1990, and Kim, 2001 an alpha coefficient of 0.6 and above is considered good for research in social sciences. Family Support, experience, institutional support are measured in terms of opinion on a five point Likert scale (1 = Strongly disagree to 5 = Strongly agree, where 3 = neutral).

TABLE I

Reliability Analysis

	Cronbach's Alpha if Item Deleted
Family support	.977
Experience	.700
Institution Support	.690

B. Descriptive Statistics

	Family Support	*Experience*	*Institution Support*
Mean	3.47	3.60	3.53
Maximum	5	5	5
Minimum	2	2	2
Std. Dev.	1.074	0.770	1.008
Sum	104	108	106
Observations	30	30	30

five-level Likert item is used : where 1 = strongly disagree, 2 = disagree, 3 = Neither agree nor disagree, 4 = agree, 5 = Strongly agree. The questions are :

Family : Without family support (either from parents/ husband) no women can start any business.

Experience : Without experience it is almost difficult to start any business for women Institution support Major barrier to start a business as a woman is no cooperation from the financial institution regarding loan or any form of financial service.

C. *Hypothesis Test*

Hypothesis 1

H_1 : There is no relation between family support and Institution support.

Institution support as dependent variable and Family support as independent variable the result is :

$$Y_{\text{Institution Support}} = 0.371 + 0.912\ X_{\text{Family support}}$$

Variables	*Coefficient*	*Std. Error*	*t-Statistic*	*Prob.*
Constant	0.371	0.150	2.467	0.020
Institution support	0.912	0.041	22.014	0.000

Value of r^2 is 0.945, so the relation between Institution support and family support is very strong. P value is < 0.01 so null is rejected in favor of alternative hypothesis. There is a strong relation between family support and Institution support.

Model Summary

Model	*R*	*R-Square*	*Adjusted R-Square*	*Std. Error of the Estimate*
1	.972(a)	.945	.943	.240

A Predictors: (Constant), without family support (either from parents/husband) no women can start any business.

Hypothesis 2

H_2 : There is a relation between experience and Institution support.

Institution support as dependent variable and experience as independent variable, the result is :

$$Y_{\text{Institution Support}} = 2.822 + 0.198\ X_{\text{Experience}}$$

Variables	*Coefficient*	*Std. Error*	*t-Statistic*	*Prob.*
Constant	2.822	0.900	3.137	0.004
Institution support	0.198	0.245	0.808	0.426

Value of r^2 is 0.023, so the relation between Institution support and experience is very weak. P value is > 0.01 so null is rejected in favor of alternative hypothesis. There is no relation between experience and Institution support.

Model Summary

Model	*R*	*R -Square*	*Adjusted R-Square*	*Std. Error of the Estimate*
1	0.151	0.023	-0.12	1.014

A Predictors: (Constant), without family support (either from parents/husband) no women can start any business

Correlations Matrix

From the correlation matrix it is learned that there is a strong correlation between family support and Institution support. But the relationship strength between experience and Institution support is not significant.

	Family support	*Experience*	*Institution support*
Family Support	1.000	.173	.983(**)
Experience	.173	1.000	.122
Institution Support	.983(**)	.122	1.000

** Correlation is significant at the 0.01 level (2-tailed).

CONCLUSION

In Bangladesh the study on women entrepreneurship is at

exploratory stage. Data scarcity and cooperation from the sample population side are the major problem to do research in this area. From this study we learn that women entrepreneurs think that family support is important than experience to get institutional support for access to finance. Welsch and Young (1984) also observe that women owners had less business experience than their male counterparts. Stevenson (1986) notes that, while male founders are able to gain experience from past work roles, women are less able to do this and only begin to obtain such experience from their own business.

Women have to play dual role so if they have support from the family it will be a great help not only to enter in to business the sample of this study believes that it will be a great help to get access to finance and this sample group believes that this support is more vital than experience. This study is based on very small sample and concentrated area so this study is suggested for extended area and more sample size for generalize this finding.

References

Aldrich, H. and Zimmer, C. (1986), "Entrepreneurship through social networks", in Sexton, D.L. and Smilor, R.W. (Eds), The Art and Science of Entrepreneurship, Ballinger Publishing Company, Cambridge, MA, pp. 3-24.

Breen, J., Calvert, C. and Oliver, J. (1995), "Female entrepreneurs in Australia: an investigation of financial and family issues", *Journal of Enterprising Culture*, Vol. 3, No. 4, pp. 445-61.

Brush, C.G., Carter, N., Gatewood, E., Greene, P.G. and Hart, M.M. (2001), An Investigation of Women-led Firms and Venture Capital Investment : A Report for the US Small Business Administration, Office of Advocacy National Women's Business Council.

Brush, C., Carter, N., Greene, P., Hart, M., Gatewood, E. and Weeks, J. (2000), Women and Equity Capital: An Exploration of the Factors Affecting Capital Access, available at: www.babson.edu/entrep/fer/XI/XIA

Business Research Services (2001), National Directory of Woman-Owned Business Firms, 11th ed., Business Research Services, Washington, DC.

Burt, R.S. (2000), "The network entrepreneur", in Swedberg, R. (Ed.), Entrepreneurship: The Social Science View, Oxford University Press, Oxford, pp. 281-307.

Carter, S. and Shaw, E. (2006), Women's Business Ownership: Recent Research and Policy Developments, *Report to the Small Business Service*, DTI Small Business Service, London.

Christopher, J. (1998), "Minority Business Formation and Survival: Evidence on Business Performance and Viability", *The Review of Black Political Economy*, Vol. 26, No. 1, pp. 37-72.

Dechant, K. and Al-Lamky, A. (2005), "Towards an Understanding of Arab Women Entrepreneurs in Bahrain and Oman", *Journal of Developmental Entrepreneurship*, Vol. 10 No. 2, pp. 123-40.

DeLollis, B. (1997), "Today's Female Passion for Entrepreneurship", *The American Enterprise*, Vol. 8, pp. 42-5.

Goldenberg, S. and Kline, T. (1999), "An Exploratory Study of Predicting Perceived Success and Survival of Small Businesses", *Psychological Reports*, Vol. 85, No. 2, pp. 365-77.

Granovetter, M. (1985), "Economic Action and Social Structure: The Problem of Embeddedness", *American Journal of Sociology*, Vol. 9 No. 3, pp. 481-510.

Humbert, A.L., Drew, E. and Kelan, E. (2009), "Gender Identity and ICT Entrepreneurship in an Irish context", in Pines, A.M. and Ozbilgin, M.F. (Eds.), Handbook of Research on High-Technology Entrepreneurs, Edward Elgar, Cheltenham.

Inman, K. (1999), Women's Resources in Business Start-up: A Study of Black and White Women Entrepreneurs, Garland Publishing, New York, N.Y.

Mattis, C. Marry (2004), "Women Entrepreneurs: Out from under the Glass Ceiling", *Women in Management Review*, Volume 19. Number 3, pp. 154-63.

Naser Kamal, Mohammed Rashid Wojoud, Nuseibeh Rana, (2009), "Factors that Affect Women Entrepreneurs: Evidence Froman Emerging Economy", *International Journal of Organizational Analysis*, Vol. 17, No. 3, pp. 225-47.

Nilufer, A. (2001), "Jobs, Gender and Small Enterprises in Bangladesh: Factors Affecting Women Entrepreneurs in Small and Cottage Industries in Bangladesh", *SEED Working Paper No. 14*, International Labor Office, Geneva.

Pines Malach Ayala, Lerner Miri, Schwartz Dafna (2010), "Gender differences in Entrepreneurship Equality, diversity and inclusion in times of global crisis", *Equality, Diversity and Inclusion: An International Journal*, Vol. 29, No. 2, pp. 186-98.

Riding, A. and Swift, C.S. (1990), "Women Business Owners and Terms of Credit: Some Empirical Findings of the Canadian Experience", *Journal of Business Venturing*, Vol. 5, No. 5, pp. 327-40.

Sinha, Shalini (2005), "Developing Women Entrepreneurs in South Asia: Issues, Initiatives and Experiences", Trade and Investment Division, UNESCAP, Bangkok, Thailand.

Shaw, E., Carter, S. and Brierton, J. (2002), "Unequal Entrepreneurs: Why Female Enterprise is an Uphill Struggle", The Work Foundation.

Smith-Hunter, A.E. (2003), Diversity and Entrepreneurship Successful Women Entrepreneurs, University Press of America, Lanham, MD.

Smith-Hunter, A.E. and Englhardt, W. (2004), "Determinants of Economic Success for Women Entrepreneurs: An Analysis Across Racial Lines", *Journal of the Academy of Business and Economics*, January.

Stevenson, L. (1986), "Against all Odds: The Entrepreneurship of Women", *Journal of Small Business Management*, Vol. 24, No. 4, pp. 30-6.

Stevenson, L. (1990), "Some Methodological Problems Associated with Researching Women Entrepreneurs", *Journal of Business Ethics*, 9 April/May, pp. 439-46.

Welsch, H. and Young, E. (1984), "Male and Female Entrepreneurial Characteristics and Behaviours: A Profile of Similarities and differences", *International Small Business Journal*, Vol. 2, No. 4, pp. 11-20.

CHAPTER

23

Micro Finance

Innovations and Growth Trends

SILKY JANGLANI, SIMRANJEET KAUR SANDHAR
AND AMITABH JOSHI

ABSTRACT

Although India's economy is diverse, encompassing agriculture, handicrafts, textile, rice, toys, manufacturing, and a multitude of services. Yet India suffers from substantial poverty. According to the World Bank's estimates on poverty, about thirds of India's more than 1 billion people live in rural areas, and almost 170 million of them are poor. Increasing stress on education, reservation of seats in government jobs and the increasing empowerment of women and the economically weaker sections of society, are also expected to contribute to the alleviation of poverty. Against this background, a need was felt for alternative policies, systems and procedures, savings and loan products, complementary services, and new delivery mechanisms that would fulfil the requirements of the poorest, especially of the women members of such households. Micro finance was one solution to these problems. The study is to analyze various growth trends and innovations in micro finance. It also studies the success of micro finance and its benefits to rural people.

Keywords: Poverty, Micro finance, Rural People, Women.

I. INTRODUCTION

1. Defining Micro Finance

Micro finance means the provision of financial services (credit, savings, insurance, etc.) to those living in poverty and excluded from the financial system. These people don't have an income nor own a property, and are therefore unable to provide bank guarantees, as a result of which they are generally forgotten by financial institutions and banks. (Goyal, 2008)

Micro finance refers to small scale financial services for both credits and deposits—that are provided to people who farm or fish or herd; operate small or micro enterprise where goods are produced, recycled, repaired or traded, provide services, work for wages or commissions, gain income from renting out small amounts of land, vehicles, draft animals, or machinery and tools, and to other individuals and local groups in developing countries in both rural and urban areas. (Marguerite S. Robinson)

2. Overview of Economy and Micro Finance

The economy of India, measured in USD exchange-rate terms, is the twelfth largest in the World/with a GDP of around $1 trillion (2008). It recorded a GDP growth rate of 9.1 for the Fiscal year 2007-08 this makes it the second fastest big emerging economy, after China, in the world. At this rate of sustained growth many economists forecast that India would, over the coming decades, have a more pronounced economic effect on the world stage. The World Bank classifies India as a low-income economy.

Although India's economy is diverse, encompassing agriculture, handicrafts, textile, rice, toys, manufacturing, and a multitude of services. Yet India suffers from substantial poverty. According to the World Bank's estimates on poverty, based on 2005 data, India has 456 million people, 41.6 of its population living below the new international poverty line of $ 1.25 per day. The World Bank further estimates that 33 of the global poor now reside in India. Moreover, India also has 828 million people, or 75.6 of the population living below $ 2 a day, compared to 72.2 for Sub-Saharan Africa. (Pronyk, Hargreaves, and Morduch, 2007)

India faces a fast-growing population and the challenge of reducing economic and social inequality. Poverty remains a serious problem, although it has declined significantly since independence.

About thirds of India's more than 1 billion people live in rural areas, and almost 170 million of them are poor. Although many rural people are migrating to cities, three out of four of India's poor people live in the vast rural parts of the country. For more than 21 per cent of them, poverty is a chronic condition. Since the early 1950s, government has initiated, sustained, and refined various planning schemes to help the poor attain self sufficiency in food production.

Probably the most important initiative has been the supply of basic commodities, particularly food at controlled prices, available throughout the country as poor spend about 80 percent of their income on food.

Eradication of poverty in India can only be a long-term goal. It is incorrect to say that all poverty reduction programmes have failed. The growth of the middle class (which was virtually non-existent when India became a free nation in August 1947) indicates that economic prosperity has indeed been very impressive in India but the distribution of wealth is not at all even. (Goyal, 2008)

While total overall poverty in India has declined, the extent of poverty reduction is often debated. While there is a consensus that there has not been increase in poverty between 1993- 94 and 2004-05, the picture is not so clear if one considers other non-pecuniary dimensions such as health, education, crime and access to infrastructure. With the rapid economic growth that India is experiencing, it is likely that a significant fraction of the rural population will continue to migrate toward cities, making the issue of urban poverty more significant in the long-run.

A 2007 report by the state-run National Commission for Enterprises in the Unorganized Sector (NCEUS) found that 77 of Indians, or 836 million people, lived on less than 20 rupees per day, with most working in "informal labour Sector" with no job or social security, living in abject poverty. (Matin, 2002)

3. Need of Finance for Eradicating Poverty

A major cause of poverty among rural people in India is lack of access for both individuals and communities to productive assets and financial resources. High levels of illiteracy, inadequate health care and extremely limited access to social services are common among poor rural people. Poverty alleviation is expected to make better progress in the next 50 years than in the past, as a trickle-down effect of the growing middle class. Increasing stress on education, reservation of seats in government jobs and the increasing empowerment of women and the economically weaker sections of society, are also expected to contribute to the alleviation of poverty. The most contributing innovation done for eradicating poverty is micro finance. Microenterprise development which could generate income and enable them .to improve their living-conditions has only recently become a focus of the government.

Empowering rural people is an essential first step to eradicating poverty. It respects the willingness and capability that each of us has to take charge of our own life and to seek' out opportunities to make it better. (Goyal, 2008)

2. MICRO FINANCE

1. Micro Finance in Rural Areas

Micro finance is one way of fighting poverty in rural areas, where most of the world's poorest people live. It puts credit, savings, insurance and other basic financial services within the reach of poor people. Through Micro finance institutions such as credit unions and some non-governmental organizations, poor people can obtain small loans receive remittances from relatives working abroad and safeguard their savings. Accessing small amounts of credit at reasonable interest rates gives people with the willingness and know-how an opportunity to set-up a small business. Records show that poor people are a good risk, with higher rates than conventional borrowers. In countries as diverse as Bangladesh, Benin and Dominica, repayment rates are as high as 97 per cent.

Micro finance is not a new idea in India. Concept of Micro finance becomes popular in 1990's with Grameen bank coming out with a useful model in Bangladesh and Mohammad Yunus winning the Nobel Prize for it. Even an Indian firm SKS Micro finance came into the news after it got 11.5 Million from Sequoia capital. Research conducted in India by the National Bank for Agriculture and Rural Development (NABARD) during the early '80s showed that despite a wide network of rural bank branches which implemented specific poverty alleviation programmes that sought creation of self-employment opportunities through link credit for almost two decades, a very large number of the poor continued to remain outside the fold of the formal banking system.

Rural development, special schemes and rural banking could not tackle the widespread poverty in rural areas. Research indicated that existing banking policies and procedures were perhaps not suited to the immediate needs of the very poor. What they really needed was better access to these services and products, rather than cheap, subsidized credit. The priority of the rural poor appeared to be consumption credit, savings, production credit and insurance. (Goyal, 2008)

Consumption needs included credit for short periods for emergent needs, which were usually met by informal sources at exploitative interest rates, as poor borrowers were unable to offer banks any security for small consumption loans. Banks in turn faced constraints due to the high transaction costs involved in processing small amounts to borrowers scattered in rural areas, as well as concerns related to loan recovery.

Against this background, a need was felt for alternative policies, systems and procedures, savings and loan products, complementary services, and new delivery mechanisms that would fulfil the requirements of the poorest, especially of the women members of such households. The Grameen Bank in neighboring Bangladesh had already proved a successful model of micro lending in South Asia. The self-help group model, pioneered by the Grameen Bank, emerged as a viable strategy to tackle these issues both for borrowers as well as banks.

With a view to developing a supplementary credit delivery mechanism to rench the poor in a cost effective and sustainable manner, the National Bank for Agriculture and Rural Development (NABARD) introduced a pilot project for linking 500 SHGs with banks in 1992 after thorough discussion with the Reserve Bank of India (the central banking authority for India), commercial banks and NGOs.

2. Micro Finance in Urban Areas

The cities in India are projecting immense development with sky scrapers, fancy, flyovers, massive shopping malls and multiplexes. But what are co-existing are urban poverty, poverty of employment, poverty of shelter, poverty of basic necessities and poverty of access to basic infrastructure like electricity, water, drainage and sanitation. Housing for the poor is so scarce and consequently slums are mushrooming everywhere, with little action on the part of the authorities to ensure cheap housing for the poor. The so-called Slum Rehabilitation authority does precious little by way of locating suitable land and constructing tenements with basic necessities.

3. HOW MICRO FINANCE WORKS?

The most common Micro finance product is a microcredit loan—usually less than $ 100. These tiny loans are enough for hardworking micro-entrepreneurs to start or expand small businesses such as weaving baskets, raising chickens, or buying wholesale products to sell in a market. Income from these businesses provides better food, housing, healthcare and education for entire families and most important, additional income provides hope for a better future. (Gonzalez, 1998)

Micro Finance institutions exist in many forms—credit unions, commercial banks, and most often non-governmental organizations. Many MFIs use social collateral in the form of peer groups to ensure loan repayment. (Roy, 2008)

I. Objectives of Micro Finance

1. *Micro Enterprise Development:* by providing financial inputs and services to informal sector entrepreneurs building their tiny businesses to the point of employing not just family members but others as well.
2. *Innovation/Investment Promotion:* by offering credit as both incentive and enabler; for Example, to small-scale farmers to adopt new inputs, practices and technologies to increase productivity of labor and land leading to more food production and/or farm income or more broadly in the population, to promote behavior change for better health and nutrition.
3. *Consumption-Smoothing:* by providing poor families with relatively inexpensive credit and convenient savings services that effectively help the family have enough cash through the year to reduce the Impact of the annual hungry season; major expenses, such as school fees or weddings; and/or the devastation of major economic shocks due to family illness, death of a breadwinner, loss of livestock or a crop, or a natural disaster.
4. *Women's Empowerment* and more generally, building of social capital, to support self-help efforts at the family and community levels and to strengthen the voice of women and other marginalized groups as rights holders and agents of local development.
5. *Financial Systems Development,* or financial sector deepening, both of which seek to lower the cost and increase the convenience of financial services so that the "unbanked" even the very poor can be reached by commercially viable enterprise.

4. OBJECTIVES OF THE STUDY

- To understand the concept of micro finance.
- To study the growth trends in micro finance.

- To study the innovations carried out in micro finance.

5. RESEARCH DESIGN

The research work is inherently based on conceptual study on the growth and innovation of micro finance. Micro finance is one of the merging issues in India as the country is facing two problems of poverty and huge population. Data had been collected from various other research papers and websites. Collectively the conclusion is drawn out. The results are summarized in discussions.

6. DISCUSSIONS

I. The Profile Micro Finance in India

India with a population over 1 billion has its 70 people staying in rural or semi urban areas with almost 260 million people living below poverty line. Approximately 75 million households need micro-finance. Of these nearly 60 million households are in rural India and the remaining 15 million are urban Slum dwellers.

In India, it began in the 1980s with the formation of pockets of informal Self Help Groups (SHG) engaging in micro activities financed by Microfinance. But India's first Micro finance Institution 'Shri Mahila SEWA Shakari Bank was set-up as an urban co-operative bank, by the Self Employed Women's Association (SEWA) soon after the group (founder Ms. Ela Bhatt) was formed in 1974.

The first official effort materialised under the direction of NABARD. (National Bank for Agriculture and Rural Development). The Mysore Resettlement and Development Agency (MVRADA) sponsored project on "Savings and Credit Management" of SHGs was partially financed by NABARD during 1986-87.

Semam Micro finance Investment Literacy and Empowerment PVT (SMILE) is the largest Grameen-model Micro finance institution in Southern India. Established originally in 1999 as Mahasemam Trust, SMILE is a non-bank financial company (NBFC) that targets poor women, offering Micro finance services including savings, loans, and insurance to promote poverty alleviation and sustainable development in the Southern Indian state of Tamil Nadu. SMILE currently has over 175 thousand active borrowers and a total loan portfolio of USD 16.4 million with total assets of USD 20 million as reported by The Mix Market. Their return on assets (ROA) was reported at 46 percent as of December 2007 with a return on equity (ROE) of 6.15 percent.

Gram-Uttham is a Micro finance institution founded in 1990 in the eastern Indian state of Orissa as part of the CARE India/Credit and Savings for Household Enterprise (CASHE) project to facilitate social and economic development in poor rural villages. Gram Uttham offers credit, savings, insurance, and self-help group services to clients, focusing on local fishing villages.

Gram-Uttham currently has over 41 thousand active borrowers and a total loan portfolio of USD 5.5 million and total assets of USD 6.6 million. Their return on assets (ROA) was reported at -.8 percent in March 2007 with a return on equity (ROE) of -221.22 percent.

2. Innovation of Micro Finance during Next Decades

It's time for Micro finance to go online with startups like Dhanax and Pie Micro finance enabling general users to make their little contribution and help those who need it. And it's no non-profit stuff; all these are pure profit-making firms. To quote from the dhanax website "Your money deposited in the savings account of a bank may fetch you anything between 2 to 3 in interest.

A fixed deposit may earn you an interest of close to 8. On the other hand, small entrepreneurs in need of micro credit pay anything between 24 to 60 as annual interest on loans to money lenders and loan sharks.

And their concept is simple, they partner with reputed MFI's and NGO's, that look at the economic needs of the poor, analyze the local situation and bring out such profit-making models which could be mutually beneficial for the investor (you) and the poor economically. As the dhanx website says "When you assume the role of a lender, your money transforms into capital which, apart from empowering individuals from the lower economic stratum, also earns you a greater return on investment." For all those who have always wanted to give back to the society, these firms now give you that platform which is not only is profitable but comes out as an overall gratifying experience for you as a lender. (Matin, 2002)

3. Bill for Micro Finance

The draft bill comes at a time when mere are differing opinions on the cost efficacy of the MFO model for reaching credit to the poor. Moreover, the bill itself contains some perplexing ideas—such as the choice of NABARD, itself an MFO, as a regulator of other such organizations. (R.S. Aubuchon, 2008)

I. Highlights of Bill

- The Micro Financial Sector (Development and Regulation) Bill, 2007 seeks to promote the sector and regulate micro financial organizations (MFO).
- National Bank for Agriculture and Rural Development (NABARD) shall regulate the micro financial sector.
- Every MFO that accepts deposits needs to be registered with NABARD. Conditions for registration include (a) net owned funds of at least Rs. 5 lakh; and (b) at least three years in existence as an MFO. All MFOs, whether registered or not, shall submit annual financial statements to NABARD.
- Every MFO that accepts deposits has to create a reserve fund by transferring a minimum of 15 of its net profit realized out of its thrift and micro finance services every year.
- The central government may establish a Micro Finance Development Council to advise NABARD on formulation of policies related to the micro financial sector.
- NABARD shall constitute a Micro Finance Development and Equity Fund to be utilized for the development of the sector.

7. CONCLUSION

1. Government Allocation to Micro Finance : 2010-11 Budget

Government is now giving due importance to micro finance sector. The corpus for micro finance development and equity Fund doubled to Rs. 400 Crore in 2010-11.

2. Areas Opened for using Micro Finance Funds

Micro finance in practical is carried out by some of the organizations such as Caspian advisors an investment managements and advisory services company based in Hyderabad, India that has been focused on managing investment funds in the Micro finance space since 2005 and Aavishkar Goodwell India Micro finance Development Company is a Micro finance development company that invests in entrepreneurial Micro finance organizations in India. It was incorporated as a Global Business License Company with Financial Service Commision, Maritius in December 2006.

3. System Recycling Government Grants by Recovery/ Return

The repayment rate of micro credit touches record high, nearly cent percent. The record is proudly advertised by the micro-credit operators. By the high rate they claim to have achieved success. A higher recovery rate and quickness turnover of capital results in higher rate of profit to the micro credit organizations.

References

Gonzalez, V.C. (1998). Micro Finance : Broader Achievements and New Challenges. *Economics and sociology*.

Goyal, N. (2008). The Changing Face of Rural India. Prestige Institute of Management. Dewas.

Matin, I. (2002). Finance for the Poor : From Micro Credit to Micro Financial Services. *Journal of International Development*, 273-94.

Pronyk, P.M., Hargreaves, J.R., and Morduch, J. (2007). Micro Finance Programs and Better Health Prospects for Sub-Sahara Africa, *The Journal of American Medical Assiciation*.

R.S. Aubuchon (2008). The Micro Finance Revolution : An Overview. Federal Reserve Bank of St. Louis Review.

Roy, M. (2008). Performance and Governance in Micro Finance Institutions, *Journal of Banking and Finance*, 662-69.

www.nabard.com

www.indiatogether.com accessed on 10th May 2011.

www.thinkchangeindia.com accessed on 10th May 2011.

www.watlog.com accessed on 10th May 2011.

www.genfinance.info.com accessed on 12th May 2011.

CHAPTER

24

Road Map to Sustainability Rests on Corporate Governance

NEHA GUPTA AND SUMBUL TAHIR

INTRODUCTION

In the recent years corporate governance has emerged as a favorite topic amongst researchers and practitioners. The origins of Corporate Governance can be traced back to 1600s when the Court of Directors was the Executive body running East India Company on behalf of Court of Proprietors. In the 1980s mergers and acquisitions became a rage leading to rising executive remuneration. Corporate governance acted as a moderator to prevent abuse of power and financial crisis. Governmental regulation and shareholder demand for information also increased. Next came the information age that gave faster access to company operations' information to the stakeholders, leading to more pressure on companies for better regulation.

The Agency theory argued that the agents of the company i.e. Managers could misuse and abuse their decision-making power for more short term gains for increasing their own remuneration at the cost of the company's long term objectives and environment. The separation of ownership and control leads to an even more pressing need for good corporate governance.

The Cadbury Code of Practice published by London Stock Exchange in 1992 brought a new realm in corporate governance. UK had witnessed a number of high profile corporate failures which had created a need for some regulatory framework. This code aimed at increasing confidence in financial reporting by companies and devising ways to improve corporate governance practices. An International code of OECD guidelines developed in partnership with World Bank and Asian Development Bank followed the Cadbury code.

One of the standard definitions of Corporate Governance given by legal and economic experts is defending shareholders' interest. It is through effective corporate governance only that the company is held accountable to its residual owners. This ideology has now become ingrained in most corporate cultures. It is further believed that if the company maximizes shareholders' value, the returns to other stakeholders' will also increase leading to overall development and success. However, in reality there have been many cases where shareholder interest do no reconcile well with stakeholders interest. Such scenarios show that overwhelming emphasis on shareholder value may push executives to lean towards short cuts and unethical conduct.

According Tirole (2001) defining corporate governance as "the design of institutions that induce or force management to internalize the welfare of stakeholders" might resolve the above conflict and pave the way for executive code of conduct. The shift from a focus on shareholders to stakeholders is in conformance with the view held by O'Sullivan (2001) who believed that the dominant perspective of corporate governance confined to shareholders has now been effectively challenged by stakeholders. A new concept of Corporate Citizenship has emerged that believes that companies can no longer be indifferent to the damage they incur on the society at large. Countries like Germany and Japan are already adopting the stakeholders' approach. Hence, the famous assertion given by Friedman (1970) and later reemphasized by Learmount (2002) that "the only business of business is business" is irrevocably refuted.

Let us consider a final comprehensive definition of Corporate Governance given by Steiner and Steiner (2003):

> Corporate Governance is the overall control of activities in a corporation. It is concerned with the formulation of long-term objectives and plans and the proper management structure (organization, systems and people) to achieve them. At the same time, it entails making sure that the structure functions to maintain the corporation's integrity, reputation and responsibility to its various constituencies.

ASPECTS

OECD (2004) has given some basic tenets of corporate governance: fairness, transparency, accountability and responsibility. These tenets are actually the benchmarks that can serve as a great tool for devising the corporate strategy for governance and code of ethics. Separating and clarifying the roles of Board of Directors and CEO, appointing independent directors and using board committees for audits, reward management and nominations are other aspects. While clarifying the roles of the Board and CEO respectively, it has to be ensured that there is scope for the directors to review and oversee the functioning of the company. This behavior is still frowned upon in most companies but unless the Board is empowered to oversee and deliberate on the company's internal working, how can the Directors be held accountable to the public for governance? Appointing independent directors especially those that have some experience in governance and socially responsible interventions, is also a necessity for creating a more mature Board of Directors. Finally, Board committees are another mechanism for ensuring some relationship and coherence between board level and managerial level decision-making.

Cadbury had also suggested two principles viz. (1) Managers must be free to drive their companies forward, and (2) this freedom must be exercised in a framework of effective accountability, effective decision-making and clear description of rights and responsibilities. Designing a lucid and legal code of ethics and control mechanisms is also an essential step. Hence, the essence of corporate governance is proper stewardship, decisions driven by integrity, openness, transparency and accountability to the public and all of his has to emerge from the company's own culture and should not be forced.

GROWING CONCERN

As we have seen the concept of corporate governance in not new, its beginning can in effect be traced back to Kautilya's Arthashastra, however, it has achieved new dimensions in a post globalization and post-recession world. Some of the factors behind this are:

1. Increasing Complexity

Organizations of today are thriving in an age marked by information technology and innovation. In an era of globalization with the threat of recession looming large, organizations have been forced to move towards lean management. Although systems theory has already shown the interdependence of sub-systems and environment in the functioning of an organization, but clubbing this with lean management makes the complexity reach even higher levels. The attraction of cutting corners and taking short cuts is increasing but so is the regulatory framework set by agencies such as the government, NGOs, UN to name a few.

2. Economic Gains

Raising capital in a globalized world is actually easier for organizations that are behaving in a socially responsible manner and have handled their investors well. Well governed companies have been proved to have higher equity returns and command higher values, with better operating performance as depicted by their balance sheets compared to their poorly governed counterparts Mir and Seboui (2008). Hence, any investment in good governance will always yield benefits in future.

3. Social Awareness

Increasing social awareness of stakeholders, consumers and public at large is also a contributing factor for good corporate governance. Many companies are now trying to capitalize on this issue by designing marketing strategies that promote them as paragons of good governance. If a company is in the habit of ethical and responsible managerial decision-making, then using the same for gaining profits through sympathy buying is no sin but if the advertising is only a gimmick used as a tool to manipulate the customers then a harsh punishment must be levied.

McKendall *et. al.* (1999) have suggested that expectations of the society along with desire for more profits may lead to encouragement of illegal activities in the company in a highly competitive internal environment. Good governance should ensure prevention and redressal of the same.

4. Legal Tangles

Despite extensive legislation on governance, there are always loopholes that are used by power hungry and dishonest executives for making a quick buck. The recent debate on introduction of a new regulation in Companies Bill, on corporate social responsibility making it mandatory for every company earning more than 5 crores as profits or having a turnover of 1000 crores to spend 2% of its net profits of preceding three years on CSR has also brought a lot of meaningful dialogue on the issue. Many believe that a mandatory spending will crush the spirit of socially responsible interventions while others want more commitment from the private sector.

5. Technological Volatility

The growth of Information Technology has led to the emergence of a decentralized society where everyone has access to information and public platforms like social networking sites and blogs to share opinions. In such a society the scope for getting away with unethical and illegal activities has become narrow. Hence, IT has increased the channels of accountability , while opening many channels of communication.

More companies are combining their strategies for increasing profit and addressing climate change.

Corporate governance and fundamental financial issues dominated Wall Street reform talk in the past year, but Ceres suggests environmental sustainability also has elbowed its way onto corporate boardroom agendas.

> "Corporate scandals and the current economic crisis have heightened demands for new approaches to governance, particularly in relation to executive compensation and risk management," says the Ceres report. "As sustainability has moved up the corporate, investor and public policy agendas, it has become more fully integrated into these governance expectations."

Companies are trying hard to reduce their carbon footprint. The first and obvious step is by controlling their energy usage. An inventory of energy used by the company has to be made and an action plan for reducing the usage levels to predetermined targets has to be developed and adhered to.

Companies like Alcoa that works in the Aluminum industry in US, conducts energy efficiency surveys at plants supported by U.S. Department of Energy. The company claims to have saved 60 million dollars in operating costs through its energy efficiency programs. Intel shows a similar story, having invested $23 million in measures for saving energy; the company has already saved $50 million.

PROMOTE EFFICIENCY, CUT WASTE

Progressive companies are realizing that profit and sustainability measures are not two ends of a rainbow rather both can be achieved at the same time. One model suggested by Ceres report says that the focus of the company has to be on five areas:

1. Sustained measures towards energy efficiency and renewable energy usage.
2. Designing closed loop systems for air and water usage that will lead to more recycling and less wastes.
3. Making sure that at least 3/4 suppliers meet sustainability performance criteria. This will create pressure on the companies that have still not understood the importance of sustainable measures.
4. Ensuring that half of the expenditure made on research and development is made on environment-friendly projects.
5. Finally, Executive remuneration should be fixed on the CEO's ability to internalize and capitalize on sustainable practices in the organizational culture. The Board should remember however that sustainable practices usually have a lag time and the profits might not be immediately apparent. Hence, a long-term view has to be taken while considering managerial performance otherwise it may lead to de-motivation of the managerial staff. It has increasingly been apparent that shareholders and other regulators are increasing pressure on boards to align executive pay with long-term objectives and profits.

In this top-down corporate governance structure, the Ceres report calls on companies to name directors who have expertise in environmental sustainability issues. Companies like Xcel Energy based out of Minnesota have linked greenhouse gas reductions and safety performance apart from shareholder earnings for annual incentives measurement for executive officers.

McDonald's has installed energy efficiency control systems for reducing annual energy expenditure. PepsiCo's Frito-Lay potato chip factory is aiming for a zero-emissions operation, and the list goes on.

Disclosure is another important facet of corporate governance. It is imperative that companies disclose a balanced view of their performance, not only painting a rosy picture but also addressing the dilemmas faced. An apt example is the 2008-09 sustainability report filed by Ford. The report mentions the challenges faced by the company during the recession including restructuring, layoffs and even closing down some factories. The company's detailed financial recovery plan and further opportunities for sustainable business practice are also mentioned.

CORPORATE GOVERNANCE AND IMPACT OF GLOBALIZATION

The Structure of Corporate Governance

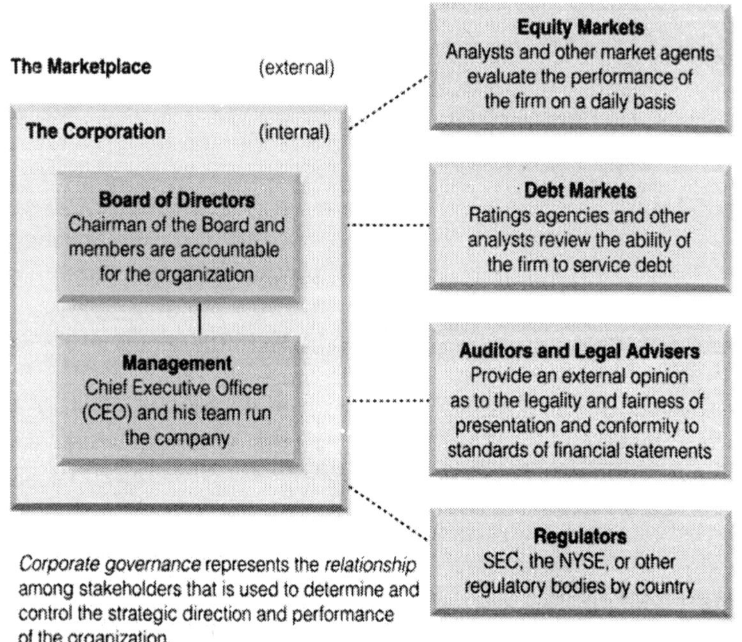

Corporate governance represents the *relationship* among stakeholders that is used to determine and control the strategic direction and performance of the organization.

Corporate Governance talks about various rules, procedures, and guidelines to be followed which affect the manner in which the company or organization is working or its working can be controlled.

Corporate governance principles and codes are developed which are in different in various countries and range from being commanded from stock exchanges, corporations or associations of directors and managers by the help of governments and various international organizations. As a rule, compliance with these governance recommendations is not mandated by any particular law. For example, companies quoted on the London, Toronto and Australian Stock Exchanges formally need not follow the recommendations of their respective codes. However, they must disclose whether they follow the recommendations in those documents and, where not, they should provide explanations concerning divergent practices. Such disclosure requirements exert a significant pressure on listed companies for compliance.

Due to Globalization there exists a need of an apex body to standardize the norms for corporate Governance. One of the most influential guidelines has been the 1999 OECD Principles of Corporate Governance. This was revised in 2004. The OECD guidelines are often referenced by countries developing local codes or guidelines. Building on the work of the OECD, other international organizations, private sector associations and more than 20 national corporate governance codes, this internationally agreed benchmark consists of more than fifty distinct disclosure items across five broad categories:

- Auditing
- Board and management structure and process
- Corporate responsibility and compliance
- Financial transparency and information disclosure
- Ownership structure and exercise of control rights

Matthew Bishop, writing in 1994 for *The Economist magazine*, admits that "predicting trends in corporate governance is a tricky business".

GOVERNANCE RANKING 2010

According to a recent report by OCED there was an

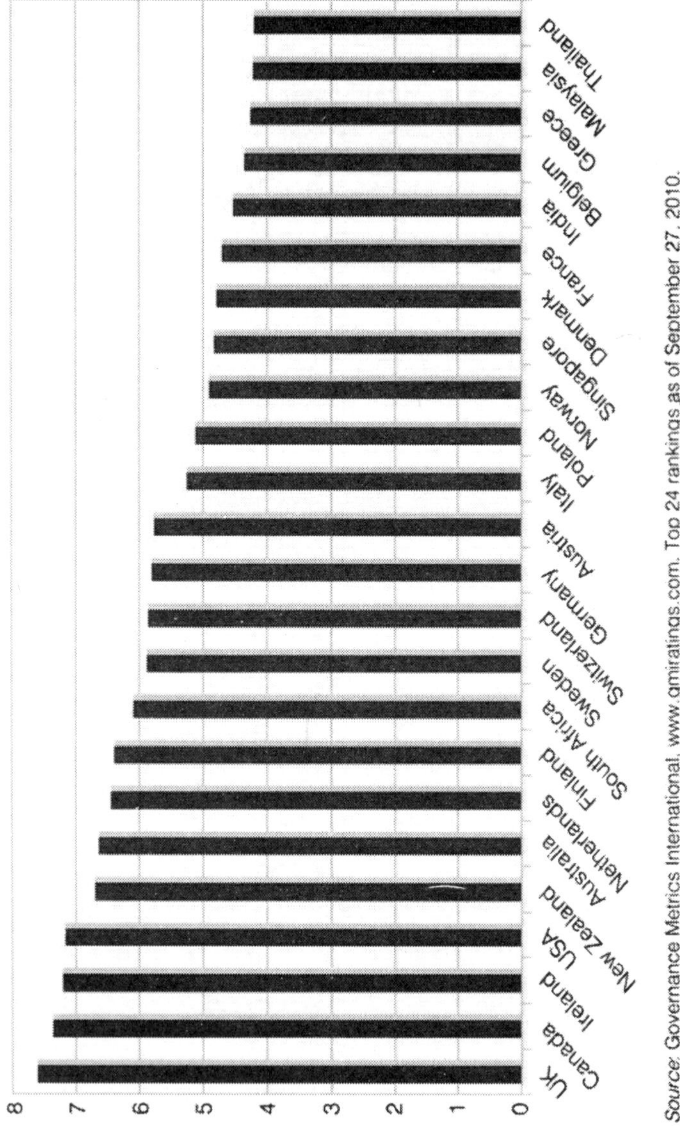

Source: Governance Metrics International, www.gmiratings.com. Top 24 rankings as of September 27, 2010.

opinion that in absence of national regulatory barriers and control techniques, the global trade seems to be increasing , which shows the lack of regulation and control over global trade practices. The OECD advisory group concludes that "the practical corporate governance agenda in different countries is converging in many vital areas, although historical and cultural differences will continue to exist" (1998a:87).

Corporate Governance Model at MacDonald's

If we talk in terms of CSR then various terms can be used interchangeably, such as corporate sustainability, corporate social investment, triple bottom line, socially responsible investment and corporate governance. Recent high profile corporate scams and deterioration have contributed to public mistrust and the demand for improved corporate governance, accountability and transparency.

COMPARATIVE CORPORATE GOVERNANCE ACROSS COUNTRIES

The topic of converging on a particular aspect out of three

Regime Basis	Characteristics	Examples
Market-based	Efficient equity markets; Dispersed ownership	United States, United Kingdom, Canada, Australia
Family-based	Management and ownership is combined; Family/majority and minority shareholders	Hong Kong, Indonesia, Malaysia, Singapore, Taiwan, France
Bank-based	Government influence in bank lending; Lack of transparency; Family control	Korea, Germany
Government affiliated	State ownership of enterprise; Lack of transparency; No minority influence	China, Russia

Source: Based on "Corporate Governance in Emerging Markets: An Asian Perspective," by J. Tsui and T. Shieh, in *International Finance and Accounting Handbook*, Third Edition, Frederick D.S. Choi, editor, Wiley, 2004, pp. 24.4–24.6.

disciplines-legal, institutional and political is still doubtful so as to select the general discipline out of three. Thus, there does not exist any particular or common aspect where Corporate Governance Systems can converge or meet due to Globalization.

References

Clarke, Thomas and Chanlat, Jean-Francois (eds.) (2009), "European Corporate Governance", London and New York: Routledge, ISBN 9780415405331.

Clarke, Thomas and dela Rama, Marie (eds.) (2006), "Corporate Governance and Globalization (3 Volume Series)", London and Thousand Oaks, CA: SAGE, ISBN 978-1-4129-2899-1.

Clarke, Thomas and dela Rama, Marie (eds.) (2008), "Fundamentals of Corporate Governance (4 Volume Series)", London and Thousand Oaks, CA: SAGE, ISBN 978-1-4129-3589-0.

Colley, J., Doyle, J., Logan, G., Stettinius, W., What is Corporate Governance ? (McGraw-Hill, December 2004) ISBN.

Guillen, Mauro F., (September, 1999), Corporate Governance and Globalization: Arguments and Evidence against Convergence (http://en.wikipedia.org/wiki/Corporate_governance.)

Tirole, J. (2001), Corporate Governance, *Econometrica*, Vol. 69, No. 1, pp. 1-35.

Cadbury, A. (2002), Corporate Governance Chairmanship: A Personal View, Oxford University Press, Great Britain.

O'Sullivan, M. (2001), Contests for Corporate Control—Corporate Governance and Economic Performance in the United States and Germany, Oxford University Press, Great Britain.

Steiner, G. and Steiner, J. (2003), Business, Government and Society: A Managerial Perspective, 10th Edition, McGraw Hill, USA.

OECD (2004), Principles of corporate governance retrieved from http://www.oecd.org/topic0,2686,en_2649_37439_1_1_1_1_37439,00.html

Mir, A.E. and Seboui, S. (2008), Corporate Governance and relationship between EVA and created shareholder value, *Corporate Governance*, Vol. 8, No. 1, pp. 46-58.

McKendall, M., Sanchez, C. and Sicilian, P. (1999), Corporate Governance and Corporate Illegality: The Effects of Board Structures on Environmental Violations, *The International Journal of Organizational Analysis*, Vol. 7, No. 3, pp. 201-23.

CHAPTER

25

Sustainability in Higher Education

A New Paradigm

SUMBUL TAHIR

INTRODUCTION

The issue of sustainability in higher education is a recently emerging theme. Though the first steps in linking environmental protection and sustainable development with higher education were taken in 1960s, but we still find a huge lacuna in this sphere with most universities and colleges still unclear or uncomfortable with the issue. This paper attempts to clarify the relationship between higher education institutions and sustainable community development and stress on the utmost need for tenacious attempts in the field. Although the top universities of the world do engage in community development initiative but none of them display an institutionalization of the concept in the DNA of the organization. Indian universities lag far behind with most of them not even displaying any relevant information on their websites.

Sustainable development is a burning issue that requires efforts and dialogue from all sections of the society with the onus of responsibility being higher on educational institutions as they are associated with the young of the society. A successful marriage between education and a positive and responsible attitude towards environment will only lead to a lasting impression for the generations to come.

The definition most widely accepted for defining sustainable development was given in Brundtland Report (1987):

> "Sustainable development is development that meets the needs of the present without compromising the ability of future generations to meet their own needs. It contains within it two key concepts:
>
> - the concept of *needs*, in particular the essential needs of the world's poor, to which overriding priority should be given; and
> - the idea of *limitations* imposed by the state of technology and social organization on the environment's ability to meet present and future needs."

The concept of sustainable development requires that we realize that the world we live in is a system composed of numerous interrelated and interdependent sub-systems. If any component of this system is harmed ultimately the entire system suffers. Hence, the materialistic culture of America has repercussions on the consumption of the poor countries of Africa and the pesticides used in South America could affect fisheries in Australia. Hence, the world is slowly and reluctantly realizing the crucial need for responsible actions.

HISTORY

The emergence of the green movement in higher education can be traced back to the late 1960s in the Western world. In India the concept is still not widely recognized. Earth Day celebrated worldwide on April 22 today, was pioneered by John McConnell in 1969 at a UNESCO Conference in San Francisco. Later the Stockholm Declaration of 1972 extended the concern for environment to education and other societal sectors. However, it is believed that the 1992 Rio Earth Summit actually made the term education for sustainable development common. Today, more than 600 universities worldwide have signed International agreements and conventions like the Bologna Charter, the Halifax Declaration, the Talloires Declaration and the Copernicus Charter for Sustainable Development.

As early as October 1977, The Tbilisi Intergovernmental Conference on environmental education, organized by United National Educational, Scientific And Cultural Organization (UNESCO) and United Nations Environment Program (UNEP) had encouraged the establishment of environment education at the university level. Talloires Declaration, in October 1990 with 66 member-states and participants had decided to implement ten steps in evolving university level education in order to put a curb on the increasing pollution and environmental degradation. The Halifax Declaration in December, 1991 was organized by International Association of Universities (IAU) and the United Nations Universities again for emphasizing on the relevance and need of universities for sustainable development. However, it was the United Nations Convention on environment and development at Rio De Janeiro (UNCED, 1992) that really brought environmental issues in the limelight making sure that the government and the universities were held responsible for maintaining a balance between economic development and environmental sustenance.

The Swansea Declaration (1993), over 400 universities participating in it, also emphasized the role of universities in saving the globe. The Kyoto Declaration in the same year was ratified by 650 university members of the international association of universities stressing the need for universities to actively participate in sustainable development. Copernicus charter was founded as a cooperative network of European higher education institutions for sustainability; today more than 290 universities from 37 European states have joined Copernicus Charter.

According to the Bologna Charter (2000), "In order to promote higher education for sustainable development four international organizations have formed a "Global Higher Education for Sustainability Partnership (GHESP)". The four founding partners of the initiative—which are the International Association of Universities (IAU), the University Leaders for a Sustainable Future (ULSF), Copernicus-Campus and UNESCO-combine forces to mobilize universities and higher education institutions in favor of a sustainable development (according to Chapter 36 of the Agenda 21)."

The WWF training center in Switzerland is also contributing a lot to enrich the relationship between sustainability and higher education. In its 57th meeting in December 2002, the United Nations General Assembly proclaimed the UN Decade of Education for Sustainable Development, 2005-14, emphasizing the importance and indispensability of education for achieving sustainable development. There is hence no doubt that the premier institutions of the world are eager to initiate and contribute to this sphere of knowledge; however, the concept has still not become accepted in many countries.

RESEARCH LEVELS

Sustainable development requires research for discovering new and innovative ways of building relationships between the various agencies active in this direction and for providing a platform for sharing the information generated. In sustainability research, three fundamental levels can be identified:

(1) analytical level, where knowledge is created or discovered;
(2) normative level, which helps in developing norms and rules for moving forward; and
(3) operative level, at which the knowledge and norms are ultimately applied.

The issue of sustainability cannot remain limited to a few selected domains. The widespread environmental and social values degradation demands a holistic and well developed approach towards rebuilding and reworking the world around us. One aspect of development in this sense can be reaching out to universities and higher education institutions for eliciting their support and commitment in this area. The higher education sector owing to its role model and knowledge disseminating function, has a special responsibility towards the cause. The target groups for the initiatives can be:

- University administrators (e.g. Rectors, Vice-Chancellors, Presidents and Principals);
- Professors, Readers, Assistant Professors, Lecturers, research fellows, research associates and other members of staff working with environmental matters;
- Staff in charge of health and safety, water and electricity consumption and transport policies; and
- Students.

For developing a comprehensive plan for sustainability on campus multiple stakeholders have to be channelized and the plan has to reflect the mission, vision and values of an institution. The organization has to imbibe sustainability in their culture and create a "campus brand" that identifies them as having done so. The beginning has to be initiated from the building of the institution itself. Universities should provide education, training and motivation to their employees on sustainability, so that they can pursue their work in an environmentally responsible manner.

GREEN INITIATIVES ON CAMPUS

For established institutions all further extensions of the existing infrastructure have to be "green". Terms like green building, natural building, sustainable design and green architecture are increasingly being used by an increasingly environmentally conscious generation. Green building refers to a structure that is developed in an environmentally responsible and resource-efficient way throughout a building's life-cycle: from design and construction, to maintenance and renovation. The main aim of all green architecture is to reduce the overall impact of the infrastructure on human beings and the natural environment. In India the IGBC, Indian Green Building Council has been set-up under CII-Sohrabji Godrej Green Business Centre. It is making inroads in sustainability development by certifying green buildings, organizing frequent conferences, training programs and conducting certification examinations.

A related concept is green cleaning that believes in using environment friendly cleaning products and methods. This might seem to be an insignificant step but considering the huge impact of using synthetic detergents for cleaning washrooms on the decomposition of sewage and ultimately effect on the ground water reserves, shows how small steps can make big impacts.

Another sustainability initiative is sustainability purchasing. Sustainability purchasing is a concept that extends the two objectives of good purchasing from price and quality to ensuring environmental, social and economic responsibility. From purchasing energy-saving light bulbs to organic locally sourced food being served in a workplace canteen—the scope for initiatives in this area are enormous. If a university believes in workforce diversity and recruits faculty and staff from all sections of society, it is an illustration of sustainability.

Zero Waste and recycling is the next sustainability mantra. Zero waste according to the definition given by Zero Waste International Alliance in 2004 is, "a goal that is ethical, economical, efficient and visionary, to guide people in changing their lifestyles and practices to emulate sustainable natural cycles, where all discarded materials are designed to become resources for others to use." Hence, Zero waste implies that all resources in the operation cycle are reused within the cycle leading to a minimal harmful impact to the environment.

Universities are also vying for carbon neutrality. Carbon neutrality also called as having a net zero carbon footprint, means balancing the carbon released during operations, transportation and energy production with the amount of carbon offset to achieve net zero carbon emissions. Buying carbon credits is also one way of achieving carbon neutrality and is a part of carbon trading. The ultimate aim remains to reduce the carbon emitted rather than devising ways of sequestering the emissions.

HIGHER EDUCATION AND SUSTAINABILITY

According to the Bologna Charter, Bachelor and Master-degree studies shall have to correspond to international educational standards for sustainable development. This implies that universities will have to ensure that their curriculum also undergo a green transformation. The idea is to provide for an enduring system for sustainable development that becomes a binding part of the campus and student life. Use of innovative learning and teaching methods with the promotion of project initiatives of students in areas like environmental and social responsibility, cooperation at local and regional processes, and so on should be accredited to encourage such initiatives.

Universities or any seat of higher education has an edge over the private sector in establishing and maintaining a successful sustainability program as they can:

- build a "critical mass" of research, education and operations expertise that is shared amongst all higher educational institutions without any fear of cut-throat competition; and
- build upon a "fusion of disciplines". Any university offering multiple disciplines can capitalize on the wide knowledge available across domains and blend across university sectors unlike private ventures that are domain specific.

INTERVENTIONS

The various areas that can be benefitted by channelizing the enthusiasm and energy of the staff and students available in higher educational institutions are:

- Environmental management systems
- Curriculum greening

- Operational aspects of universities
- Energy, water, recycling, waste management
- Planning and design of campuses
- Environmental reports
- Environmental policies and action plans
- Staff and student initiatives
- Community Engagement

There are many more ways of ensuring that the human resources associated with the education sector are contributing to the betterment of society. All that is required is providing genuine opportunities for dialogues and debates on this issue and supporting student initiatives at the administrative level.

WHAT SOME UNIVERSITIES ARE DOING?

A study of the sustainability interventions listed on the respective websites of the top universities of the world generated the following data:

1. *Harvard University*: Harvard is organizing arts, sports, lectures, and religious services on campus. It is also engaging in community partnership programs and planning.
2. *Cambridge University*: Students and staff devote about 4 lakh hours every year in voluntary and outreach work, benefitting more than 1 million people annually.
3. *Oxford University*: Community activities related to education, museums, organizing events and voluntary work on part of students.
4. *Yale University*: The University encourages staff and student volunteers in interventions like American Red Cross, community programs for children, etc.
5. *Imperial College, London*: The University has set-up a volunteer center open for all people, for persons with special needs and environment.
6. *Princeton University*: The University promotes a sense of ethic and community awareness among students, believes in building a relationship with surrounding

communities, and initiating and encouraging dialogues between academia and other participants.

7. *California Institute of Technology*: Promotes volunteer programs in clearing trails of hiking, supporting HIV AIDS affected population, and preparing and serving meals for the homeless people.
8. *University of Chicago*: Believes in having a strong relationship with surrounding communities and contributing to the same through providing healthcare, safety and other amenities, affordable housing and support education initiatives.
9. *University College, London*: It has set-up a Volunteering Services Unit to encourage student volunteers. It also organizes volunteer fairs, provides training and grants and has a global citizenship agenda.
10. *Massachusetts Institute of Technology (MIT)*: Volunteering programs for students for contributing to the community in areas like technology, health, psychology, science and others.

Unfortunately information on sustainability interventions done by Indian universities and institutes of higher education are not available as easily on their websites, raising the question that there is perhaps a long way for them to travel in this direction.

KEY CHALLENGES

1. *Data benchmarking and tracking across universities*: Knowledge management initiatives are critically required to avoid duplication and overlapping of sustainable initiatives and to build upon everyone's strengths.
2. *Communication, awareness and education*: To achieve synergy of efforts, communication through public forums, seminars, conferences and other events is a must. Not only do we need specialists learning from each other but also, the general public and students have to be educated and mobilized as well.

3. *Buy-in across the university*: The administrative machinery of the institution has to support and drive the sustainability effort. Hence, a complete belief and commitment is required at all levels.
4. *Competing values and objectives*: In an era where foreign universities are soon to be allowed access to Indian education market and where education is turning into a lucrative business model, the competing values of profit maximization at all costs have to be challenged and replaced.
5. *Third Party relationships*: The institutions have to initiate (if not present already) relations with various governmental, social sector and corporate sector agencies for a comprehensive long-term sustainability program.

CONCLUSION

Any initiative taken seriously by an organization demands the support and commitment of top management. The same remains true in the current regards as well, if the institution is serious about sustainability then the top management has to be educated, mobilized and driven towards the cause. Case in point is the Texas technological University that has not only appointed a sustainability liaison to its President but also launched a "Spring into Green" initiative along with a slogan of Good stewardship, good citizenship, good business! Closer home, Jamia Millia Islamia, a Central University of India has launched initiatives like "Book Donation program" where used books can be donated to be of use to the needy students who cannot afford them. Higher education institutions can serve as seats of discussions and deliberations where people from academia and corporate can both come together to improvise new ways and means of driving the cause of sustainability. Students studying in universities should be encouraged to not only think but also live green. Using bicycles to transport, recycling and waste management in hostels, and encouragement to take up green jobs are some such initiatives. It is not enough if the biology department has a rain water harvesting plant, motivating students to build, use and maintain the plant is a better idea. Organizing "Green Week" or establishing student councils are also some ways of making sure that sustainability does not remain a high brow topic discussed by top managers with no relevance for people at the grass-roots.

References

Sustainable Bologna [online] Available at http://www.aic.lv/bolona/Bologna/contrib/Statem_oth/Copernicus-Campus.pdf [September 30, 2011].

A Report on Ethical framework for a sustainable world, 2010, [online] Available at http://www.desd.org/EC+10%20Report.pdf [September 30, 2011].

Kagan, S. and Kirchberg, V. *et. al.*, 2008, Sustainability: A new frontier for the arts and cultures, Verlag für Akademische Schriften, Germany.

CHAPTER

26

Growth of Banking Sector in India

An Overview

G. Prasad Babu, Talata C. Ratnayake
and K.S. Kadian

INTRODUCTION

India has had a long history of banking in so far as providing credit is concerned. There are references to lending for interest and the social religious sanctions governing the norms relating to these activities even in the ancient Indian scriptures like Manusmriti and Arthasastra. However, establishment of banking of the western type was attempted only as late as 1683 by the East India Company. Today Indian banking has come a long way since then in terms of complexity of operations and the elaborateness of the structure. Moreover, Indian banking system the way it has evolved has come to acquire certain peculiarities of its own not found in the banking system in the other countries. For understanding the banking structure in India, it will be essential to first know what constitutes banking activity. The banking regulation act 1949 defines banking as "accepting for the purposes of lending or investment, deposits of money from the public, repayable on demand or otherwise and withdrawable by cheque, draft, order or otherwise". The definition thus rules out form its scope the vast unorganized network of the indigenous village bankers who do not generally accept deposits and the mostly urban-based financial bodies who accept deposits for the purpose of lending but who do not offer withdrawal either on demand or by cheque and draft.

DIFFERENT STAGES OF THE DEVELOPMENT OF INDIAN BANKING

- Establishment of the RBI in 1935 through RBI Act 1934.
- Nationalization of RBI in January 1st, 1949.
- With a view to have the coordinated regulation of Indian banking, the banking regulation act was passed in March 1949.
- Imperial bank of India was partially nationalized in 1st July 1955 and it was named as the "State Bank of India". Along with it other 8 (at present 7) banks were converted as its associate banks which form what is named as the state bank group.
- IDBI established under industrial development bank of India act. 1964 for providing credit and other facilities for developing industries. Of course later it has been converted into as a banking company.
- 14 large commercial banks whose reserves were more than Rs. 50 crore each were nationalized on 19th July, 1969.
- 1971: Creation of credit guarantee corporation.
- RRB's came into existence on 2nd October, 1975 and are being governed by RRB Act 1976.
- After one decade of first nationalization of 14 banks, on April 15th, 1980, those 6 private sector banks

FIG. 1
Structure of Banking Sector in India

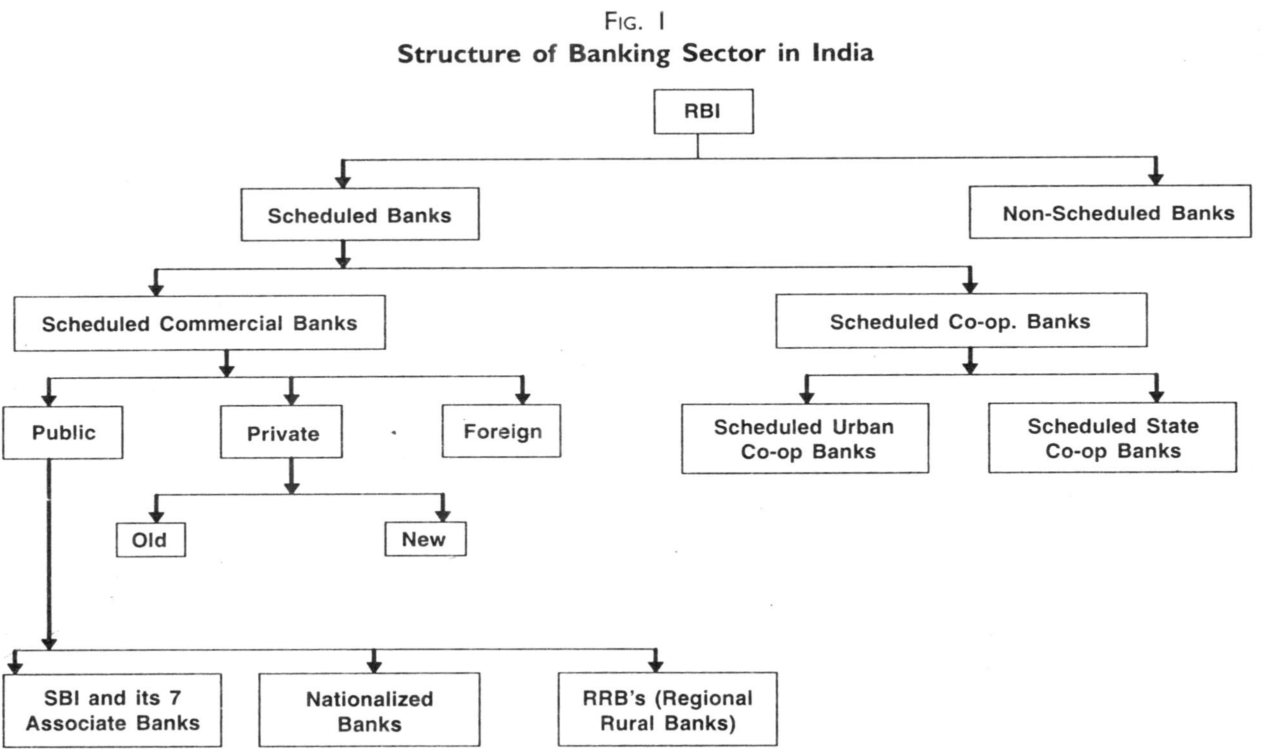

whose revenues were more than Rs. 200 crores each were nationalized.

- EXIM bank was established in January 1st, 1982 for financing, facilitating, and promoting foreign trade in India.
- Establishment of NABARD in July 12th, 1982.
- SIDBI was established in 1989 under Small Industries Development Bank of India Act. 1989.
- Setting up of CGTMSE (Credit Guarantee Fund Trust for Medium and Small Enterprises) in August 2000 to provide guarantee support to banks and lending institutions for their exposure to the MSE sector. This is the only credit guarantee institution in the country exclusively set-up for the benefit of entrepreneurs in the MSE sector.

TABLE I

Progress of Banking Sector

Progress	*1969*	*March 2009*
No. of branches	8260	More than 86,640
Percentage of rural branches	22%	48%
Bank Deposits	3896 crore	39.23 lakh crores (June-2009)
Bank Credit	3030 crore	27.46 lakh crores (June-2009)
Percentage of priority sector advances by public sector banks to their total bank credit	15%	42.5%

BANKING SECTOR REFORMS

Despite the commendable progress, serious problems have emerged, reflecting a decline in efficiency and erosion of the profitability of the banking sector. The major factors responsible for these were :

- High degree of regulation,

- Unacceptable level of subsidization of interest rates,
- Complex structure of administered interest rate system,
- Govt./RBI control over credit allocation,
- Preemption of funds by high SLR and CRR,
- Growth in non-operative assets,
- Absence of efficient payment system, and
- Weaknesses in the banking sector due to high cost of rapid expansion, organizational inadequacies and lags in introducing computer technologies, etc.

REFORMS

Different committees were appointed to give recommendations to overcome these problems :

1. Narasimham committee in 1991,
2. Second Narasimham committee in 1998, and
3. Verma committee on restructuring of weak PSB's.

SOME OF THE RECOMMENDATIONS IMPLEMENTED BY GOI BASED ON THESE COMMITTEES REPORTS

- SLR has been slowly and sturdily reduced to 25% of demand and time liabilities of the bank. This helped the banking sector to expand their lending programme and to promote Agricultural trade and industries.
- While using the CRR as principle instrument of monitory and credit control, RBI is also keeping a track on open market operations to control inflationary pressure.
- The bank rate is being used as the anchor rate and all other rates of interest are closely connected to it.
- RBI has the authority to simplify the structure of the interest rate.
- The business of RRB's predominantly engaged in financing Agricultural and allied activities.
- Government had allowed the foreign banks to open offices in India either as branches or subsidiaries.

- Prior to recommendations there was dual control over the banking system between RBI and banking division of ministry of finance. After the recommendations the control power of the ministry has been minimized and RBI is primary agency for the regulation of the banking system.
- Liberalized new branch licensing and new bank licensing policy.
- Implementation of capital adequacy norms.
- Prescription of uniform accounting norms with respect to asset classification, enactment of a statute providing for setting up of tribunals for expeditious adjudication and recovery of bank loans.
- Establishment of separate branch for financial supervision of banks.
- Rationalization and deregulation of interest rates, etc.

TRANSFORMATION IN INDIAN BANKING

Prudential measure which have been implemented covered fulfilment of capital adequacy norms; new accounting, income recognition, providing and exposure norms. Measures initiated to strengthen risk management included assignment of risk weights to different categories assets, norms on connected lending, credit concentration norms, application of marked-to-market principle for investment portfolio and fixation of limits for deployment of funds in sensitive sectors and activities. In addition, KYC (Know Your Customer) guidelines, AML (Anti Money Laundering) standards, introduction of capital change for market risk, higher graded provisioning of NPA's, etc. were adopted from implementation. Institutional and legal measures introduced for improving bank's performance in the area of recovery and for asset quality upgradation included setting up of Lok Adalats, Debt Recovery Tribunals (DRT), Asset Reconstruction Companies (ARC), settlement advisory committees, corporate debt restructuring mechanisms, etc. Enactment of Securitization of Reconstruction of Financial Assets and Enforcement Security interest act (SARFAESI Act) was another important milestone in reforms. Setting up of Credit Information Bureau (India)

Limited (CIBIL) for sharing of credit information and establishment of the Clearing Corporation of India Ltd. (CCIL) to act as central counter-party for facilitating payments and settlement system relating to fixed income securities and money market instruments extended support to banks. Certain supervisory measures such as establishment of a separate board for financial supervision in RBI, recasting the role of statutory auditors and increased internal control through strengthening of corporate governance etc. were also initiated. The technology-related measures included setting up of Indian Financial Network (INFINET) as the communication backbone for the financial sector, introduction of negotiated dealing system for screen-based trading in Government securities and implementation of Real Time Gross Settlement (RTGS), National Electronic Fund Transfer (NEFT), Core Banking Services (CBS), cash tree, cash net, Structured Financial Messaging System (SFMS), etc. have been done.

IT INITIATIVES

Banks are striving hard to extend CBS to all branches in a phased manner. In post-reform era we have seen strategic alliance among banks in areas like sharing ATM's and funds transfer, etc. bringing all the branches, including rural ones, with the CBS network, establishment of biometric rural ATM's and introduction of internet and mobile banking are some of the major developments. The number of branches providing "core banking solutions" (CBS) rose rapidly to 67.0 per cent as of end-March 2008 from 44.4 per cent at end-March 2007. The number of automated teller machines (ATMs) at the end-March 2008 was 34,789 compared to 27,088 at end-March 2007.

VALUE-ADDED SERVICES

As a result of reforms, the trend is clearly towards providing value-added services such as credit cards, insurance products, mutual funds, and demats accounts with trading plat-form.

FOCUS OF QUALITY ASPECTS

There is a graded shift in focus from "size-related" issues to concerns in respect of productivity, efficiency, profitability; return on capital, net interest margin and return on assets, etc. in the day to come, there will be greater stress on these concerns

RISK-BASED MANAGEMENT

Banks in India have adopted comprehensive risk management system for focusssed attention to various types of risks such as interest rate risk, credit risk, liquidity risk, market risk, operational risk. These risk management systems spell out internationally accepted risk measurement methods for various types of risk to calculate capital charge required for meeting prescribed capital adequacy ratio. Capital adequacy of a bank means the availability of adequate capital as a percentage of its risk weighted assets. It is indicated formally by Capital-to-Risk Weighted Assets (CRAR) ratio. RBI fixed this rate as 8 percent in 1992. It was raised to 9 percent subsequently. All the scheduled commercial banks exceeded this ratio in their performance (except two old two private sector banks) and achieved overall CRAR of 13.19 percent by March 2009. This was made possible by augmenting capital base of the banks by tapping domestic as well as international capital markets to meet the sharp increase in the risk weighted assets. BASEL norms; they are internationally accepted prudential norms for financial system. BASEL-I is very simplistic in its approach towards credit risks. It does not distinguish between collateralized and non-collateralized loans, while BASEL-II tries to ensure that the anomalies existed in BASEL-I are corrected. For instance, BASEL-I norms for capital adequacy is a CRAR of 8 percent. The Indian banks achieved BASEL-I norms long ago. Now the banks and other financial institutions are required to confirm to BASEL-II, which are more stringent. BASEL-II accord of 1999 specified a three-tier capital structure for banks. To enable banks confirm to this, RBI issued guidelines for raising capital funds to meet market as well as credit risks.

EFFICIENCY PARAMETER

In the post-reform period, we find a complete change in efficiency parameters. Today, what is important is the strength of Balance Sheet, Return on Asset, NPA percentage, per employee business and overall per employee productivity and proportion of low cost deposits. The following table shows the comparison of India with other major countries *vis-à-vis* some efficiency parameters.

TABLE 2
Financial Soundness Indicators—2007
(Figures in percentages)

Country	*CRAR*	*ROA*	*Capital to assets*	*NPA's*	*Provisioning to NPA's*
India	12.3	0.9	6.4	2.8	56.1
USA	12.8	0.6	10.5	1.1	104.8
UK	12.9	0.8	8.9	0.9	54.6
Japan	12.9	0.3	5.0	1.5	28.8
Canada	12.1	0.3	5.1	0.4	44.9
Australia	10.3	1.0	4.7	0.2	188.9

Source : Global Financial Stability Report, 2008.

INCREASED STRENGTH

Consequent to banking sector reforms, Indian banks have emerged relatively stronger in terms of range of products and services, capital adequacy, asset quality, profitability, productivity, and overall balance sheet strength *vis-à-vis* their counterparts in other Asian countries. An analysis by standard and poor's has shown that the Indian banking is ahead of China, Indonesia, Philippines and Vietnam. Another study undertaken by Moody's investor services revealed that Indian banking is qualitatively better than its counterparts even in developed countries like, Japan, Singapore, and Australia. There has been a distinctly improvement in the performance of

Indian banks on various fronts. But, the acquisition of a globally competitive size for Indian banks in a major challenge.

FUTURE CHALLENGES OF BANKS IN INDIA

The Indian banks are hopeful of becoming a global brand, as they are the major source of financial sector revenue and profit growth. The financial services penetration in India continues to be healthy, thus the banking industry is also not far behind. As a result, of this, the profit for the Indian banking industry will surely surge ahead. The profit pool of the Indian banking industry is probable to augment from US$ 4.8 billion in 2005 to US$ 20 billion in 2010 and further to US$ 40 billion by 2015. This growth and expansion pace would be driven by the chunk of middle class population. The increase in the number of private banks, the domestic credit market of India is estimated to grow from US$ 0.4 trillion in 2004 to US$ 23 trillion by 2050. Third largest banking hub of the globe by 2040—is that vision too far away.

REFERENCES

www.iba.org.in
Nabara.org.in
Rbi.org.in
http://www.theindianbanker.co.in/

CHAPTER

27

SHGs and Empowerment of Rural Women

Issues and Challenges

TOSIB ALAM AND ZEESHAN

ABSTRACT

In India, there has been impressive growth in micro finance activities over the three decades or more. Micro finance in India has gathered momentum to become a major force. Micro finance does not directly address some structural problems facing Indian society and the economy, and it is not yet as efficient as it will be when economies of scale are realised and a more supportive policy environment is created. Micro finance is one of the few markets-based, scalable anti-poverty solutions that are in place in India today, and the argument to scale it up to meet the overwhelming need is compelling.
Keywords: Poverty, Microfinance, Self-help groups, Women-empowerment, NABARD.

INTRODUCTION

Alleviation of poverty, the core of all development efforts, has remained a very complex and critical concern among developing countries. Poverty is deep-rooted covering several interlocked aspects such as assetlessness, under-employment, uncertain and relatively unproductive employment, and low remuneration, lack of bargaining power, economic vulnerability, literacy, and proneness to disease, social disadvantage and political powerlessness. To fully exploit India's potential and improve living standards for all parts of society, a mass-mobilization of the downtrodden population into productive and sustainable jobs, mostly through self-employment and entrepreneurship, is required. Micro finance is fast emerging the world over as an effective tool for poverty alleviation, equitable and inclusive growth, and women empowerment in developing world. There has been impressive growth in micro finance activities over the three decades or more in India (Khan and Alam, 2011).

Today, when the majority of the world's population is living below subsistence level, more than 3,000 organizations are providing micro finance services to the millions of the world's poor. Providing employment opportunities to the rural women and developing the living status of the rural folk by providing credit with less interest is the major concern of the microfinance. Micro financers use innovative contractual practices and organizational forms to reduce the risk and costs of making loans, such as lending to groups, rather than just to one person. Some micro credit organizations give their clients more than loans, offering education, training, health care, and other social services. In spite of the impressive figures micro finance in India is still presently too small to create a massive impact in poverty alleviation, but if pursued with skill, it holds the promise of to alter the socio-economic face of the India's poor.

Micro finance movement is broadly defined on group based institution. In group lending programmes, the function of screening, monitoring, and enforcement of repayment are to a large extent transferred from the bank to the borrower—the group member themselves (Sharma and Zeller, 1997). These perceived advantages of collective actions during the time of screening of loan application and monitoring of borrowers. Even in the area of 'social banking' banks were highly unapproachable for the rural poor. Due to worldwide wave of economic reforms, the access to credit has fallen further. In this regard micro-finance explores new avenue of credit for the rural poor. In India the model of micro finance delivery can be broadly classified as the Self Help Groups (SHGs) model which is actually a Grameen Bank replication model (Mukherjee and Kundu, 2009). It has been observed that Micro finance often gets equated merely as credit for micro-enterprises while the poor also need savings, consumption loans, housings loans and insurance services. Micro finance does not directly address some structural problems facing Indian society and the economy, and it is not yet as efficient as it will be when economies of scale are realised and a more supportive policy environment is created. Micro finance is one of the few markets-based, scalable anti-poverty solutions that are in place in India today, and the argument to scale it up to meet the overwhelming need is compelling.

STATUS OF POVERTY IN INDIA

India remains predominantly a rural nation, with 71 percent of its people living in rural areas as of 2004-05 and the incidence of poverty is much higher in rural areas affecting the rural economy as well as the overall economy of the nation. India has entered the Eleventh Plan Period with an impressive record of economic growth: As far as poverty concerned the percentage of the population below the poverty line has come down from 36 percent in 1993-94 to 27.5 percent in 2004-05 but the rate of decline in poverty has not accelerated along the growth in GDP, and the incidence of poverty among certain marginalised groups (Hazra, 2009).

The poverty ratio may be strictly comparable to the earlier ratio of poverty because of some changes in methodology of data collection from time to time. An important feature of poverty ratio in India is that its incidence is far greater in rural areas than in urban areas. Likewise, there has been significant

TABLE I
Trends in Poverty in India

Years	*Rural Sector Poverty Ratio (%)*	*Urban Sector Poverty Ratio (%)*	*All India Poverty Ratio (%)*
1973-74	56.44	49.01	54.88
1977-78	53.07	45.24	51.32
1983-84	45.85	40.79	44.48
1987-88	39.09	38.20	38.86
1993-94	37.27	32.36	35.97
1990-00	27.09	23.62	26.10
2004-05 URP	28.3	25.7	27.5
2004-05 MRP	21.8	21.7	21.8

Note : Uniform Recall Period (URP), Mixed Recall Period (MRP).
Source : Planning Commission estimates based on NSS round.

decrease in the all India overall poverty ratio which has come down to about 21.8 compared to 54.9 in the year 1973-74.

GROWTH AND DEVELOPMENT OF MICRO FINANCE IN INDIA

Provision of credit to poor people has been one of the main concerns of policy planners in India. Government of India, since independence has been making concerned efforts in the direction viz, nationalization of existing private commercial banks in 1969 in terms of massive expansion of branch networks in rural areas, mandatory directed credit to priority sectors of the economy, subsidized rates of interest and creation of a new set of rural banks at district level and an apex bank for Agriculture and Rural Development (NABARD) at national level in 1982. As a fillip to rural delivery mechanism, Regional Rural Banks (RRBs) had been set-up in India 1975 as a unique institution, in the sense that it is meant to be local institution, familiar to the local conditions and at the same time being commercial in its operations. Despite their massive infrastructure of banks, about 30 percent of the rural indebted households are still dependant on informal sector. The institutional structure was neither profitable in rural lending nor serving the needs of the poorest. In short, it had created a structure "quantitative impressive but qualitatively week". Because of existing banking policies, systems and procedures, and deposit and loan products were not will suited to meet the most immediate needs of the poor (Singh, 2007).

Micro credit institutions are seen as being able to rectify these weaknesses. Micro finance is the new mantra in rural finance. It has been recognised world over as an effective tool for poverty alleviation and improving socio-economic status of rural poor. Micro finance refers to the programme that provides credit or self-employment and other financial and business services, including saving and technical assistance to the poor persons. The micro finance industry in India emerged in the 1970s to provide poor people with access to credit without restoring to the usurious interest rates fixed by informal money lenders. In 1974, SEWA cooperative Bank was established to help low income women escape their trap and reduce their dependence on money lenders. Much like Grameen bank in Bangladesh SEWA Bank relied on peer pressure groups ensure high loan repayment rates. Through its success, SEWA Bank proved that the poor were bankable and helped pave the way for the emergence of hundreds of micro-finance institutions during the 1980s and 1990s (Rajesh and Venkatamma, 2009). The beginning of the micro-finance movement in India could be traced to the self-help group (SHG) Bank linkage programmes (SBLP) stated as a pilot project in 1992 by National Bank for Agriculture and Rural Development (NABARD) this programme not only proved to be very successful, but has also emerged as the most popular model of micro-finance in India. From the pilot project, the self-help Group-Bank linkage became a full-fledged model.

Recognising the potential of micro-finance through SHGs to positively influence the development of the poor, the Reserve Bank, NABARD and Small Industries Development Bank of India (SIDBI) have taken further fillip to the micro-finance in India. The basic purpose of the linkage is to strengthen the financial health of SHGs by ensuring adequate flow of bank credit to these institutions (Kumar, S., 2010).

SHGS AND WOMEN EMPOWERMENT

Empowerment is a continuous process for realizing the ideals of equality, human liberation and freedom for all. It is the process of challenging existing power relations and gaining control over the source of power. Empowerment of women involves many things, economic opportunity, property rights, political representation, social equality, personal right and so on. Empowerment as a form of development change is brought about by local problem-solving efforts and techniques. The term empowerment is frequently used to describe a process where the powerless members gain greater share of control over resources and decision-making, and women are generally accepted as being the most powerless members of the depressed classes (Sharma, 2006). The self help group is a viable organized set up to disburse micro credit to the rural women for the purpose of making them enterprising and encouraging to enter into entrepreneurial activities. The formation of SHGs is not ultimately a micro credit project but an empowerment process. Community Bank, NGOs and grass-root saving and credit groups around world have shown that these micro-enterprises loans can be profitable for borrowers and for the lenders making micro finance one of the most effective poverty reducing strategies. (Mahalakshmi, M. 2010). Micro finance is a human right and way to end poverty though socio-empowerment has been considered as best alternative for empowerment of rural poor and social change.

It shows that access and efficient provision of micro credit can enable the poor to smooth their consumption, better manage their risks better gradually build their assets, develop their micro-enterprises, enhance their income earning capacity and enjoy an improved quality of life. Micro finance services can also contribute to the improvement of resources allocation, promoting of markets, and adoption of better technology. Micro Finance is expected to play a significant role in poverty alleviation and development (Bakhtiari, 2006).

SELF-HELP GROUPS

India has been experiencing micro credit in the form of

Self-Help Groups (SHGs) as a part of formal credit delivery system giving lot freedom to Non-Government Organizations (NGOs) to set-up SHGs on various models. The self-help group is a registered or unregistered group of wall and economically homogeneous and affinity group of poor, Voluntary coming together to save small amounts regularly, to mutually help basis, which are deposited in a common fund to meet members' emergency needs and to provide collateral free loans decided by the group. They have been recognized as useful tool to help the poor and as alternative to meet the urgent credit needs of poor through thrift. SHGs enhance the equality of status of women as participants, decision-makers and beneficiaries in the democratic, economic, social and cultural spheres of life (Singh, *et. al.*, 2010).

NGOs create a strong base for the members in forming SHGs where the members contribute their saving to a common pool and money is lent to the members on rotation basis according to their need and preference. NGOs also contribute some initial funds to strengthen the financial resources of the group and encourage the financial institutions to develop confidence and establish lending relationship with the groups (Roheeni, 2006). The groups are eligible for the loans from the banks after six months of saving and credit operations. The banks assess the strengthen of the groups in terms of successful rotation of saving of the groups as loans, regularity in conducting and attending meeting savings mobilization numbers of loan issued to the groups as replacement of loans. The opportunity provided in safe saving as well as availability of need-based credit has led to more and poor people keen to join SHGs. The members use the credit for a variety of purposes like small business, agriculture, health, education of children, festivals and so on (Kour, 2008).

SALIENT FEATURES OF THE SELF-HELP GROUPS

1. It is formed either by NGOs or Government agencies or by banks.
2. Members are from neighbourhood with homogeneous financial background.
3. The members of the group meet frequently.

4. They identify the problems among themselves and find solutions with alternatives.
5. They save small amounts and lend the same among the members.
6. They operate single bank account only.
7. 90% are women SHGs.

TABLE 2

Progress of Self-help Groups

Year	*(Credit (Rs. Crore)*	*Self-Help Groups (in lakh)*	*No. of Self-Employment (in lakh)*
1999-2000	192.98	1.15	9.31
2000-01	480.87	2.64	9.78
2001-02	10,26.34	4.61	NA
2002-03	20,48.70	7.17	32.48
2003-04	39,04.21	10.80	45.67
2004-05	6898.46	16.18	NA
2005-06	11,397.55	22.38	62.75
2006-07	12,366.49	28.94	73.25
2007-08	16,999.90	36.26	93.21
2008-09	22,679.85	42.24	120.89

Source : Status of Micro Finance in India 2009-10, NABARD, Economic Survey, 2009-10.

Table shows that cumulative number of SHGs finance by banks has jumped to 42.24 lakh in the year 2008-09 from 1.15 lakh in 1992-2000. Banks extended loans of Rs. 22,679 crore in 2008-09 as against 192.98 crore in 1990-2000. Significant progress was made during the year 2005-06 with 4499.09 new SHGs financed by banks. The number of poor families benefiting through SHGs increased from 9.31 lakh as on 1999-2000 to 120.89 lakh on 2008-09 registering a growth of 11.98 percent of the SHGs are women groups.

As compared to the socio-economic conditions of members in the pre and post SHG situations and the members have improved the business turnover in the post-SHG

TABLE 3

Position of Women SHGs (As per March, 2010)

(in Crore)

Particulars	*Total SHGs*		*Exclusive Women SHGs*		*%age of Women SHGs to total SHGs*	
	No.	*Amount*	*No.*	*Amount*	*No.*	*Amount*
(1)	*(2)*	*(3)*	*(4)*	*(5)*	*(6)*	*(7)*
Saving liked SHGs	6953250	6198.71	5310436	4498.66	76.4	72.6
Loans Disbursed	1586822	14453.30	1294476	12429.37	81.6	86.0
Loans Outstanding	4851356	28038.28	3897797	23030.36	80.3	82.1

Source : Status of Micro Finance, 2009-10, NABARD.

situations and in turn the net income. The widespread formation of the SHGs means that it has also taken the form of a movement for women's social development in India. Self-help groups, as a strategy for women's development, have arisen out of the perceived problem of women's development has in India (Qazi, 2007).

It may seen that of the total number of saving linked and credit linked SHGs, exclusive women SHGs with banks were 76.4 percent and 81.6 percent respectively. Further, the percentage of loans outstanding of exclusive women SHGs to loans outstanding of total SHGs which was 81.9 percent as of March, 2009 has increase to 82.1 percent as of March, 2010.

SHGS-BANK LINKAGE PROGRAMME

The SHG-bank linkage programme is the flagship micro finance intervention mechanism of NABARD. NABARD with the policy back up of the RBI designed of linking these groups with banks to overcome the financial constraints. With the NABARD programmes on self-help groups, the emphasis shifted to loans without collateral, 100 percent repayment norms and lending to groups of people who would also invest their saving and regulate their groups and group's loans, thus reducing transaction costs for the borrowers and for the banks. The programme has come a long way since 1992 passing through stages of pilot study (1992-95), main streaming (1995-98) and expansion phase (1998 onwards). RBI and NABARD have tried to promote 'relationship banking, i.e. improving the existing relationship between the poor and bankers with the social after meditation NGOs. The programme initiated by NABARD inactive collaboration with NGOs aimed at enhancing the courage of rural poor under institutional credit there by forcing of poverty alleviation and empowerment (Karunaiathal, 2009).

Under the SHG-Bank Linkage Programme as on March 2010, 69.53 lakh SHGs held saving bank accounts with total savings of Rs. 6198.71 crore as against 61.21 lakh SHGs with savings of Rs. 5545.62 as on March, 2009. Thereby showing a growth rate of 13.6 percent and 11.8 percent. Thus more than 97 million poor households were associated with banking agencies

TABLE 4

SHG-Bank Linkage Progress Last Two Years

(in Crore)

Particulars	2008-09		2009-10		Growth Rate	
	No. of SHGs	Amount	No. of SHGs	Amount	No. of SHGs	Amount
(1)	(2)	(3)	(4)	(5)	(6)	(7)
Savings SHGs with Banks	6121147	5545.62	6953250	6198.71	13.6	11.8
Bank Loans Disbarred to SHGs	1609586	12253.51	1586822	14453.30	-1.4	17.9
Bank Loans Outstanding with SHGs	4224338	22679.84	4851356	28038.38	14.8	23.6

Source : Status of Micro Finance in India, 2009-10, NABARD.

under this programme. The share under SGSY was 16.94 lakh SHGs with saving of Rs. 1,292.62 crore forming 24.4 percent of the total SHGs having saving accounts with the banks and 20.8 percent of their total saving account. During 2009-10, banks have financed 15.87 lakh SHGs, including repeat loan to te existing SHGs with bank loans of Rs. 14,453.30 crore as against 16.10 lakh SHGs with bank loans of Rs. 12,253.51 crore during 2008-09, registering a decline of 1.4 percent of SHGs but a growth of 17.9 percent in bank loans disbursed. As on March 2010, the total number of 48.51 lakh SHGs were having outstanding bank loans of Rs. 28,28,038.28 crore as against 42.24 lakh SHGs with bank loans of Rs. 22,679.85 crore as on March 2009, representing a growth of 14.8 percent in number of SHGs and 23.6 percent in bank loans outstanding against SHGs. The share of SHGs under SGSY was 25.7 percent with outstanding bank loans of 22.3 percent as against 23.1 percent SHGs with outstanding bank loans of 25.8 percent as on March 2009.

TABLE 5

Bank Loan Outstanding against SHGs—Agency-wise Position (As on March 31, 2010)

Agency	*No. of SHGs*	*Share in % (Rs. Core)*	*Amount*	*Share in %*	*Per SHG outstanding Loan (Rs.)*
Commercial Banks (Public and Private Banks)	3237263	66.7	20164.71	71.9	62,289
Regional Rural Banks (RRBs)	1103980	22.8	6144.58	21.9	55,658
Cooperative Banks	510113	10.5	1728.99	6.2	33,894
Total	4851356	100.0	28038.28	100.0	57,795

Source : Status of Micro Finance, 2009-10, NABARD.

It may be observed from table that commercial banks (CBs) had the maximum share of 66.7 percent in outstanding bank loans to SHGs followed by RRBs with a share of 22.8 percent and cooperative banks with a share of 10.5 percent. The average bank loan outstanding per SHG had increased from Rs. 53,689 as on Mach 2009 to Rs. 57,795 as on March 2019. It varied between Rs. 62,289 per SHG in case of CBs and Rs. 33,894 per SHG in care of cooperative banks as on March, 2010. The commercial banks had the maximum share of SHGs with saving amount (59.3%) followed by RRBs (21.0%) and cooperative banks (19.8%).

TABLE 6

Non-Performing Assets of Bank Loans to SHGs

Agency	*Outstanding Loans against SHGs (crore)*	*Amount of NPAs (crore)*	*% of NPA to Outstanding Bank Loans*
CBs (Public Sector)	19724.42	513.53	2.60
CBs (Private Sector)	440.29	23.93	5.44
RRBs	6144.58	218.53	3.56
Cooperative Banks	1728.99	67.04	3.88
Total	28038.28	823.04	2.94

Source : Status of Micro Finance, 2009-10, NABARD.

Total 221 banks had reported data on Non-Performing Assets (NPAs). NPAs to total bank loans outstanding against SHGs as on March 2010, stood at 2.94 percent, amounted to Rs. 823.04 crore. Out of 302 banks which have reported the survey data, about 70 percent of banks had more than 80 percent recovery of SHG loans as on March, 2010. the banks also financed NGOs and micro finance institutions (MFIs) for on-lending under MFIs that has outstanding bank loans was 1513 amounting to Rs. 10,147 crore.

MODELS OF LINKAGE

SHGs "linked" with banks functions as micro-banks were able to access funds from the formal banking system. The linkage has resulted in the reduction of transaction costs of banks through the externalization of costs of servicing individually loans and also ensuring their repayment through the peer pressure mechanism. The three broad models of linkage programmes.

First type: Bank takes the initiative to form the groups, open their savings account and provide them credit.

Second type: Groups are formed and developed by government agencies, NGOs or communities are given by the banks

Third type: The NGOs that forms and developed the SHGs also act as financial intermediary and the banks lend to three financial intermediaries for onwards lending to the member-SHGs and their members. In several cases, federation of SHGs act as financial intermediaries.

The second type has emerged at the most popular model accounting for over 70 percent of the total SHGs financed under their category, followed by model I and model III, confirming the popularity of model II as preferred by the bankers (Kamdar, 2007). SHG-Bank Linkage Programmes has been in the forefront in the Southern Region as compared to all other regions. Andhra Pradesh has had more number of SHGs linked with banks and maximum amount of bank loan disbursed, compared to all other status in the Southern Region as well as in all other regions. Certain states, namely, Andhra Pradesh, Karnataka and Tamil Nadu account for 50 percent of the SHG credit linkage. The other two states viz., Karnataka and Tamil Nadu, South India are supported by large NGOs like MYRADA and SHARE. These NGOs have greater creditability which has enabled them to leverage bank finance easily. Moreover, as the micro finance movement had "originated" in South India, the awareness and acceptability of the programme has relatively been higher. Rajasthan, Meghalaya, Orissa, Bihar, West Bengal, Madhya Pradesh and Gujarat have been identified by NABARD for having higher potential of increasing SHG outreach. The states which have suffered from inadequate due to inherent lack of institutional framework non-availability of good infrastructure and poor presence of NGOss continued to receive special attention from NABARD (Kumaresan and Chitrakala, 2009).

DEVELOPMENTAL POLICIES OF NABARD

NABARD has been playing the role of propagator and facilitator by providing conducive policy environment, training and capacity building besides extending financial support for the health growth SHG linkage programme.

NABARD REFINANCE SUPPORT TO BANKS

NABARD provides refinance support to banks to extent of 100 percent of the bank loans disbursed to SHGs. The total refinance disbursed to banks against bank loans to SHG during 2009-10 was Rs. 3173.56 crore, registered a growth of 21.1 percent from Rs. 2620.03 crore in 2008-09. The cumulative refinance disbursed under SHG-bank linkage programme by NABARD to banks up to 31 March, 2010 stood at Rs. 12,861.65 crore (NABARD, 2009-10).

MICRO FINANCE DEVELOPMENT AND EQUITY FUND

The Micro finance Development and Equity Fund is being utilised for promotion of various micro finance activities such as formation and linkage of SHGs through SHPIs, training and capacity building of stakeholders, capital and soft loan assistance to MFIs, livelihood propagation, studies, documentation, etc. During 2009-10, an amount of Rs. 80.91 crore was released, of which Rs. 20.49 crore grant was for capital support/Revolving Fund Assistance (RFA) to MFIs, as against Rs. 18.73 crore and 15.93 crore in the previous year, respectively.

SUPPORT FOR PARTNER AGENCIES FOR PROMOTION AND NATURE OF SHGs

NABARD continued to extend grant support to NGOs, RRBs, DCCBs, FCs and Individual Rural Volunteers (IRVs) for promoting and nurturing quality SHGs. During 2009-10, grant assistance of Rs. 2,878.17 lakh was sanctioned to various agencies for promoting 71,268 groups, taking the cumulative assistance sanctioned to Rs. 10,766.07 lakh for 4,92,746 groups.

As on 31 March 2010, Rs. 4,037.74 lakh was released and 2,36,863 SHGs credit linked to banks.

CAPABILITY BUILDING AND TRAINING OF PARTNER AGENCIES

To fine-tune the strategies for up-scaling support to the micro finance sector, NABARD conducted many awareness creation and sensitization programmes and arranged exposure visit for SHG members, NGOs, bankers, trainers, Panchayati Raj Institutions (PRIs) representatives, NABARD officials, IAS officers and micro-entrepreneurs throughout the year.

JOINT LIABILITY GROUPS (JLGs)

It needs simplified documentation, group dynamics timely repayment culture and prospects of credit enhancement to quality clients. NABARD has issued comprehensive guideline on Joint Groups to banks focusing on small and marginal farmers, tenant farmers engaged in farm sector and other clients under non-farm activities. Banks may use the services of JLG-promoting agencies.

MICRO-ENTERPRISE DEVELOPMENT PROGRAMME FOR SKILL DEVELOPMENT

The Micro-Enterprise Development Programme (MFDP) was launched by NABARD in 2006 with the basic objective to enhance the capability of the number of matured SHGs to take up micro-enterprises through appropriate skill upgradation/development in the existing or new livelihood activities both in farm and non-farm sectors by way of enriching knowledge of participants on enterprise management business dynamics and rural markets. In 2009-10, a total of 1530 MEDPs, both under farm and non-farm activities were conducted across the country covering 38,313 numbers of the matured SHGs, cumulatively so far covering 93,777 participants (NABARD, Report 2009-10).

PILOT PROJECT ON SHGS—POST OFFICE LINKAGE PROGRAMME

The result of SHG-Post Office Linkage Programme in Tamil Nadu has been very encouraging. NABARD sanctioned additional Rs. 200 lakh Revolving Fund Assistance (RFA) to India post for onward landing to SHGs, taking the total RFA sanctioned to Rs. 500 lakh. Cumulatively, 2, 828 SHGs have opened interest saving accounts with relent Post Office in Tamil Nadu and 1195 SHGs have been credit linked by post offices, with loan amounting to Rs. 321.25 lakh.

SUPPORT TO ACTIVITY-BASED GROUPS (ABGs)

NABARD continued to support the scheme for small-scale activity-based groups wherein capacity building, credit and market-related support will be extended. The focus is on farming and nurturing groups engaged in similar economic activities, i.e. farmers, handloom weavers, craftsmen, fishermen, etc. to improve production and realising better price for produce. The scheme has both graft and loan components. NABARD may provide loans directly to registered groups or through agencies promoting the groups, to establish a few initial projects where have exists (NABARD, Annual Report, 2009-10).

PROVIDING TECHNOLOGY SUPPORT TO NGOs

The scheme of supporting NGOs for computerisation of MIS of the SHG-Bank linkage programme has been revised. NGOs promoting a minimum of 250 SHGs would now be eligible for a maximum grant assistance of Rs. 50,000 for hardware components.

SUPPORT TO SHGs FEDERATION

Recognizing the emerging role of the SHGs Federation in nurturing of SHGs, enhancing the bargaining powers of groups members and livelihood promotion, NABARD introduced during 2007-08, a flexible scheme support such federations, irrespective of their model. The broad norms prescribed for supporting SHG federation stipulate that the federations should be need-based. Members-owned, democratically managed, become self-managed over three years, etc. NABARD extends grant support to the federation for training, capacity building and exposure visits of SHG members, etc. (Khan and Alam, 2011).

THE ISSUES AND CHALLENGES

The mainstream financial institutions are generally seen as flushed with funds and have access to enormous amounts of low-cost savings deposits. It is found that the poorer the region, the lower the credit-deposit ratio. Most of eastern Uttar Pradesh, Bihar, Orissa and the North-East regions have credit deposit ratios of 20-30 per cent. Since most of the poor and needy are illiterate and prefer loans for consumption rather than productive purposes, majority of the poor find it hard to get loans sanctioned for taking up economic activities, even if they want to. Sometimes, the loanees are asked to furnish some documents and collateral security against the loan sanctioned, contrary to the directives of the Government and the RBI. The rigid systems and procedures for sanctioning loans and disbursing them to the beneficiaries result in a lot of delay in time for the borrowers, which de-motivate them. Although the interest rate offered to the borrowers is regulated, the transaction costs in terms of the number of trips to be made, the documents to be furnished, etc. plus the illegal charges demanded by the lending institutions clandestinely, result in increasing the cost of borrowing, thus, making it less attractive to the borrowers.

The status of women has generally improved as they have developed stronger confidence which has changed gender dynamics and their role in the household. Further, SHGs are becoming more than just financial intermediaries, instead they have emerged into a more political and social unit of society. More importantly, the penetration of micro finance to the poorest of the poor is still weak and needs a wider reach. The need for a coordinated and comprehensive support strategy is imperative as the financial management issues of SHGs need to be addressed otherwise the benefits of the civil society impacts will be lost as SHGs will become overburdened and un-sustainable.

Micro finance has been seen as a social obligation rather than a potential business opportunity. Sometimes, a few financial institutions charge the beneficiaries of a group high interest rate which makes the repayment difficult for the very poor. The poorest of the poor are, therefore, unable to access the micro-finance benefits. In most of the cases, it has been found that members of a group take up certain economic activities for their sustenance which are not preceded by relevant training. After the pioneering efforts of the last few years by the government, banks, NGOs, and so on, the micro-finance scene is reaching the take-off point (Tripathy, 2003).

CONCLUDING REMARKS

As a sector, micro finance has shown very fast growth across the country in terms of geographical coverage, increased clientele, portfolio, institutional involvement, etc. Increasingly more and more promoting organizations, financial institutions, donors and clients are getting associated with the programme, mainly because of its contributions to alleviating poverty and empowering women. Micro finance programmes like the Self-Help Bank Linkage Programme (SHG) in India have been increasingly hailed for their positive economic impact and the empowerment women. The assumption is that increasing women's access to micro finance will enable women to make a greater contribution to household income, either through their own economic activity or equality becoming a channel for loans to household activity. This contribution and subsequent increase in status in the household will in turn give women the support they need to enable women to bring about wider changes in gender inequality in the community. Self-Help Group Programme is the right approach to create Self-employment opportunities so as to supplement the income and assets of rural poor.

The SHG programme show a much skewed growth pattern in the country. The programme is largely concentrated in southern region of the country. It is important that the micro finance programme spread more evenly so that the benefits are available especially in regions where the need is more accurate. The challenge for NGOs and MFIs is to achieve their own financial self-sufficiency without transferring all the overhead costs to their poor clients. They need to ensure sufficient investment to provide diversified livelihood options and employment creation by optimizing existing resources through timely credit, technical inputs, skill training and knowledge transfer. It is crucial to arrive at the right trade-off between the needs of the poor and the sustainability of the MFIs. Challenge is to have financial inclusion with an inclusive growth. The banking sector can play a lead and proactive role in ensuring financial inclusion through SHG-Bank Linkage Programme and Business Correspondent model. SHG quality must improve, and all stakeholders need to work towards it. Use of technology would be a major driving force in the future as it would reduce cost, and there is a need to come on a common platform for that. To ensuring a monitoring mechanism and adopting standard accounting practices in SHGs to bring uniformity and transparency in transactions. The members should be provided training in micro-enterprises so that credit availed by them can be used productively.

The commercial banks must provide a greater linkage to SHGs in providing them higher amount of bank loans. The absence of quality agencies or individuals for social intermediation is limiting the spread of the programme. So there is a need for substantial scaling up of micro finance which includes credit, saving and insurance. As the banking sector is not able to meet the entire credit needs of the poor, it is necessary to encourage the growth of MFIs, subject to appropriate regulation which should not be too restrictive. In order to achieve these, emphasis should be given to creation of adequate infrastructure, efficient extension services, processing and marketing facilities, etc. Micro-finance ombudsmen may be set-up at district levels to decide on complaints regarding exploitative and illegal practices by the lenders. Government institutions like NABARD, SIBDI, etc. should create a credit enhancement structure where they can enhance the bonds or instruments to be issued by the MFIs to raise money from public at large. This could really catalyze further investment in the sector and ultimately lead to lowering of interest rates charged to the end borrowers.

REFERENCES

Acharya, N. (2008), "Micro finance and Rural Poor in Orissa", Micro finance and Rural Development in India (ed.) S.K Das, *et. al.*, New Century Publication, New Delhi, pp. 8-14.

Anand, V. Vijay (2008), "Micro finance for Rural Development", *Yojana*, Vol. 52, January, pp. 63-64.

Bakhtiari, Sadegh (2006), "Micro finance and Poverty Reduction: Some International Evidence", *International Business and Economics Research Journal*, Vol. 5, No. 12, December, p. 17

Hazra, Anupan (2009), "Poverty in Rural India : Jeopardizing the Future Growth", *Kurukshetra*, November, pp. 32-35.

Kamdar, Sangita (2007), "Micro finance in India : Issues and Challenges", Micro finance Self-help Employment and Poverty Alleviation (ed.) Himalaya Publishing House, New Delhi, pp. 14-51.

Karmakar, K.G. (2008), "Micro finance Revisited", Micro finance in India, (ed.) K.G. Karmakar, Sage Publication, New Delhi, pp. 33-54.

Karuraiathal, A. (2009), "Linkage between Self-help Groups (SHGs) and Banks in India", Banking, Micro finance and Self-help groups in India (ed.) A. Vijay Kumar, New Century Publications, New Delhi, pp. 161-173.

Khan, Mohd. Azam and Alam, Tosib (2011), Micro Finance in India: A Step towards Rural Prosperity, *Financing Agriculture,* Vol. 43, Issues 7, July, pp. 26-28.

Kour, Amarjeet (2008),"Self-help groups (SHG) and Rural Development, *Kurukshetra*, December, pp. 25-29.

Kumar, S. Mahendra and S. Srinivasa (2010), "Reflection of Micro finance in India", Macro Dynamics of Micro finance (eds.) Daniel Lazar, *et. al.*) Excel Books, New Delhi, pp. 198-201.

Kumaresan, A. and Chitrakala, I. (2009), "Micro financing and Banking Sector", *op. cit.*, pp. 183-206.

Mahalakshmi, M. (2010), "Microfinance—A Poverty Measurement Tool of Self-help Members in Kanyakumari District and its Impact on Saving and Borrowings", Macro Dynamics of Micro finance (eds.) Daniel Lazar, *et. al.* Excel Books, New Delhi, pp. 251-60.

NABARD, Annual Report, 2009-10, pp. 47-42.

NABARD, Report, (2009-10), Status of Micro finance in India, NABARD, p. xi.

Panday, Bharat, *et. al.* (2009), "Growth of Micro finance in India: Opportunities and Challenges", Micro finance—Performance

Evaluation and Enterprise Development (eds.) Daniel Lazar and Malabika Deo, Allied Publishers, New Delhi, pp. 83-95.

Pawar, Anand and Chary, D. Thiruvengala (2010), "Impact of Micro finance on Tribal Development in Andhra Pradesh", Macro Dynamics of Micro finance (eds.) Daniel Lazar, *et al.*, Excel Books, New Delhi, pp. 34-45.

Raheem, A. Abdul (2006), "Role of SHGs", *Yojana*, October, pp. 58-60.

Rajesh, S. and Venkatamma, G. (2009). "Micro finance Institutions in India", *Kurukshetra*, November, pp. 11-13.

Samal, A.P. (2009), "Building Social Capital for Combating Poverty", Micro Finance and Rural Development in India, (eds.) S.K. Das, *et. al.*, New Century Publications, New Delhi, pp. 84-92.

Sharma, M. and M. Zeller (1997), "Repayment Performance in Group-based Credit Programmes in Bangladesh: An Empirical Analysis," *World Development*, Vol. 25, No. 10, pp. 1731-42.

Singh Sukhbir (2007), "Towards Inclusive Rural Financial Services—Micro finance in India", Microfinance, Self-employment and Poverty Alleviation, (ed.) Sangita Kamdar, Himalaya Publishing House, New Delhi, pp. 53-74.

Singh, Pankaj, *et. al.* (2010), "Impact of Women SHGs on Scio-economic Development", *UPUEA Economic Journal*, Vol. 6, Conference No. 6, 23-24 December, pp. 86-89.

Thakur, K.S., *et. al.* (2010), "Microfinance—A Tool for Poverty Control (with special reference to Gwalior and Chambal division of Madhya Pradesh)", *op. cit.*, pp. 142-47.

Tripathy, K.K., (2003), Poverty Alleviation: Making Micro finance Sustainable.

www.thehindubusinessline.com/2003/11/...

CHAPTER

28

Sustainable Development and the Indian Garments Industry

SHAHID ALAM

ABSTRACT

Sustainable development is termed as a development path along with the maximization of human well-being for today's generations which requires securing those public goods that are essential for economic development to last, such as those provided by well-functioning ecosystems, a healthy environment and a cohesive society. Indian apparel market is one of the fastest growing market in the world and is expected to become one of the major consumption bases in near future. It offers enormous opportunity going forward due to various consumption growth drivers inherent in the Indian economy. A scan of the apparel market throws out some important opportunities that companies need to look more closely. Promising apparel segments like Women's wear, Casual wear, Kids wear, Inner wear, Plus size clothing, School Uniforms, Active wear and youth fashion offer huge opportunity for apparel companies/brands/retailers as consumer demands get more specific going forward. The increasing presence of foreign retailers in the domestic market is also expected to influence domestic players to improve their operations and offering to the customers. To tap the opportunities and sustain businesses in this changing consumption scenario, companies need to align themselves with the market requirements and develop required competencies. Manufacturers need to get more service-oriented and look to develop a niche positioning for themselves amongst their buyers. With growing competition suppliers also need to have orientation towards innovation across their business in terms of products, processes and adopt best manufacturing practices to increase competitiveness.

Keywords: Sustainable Development, Indian Garments Industry, Domestic and Export Market

INTRODUCTION

Sustainable development can be defined in technical terms as a development path along with the maximization of human well-being for today's generations which does not lead to declines in future well-being. Attaining this path requires eliminating those negative externalities that are responsible for natural resource depletion and environmental degradation. It also requires securing those public goods that are essential for economic development to last, such as those provided by well-functioning ecosystems, a healthy environment and a cohesive society. Sustainable development also stresses the importance of retaining the flexibility to respond to future shocks, even when their probability, and the size and location of their effects, cannot be assessed with certainty. Beyond this technical definition, the notion of sustainable development has gained a broader political usage.

Here, it embodies a concern for taking a broad view of what human welfare entails, and for balancing the goals of economic efficiency, social development and environmental protection. Sustainable development also underscores the importance of taking a longer-term perspective about the consequences of today's activities, and of global co-operation among countries to reach viable solutions. These elements have made sustainable development a key objective for domestic and regional policy formulation, as well as for international relations between countries in the 21st century.

The present size of Indian Textile and Apparel market is US$ 62 Billion out of which US$ 22 Billion is contributed by exports while the rest US$ 40 Billion is domestic market. Growing Textile and Apparel Exports in Textiles and Apparel have registered a strong growth in the last few years with 11% CAGR from 2004-05 to 2007-08. The single largest category is woven apparel followed by knitted apparel, made-ups and cotton-based textiles.

GROWING MARKET OF INDIAN GARMENTS INDUSTRY

Indian domestic textiles and apparel market is one of the fastest growing market in the world and offers huge market potential for textile and apparel manufacturers. It is expected to become one of the major consumption bases in near future. Out of the total market size of US $ 40 Billion, Clothing contributes US $ 30 Billion, while rest US$10 billion is contributed by Textiles (Home textiles, Technical textiles and other textiles end-uses). The domestic market has shown a significant growth in past few years registering a Compounded Annual Growth Rate (CAGR) of ~13%. Despite the recent demand slump, the domestic market is expected to grow at around 9% in the next 5 years. In this context, the industry needs to focus on the domestic market more intensely and understand the market dynamics in more detail in order to tap the complete potential. Further we discuss these opportunities for Indian textile and apparel companies in the domestic market and strategies for developing sustainable businesses with the changing requirements of the domestic market.

The post-quota period for Indian Apparel exports has marred with high volatility. Initially, the currency fluctuations in 2007-08, and then the global meltdown in 2008-09, have pulled down apparel exports growth to single digit (5%). The estimated figure for April-September 2009-10 is US$ 4840 million. India's percentage share in World apparel exports have dipped over the last five years (including estimated figures for 2009-10). From 31% in 2005-06, it has declined to negative growth of 7 per cent. In the fiscal year, 2007-08, the readymade garment export amounted to US$ 9.7 billion. USA, UK, Germany were the top three destinations with the cumulative share of 51%.

SEGMENTS OF INDIAN GARMENTS INDUSTRY WITH HIGH GROWTH POTENTIAL

It is evident that the Indian consumer is ready for change, demanding options and looking out for product that suits and matches their needs and aspirations. With the back drop of changes, Indian apparel market is moving away from the traditional segmentation to a much deeper and wider segmentation based on consumer needs. Indian apparel market can be broken up into men, women and kids, but within each there are a number of segments that are emerging reflecting changing needs. Some of the segments that are potential opportunities to watch out for are:

1. Women's wear
2. Casual wear
3. Kids wear
4. School Uniforms
5. Inner wear
6. Plus size clothing
7. Active wear/Exercise wear/Swim wear
8. Youth fashion/College fashion

All above segments are discussed further in detail:

1. Women's Wear

Women's formal wear and ethnic wear markets are still ruled by unorganized players. With more women expected to enter corporate world, both these segments are good opportunities because of the market size.

2. Casual Wear

Casual wear segments are expected to grow between 10-15% as compare to 9% growth of overall Indian Apparel Market. More than 50% of the clothes in this category are bought by youth (age 13-30). Increase of buying frequency of casual wear is spurred by:

- Preference for more comfort wears,
- Increase in employability, and
- Acceptance of Casual wear in work places.

3. Kids Wear

Kids wear is a major category with few established players. Very few brands namely Lilliput, Gini and Jony, Catmoss, Benetton, Disney, Barbie. Some brands have extended into this category though not very successfully, i.e. OYO by Spykar, Zapp by Raymond. It still holds a large opportunity which is clearly untapped.

4. School Uniforms

Scope in organized retail of good quality uniforms is very high with very few organized players in this high growth potential segment Uniforms form almost 40% of the Rs. 32,000 Crore Kids wear market in India. With literacy rates increasing and the private education market estimated at Rs. 172,000 crore, uniforms form an essential part of the apparel market. The impetus will come not only from sheer numbers at the lower price brackets, but from the rise of high end schooling education in the form of world schools and international schools. Present state of the market in this category are:

- This category is highly fragmented and unorganized with hardly any large players. SKNL is the only organized player and they are able to cater to a small part of the market.
- Uniforms available are sub-standard quality of stitching and lack standardization.
- Shopping for uniforms is a bad Shopping experience and uniform retailers are found in very low key markets Internationally, most brands like Marks and Spencer, Next, JC Penny have brand extensions into uniforms while there are some standalone uniform brands like K-12 gear, Academy Uniforms, First In Class, etc.

5. Inner Wear

Inner wear market in India, estimated at Rs. 14,000 Crores, is largely unorganized with more than 75% of the industry dominated by unorganized indigenous players. However, there is a growing awareness of physical appearances among consumers leading to demand for more variety and designs which is driving the organized market growth. Some of the bottlenecks for growth of innerwear and subsequent opportunity for modern retailers include:

- Lack of innovation and product differentiation in this product
- Lack of standard sizing
- Low penetration and distribution levels

6. Plus Size Apparel

Plus size apparel market (Rs. 11,000 Crores) is virtually untapped. It is estimated that ~8% of the Indian population comprises plus sizes, hence the potential market for plus size is 8% of Indian apparel market, but only 0.15% of present market consists of this segment. India only has a handful of brands in this category like Revolution, mustard, and, etc. None of the western wear brands have extended into the plus sizes. Internationally besides stand alone plus size brands like Brylane, Evans, Igigi, most regular brands like Next, M&S have plus sizes.

7. Active Wear/Exercise Wear/Swim Wear

Indians get more and more health conscious and look for sports and games to address this need. They are also looking to live fuller lives by participating a lot more in outdoor activities as a way to connect to family, friends and their unfulfilled aspirations. Active wear for various sports such as football, tennis, golf, rock-climbing, cricket, swimming is finally gaining acceptance. Exercise wear especially for gyming, exercising, walking and jogging is also becoming important besides apparel for more spiritual inclinations like yoga, meditation, etc. Currently, the market for active wear is estimated to be Rs. 1100 crores and growing at 13%.

While India is already home to brands like Reebok, Adidas, Nike and Puma who are showing tremendous growth figures, there still exists potential for brands focusing on specific sporting categories. Besides brand-based retailing, another important concept is the event centric merchandise retailing which is very popular in the sporting industry, for example, FIFA apparel, etc.

8. Youth Fashion/College Fashion

There is also significant potential in youth fashion market as college going youngsters are getting more fashion conscious. Internationally there are brands like American Eagle Outfitters, Aeropostale, True religion, etc. which are positioned as fashion labels specifically for the youth. In India, there are approximately, 11 million youth (15-24 years of age) in top consuming strata in 70 cities and this segment offers an opportunity for brands to position themselves for specific age groups like 13-19 years, 20-25 years, etc. and establish their brands amongst these specific consumers.

INCREASING PRESENCE OF INTERNATIONAL PLAYERS

With more and more international brands and retailers looking at India as their next destination, the competition in the domestic market is expected to shoot up significantly. However, at the same time the international brands/retailers like Zara, Wal-mart, Tesco, etc. will also bring with them superior technology and economies of scale across the supply chain, thus making it imperative for the domestic players to tighten up their operations. Already established retailers in India are looking to upgrade their existing systems, for example, Future Group is making investments worth crore of rupees in new technology and processes with a view to sustain its potential growth in the Indian market and also looking at partnerships with global majors for improving supply chain scales and efficiencies. As a result, the productivity and efficiencies of domestic players will improve along with skill upgradation. Also the competition from these international retailers/brands will eat up substantial portion of the market pie. Hence, in this backdrop, domestic players need to be efficient and forward thinking in terms of their offering to the customer and establish an upper hand in the market *vis-à-vis* these MNCs.

For the manufacturers it offers enormous market potential since the international players would be looking at sourcing from local players. Hence, in this context manufacturers need to align themselves as per the international players sourcing requirements.

INTERNATIONAL PLAYERS EXPANDING IN INDIA

- Wal-Mart (already present with Bharti)
- Tesco (planning)
- Arcadia (Topshop, Topman)
- Inditex (Zara)
- M&S
- Carrefour (planning)
- Gucci (already present)
- Mother care (already present)
- Etc.

GROWING VALUE RETAIL IN INDIA

Rural India constitutes more than half of India's apparel market. The rural consumption is also growing significantly and is expected to provide much of the economic growth in coming years. Consequently, there is huge potential for value retailing which has so far been unexplored by majority of Indian apparel retailers. Also with entry of Zara into India by next year it won't be surprising to see the "Zara like" fast fashion business model emerge in the Indian market. Already many apparel companies have taken note of this opportunity and are foraying into the mass market, with some like Koutons already having significant presence (78% of their stores already present in below top 35 cities).

Subsequently, this means a huge opportunity for Indian textile and apparel manufacturers to look towards catering to the domestic value market. For manufacturers this means more emphasis on fashion at low prices. Hence, firms need to take designing more seriously along with improving operational efficiencies. Companies also need to establish strong supply relationships with these upcoming "value retailers" to become first partners of choice for their fast fashion requirements.

Some examples of Indian apparel companies looking towards mass market :

- SKNL—Planning to launch a 'mass brand' for the tier 3 and tier 4 cities.
- Arvind—Planning to locate a significant share of 30 outlets to be added this year in tier 3 cities.
- Alok—Planning to triple its H&A store count by next March, with a strong focus on the tier 2 and tier 3 cities. It already has outlets in Moga and Firozepur in Punjab, and Latur in Maharashtra.
- Welspun Retail—Planning to add 70-80 'Welhome' stores in FY11, with 30 percent focused on villages.

PROVIDING VALUE ADDED SERVICES AND DEVELOPING NICHE POSITIONING

Service Orientation

With the growing domestic market and growing presence of international retailers suppliers need to align themselves as per requirements of the retailers. The big retailers would also be looking at sourcing from established partners in the supply chain and would be expecting certain pre-requisites from their suppliers. In this regard suppliers need to look at integrating and offering value-added services to retailers like design, logistics, warehousing, etc. in order to establish long-term supply chain partnerships. Particularly logistics and warehousing play a significant role in the Indian domestic market due to the long distances between supply bases and markets, and suppliers should look towards working closely with retailers in these areas. Also textile and apparel companies should look at investing in IT and developing linkages across the supply chain for driving efficiencies.

Niche Positioning

With growing specialization at the retail level, suppliers should also look at developing niche/specialized product competencies and offer customized solutions for respective retailers/brands based on their specific requirements. Innovating to "Survive" with increasing global competition and evolving consumerism it is slowly becoming a must for textile manufacturer to be innovative. Firms need to explore innovation both in terms of processes, marketing and products. Activities like R&D and designing should be treated as key success factors and a pre-requisite rather than an afterthought. Apart from process-based innovations companies should also not shy away from exploring new business models in the context of the ever changing consumption space. In this regard there are many apparel companies who have already realized the importance of "business" innovation to "survive" in the increasingly competitive market place and are looking to differentiate their product offering across various levels.

Adopting Global Best Practices

Companies also need to adopt best management practices like lean manufacturing, Kaizen, six sigma, etc. for improving overall efficiencies and productivity. This would not only improve the financial returns for companies but also make them more cost competitive in the market. In this textile and apparel companies can take a cue from other industries in reaping respective benefits of best management practices.

Developing Manpower

With so many new industries growing like telecom, IT, automobiles, banking, etc., one of the challenges for the industry today is attracting skilled and qualified manpower and staff to work in the textile industry. While, many of the big textile companies regularly recruit from major textile institutes in technical grade (engineering, design, merchandising), there is still a general lack of interest amongst most of the Managerial grade students joining the industry. In this except for a few big firms like ITC, Arvind, etc. not many companies have been able to recruit students from premier MBA/Engineering institutes like IIM/IIT.

The industry needs fresh and innovative thoughts to improve its existing work practices and drive efficiencies in manufacturing and supply chain. The best way to do this is by reaching out to the young managerial talent and give them the right 'incentives' to join the T&A industry.

T&A companies also need to increase the industry-academia interaction to nurture talent at the base level and for other purposes also like Research and Development, training existing staff in best practices, etc. The industry needs to reach out to the academia and in this regard can take cue from companies in other industries which are collaborating with academia in many ways.

Such industry-academia interaction helps in developing affinity for students to work in the industry in future. There are 103 textile institutes in India along with 118 National Institutes of Fashion Technology, which can be tapped for this purpose. The industry must make best efforts to attract higher and highest quality talent—at all levels—to provide the intellectual backbone for engineering a renaissance for itself in the next 10 years.

Environmental Sustainability

Environmental sustainability is the ability to maintain the qualities that are valued in the physical environment. It is clearly emerging that the world's coastline and watersheds are increasingly affected by economic changes and environmental degradation; consumers have become edgy about the effect of human activity on the environment. In such a scenario, environment sustainability has become an industry in itself.

With increasing concerns regarding the effect of the textile industry on the environment, at all stages of its chain, i.e. raw material, fiber, fabric, apparel, processing; more and more textile researchers, producers and manufacturers are looking to biodegradable and sustainable fibers as an effective way of reducing the impact textiles have on the environment.

More and more people are now focusing on the responsibility of industry and consumer priorities, and introducing new measuring tools for electricity and water usage, carbon footprint and traceability. As consumers in the other countries get aware of sustainability issues, it is going to put tremendous pressure on Indian manufacturers to comply. The young consumer is moving from the industrial economy to the sustainable economy and manufacturers/retailers globally have to build that into our processes.Hence companies need to gear up towards going green and give more weightage to environmental friendliness going forward. Leveraging FTA's Historically, Free Trade Agreements have played a significant role in determining trade dynamics across the World. Many trade agreements like NAFTA, EFTA, AGOA, GSP benefits have been instrumental in developing the textile and apparel industry of respective countries. India has also established a few trade agreements with countries like Sri Lanka, Thailand, ASEAN, etc. and further negotiations are in progress with many countries like EU, Australia, Japan, etc. The major benefits of these FTA's include:

- Decreased sourcing costs of key products included in the agreements.
- Availability of variety of products for the domestic market.

Hence, it is important for firms to keep track of these agreements and understand the key benefits that can be leveraged from the respective countries both in terms of sourcing as well as marketing in those countries.

CONCLUSION

The Indian domestic apparel market offers enormous opportunity going forward due to various consumption growth drivers inherent in the Indian economy. Overall consumption patterns are changing with decreasing apparel share of wallet and increase of more products in consumption basket. In this context apparel companies need to study the domestic market dynamics more intensely in order to sustain apparel's share in the consumption basket.

A scan of the apparel market throws out some important opportunities that companies need to look more closely. Promising apparel segments like Women's wear, Casual wear, Kids wear, Inner wear, Plus size clothing, School Uniforms, Active wear and youth fashion offer huge opportunity for apparel companies/brands/retailers as consumer demands get more specific going forward. Also the mass market offers significant opportunity for companies as value retailing takes its root in India. The increasing presence of foreign retailers in the domestic market is also expected to influence domestic players to improve their operations and offering to the customers. To tap the above opportunities and sustain businesses in this changing consumption scenario, companies need to align themselves with the market requirements and develop required competencies. Manufacturers need to get more service-oriented and look to develop a niche positioning for themselves amongst their buyers. With growing competition suppliers also need to have orientation towards innovation across their business in terms of products, processes and adopt best manufacturing practices to increase competitiveness. There also needs to be more focus given to hitherto overlook areas like manpower development, environment friendliness and leveraging trade agreements for reducing sourcing costs.

References

Abernathy, F.H., A. Volpe, and D. Weil (2004), The Apparel and Textile Industries after 2005: Prospects and Choices, Harvard Center for Textile and Apparel Research, Draft, December.

Abernathy, F. and D. Weil (2004) Apparel Apocalypse? The America's Textile Industries won't die when quotas do, *The Washington Post*, 18 November 2004.

Adhikari, R. (2005), Sense and Nonsense of Rules of Origin. *Trade Insight*, Vol. 1, No. 2. Kathmandu: South Asia Watch on Trade, Economics and Environment (SAWTEE).

S. Kelegama and M. Rahman (eds.), Multilateralism at Cross-roads: Reaffirming Development Priorities', South Asian Yearbook of Trade and Development, 2006, Delhi: Centre for Trade and Development and Wiley India.

Ahmad, M. (2005), Developments in Textiles and Clothing Trade, Post-ATC: Modellers Offmark—EU/US trade policy remains the predominant influence, Paper Presented at a Panel Discussion on Textiles and Clothing: One Year of Evidence after the Phasing out of Quotas in Hong Kong, 16 December 2005.

Baldwin, R.E. (2000), Regulatory Protectionism, Developing Nations and a Two-Tier World Trade System, Brookings Trade Forum. The Textile and Clothing Industry, 230 Industrial Development for the 21st Century.

Bennet, M. (2006), Lesotho's export textiles and garment industry in H. Jauch and R. Traub-Merz (eds.) The Future of the Textile and Clothing Industry in Sub-Saharan Africa. Bonn: Friedrich-Ebert-Stiftung.

Berger, S. (2006), How We Compete, New York: Currency/Doubleday.

Bhatt, S.R., B. Shakya, M. Udas, S. Thapa, G. Sharma, M. Pradhananga and A. Shrestha (2006), Human Development Impact Assessment in the Post ATC period: The case of Nepal, a revised draft report submitted to UNDP RCC APTII, September, Kathmandu: SAWTEE and Action Aid, Nepal.

Chandra, P. (1998), Competing through Capabilities: Strategies for global competitiveness of Indian Textile Industry. *Economic and Political Weekly,* 34 (9):M-17-M-24, February 27.

Amsden, Alice, 2001. *The Rise of 'The Rest': Challenges to the West from Late Industrializing Economies.* Oxford: Oxford University Press.

Berger, Suzanne. 2006. *How we Compete.* New York: Currency/Doubleday.

Feenstra, R.C., 1998, "Integration of Trade and Disintegration of Production in the Global Economy," *Journal of Economic Perspectives,* Vol. 12; No. 4, pp. 31-50.

Imbs, J. and R. Wacziarg (2003), 'Stages of diversification', *American Economic Review,* 93(1): 63-86.

Kuznets, Simon (1971): *Economic Growth of Nations: Total Output and Production Structure,* Cambridge Mass.

Mazumdar, Dipak and Sandip Sarkar (2009), The employment problem in India and the Phenomenon of the 'Missing Middle', *Indian Journal of Labour Economics,* Vol. 52, No. 1, pp. 43-55.

Sreenivasan, Kasthuri (1984), *India's Textile Industry: A Socio-economic Analysis,* Coimbatore: The South Indian Textile Research Association.

Tewari, Meenu (2006), 'Is Price and Cost Competitiveness Enough for Apparel Firms to Gain Market Share in the World after Quotas? A Review', *Global Economy Journal,* Vol. 6, Issue 4, Article No. 5.

UNCTAD (2005), 'TNCs and the Removal of Textiles and Clothing Quotas', *United Nations,* Geneva.

A Project Report by Techno Park Advisors Pvt. Ltd., Mumbai, "Building Sustainable Businesses in the Growing Domestic Market".

CHAPTER

29

An Analysis of Human Resource Strategy in Micro Finance Sector

SASWAT BARPANDA

ABSTRACT

Micro finance is gathering momentum to become a significant force in India. With its challenging growth, HR is the most neglected function of Micro finance Institutions (MFIs) which implies it demands more orientation in future because of its complexities and dynamics. Now there are more than 1000 MFIs currently operating in India and have disbursed only for 10% of potential demand of over $50 bn as a large proportion of Indians are living below the poverty line and the demand for credit for the poor is still surge ahead. Human resources are often seen as one of the most important assets of MFOs. Numerous studies have examined how a proper HR system can be design to contribute to the organizational bottom line. This paper presents the challenges especially of Human Resource in the process of growth and transformation of micro finance organisations (MFO) in India. HRM processes refer to the deeply-embedded, firm specific, dynamic routines by which a firm attracts, socialize trains, motivates, evaluates, and compensates its human resources. It provides new lenses on the tactic and aspects of HRM and the value it creates. This article is a structured review of the literature regarding key human resources management (HRM) issues in the micro finance industry. Based on this review, the authors offer an assessment of emerging trends in HRM and a summary of what has been advocated in the literature for improving HR value. This article explains resource-based view (RBV) of the firm has influenced the field of strategic human resource management (SHRM) and the author tried to apply the concept of RBV to SHRM as characteristics necessary for a sustainable competitive advantage. The author depicts various human resource issues and a strategy involved in this sector and tries to find out a new direction of research by critically analyzing various papers and identifies various gaps in the literature.

Keywords: Microfinance, strategic human resource management, Resource-based view, competitive advantage, intellectual capital, social capital

INTRODUCTION

Micro finance is gathering momentum to become a significant force in India. With its challenging growth, HR is the most neglected function of Micro finance Institutions (MFIs) which implies it demands more orientation in future because of its complexities and dynamics. Now there are more than 1000 MFIs currently operating in India and have disbursed only for 10% of potential demand of over $ 50 bn as a large proportion of Indians are living below the poverty line and the demand for credit for the poor is still surge ahead. Human resources are often seen as one of the most important assets of MFOs. Numerous studies have examined how a proper HR system can be design to contribute to the organizational bottom line. Micro finance offers poor people access to basic financial services such as loans, savings, money transfer services and micro insurance, according to the Consultative Group to Assist the Poor. The industry emerged to alleviate poverty on the premise that poor people, like everyone else, need a diverse range of financial services to run their business, build assets and reduce vulnerability to fluctuations in their income. Their needs for financial services have been traditionally met through a variety of financial relationships, mostly informal. In the past two decades, different types of financial services providers for poor people have emerged, including non-government organizations, or NGOs; cooperatives; community-based development institutions like Self Help Groups, or SHGs, and credit unions; commercial and state banks and micro finance institutions, or MFIs, offering new possibilities. The ultimate goal of micro finance is to enable the poor to build assets, increase incomes, reduce vulnerability to shocks and economic stress and improve quality of life by enabling better access to education and healthcare. The micro finance industry has grown at a rapid pace across the world and has created a positive impact in the lives of millions of poor people

LITERATURE REVIEW

Benjamin, B. Dunford, Scott A. Snell and Patrick M. Wright (2001) in the paper, "Human Resources and the Resource Based View of the Firm" discussed the concepts of core competencies, dynamic capabilities, and Knowledge as bridge constructs connecting the fields of strategy and SHRM. They proposed that both fields could benefit greatly from sharing respective areas of expertise. In fact, at the risk of oversimplification, the strategy literature has generated significant amounts of knowledge regarding who (i.e., employees/executives or groups of employees/executives) provides sources of competitive advantage.

The resource-based view (RBV) of the firm has influenced the field of strategic human resource management (SHRM) and the author tried to apply the concept of RBV to SHRM as characteristics necessary for a sustainable competitive advantage. It says sustained competitive advantage is not just a function of single or isolated components, but rather a combination of human capital elements such as the development of stocks of skills, strategically relevant behaviors, and supporting people management systems. It says about how SHRM help to realize the role of Human Resource in organization. Though the field of SHRM was not directly born out of the RBV, it has clearly been instrumental to its development. This was largely due to the RBV shifting emphasis in the strategy literature away from external factors (industry) toward internal firm resources as sources of competitive advantage (Hoskisson, Hitt, Wan, and Yiu, 1999). RBV has helped to put "people" (or a firm's human resources) on the radar screen. Concepts such as knowledge, dynamic capability, learning organizations, and leadership as sources of competitive advantage turn attention toward the intersection of strategy and HR issues. Wright and McMahan (1992) reviewed the theoretical perspectives that had been applied to SHRM and presented the RBV as one perspective that provided a rationale for how a firm's human resources could provide a potential source of sustainable competitive advantage. Individual HRM practices may be imitable but HRM systems and routines, which develop over time, may be unique to a particular firm and contribute to the creation of specific human capital skills. (Barney, Wright, Ketchen, 2001).

This paper also says that most models of SHRM based on fit assume that a certain business strategy demands a unique set of behaviors and attitudes from employees and certain human resource policies produce a unique set of responses from employees. They further argued that many within strategy have implicitly assumed that it is easier to rearrange complementary assets of strategy than it is to rearrange strategy given a set of assets/resources, even though empirical research seems to imply the opposite. Thus, they proposed that the resource-based view might provide a theoretical rationale for why HR could have implications for strategy formulation as well as implementation. Wright *et al.* (1994) mentioned a clear distinction between the firm's human resources (i.e. the human capital pool) and HR practices (those HR tools used to manage the human capital pool).

Boxall (1996), suggesting that human resource advantage (i.e., the superiority of one firm's HRM over another) consists of two parts. First, human capital advantage refers to the potential to capture a stock of exceptional human talent "latent with productive possibilities". Human process advantage can be understood as a "function of causally ambiguous, socially complex, historically evolved processes such as learning, cooperation, and innovation. A second task is to develop employees and teams in such a way as to create an organization capable of learning within and across industry cycles. Successful accomplishment of this task results in the organizational process advantage".

The RBV has also effectively put "people" on the strategy radar screen (Snell *et al.*, in press). In the search for competitive advantage, strategy researchers increasingly acknowledge human capital (Hitt, Bierman, Shimizu, and Kochar, 2001), intellectual capital (Edvinsson and Malone, 1997) and knowledge capital (Grant, 1996; Leibeskind, 1996; Matusik and Hill, 1998) as critical components. In so doing, the RBV has provided an excellent platform for highlighting the importance of people to competitive advantage.

Raphael Amit and Monica Belcourt (1999) in their paper, "Human Resources Management Processes: A Value-Creating Source of Competitive Advantage" states that value to a firm's stock of human-capital as a way of measuring the contribution of human resources to firm performance (Stewart, 1997). It has been recognized that most of the jobs have been knowledge-based (Quinn *et al.*, 1996) and this knowledge asset is not formally recognized in balance sheets of organizational assets. The human-capital advocates in this first paradigm attempt to formalize capture and leverage this asset (intellectual capital) to produce a higher-valued product (Stewart, 1997). This article introduces a new perspective on the contribution of HRM to a firm's financial performance. The 'process' perspective of HRM developed here, which is fixed in both the resource-based view of the firm and in institutional theory, links the human capital and social norms to gear up its human resources. Moreover, it builds on the organizational capital perspective, which views systems as ways to capture and deploy human-capital. This paper explains how adapting a 'process' perspective of HRM leads to the conclusion that an organization's ability to build, deploy, and renew its productive human-capital through transformational routines in ways that cannot be easily replicated by other organizations generates a competitive advantage in the market

Resource-Based View (RBV) theory is anchored in the notion that a firm's resources and capabilities are heterogeneous. It is this heterogeneity that explains variability in performance across firms within an industry (Amit and Schoemaker, 1993; Peteraf, 1993; Barney, 1991). A firm's resources are stocks of transferable input factors owned or controlled by the firm. Examples of input factors include tradeable 'knowhow', financial and physical assets, and human-capital. 'Capabilities', i.e firm's ability to deploy and coordinate its resources to reach a desired end is information-based, tangible and intangible firm-specific decision-making patterns (routines) that an organization develops through experience. Capabilities thus refer to the mechanisms used by firms to develop, combine, deploy and protect resources to convert them into outputs. Dynamic capabilities reflect the organization's capacity to draw on its past experiences to renew, reconfigure, and integrate new processes to remain competitive in a changing market environment (Teece *et al.*, 1997).

As far as the Human resource challenges in MFIs is concern, N. Sudhir Kumar and G. Susmitha (2011) in the paper "HR Challenges in Micro finance institutions" basically trying to convey the challenges especially of Human resource in the process of growth and transformation of micro finance organisations (MFO) in India. Micro finance is gathering momentum to become a significant force in India. With its challenging growth, HR is the most neglected function of MFIs which implies it demands more orientation in future because of its complexities and dynamics. Now there are more than 1000 MFIs currently operating in India and have disbursed only for 10% of potential demand of over $ 50 bn as a large proportion of Indians are living below the poverty line and the demand for credit for the poor is still surge ahead. In this article the author tries to depict various human resource issues and strategies involves in this sector. The quality of service delivery in the MFIs is depends on person to person contact and relationship. Hence, it demands more human resource intensive. HR is the more neglected function in Indian MFIs where there is a great dearth of HR planning where finding the right people for different MFI function. There are very few people available with relevant experiences because this sector has been scale up recently and there are limited training institutes and business schools to churn out people with required skill sets. Micro finance is a complicated business because there are large numbers of very small transactions. One needs to keep meticulous records for these transactions. The margins are thin and there is pressure to maintain portfolio quality. One needs to keep track of estimated and actual repayments on a daily basis. There is high amount of risk due to cash transactions. Also there are large number of units (field staff, branches, regions) whose performances have to be managed. As the scale of operations of an MFI increases, the task of managing operations becomes enormous which would make it imperative for the MFI to use the services of professionals. The most critical issue in HR planning is the finding right people for different functions in MFIs as there is a dearth of talents with relevant experience.

This author also referred the paper of Craig Churchill (1997), Managing Growth: the Organizational Architecture of Micro finance Institutions", where it depicted there elements i.e. organizational structure, Human resource development and institutional culture for making of successful and sustainable MFIs. It basically focuses on the formal structure of organization like design of work process, operation cycle and the process for selection, development and socialization of employees. Human resource process may be a pivotal element in gaining competitive advantage. Human resource development plays a vital role building institutional culture and organizational structure. Thus, it's important to align the firm's code of conduct, value system with its mission and vision. The different HR process must create an impression and portray of reputation. The organization structure can be a flat type where team-based work can only considered as the best procedure in every organization. During expansion the MFIs should built a lively and decentralized organizational structure to give confidence in various branch offices.

The various HR challenges can be broadly classified into three levels, namely, sectoral level, organizational level and individual level of challenges. In the former, their interpersonal relationship and service quality to customer will make a large difference in developing an organizational wealth. The organization level challenges include un-alignment of growth of Human Resource with that of organization what lead s to improper ratio of clients per officer which result in to low morale, turnover and declining of portfolio quality. Even the unprofessional way of hiring also creates lots of anomaly in the process. The individual level challenges in employees who mostly reluctant to work in remote areas. Lack of induction, training and skill enhancement is another challenging issue. So it identifies the various challenging issues like recruitment of qualified staff, training and capacity building, managing turn over and designing incentives, etc.

Deepak Alok (2006) in his article "HR Planning, Recruitment and Deployment (Challenges related to recruitment policies, HR policies and practices)" tried to highlight the growth of micro finance in India and the huge HR requirement in this sector in India. It explains about various job responsibilities of line a manger and staff managers as par as their functionalities are concern. It focuses on the importance of HR planning when it grows to a bigger MFI. An MFI which has reached a considerable size must follow a systematic approach to HR planning. The size of workforce required would essentially depend on the planned outreach of the MFI. Assuming an average productivity of the staff the planned size of the workforce can be determined easily. The next stage is to break-down the personnel requirement into different functional areas (e.g. field operations, accounts, finance, MIS, IT, Internal Audit, planning, legal). This would require lots of foresight to imagine the complications involved as the scale of operations increase. (For example, at a smaller scale of operations one may not require a specialized legal functions, but as the scale of operations would increase, increasing litigations and compliance issues would require that the MFI has a specialized legal functions). The number of staff required in different functional areas can be determined by using certain assumptions and thumb rules. (for example, each set of 10,000 clients, the MFI would require an Internal Auditor). The next part of this paper is regarding the characteristics of personnel. This would require further analysis and foresight. The MFI would have to further breakdown the functional areas into different levels and will have to identify the skills required on the basis of the anticipated job description. For example, the Internal Audit department would require some Audit Assistants, some Audit Supervisors and one Internal Auditor. Each of these categories of people will have a different job description and skill requirements. Regarding training and induction system, it says of Training and induction system for the staff will have to be customized for each category and level of staff. For example, a field staff may require training in processes and procedures but a person joining at the middle management level would require training in operational and financial analysis. Exposure visits could be planned for the personnel who are new to the micro finance sector. A combination of in-house and external trainings as well as exposure visits can also be planned.

Soderquist, Papalexandris, Ioannou and Prastacos (2009) in their paper, "From Task-based to Competency-based: A Typology and Process Supporting a Critical HRM Transition" seeks to develop a competency typology and propose a methodology for identifying competencies to aid the transition from a task-based to a competency-based logic for human resource management. This paper says that competencies as characteristics of an organization as a whole, with particular emphasis on core competencies and dynamic capabilities. The author of this paper has given a multidimensional view to understand the term competency. They reviews and compares different competency perspectives proposed in the literature, identifying their key components and analyzing major advantages and disadvantages. The Competency-based HRM is human-centered and concentrates on how objectives are met or how work is accomplished successfully, rather than on what is accomplished. It also seeks to identify those competencies that will enable long-term organizational fit with evolving business conditions, rather than achieving a short-term task match. It also allows behavioral traits to be integrated in HRM models, rather than focusing merely on technical skills. The paper also draws a clear line between managerial and operational competencies.

References

Sudhir, K.N. and Susmitha, G. (2011), "HR Challenges in Micro finance Institutions", *HRM Review*, IUP Publications, Vol. XI, Issue II, pp. 31-38.

Raphael, A. and Belcourt, M. (1999), "Human Resources Management Processes: A Value-Creating Source of Competitive Advantage", *European Management Journal*, Vol. 17, No. 2, pp. 174-81.

Sandhawalia, B.S. and Dalcher, D. (2010), "Developing Knowledge Management Capabilities: A Structured Approach", Vol. 15, No. 2, 2011, pp. 313-28.

Dunford, B.B., Snell, S.A. and Wright, P.M. (2001), "Human Resources and the Resource-based View of the Firm", *CAHRS Working Paper Series*. Paper 66. Available at: http://digitalcommons.ilr.cornell. edu/ cahrswp/66.

Barney, J., Wright, M., David, J., Ketchen Jr., D.J. (2001), "The Resource-based View of the Firm: Ten years after 1991", *Journal of Management*, 27, pp. 625-41.

Soderquist, K.E., Papalexandris, A., Ioannou, G., and Prastacos, G. (2008), "From task-based to Competency-based: A Typology and Process Supporting a Critical HRM Transition", *Personnel Review*, Vol. 39, No. 3, pp. 325-46.

CHAPTER

30

Impact of Index Futures on Indian Market Volatility

An Application of Garch

HARISH HANDA AND POOJA TALWAR

ABSTRACT

The paper attempts to examine whether, and to what extent, the introduction of Index Futures contracts trading has changed the volatility structure of the underlying BSE Sensex and NSE Nifty Index. It has also delved into the behavior of volatility in equity market in pre and post-derivatives period in India using conditional variance. Conditional volatility is modeled using GARCH (1, 1). The study is based on daily closing values of S&P CNX Nifty and BSE Sensex (broadly representing the Indian) indices from 1st Jan. 1998 to 31st Dec. 2002, i.e. pre and post-introduction of derivatives in India. While studying conditional volatility it was observed that the volatility has come down in the post-derivative period. The paper concludes that the volatility of the market as measured by benchmark indices likes S&P CNX NIFTY and SandP CNX NIFTY JUNIOR have fallen in the post derivatives period.

PROLOGUE

In the last decade, many emerging and transition economies have started introducing derivative contracts. As was the case when commodity futures were first introduced on the Chicago Board of Trade in 1865, policy-makers and regulators in these markets are concerned about the impact of futures on the underlying cash market. One of the reasons for this concern is the belief that futures trading attract speculators who then destabilize spot prices. This concern is evident in the following excerpt from an article by John Stuart Mill (1871):

> "The safety and cheapness of communications, which enable a deficiency in one place to be, supplied from the surplus of another render the fluctuations of prices much less extreme than formerly. This effect is much promoted by the existence of speculative merchant. Speculators, therefore, have a highly useful office in the economy of society."

Since futures encourage speculation, the debate on the impact of speculators intensified when futures contracts were first introduced for trading; beginning with commodity futures and moving on to financial futures and recently futures on weather and electricity. However, this traditional favorable view towards the economic benefits of speculative activity has not always been acceptable to regulators. For example, futures trading were blamed for some of the stock market crash of 1987 in the USA, thereby warranting more regulation. However, before further regulation is introduced, it is essential to determine whether in fact there is a causal link between the introduction of futures and spot market volatility. It therefore becomes imperative that one seeks answers to the questions like: What is the impact of derivatives upon market efficiency and liquidity of the underlying cash market? To what extent do derivatives destabilize the financial system, and how should these risks be addressed? Can the results from studies of developed markets be extended to emerging markets?

This paper seeks to contribute to the existing literature in many ways. The paper attempts to examine the impact of financial derivatives introduction on cash market volatility in an emerging market in India. Further, the study improves upon the methodology used in prior studies by using a framework that allows for generalized auto-regressive conditional Hetroskedasticity (GARCH) i.e., it explicitly models the volatility process over time, rather than using estimated standard deviations to measure volatility. This estimation technique enabled us to explore the link between information/ news arrival in the market and its effect on cash market volatility. The study also looks at the linkages in ongoing trading activity in the futures market with the underlying spot market volatility by decomposing trading volume and open interest into an expected component and an unexpected (surprise) component.

LITERATURE REVIEW

Analyzing the Structure of Volatility using GARCH

The general approach adopted in the literature to examine the effect of onset of futures trading is to compare the spot price volatility prior to the event with that of post-futures. In analyzing the behavior of pre- and post-futures volatility, one should attempt to explicitly capture the temporal dependency phenomena and time-varying nature of volatility. In addressing these issues, following Chan and Karolyi (1991), Lee and Ohk (1992), Antoniou and Holmes (1995), within the framework of the Generalized Autoregressive Conditional Hetroskedasticity (GARCH) model is performed. By providing a detailed specification of volatility, this technique enables one to not only check whether the volatility has changed but also provides the endogenous sources of change in volatility.

Following Pagan and Schwert (1990) and Engle and Ng (1992), the first step in GARCH modeling of daily returns series, which does not possess a unit root, is to remove any predictability associated with lagged returns and holiday/ week-end effects by accommodating sufficient number of

(ARMA) terms and holiday/weekend dummies in the mean equation respectively. Thus, for NSE Nifty logarithmic daily returns, the conditional mean equation is specified as:

$$R_t = \Phi + \sum_{i=1}^{l} \Phi R_{t-i} + \sum_{j=1}^{m} \theta_j \varepsilon_{t-j} + \nu HOL_t + \sum_{k=1}^{n} \gamma_k RW_{t-k} + \varepsilon_t \quad (1)$$

where R_t is the daily logarithmic return on the NSE Nifty index, HOL_t corresponds to week-end/holiday dummy. Graphical analysis and the computation of some basic statistical measures like the kurtosis, descriptive analysis and Ljung-Box Q-statistics for squared returns provide evidence about the presence of volatility clustering phenomenon, which calls for GARCH modeling. To model the conditional variance, Bollerslev (1986) introduced GARCH models that relate conditional variance of returns as a linear function of lagged conditional variance and past squared error.

The standard GARCH (p, q) model can be expressed as follows:

$$\varepsilon_t / \Omega_{t-1} \sim N(O, h_t)$$

$$h_t = \alpha_o + \sum_{i-1}^{p} \alpha_i \varepsilon^2 + \sum_{j=1}^{q} h_{t-j} \quad (2)$$

where, is the same error term Ot is the information set till time t, ai's are news coefficients measuring the impact of recent news on volatility and ßj's are the persistence coefficients measuring the impact of "less recent" or "old" news on volatility. These interpretations of ai's and ßj's can be found, for instance, in Antoniou and Holmes (1995) and Butterworth (2000).

First separate models been fitted for the before and after Nifty time series using the ARMA-GARCH model of (1) and (2) and it is found that the ARMA-GARCH orders of the two models are same. This facilitates writing a single model for the entire series including both before and after components by introducing a dummy variable, Dt, taking value 0 for before period and 1 for after. By including individual dummies, instead of additive or multiplicative dummy, as suggested in Butterworth (2000) and Gulen and Mayhew (2000), the proposed ARMA-GARCH model allows one to identify and study the nature of potential impacts of introduction of the futures contracts on the structure of both mean level and volatility of the spot market in general terms. By examining the significance of dummy coefficients, one can test whether there is a change in both the speed and persistence with which the volatility shocks evolve. Following the onset of futures trading, a positive significant value of aid would suggest that news is absorbed into prices more rapidly, while a negative and significant value of ßj, d implies that "less recent news" has less impact on today's price changes. This means that the investors attach more importance to recent news leading to a fall in the persistence of information. Thus, the ARMA-GARCH framework enables one to model changes that might occur both in the mean level and structure of volatility, which can be detected by checking the sign and significance of the coefficients attached to dummy variables.

Stein (1987) develops a model in which prices are determined by the interaction between hedgers and informed speculators. In this model, opening a futures market has two effects : (1) The futures market improves risk sharing and therefore reduces price volatility, and (2) If the speculators observe a noisy but informative signal, the hedgers react to the noise in the speculative trades, producing an increase in volatility.

In contrast, models developed by Danthine (1978) argue that the futures markets improve market depth and reduce volatility because the cost to informed traders of responding to mispricing is reduced. Froot and Perold (1991) extend Kyleís (1985) model to show that market depth is increased by more rapid dissemination of market-wide information and the presence of market makers in the futures market in addition to the cash market. Ross (1989) assumes that there exists an economy that is devoid of arbitrage and proceeds to provide a condition under which the no-arbitrage situation will be sustained. It implies that the variance of the price change will be equal to the rate of information flow. The implication of this is that the volatility of the asset price will increase as the rate of information flow increases. Thus, if futures increase the flow of information, than in the absence of arbitrage opportunity, the volatility of the spot price must change.

Overall, the theoretical work on futures listing effects offer no consensus on the size and the direction of the change in volatility. We therefore need to turn to the empirical literature on evidence relating to the volatility effects of listing index futures and options.

OBJECTIVES OF THE STUDY

The objective of this study is to test, whether the introduction of Index Futures had any impact on the volatility of Indian stock market and if confirmed, the effect was immediate or delayed.

RESEARCH METHODOLOGY

Data for the present study were time series secondary data showing hetroskedasticy. Data has been collected from National Stock Exchange and Bombay Stock Exchange websites. Incidentally, BSE Sensex Futures started on 5th June 2000 and NSE Nifty Futures started on 12th June 2000. There are no index futures for Nifty Junior. Thus, around the date of introduction of Futures there has been a sudden turn in BSE Sensex and NSE Nifty daily squared returns and needs further examination to conclusive evidence.

The data employed in study consists of daily prices of the S&P CNX Nifty Index, and Nifty Junior for the period Jan. 1, 1998 to Dec. 31, 2002. The prices used are daily open and close prices.

STATISTICAL PROCEDURE: UNIT ROOT TEST BY AUGMENTED DICKEY FULLER (ADF) TEST

The first step in analysis of time-series is to find out whether the data is stationary or non-stationary. This is achieved by applying Unit Root ADF test. The Augmented Dickey-Fuller (ADF) test which is a common method for determining unit roots is used. The DF Unit Root Test is based on the following three regression forms:

Without Constant and Trend

$DY_t = dY_{t-1} + u_t$

With Constant

$DY_t = a + dY_{t-1} + u_t$

With Constant and Trend

$DY_t = a + bT + dY_{t-1} + u_t$

The hypothesis is:

$H_0 : d = 0$ (Unit Root)
$H_1 : d \neq 0$

Decision rule:

If t* > ADF critical value, ==> null hypothesis accepted, i.e., unit root exists.
If t* < ADF critical value, ==> reject null hypothesis, i.e., unit root does not exist.

Augmented Dickey Fuller (ADF) Test, the regression equation is based:

$DY_t = a + bT + dY_{t-1} + g_i \Sigma DY_{t-1} - e_t$

If the series is correlated at high order lags, the assumption of white noise disturbances is violated. The ADF controls for high-order correlation by adding lagged difference terms of the dependent variable to the right-hand side of the regression.

$$\Delta yt = C + \gamma_{t-1} + \delta_1 \Delta y_{t-1} + \delta_2 \Delta y_{t-2} + ...+ \delta p \Delta y_{t-p} + \varepsilon_t$$

ARCH AND ARCH LM TEST

The second objective is to find out whether the data is hetroskedastic or not. Hetroskedastic means that variance of error term is non-constant, thereby implying that Volatility Exists. If the data is homoskedastic then there is no need of applying the GARCH model. For this, we check whether volatility actually exists in Indian Market, using ARCH test. Further, Hetroskedasticity was also confirmed using ARCH LM test as well.

General Autoregressive Conditional Hetroskedastic (GARCH) with Variance Regressor (Dummy variable)

The third objective of finding out whether the introduction of stock index futures reduces stock market volatility will be tested by amending the variance equation of the GARCH model with a Variance Regressor or Dummy variable, which takes values zero for the pre-futures period and one for the post-futures period.

The GARCH (1, 1) Model

The simplest GARCH (1, 1) specification:

$$Y_t = X_t\theta + \epsilon_t \quad (1)$$

$$\sigma_t^2 = \omega + \alpha\epsilon_{t-1}^2 + \beta\sigma_{t-1}^2 \quad (2)$$

The mean equation given in (1) is written as a function of exogenous variables with an error term. Since σ_t^2 is the one-period ahead forecast variance based on past information, it is called the conditional variance. The conditional variance equation specified in (2) is a function of three terms:

A constant term ω: News about volatility from the previous period, measured as the lag of the squared residual from the mean equation :

ϵ^2_{t-1} (the ARCH term).

Last period's forecast variance: σ^2_{t-1} (the GARCH term).

The (1, 1) in GARCH (1, 1) refers to the presence of a first-order autoregressive GARCH term (the first term in parentheses) and a first-order moving average ARCH term (the second term in parentheses).

$$\sigma_t^2 = \omega + \sum_{j=1}^{q} \beta_j \sigma_{t-j}^2 + \sum_{i=1}^{p} \alpha_i \epsilon_{t-i}^2$$

The above is the general GARCH equation. GARCH (p, q) can be estimated by choosing p and q where q is the order of the autoregressive GARCH terms and p is the order of the moving average ARCH terms.

EViews 5.0 software has been used to conduct the Augmented Dickey Fuller Unit root and GARCH test.

DATA ANALYSIS AND INTERPRETATION

Daily closing prices for S&P CNX Nifty, and CNX Nifty Junior were obtained respectively from www.nseindia. com over the period Jan. 1, 1998 to Dec. 31, 2002. The data comprises 613 observations related to the period prior to the introduction of futures trading and the remaining 641 observations to the period after the introduction of futures trading. Continuously compounded percentage returns are estimated as the log price relative. That is for an index with daily closing price P_t, its return R_t is defined as ln (P_t/P_{t-1}). All the return series (before, after and full period) are subjected to Augmented Dickey Fuller test and the null hypothesis of unit root is rejected in all cases. Figures 1, 2 and 3 plots the returns

FIG. 1

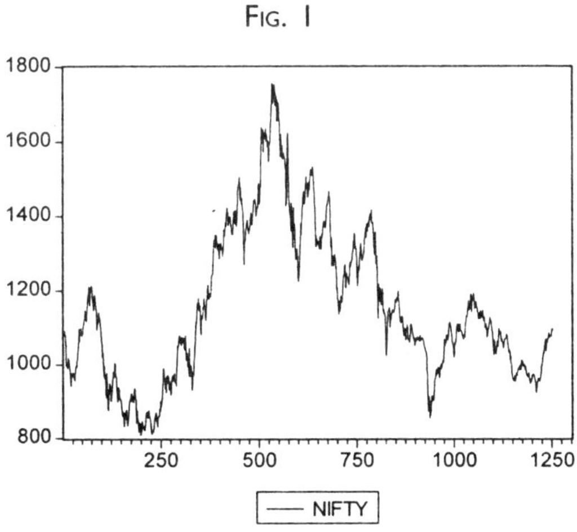

of Nifty daily closing price, Nifty Junior and BSE Sensex daily closing price respectively.

FIG. 2

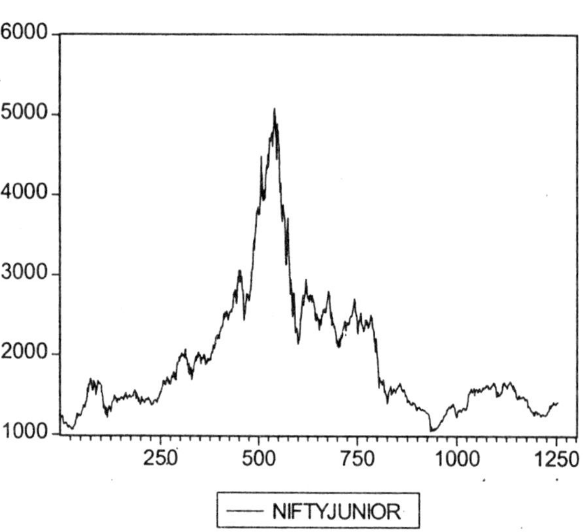

FIG. 3

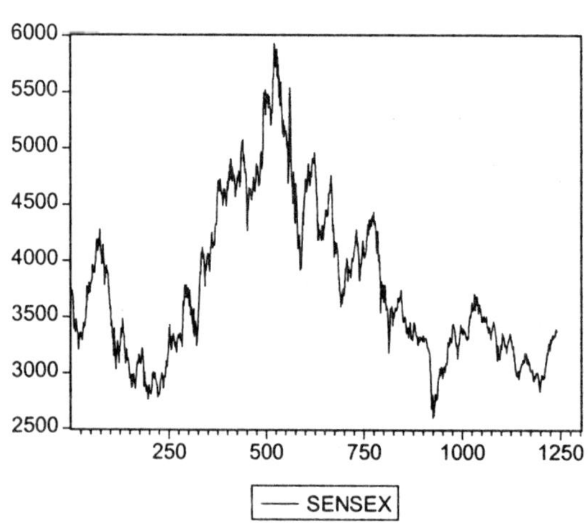

Figures 4, 5 and 6 plot the log price relative for Nifty, Nifty Junior and BSE Sensex clearing indicating that the price change volatility is very high.

FIG. 4

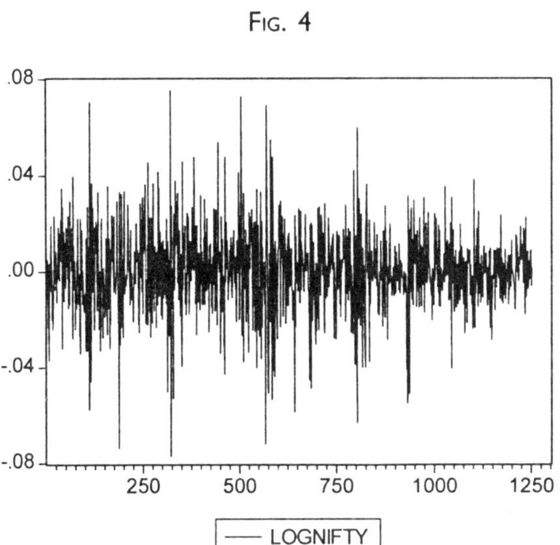

FIG. 5

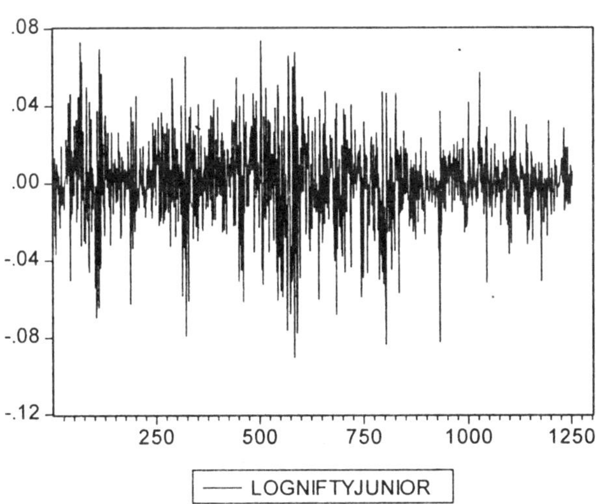

FIG. 6

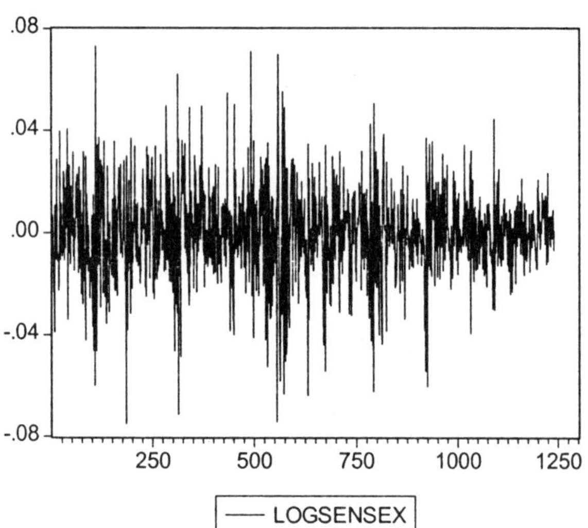

The study of these graphs provides an initial view of volatility for NSE Nifty, Nifty Junior and BSE Sensex indices. It can be observed from the graph that the pre-futures NSE Nifty and BSE Sensex volatility is greater than that of post-futures. This broadly suggests that the introduction of index futures has not destabilized the spot market. However, inferences cannot be drawn from these figures alone, as they are not supported by any statistical data. The Figure 4, Figure 5 and Figure 6 displays the volatility-clustering phenomenon, namely, large (small) shocks of either sign tend to follow large (small) shocks. These preliminary findings motivate and call for further investigation by GARCH modeling.

Augmented Dickey Fuller Test (ADF) Unit Root Test

Series Name	*ADF Statistic*	*Critical Value 1%*	*Critical Value 5%*	*Critical Value 10%*	*Inter-pretation*
NIFTY	-33.61922	-3.435365	-2.863642	-2.567939	Stationary
NIFTY Junior	-31.06373	-3.435365	-2.863642	-2.567939	Stationary
BSE Sensex	-33.69100	-3.435415	-2.863664	-2.567951	Stationary

ARCH-LM TEST FOR HETROSKEDASTICITY

One of the key assumptions of the ordinary regression model is that the errors have the same variance throughout the sample. This is also called the homoskedasticity model. If the error variance is not constant, the data are said to be hetroskedastic. Since ordinary least-squares regression assumes constant error variance, hetroskedasticity causes the OLS estimates to be inefficient. Models such as ARCH/GARCH that takes into account the changing variance can make more efficient use of the data. In the past, studies of volatility have used constructed volatility measures like estimated standard deviations, rolling standard deviations, etc., to discern the effect of futures introduction. These studies implicitly assume that price changes in spot markets are serially uncorrelated and homoskedastic.

However, findings of hetroskedasticity in stock returns are well documented. Performing an *ARCH-LM* on the daily stock returns of BSE Sensex, S&P CNX Nifty and Nifty Junior proves the hetroskedastic nature of the above data. As seen below (see appendix) from the analysis it can concluded that the variance of the ten periods is different thus proving that the data considered is hetroskedastic.

GARCH TEST

To determine the impact of index futures on the volatility of the underlying stock market GARCH (1, 1) model has been used. It determines the conditional volatility of the benchmark indices as well as stocks in question. It can be seen that for almost all stocks as well as the benchmark indices, the static volatility for the period before introduction of derivatives was higher (see appendix).

RESID (-1)^2 represents news about volatility from the previous period, measured as the lag of the squared residual from the mean equation. GARCH (-1) represents last periods forecast variance. There is a substantial increase in news incorporation coefficient RESID (-1)^2, GARCH (-1) which are positive, implying increase in market efficiency, measured by its ability to quickly incorporate new information. The results of Nifty Junior which acts as the control for the Nifty where the futures index are not introduced shows GARCH (-1) are less than that in Nifty, thus proving that the introduction of the index futures trading led to a more rapid absorption of news into prices.

The sum of RESID (-1)^2 and GARCH (-1) coefficients is very close to one, indicating that volatility shocks are quite persistent (as observed from results). As the sum of C, RESID (-1)^2, GARCH (-1), and dummy approaches one or equal to one the Mean reversion is a slow process. This means that the shocks tend to cause a very high degree of volatility. The sum C, RESID (-1)^2 and GARCH in Nifty (0.85) is lesser than that of Nifty Junior (0.93) marginally thus suggesting that introduction of Index futures does impact the underlying spot volatility and has reduced it. Hence, on the whole, the volatility of the Nifty series has decreased but the change is marginal. The above can be better explained with the help of a dummy variable introduced during the GARCH test. This variable takes value "0" before the introduction of the Index Futures and "1" after the introduction of Index Futures.

Indices	*Dummy Variable*
NIFTY	-3.53E-05
NIFTY Junior	-2.09E-05
BSE Sensex	-3.87E-05

As the coefficient of the dummies in the variance equation of NSE Nifty Junior is higher than the Nifty, it can be concluded that the volatility has reduced after the introduction of the Index Futures. Also, BSE Sensex has a similar value to Nifty, which would imply the similar result.

CONCLUSION

The paper concludes that the conditional volatility has come down in the post-derivative period. This suggests that the volatility of the market as measured by benchmark indices like S&P CNX NIFTY and S&P CNX NIFTY JUNIOR have fallen in the post-derivatives period.

CHAPTER

31

Ethical Issues in Corporate Governance and Social Responsibility

K. HEMA DIVYA

ABSTRACT

India has become one of the fastest emerging nations to have aligned itself with the international trade in corporate governance. As a result, Indian companies have increasingly been able to access to newer and larger markets around the world as well as able to acquire more businesses. With the integration of Indian economy with global markets. Industrialists and corporates in the country are being increasingly asked to adopt better and transparent corporate practices. The liberalization and de-regulation world over gave greater freedom in management which would imply greater responsibilities. The players in the field are many. Competition brings in its wake weakness in standards of reporting and accountability. The failure of corporate due to lack of transparency and disclosures and instances of falsification of accounts and the effect of such undesirable practices in other companies demands ethical practices in corporate governance.

INTRODUCTION

Corporate governance encompasses commitment to values and to ethical business conduct to maximize shareholder value on a sustainable basis while ensuring fairness to all shareholders including customers, employees and investors, vendors ,government and society at large. It is about promoting corporate fairness, transparency and accountability.

In a company, shareholders leave management of the firm to professional managers (agents). In general, one would expect that the agent—the professional manager—would work in the interest of the principal—the owner. In practice, however that has not always happened. So, an important theme of corporate governance is to ensure the accountability of certain individuals in an organization through mechanisms that try to reduce or eliminate the principal-agent problem.

Corporate Governance is about ethical conduct in business. Managers has to make decisions based on a set of principles influenced by the values, context and culture of the organization. Ethical leadership is good for business as the organization is seen to conduct its business in line with the expectations of all stakeholders.

Social responsibility can be an example of ethical behavior. It is enhancing society in general. However, a business can't afford to go around doing good deeds if there is no potential pay-off. If the business were to loose too much money, then it would cease to exist, hurt customers, and leave employees jobless. There are some that argue that social responsibility is shown only when companies go beyond what is optional, and really intend to create a benefit for others besides the company. Additionally, some companies may not benefit from some forms of social responsibility. These businesses should focus on what they do best as a business and give back what they can. Examples of socially responsible behavior range from projects that raise money for research on diseases, raising money for the needy, requiring workers to volunteer within the community, recalling products that may be dangerous, promoting recycling, and offering free services to the disadvantaged.

FACTORS INFLUENCING CORPORATE GOVERNANCE

1. The Ownership Structure

The structure of ownership of a company determines, to a considerable extent, how a Corporation is managed and controlled. The ownership structure can be dispersed among individual and institutional shareholders as in the US and UK or can be concentrated in the hands of a few large shareholders as in Germany and Japan. But the pattern of shareholding is not as simple as the above statement seeks to convey. The pattern varies across the globe.

Our corporate sector is characterized by the co-existence of state owned, private and multinational Enterprises. The shares of these enterprises (except those belonging to a public sector) are held by institutional as well as small investors. Specifically, the shares are held by :

(1) The term-lending institutions,
(2) Institutional investors, comprising government-owned mutual funds, Unit Trust of India and the government-owned insurance corporations,
(3) Corporate bodies,
(4) Directors and their relatives, and
(5) Foreign investors. Apart from these block holdings, there is a sizable equity holding by small investors.

2. The Structure of Company Boards

Along with the structure of ownership, the structure of company boards has considerable influence on the way the companies are managed and controlled. The board of directors is responsible for establishing corporate objectives, developing broad policies and selecting top-level executives to carry out those objectives and policies.

3. The Financial Structure

Along with the notion that the structure of ownership matters in corporate governance is the notion that the financial structure of the company, that is proportion between debt and equity, has implications for the quality of governance.

4. The Institutional Environment

The legal, regulatory, and political environment within which a company operates determines in large measure the quality of corporate governance. In fact, corporate governance mechanisms are economic and legal institutions and often the outcome of political decisions. For example, the extent to which shareholders can control the management depends on their voting right as defined in the Company Law, the extent to which creditors will be able to exercise financial claims on a bankrupt unit will depend on bankruptcy laws and procedures, etc.

CORPORATE GOVERNANCE FAILURES

The creation of corporate regulation is often linked to perceived failures of corporations and their management to behave in the way society expect them to. Corporate governance is not an exception to this trend, and, as with accounting, different countries may well experience difficulties at different times. For example, the development of British codes of best practice, which began with the Cadbury Committee, can be related to governance scandals such as Polly Peck and Coloroll in the late 1980s and early 1990s. However, the wave of corporate scandals, mostly in the USA, at the turn of the century has been marked not only by the number of cases but also by the effect they have had on investor confidence and market values worldwide.

The combined impact of various US corporate scandals caused the Dow Jones Index to drop from a high for 2002 of 10,632 on 19 March to 7,286 on 9 October, wiping out trillions of dollars in market value. Investor confidence in the fairness of the system and the ability of corporations to act with integrity was ebbing. According to a poll in July 2002, 73 per cent of respondents said that Chief Executive Officers (CEOs) of large corporations could not be trusted (Conference Board, 2003). Amongst the many negative effects of this was a worsening of the pension funding crisis caused by the dramatic drop in the value of pension fund assets. It also increased the cost of capital and caused a virtual cessation in new securities offerings. The International Federation of Accountants (IFAC) claims that while there has been a lot of strategic guidance for business, there has been too little said about the need for good corporate governance. These authors emphasize the fact that successful companies were visionary companies, with a long track record of making a positive impact on the world. They did more than focus on profits; they focused on continuous improvement. They took a long-term view and realised that they were members of society with rights and responsibilities.

However, the long-term view is something of a rarity in many companies. A critical factor in many corporate failures was:

1. Poorly designed rewards package
2. Including excessive use of share options (that distorted executive behaviour towards the short-term)
3. The use of stock options, or rewards linked to short-term share price performance (led to Aggressive earnings management to achieve target share prices)
4. Trading did not deliver the earnings targets, aggressive or even fraudulent accounting tended to occur. This was very apparent in the cases of Ahold, Enron, WorldCom and Xerox (IFAC, 2003).

Adelphia manipulated its earnings figures for every quarter between 1996 and 2002 to make it appear to meet analysts' expectations. Some of the better known cases of financial irregularities are summarised in following table :

Company	*Country*	*What went wrong*
Ahold	NL	Earnings overstated
Enron	USA	Inflated earnings, hid debt in SPEs
Parmalat	Italy	False transactions recorded
Tyco	USA	Looting by CEO, improper share deals, evidence of tampering and falsifying business records
WorldCom	USA	Expenses booked as capital expenditure
Xerox	USA	Accelerated revenue recognition

In terms of corporate governance issues, Ahold, Enron and WorldCom all suffered from :

1. Questionable ethics
2. Behaviour at the top
3. Aggressive earnings management
4. Weak internal control
5. Risk management
6. Shortcomings in accounting and reporting
7. Corporate governance failure at Enron

Every time you turn a stone, another worm creeps out. That seems to be the story of the Enron debacle. Not a day goes by without a new expose of wrong doing in the company that one begins to wonder if there is anything in our system and structure of an enterprise that can prevent such a catastrophe.

Enron is an excellent example where those at the top allowed a culture to flourish in which secrecy, rule-breaking and fraudulent behaviour were acceptable. It appears that performance incentives created a climate where employees sought to generate profit at the expense of the company's stated standards of ethics and strategic goals (IFAC, 2003). Enron had all the structures and mechanisms for good corporate governance. In addition, it had a corporate social responsibility task force and a code of conduct on security, human rights, social investment and public engagement. Yet no one followed the code. The board of directors allowed the management openly to violate the code, particularly when it allowed the CFO to serve in the special purpose entities (SPEs); the audit committee allowed suspect accounting practices and made no attempt to examine the SPE transactions; the auditors failed to prevent questionable accounting.

The use of questionable accounting and disclosure practices, their approval by the board and their verification by the auditors arose from a variety of forces, including:

1. Pressure to meet quarterly earnings projections and maintain stock prices after the expansion of the 1990s
2. Executive compensation practices
3. Outdated and rules-based accounting standards

4. Complex corporate financial arrangements designed to minimise taxes and hide the true state of the companies, and the compromised independence of public accounting firms.

CORPORATE GOVERNANCE FAILURE AT WAL-MART

It has co-filed a shareholder proposal over concerns that Wal-Mart Stores Inc, the US supermarket group, is failing to comply with its own governance standards. Karina Litvack, head of governance and sustainable investment.

1. Despite strong policies on paper, Wal-Mart has struggled to implement its standards across its US business.
2. 'Weaknesses in internal controls have eroded the company's reputation as an attractive employer and are adding fuel to the fires of Wal-Mart's critics.
3. Its failure to deliver on these policy commitments is inhibiting Wal-Mart's ability to expand into new domestic markets.
4. Over 'the past several years', it has become increasingly concerned by signs of failure in internal controls that have led to government investigations and class action lawsuits by employees.
5. Allegations include requiring employees to 'work-off the clock'—during breaks and after shifts—systematic discrimination against women, and alleged questionable tactics to prevent workers from voting for union representation.
6. It got-off to a promising start in 2005 with expectations of a dialogue with the independent directors on the audit committee. But when this simply withered on the vine, Wal-Mart had little choice but to bring concerns about internal controls, labour violations and the erosion of the company's reputation to fellow shareholders.
7. Company was not interested in engaging in a productive discussion about how it builds and supports a compliance culture and, as a result, they

have joined an international group of large filers led by the New York City Employees' Retirement System to file a shareholder proposal.

CORPORATE GOVERNANCE FAILURE AT SATYAM

It is one of Corporate India's worst unfolding chapters, What could be the reason behind such a huge collapse? The top level management failed to estimate the intensity of the gangrene in the organization. Questions also arise on the role of the auditors, and how such a magnitude of financial fraud could have gone unnoticed. Corporate governance is a field which constantly investigates how to secure and motivate efficient management of corporations. It has began as a corporate governance issue back in December has now turned into a major financial scandal for the ages in India. The shares of Satyam Computer Services has plummeted more than 90% in trading at the NYSE today, a stark reminder that investors must always cover their backs or else get racked even by the big names in the industry. NYSE today halted trading in Satyam Computer at its bourses in the US as well as in Europe after the Chairman disclosed financial bungling at the Indian IT major.

A business will always have two sides, its not necessary to gain profits every time, but to sustain in the market the integrity is vital. Every day in some or the other place there is a merger or an acquisition happening, but due to the projected image the co-players in the market are dropping out their plans of taking over Satyam.

Undoubtedly there will be intense focus directed at the other Indian IT Services companies as well. The Satyam corporate governance failure may also make its competitors bolder in terms of acquiring market share created by its fallout provided the industry can regain the trust of the same investors that Satyam has deceived.

From this necessarily brief review of the evidence, and particularly of the sources of failure in financial firms, draw some tentative conclusions. It is important to recognize, however, the evidence base for firm recommendations on corporate governance in financial institutions is thinner than one would like, and certainly not robust enough to offer a standardized set of recommendations valid at all times and in all places.

Principal conclusions are:

First, that people are more important than processes. Many of the failed firms, or near failed firms which we have encountered, had Boards with the prescribed mix of executives and non-executives, with socially acceptable levels of diversity, with directors appointed through impeccably independent processes, yet where the individuals concerned were either not skilled enough for, or not temperamentally suited to, the challenge role that came to be required when the business ran into difficulty.

Secondly, and in spite of first conclusion, there are some good practice processes worth having. Properly constituted audit committees, and Board risk committees can play an important role, as long as they are prepared to listen carefully to sources of advice from outside the firm.

Third, this is a foundation stone of the FSA's approach, a regulatory regime built on senior management responsibilities is absolutely essential. In some of the cases we have wrestled with, senior management did not consider themselves to be responsible for the control environment and indeed, in the old pre-FSA regime, were able successfully to claim that they were not responsible even if the business failed. So our regulation is built on a carefully articulated set of responsibilities up and down the business. It is important that they are not unrealistic. We do not expect the CEO to check in the bottom drawers of each of his traders for unbooked deal tickets. But we do expect the CEO to ensure that there is a risk management structure and a control framework throughout the business which ought to identify aberrant behaviour, or at least prevent it going on unchecked for any length of time.

One consequence of this senior management regime, *fourth point,* is that regulators must focus attention on the top level of management in the firm. For the major firms we regulate we insist that our supervisors have direct access to the Board, and that they present to the Board their own unvarnished view of the risks the firm is running, and of how good the control systems are by comparison with the best of breed in their sector. Unfortunately, we find some resistance to this approach. The management of some of our firms want to negotiate the regulators assessment, so that when it reaches the Board it is an agreed paper and sufficiently bland to cause no debate. Well-structured Board, and a confident management, should welcome an independent view, even expressed at the Board level, which they may challenge and contest if they wish. And non-executive directors should find it helpful to see a knowledgeable view of the institution which does not come from or through its own senior management.

Fifth and penultimate point may not be a popular one. Boards should take more interest in the nature of the incentive structure within the organisation. I am not talking solely about the pay of the CEO, important though that is to get right—as some firms in Britain have recently discovered. Talking about ensuring that the incentives within the firm, and pay is a very powerful one, are aligned with its risk appetite. A number of our most problematic cases have their roots in a misalignment of incentives. *Lastly*, no corporate governance system will work well unless there is some engagement on the part of shareholders. Boards are responsible to shareholders. That is the received wisdom in Anglo-American capitalism, at least. But if those shareholders are not prepared to vote their shares, and show little interest in business strategy, then that accountability is somewhat notional, and unlikely to be effective. Certainly, regulators cannot hope to substitute for concerned and challenging shareholders, though in some senses they may complement them.

CORPORATE GOVERNANCE FAILURE AT CADBURY

Adrian Cadbury, Successor to and Chairman of the Cadbury Schweppes Confectionary Group

Mr. Cadbury's visit and interactions with Indian industry triggered the first serious discussions on the subject of corporate governance. All in all, it seemed like a promising new way of looking at the evil that was single promoter-run firms in India then, who, among other things, ran their companies like fiefdoms and were loath to give up control even if their shareholdings were low.

Recognise that it was a not so competitive environment, the grip of the license raj was still fairly firm and companies and their promoter/founders could pretty much do what they wanted, with public money. The real pain of liberalisation was yet to set in and the Infosys way of boardroom discipline was some way from making its presence felt.

History it seems is repeating itself. Indian companies have exposed themselves to billions of dollars worth of forex derivative contracts over the last few years. Precise numbers are hard to come by and will perhaps never will. What is clear is that companies have taken financial risks they could or should have avoided.

What is clearer is that there was no compelling reason to take these risks. And to that extent, it's a failure of corporate governance and must be treated and then addressed as such. There is of course the other issue of how the Institute of Chartered Accountants or the accounting regulator figuring out how to treat derivative losses as they stand on scores of balance sheets today.

How did it happen? Companies have been steadily stepping up their exposure to currency swaps and the like for at least four years now. Over time, as the stock markets (which bolster sentiment) have held their own and the prospect of any downside risk appeared more and more distant with every passing day, chief financial officers (CFOs) of companies have got braver.

If a company entered into, let's say, a transaction to convert a local currency borrowing into the Japanese yen or Swiss franc borrowing through the swap route, then the company is inducing a risk into the system where there is not. No two ways about that.

Managements ought to have, in the interests of corporate governance, clearly informed their boards of all foreign exchange exposures, the risks arising out of that and the measures to mitigate them were something to go wrong.

Moreover, under the relevant Securities and Exchange Board of India regulations, in the absence of an applicable standard in India for derivatives, the companies' Audit Committees should have examined international standards and disclosed the losses in the Governance report and indicated that these would have been provided for had the country adopted international standards as applicable.

Its possible many companies did keep their boards informed and made the appropriate references in their balance sheets. Though this does seem unlikely, even if they did, no one was watching. It's also possible that some companies are in violation of law. Either way, shareholders must perhaps shoulder some part of the blame.

To conclude is another Enron waiting in the wings? Not quite but it does raise some fundamental questions on what companies do with their shareholders' funds. It's also about how when the good times roll, everyone forgets to look at the figures closely. There is something in the original Cadbury committee definition of corporate governance. "Corporate governance is the system by which companies are directed and controlled."

Getting down to the Details of Governance, we can focus on five issues

Chairman and CEO: It is considered good practice to separate the roles of the Chairman of the Board and that of the CEO. The Chairman is head of the Board and the CEO heads the management. If the same individual occupies both the positions, there is too much concentration of power, and the possibility of the board supervising the management gets diluted.

Audit Committee: Boards work through sub-committees and the audit committee is one of the most important. It not only oversees the work of the auditors but is also expected to independently inquire into the workings of the organisation and bring lapse to the attention of the full board.

Independence and conflicts of interest: Good governance requires that outside directors maintain their independence and do not benefit from their board membership other than remuneration. Otherwise, it can create conflicts of interest by having a majority of outside directors on its Board.

Flow of information: A board needs to be provided with important information in a timely manner to enable it to perform its roles. A governance guideline of General Motors, for instance, specifically allows directors to contact individuals in the management if they feel the need to know more about operations than what they are being told.

Too many directorships: Being a director of a company takes time and effort. Although a board might meet only four or five times a year, the director needs to have the time to read and reflect over all the material provided and make informed decisions. Good governance, therefore, suggests that an individual sitting on too many boards looks upon it only as a sinecure for he or she will not have the time to do a good job.

CONCLUSION

Good corporate governance makes for good business sense. It increases the confidence of shareholders in your company. This leads to better stock prices. Research has shown that good corporate governance brings down the cost of capital for the company. Good disclosure practices lead to a more liquid market for the company. This lowers cost of debt for the company. Thus for CEOs of today, there is a clear business case for complying with principles of good corporate governance.

References

Corporate Governance, *International Journal*, "A Board Culture of Corporate Governance, Vol. 6, Issue 3 (2003).

SSRN—Good Corporate Governance: An Instrument for Wealth Maximisation by Vrajlal Sapovadia.

National Association of Corporate Directors (NACD)—Directors Monthly, "Enlightened Boards: Action Beyond Obligation", Vol. 31, Number 12 (2007), p. 13.

Business for Development: Fostering the Private Sector, OECD Development Centre. Paris: OECD Publications, 2007 (149-52).

"International Standards of Accounting and Reporting, Corporate Governance Disclosure". UNCTAD.

http://www.indianmba.com/Faculty_Column/FC974/fc974.html

Corporate Governance and Ethics—Challenges and Imperatives, a note by Smt. Ranjana Kumar, Vigilance Commissioner.

APPENDIX

I. Augmented Dickey-Fuller Test (ADF) Unit Root Test : Nifty

Null Hypothesis: LOGNIFTY has a unit root

Exogenous: Constant

Lag Length: 0 (Automatic based on SIC, MAXLAG=22)

		t-Statistic	*Prob.**
Augmented Dickey-Fuller test statistic		-33.61922	0.0000
Test critical values:	1% level	-3.435365	
	5% level	-2.863642	
	10% level	-2.567939	

*MacKinnon (1996) one-sided p-values.

Augmented Dickey-Fuller Test Equation

Dependent Variable: D(LOGNIFTY)

Method: Least Squares

Date: 01/17/10 Time: 22:04

Sample (adjusted): 2 1252

Included observations: 1251 after adjustments

Variable	*Coefficient*	*Std. Error*	*t-Statistic*	*Prob.*
LOGNIFTY(-1)	-0.950063	0.028260	-33.61922	0.0000
C	4.96E-06	0.000479	0.010359	0.9917

R-squared	0.475045	Mean dependent var	-2.55E-06
Adjusted R-squared	0.474625	S.D. dependent var	0.023362
S.E. of regression	0.016934	Akaike info criterion	-5.317430
Sum squared resid	0.358149	Schwarz criterion	-5.309226
Log likelihood	3328.053	F-statistic	1130.252
Durbin-Watson stat	1.995669	Prob (F-statistic)	0.000000

2. Augmented Dickey-Fuller Test (ADF) Unit Root Test: Nifty Junior

Null Hypothesis: LOGNIFTYJUNIOR has a unit root

Exogenous: Constant

Lag Length: 0 (Automatic based on SIC, MAXLAG=22)

		t-Statistic	*Prob.**
Augmented Dickey-Fuller test statistic		-31.06373	0.0000
Test critical values:	1% level		-3.435365
	5% level		-2.863642
	10% level		-2.567939

*MacKinnon (1996) one-sided p-values.

Augmented Dickey-Fuller Test Equation

Dependent Variable: D(LOGNIFTYJUNIOR)

Method: Least Squares

Date: 01/17/10 Time: 23:35

Sample (adjusted): 2 1252

Included observations: 1251 after adjustments

Variable	*Coefficient*	*Std. Error*	*t-Statistic*	*Prob.*
Lognifty junior(-1)	-0.871690	0.028061	-31.06373	0.0000
C	0.000105	0.000604	0.173234	0.8625

R-squared	0.435851	Mean dependent var	-9.18E-07
Adjusted R-squared	0.435400	S.D. dependent var	0.028434
S.E. of regression	0.021365	Akaike info criterion	-4.852528
Sum squared resid	0.570123	Schwarz criterion	-4.844324
Log likelihood	3037.256	F-statistic	964.9553
Durbin-Watson stat	1.992845	Prob (F-statistic)	0.000000

3. Augmented Dickey-Fuller Test (ADF) Unit Root Test: BSE Sensex

Null Hypothesis: LOGSENSEX has a unit root

Exogenous: Constant

Lag Length: 0 (Automatic based on SIC, MAXLAG=22)

		t-Statistic	*Prob.**
Augmented Dickey-Fuller test statistic		-33.69100	0.0000
Test critical values:	1% level		-3.435415
	5% level		-2.863664
	10% level		-2.567951

*MacKinnon (1996) one-sided p-values.

Augmented Dickey-Fuller Test Equation

Dependent Variable: D(LOGSENSEX)

Method: Least Squares

Date: 01/17/10 Time: 23:53

Sample (adjusted): 2 1240

Included observations: 1239 after adjustments

Variable	*Coefficient*	*Std. Error*	*t-Statistic*	*Prob.*
LOGSENSEX(-1)	-0.956976	0.028404	-33.69100	0.0000
C	-7.48E-05	0.000507	-0.147540	0.8827

R-squared	0.478517	Mean dependent var	-4.94E-06
Adjusted R-squared	0.478096	S.D. dependent var	0.024713
S.E. of regression	0.017853	Akaike info criterion	-5.211627
Sum squared resid	0.394289	Schwarz criterion	-5.203358
Log likelihood	3230.603	F-statistic	1135.083
Durbin-Watson stat	1.999685	Prob (F-statistic)	0.000000

4. ARCH-LM Test for Hetroskedasticity : Nifty

ARCH Test:

F-statistic	58.45890	Probability	0.000000
Obs* R-squared	55.93258	Probability	0.000000

Test Equation:

Dependent Variable: RESID^2

Method: Least Squares

Date: 01/17/10 Time: 23:42

Sample (adjusted): 3 1252

Included observations: 1250 after adjustments

Variable	*Coefficient*	*Std. Error*	*t-Statistic*	*Prob.*
C0.000226	1.84E-05	12.25842	0.0000	
RESID^2(-1)	0.211532	0.027666	7.645842	0.0000

R-squared	0.044746	Mean dependent var	0.000286
Adjusted R-squared	0.043981	S.D. dependent var	0.000601
S.E. of regression	0.000587	Akaike info criterion	-12.04084
Sum squared resid.	0.000430	Schwarz criterion	-12.03263
Log likelihood	7527.523	F-statistic	58.45890
Durbin-Watson stat	2.045718	Prob (F-statistic)	0.000000

5. ARCH-LM Test for Hetroskedasticity: Nifty Junior

ARCH Test:

F-statistic	123.5630	Probability	0.000000
Obs* R-squared	112.6115	Probability	0.000000

Test Equation:

Dependent Variable: RESID^2

Method: Least Squares

Date: 01/17/10 Time: 23:44

Sample (adjusted): 3 1252

Included observations: 1250 after adjustments

Variable	*Coefficient*	*Std. Error*	*t-Statistic*	*Prob.*
C	0.000318	2.64E-05	12.04258	0.0000
RESID^2(-1)	0.300148	0.027002	11.11589	0.0000

R-squared	0.090089	Mean dependent var	0.000455
Adjusted R-squared	0.089360	S.D. dependent var	0.000867
S.E. of regression	0.000827	Akaike info criterion	-11.35496
Sum squared resid.	0.000854	Schwarz criterion	-11.34675
Log likelihood	7098.852	F-statistic	123.5630
Durbin-Watson stat	2.115185	Prob (F-statistic)	0.000000

6. ARCH-LM Test for Hetroskedasticity : BSE Sensex

ARCH Test:

F-statistic	60.18434	Probability	0.000000
Obs* R-squared	57.48273	Probability	0.000000

Test Equation:

Dependent Variable: RESID^2

Method: Least Squares

Date: 01/18/10 Time: 00:14

Sample (adjusted): 3 1240

Included observations: 1238 after adjustments

Variable	*Coefficient*	*Std. Error*	*t-Statistic*	*Prob.*
C	0.000250	1.94E-05	12.86992	0.0000
RESID^2(-1)	0.215484	0.027776	7.757857	0.0000

R-squared	0.046432	Mean dependent var	0.000318
Adjusted R-squared	0.045660	S.D. dependent var	0.000622
S.E. of regression	0.000608	Akaike info criterion	-11.97124
Sum squared resid.	0.000457	Schwarz criterion	-11.96296
Log likelihood	7412.195	F-statistic	60.18434
Durbin-Watson stat	2.066100	Prob (F-statistic)	0.000000

7. GARCH Test with Dummy Variable: Nifty

Dependent Variable: LOGNIFTY

Method: ML-ARCH (Marquardt)—Normal distribution

Date: 01/17/10 Time: 23:47

Sample (adjusted): 2 1252

Included observations: 1251 after adjustments

Convergence achieved after 17 iterations

MA backcast: 1, Variance backcast: ON

GARCH = C(4) + C(5)*RESID(-1)^2 + C(6)*GARCH(-1) + C(7)*DUMMY

Variable	Coefficient	Std. Error	t-Statistic	Prob.
C	0.000670	0.000439	1.526566	0.1269
AR(1)	-0.245926	0.281505	-0.873612	0.3823
MA(1)	0.341319	0.274454	1.243630	0.2136

Variance Equation

C	5.90E-05	1.29E-05	4.575634	0.0000
RESID(-1)^2	0.164348	0.025794	6.371691	0.0000
GARCH(-1)	0.699481	0.046398	15.07556	0.0000
DUMMY	-3.53E-05	8.98E-06	-3.934306	0.0001

R-squared	0.000969	Mean dependent var	5.35E-06
Adjusted R-squared	-0.003849	S.D. dependent var	0.016948
S.E. of regression	0.016981	Akaike info criterion	-5.470844
Sum squared resid	0.358696	Schwarz criterion	-5.442129
Log likelihood	3429.013	F-statistic	0.201193
Durbin-Watson stat	2.082106	Prob (F-statistic)	0.976462

Inverted AR Roots	-.25
Inverted MA Roots	-.34

8. GARCH Test with Dummy Variable: Nifty Junior

Dependent Variable: LOGNIFTYJUNIOR
Method: ML -ARCH (Marquardt)—Normal distribution
Date: 01/17/10 Time: 23:48
Sample (adjusted): 2 1252
Included observations: 1251 after adjustments
Convergence achieved after 34 iterations
MA backcast: 1, Variance backcast: ON
GARCH = C(4) + C(5)*RESID(-1)^2 + C(6)*GARCH(-1) + C(7)*DUMMY

Variable	*Coefficient*	*Std. Error*	*t-Statistic*	*Prob.*
C	0.000761	0.000476	1.600621	0.1095
AR(1)	-0.901702	0.024344	-37.04063	0.0000
MA(1)	0.956661	0.012657	75.58246	0.0000

Variance Equation

C	4.01E-05	7.59E-06	5.287383	0.0000
RESID(-1)^2	0.196157	0.024844	7.895602	0.0000
GARCH(-1)	0.748544	0.026730	28.00404	0.0000
DUMMY	-2.09E-05	5.63E-06	-3.716094	0.0002

R-squared	0.009561	Mean dependent var	0.000120
Adjusted R-squared	0.004784	S.D. dependent var	0.021534
S.E. of regression	0.021483	Akaike info criterion	-5.084505
Sum squared resid	0.574124	Schwarz criterion	-5.055791
Log likelihood	3187.358	F-statistic	2.001529
Durbin-Watson stat	1.841113	Prob (F-statistic)	0.062624

Inverted AR Roots	-.90
Inverted MA Roots	-.96

9. GARCH Test with Dummy Variable: BSE Sensex

Dependent Variable: LOGSENSEX
Method: ML-ARCH (Marquardt)—Normal distribution
Date: 01/18/10 Time: 00:17
Sample (adjusted): 2 1240
Included observations: 1239 after adjustments
Convergence achieved after 15 iterations
MA backcast: 1, Variance backcast: ON
GARCH = C(4) + C(5)*RESID(-1)^2 + C(6)*GARCH(-1) + C(7)
*SENSEXDUMMY

Variable	*Coefficient*	*Std. Error*	*t-Statistic*	*Prob.*
C	0.000574	0.000469	1.226189	0.2201
AR(1)	-0.060381	0.324764	-0.185921	0.8525
MA(1)	0.150389	0.322463	0.466374	0.6409

Variance Equation

C	6.46E-05	1.27E-05	5.081901	0.0000
RESID(-1)^2	0.175477	0.028378	6.183590	0.0000
GARCH(-1)	0.691265	0.046854	14.75369	0.0000
SENSEXDUMMY	-3.87E-05	8.63E-06	-4.481529	0.0000

R-squared	-0.001554	Mean dependent var	-7.80E-05
Adjusted R-squared	-0.006432	S.D. dependent var	0.017863
S.E. of regression	0.017920	Akaike info criterion	-5.371618
Sum squared resid	0.395634	Schwarz criterion	-5.342680
Log likelihood	3334.718	Durbin-Watson stat	2.092002

Inverted AR Roots	-.06
Inverted MA Roots	-.15

Bibliography

Impact of Futures Introduction on Underlying Index Volatility: Evidence from India—*Kotha Kiran Kumar. and Chiranjit Mukhopadhyay.*

Behaviour of Stock Market Volatility after Derivatives— *Golaka C. Nath.*

Do Futures and Options Trading Increase Stock Market Volatility?—*Dr. Premalata Shenbagaraman.*

Effect of Introduction of Index Futures on Stock Market Volatility: The Indian Evidence—*O.P. Gupta.*

Index